# Lecture Notes in Computer Science 4084

Maria A. Wimmer   Hans J. Scholl
Åke Grönlund   Kim Viborg Andersen (Eds.)

# Electronic Government

5th International Conference, EGOV 2006
Kraków, Poland, September 4-8, 2006
Proceedings

Springer

Volume Editors

Maria A. Wimmer
University of Koblenz-Landau
Universitätsstrasse 1, 56070 Koblenz, Germany
E-mail: wimmer@uni-koblenz.de

Hans J. Scholl
University of Washington
Mary Gates Hall, Suite 370C, Box 352840, 98195-2840 Seattle, USA
E-mail: jscholl@u.washington.edu

Åke Grönlund
Örebro University
ESI/Informatics
70182 Örebro, Sweden
E-mail: ake.gronlund@esi.oru.se

Kim Viborg Andersen
Copenhagen Business School
Department of Informatics
Howitzvej 60, 2000 Frederiksberg, Denmark
E-mail: andersen@cbs.dk

Library of Congress Control Number: 2006931355

CR Subject Classification (1998): K.4, K.6.5, K.5, K.3, C.2, H.5, H.4

LNCS Sublibrary: SL 3 – Information Systems and Application, incl. Internet/Web and HCI

ISSN 0302-9743
ISBN-10 3-540-37686-0 Springer Berlin Heidelberg New York
ISBN-13 978-3-540-37686-6 Springer Berlin Heidelberg New York



Springer is a part of Springer Science+Business Media

springer.com


Printed in Germany

Typesetting: Camera-ready by author, data conversion by Scientific Publishing Services, Chennai, India
Printed on acid-free paper SPIN: 11823100 06/3142 5 4 3 2 1 0

# Preface

Over the years the international EGOV conferences have gained the reputation of presenting and representing the current status of e-Government research. In a sense, the EGOV conference series provides a log for the unfolding of this particular domain of study and practice. This fifth EGOV conference promises to be as special and as unique a milestone as its four predecessors. Every past conference marked a specific major accomplishment: The first conference at Aix-en-Provence, France, established the conference and its format within the DEXA cluster of conferences. The second conference in Prague, the Czech Republic, saw a drastically increased number of submissions, and many more scholars became involved in a decentralized paper review process. The third conference in Zaragoza, Spain, witnessed another increase in submissions from around the world (among which were also a higher number of contributions from North America) leading to an increased attention to the many different flavors of governance and e-Government around the world. The 2005 conference in Copenhagen, Denmark, with an increased volume (again) established a rigorous double-blind review process and also introduced the distinction between full (and finished) research papers (published in Springer's *Lecture Notes in Computer Science*), on the one hand, and posters, work in progress, as well as workshops (published by Trauner Druck, Linz, Austria), on the other hand. Also, a pre-conference PhD colloquium was added to the schedule.

The Copenhagen conference was instrumental in greatly furthering the research collaboration between Europe-based researchers and scholars from other parts of the world. Along with the International Conference on Digital Government Research (dg.o) and the e-Government Track at the Hawaii International Conference on System Sciences (HICSS), the EGOV series of conferences has firmly established itself as one of three leading annual conferences on e-Governance and e-Government with a global reach. Unlike in other fields, the organizers of these three annual conferences collaborate rather than compete against each other. This has had many positive impacts on the study domain of e-Governance and e-Government, which none of the three conferences could have ever achieved alone. Some of these impacts are:

1. The community of professionals and scholars meets on a regular four-month basis (January: HICCS; May: dg.o; and September: EGOV) with ample opportunity for face-to-face exchanges.
2. The four-month interval provides sufficient time for progressing in research endeavors.
3. As a consequence, work initiatives. and collaborative projects are carried forward in a timely fashion providing participating professionals and scholars with a predictable short-term schedule for reunion.

4. Professionals and scholars develop an intimate knowledge of each others' projects fostering tremendous cross-pollination and collaboration.
5. Both a global and a multi-local perspective of, and in, the study domain are unfolding (for example, scholars from around the world collaborate on the European Union's Roadmap 2020 project eGovRTD2020, www.egovrtd2020.org).
6. The three conferences provide a research and publishing rhythm that reinforces the intensity and diversity of research.
7. A shared research culture and a sense of a global scholarly and practice community is developing.

As a result of this collaboration, in the summer and fall of 2005 the global e-Gov community of practitioners and researchers discussed and voted on the mission statement of a future professional Digital Government Society. Late in the fall of 2005 and in early winter 2005/2006, the global community also voted on both the North American and Global Digital / E-Government Society constitutions. In May 2006 at dgo2006 the Digital Government Society of North America was formed, and its elected officers met for the first time in their new capacity.

The 2006 EGOV conference, EGOV – The Digital Government Society of Europe was formed, and its elected board was presented to the public. Soon, an Asian Digital Government Society will appear. In other words, the global community of e-Government practitioners and researchers will have professional societies, which equip "its members with a professional support network focused on both scholarship and effective practices that nurture technical, social, and organizational transformation in the public sector" (cf. Mission Statement of the Digital Government Society, www.dgrs.org).

So far, e-Government research appears to be multi- and interdisciplinary in nature. The 2006 EGOV conference underlined and exposed this nature of the study domain. However, there is a lively debate on whether or not e-Government research should develop into a discipline or rather stay away from disciplinary organization. The future will tell whether or not we remain a study domain or develop into the disciplinary direction.

In the Call for Papers of EGOV 2006, seven topical threads were highlighted, which attracted a large number of paper submissions:

- The e-Government environment
- E-Government implementation
- Conceptual design and frame for e-Government
- Assessment of e-Government
- Emerging technologies in e-Government
- E-Government and development
- E-Government research and learning

Thirty-one full research papers (empirical and conceptual) were accepted for the conference and cover those topical threads. According to the reviewers' assessments, the overall quality of papers has risen again. For better readability, the papers have been clustered under the following headings:

- Research Review and Outlook
- Participation and Democracy
- Designing Government Services
- Legal Dimensions in E-Government
- Procurement and Governance Issues in Networked Governments
- Evaluation and Assessment

As in the previous years, many people made this conference happen by reviewing and by preparing both the program and the proceedings. Gabriela Wagner for the DEXA organization as well as the members of the Program Committee deserve special thanks. Gerti Orthofer of the University of Linz, Austria, was a cornerstone of support and organization in preparing the review process, the program and proceedings.

Finally, this year's conference provided a great opportunity for honoring our great mentor, inspirer, communicator, founder of the EGOV conferences and wonderful colleague, Roland Traunmüller, who has been leading the community with advice, vision, and practical initiatives for many years. Without him, the community would not have developed the same spirit, productivity, and sense of shared meaning that it has developed on a global scale. Roland Traunmüller has truly carried the Prometheus torch enlightening the e-Government community for longer than anybody else. We are greatly indebted to him and hope that he may continue leading us for many years to come!

Koblenz, Seattle, Ørebrø, Copenhagen
September 2006

Maria A. Wimmer
Hans J. (Jochen) Scholl
Åke Grönlund
Kim Viborg Andersen

# Organization

## Program Committee

General Chair: Roland Traunmüller, University of Linz (Austria)
Program Chairs: Åke Grönlund, Ørebrø University (Sweden)
Maria A. Wimmer, University of Koblenz- Landau (Germany)
Kim V. Andersen, Copenhagen Business School (Denmark)
Jochen Scholl, University of Washington (USA)

## Program Committee Members

Georg Aichholzer, Austrian Academy of Science, Austria
Vincenzo Ambriola, University of Pisa, Italy
Kim Viborg Andersen, Copenhagen Business School, Denmark
Ari-Veikko Anttiroiko, University of Tampere, Finland
Yigal Arens, Digital Government Research Center USC/Information Sciences Institute, USA
Mahwood A. Awan, Dubai University College, Dubai
Frank Bannister, Trinity College Dublin, Ireland
Lasse Berntzen, Vestfold University College, Norway
Jean-Loup Chappelet, Swiss Graduate School of Public Administration Lausanne, Switzerland
Wichian Chutimaskul, King Mongkut's University of Technology Thonburi, Thailand
Laurens Cloete, CSIR, South Africa
Tony Cresswell, CTG, USA
Ahmed M. Darwish, Arab Republic of Egypt E-Government Program Director, Egypt
Sharon Dawes, CTG, University at Albany, USA
Lois Delcambre, Portland State University, USA
Rahul De, Indian Institute of Management Bangalore, India
Sara Eriksén, Blekinge Institute of Technology, Sweden
Patrizia Fariselli, Nomisma, Italy
Jose Fortes, University of Florida, USA
Fernando Galindo, University of Zaragoza, Spain
Thomas F. Gordon, Fraunhofer Institute for Open Communications Systems (FOKUS), Germany
Dimitris Gouscos, University of Athens, Greece
Åke Grönlund, Ørebrø University, Sweden
Luis Guijarro-Coloma, University of Valencia, Spain
Richard Heeks, University of Manchester, UK

Helle Zinner Henriksen, Copenhagen Business School, Denmark
Hermann Hill, German University of Administrative Sciences, Germany
Ian Holliday, City University of Hong Kong, Hong Kong
Eduard Hovy, USC/Information Sciences Institute, USA
Luiz Antonio Joia, Public and Business Administration – Getulio Vargas Foundation, Brazil
Peter Kawalek, Manchester Business School, UK
Ralf Klischewski, German University in Cairo, Egypt
Robert Krimmer, Austria
Mário Jorge Leitão, INESC Porto, Portugal
Christine Leitner, Danube University, Krems, Austria
Klaus Lenk, Danube University, Krems, Austria
Claire Lobet-Maris, FUNDP Namur, Belgium
Euripides Loukis, University of the Aegean, Greece
Ann Macintosh, Napier University, UK
Josef Makolm, Federal Ministry of Finance, Austria
Peter Mambrey, Fraunhofer Institute for Applied Information Technology (FIT), Germany
Manuel de Jesus Mendes, University of Campinas, Brazil
Gregoris Mentzas, National Technical University of Athens, Greece
Jeremy Millard, Danish Technological Institute, Denmark
Carl Erik Moe, Adger University College, Norway
Enrico Nardelli, NESTOR – University of Rome "Tor Vergata," Italy
Monica Palmirani, University of Bologna, Italy
Rimantas Petrauskas, Law University of Lithuania, Lithuania
Reinhard Posch, Federal Chancellery of Austria, Austria
Alexander Prosser, Vienna University of Economics, Austria
Gerald Quirchmayr, University of Vienna, Austria
Peter Reichstädter, Federal Chancellery of Austria, Austria
Reinhard Riedl, University of Zurich, Switzerland
Tomas Sabol,TU Kosice, Slovakia
Airi Salminen, University of Jyväskylä, Finland
Hans Jochen Scholl, University of Washington, USA
Erich Schweighofer, University of Vienna, Austria
Maddalena Sorrentino, University of Milan, Italy
Dieter Spahni, University of Applied Sciences Bern, Switzerland
Witold Staniszkis, Rodan Systems S.A., Poland
Efthimios Tambouris, University of Macedonia, Greece
Roland Traunmüller, University of Linz, Austria
Tom M. van Engers, University of Amsterdam, The Netherlands
Mirko Vintar, University of Ljubljana, Slovenia
Francesco Virili, University of Cassino, Italy
Rene Wagenaar, Technical University Delft, The Netherlands
Sue Williams, The University of Sydney, Australia
Maria A. Wimmer, University of Koblenz-Landau, Germany

## Additional Reviewers

Niklas Auerbach
Molnár Bálint
Victor Bekkers
Francesco Bolici
Lemuria Carter
Giovanni A. Cignoni
Tony Elliman
Fabio Fioravanti
Leif Flak
Simon French
Andreás Gábor
Javier Garca Marco
Helene Gieber
Olivier Glassey
Meliha Handzic
Catherine Hardy
Charles Christopher Hinnant
Chris Holland
Vincent Homburg
Marcel Hoogwout
Marijn Janssen
Bernhard Karning
Auli Keskinen
Trond Knudsen
Herbert Kubicek
Jukka Kultalahti
Pilar Lasala
Virpi Lyytikäinen
Guirong Mao
Oliver Märker
Robert Müller-Török
Thomas Mundt
Anna Ni
Gerti Orthofer
Theresa Pardo
Peter Parycek
Vassilios Peristeras
Wolfgang Polasek
Siegmund Prieglinger
Stefanie Röder
Øystein Sæbø
Andreas Schaad
Ella Smith
Ignace Snellen
Joergen Svensson
Jukka Tuomela
Réka Vas
Costas Vassilakis
Morten Wellendorf
Rolf Wigand
Peter Wolcott

# Table of Contents

## Research Review and Outlook



## Participation and Democracy

## Designing Government Services



## Legal Dimensions in E-Government

## Procurement and Governance Issues in Networked Governments



## Evaluation and Assessment

# e-Gov Research Quality Improvements Since 2003: More Rigor, but Research (Perhaps) Redefined

Åke Grönlund and Annika Andersson

Örebro University, Informatics/ESI
{ake.gronlund, annika.andersson}@esi.oru.se

**Abstract.** This paper follows up on an earlier study [1] by assessing the nature of 80 papers from EGOV 05 in terms of rigor and relevance criteria. Both studies use the same method and makes comparison between the results. We find that however still focusing overwhelmingly on descriptions and little on theory testing and creation, paper quality appears much better in that references to literature have increased grossly, there are very few dubious claims, philosophical research and theoretical arguments are virtually extinct, and the number of case stories is vastly reduced. However, the number of product descriptions is more than doubled to just over 30 %. The reasons for this are discussed, and as most of these papers are based on EU research funding we propose that an important reason may be the funding mechanism where researchers are employed as helpers in product development rather than critical scrutiny and analysis.

## 1 Introduction

Grönlund [1] made a survey of 170 papers at three main (2003) Electronic Government (eGov) conferences for the purpose of measuring the maturity of the field as a research area., and at the same time at a general level, the quality of papers. Maturity, we proposed, could be assessed by charting the nature of the research done. A scientific field is usually characterized by not just a common object of study, but also a set of theories which can be used to understand the general conditions of the field. More of theory generating and testing would indicate a more mature field, more of pure description and case story telling would be signs of a less mature field. Paper quality was measured at a cursory level by some rigor and relevance-oriented criteria. In the 2004 study we found that as concerns rigor, theory generation and theory testing were not frequent, whereas case stories (no theory, no data) and product descriptions (no analysis or test) were very frequent. Dubious claims (beyond what is reasonable given the method used) were also frequent, appeared in 29 % of the papers As concerns relevance, we found that only a few of the cases where theories were either tested or generated concerned the role and nature of government, most concerned general

M.A. Wimmer et al. (Eds.): EGOV 2006, LNCS 4084, pp. 1–12, 2006.

organizational issues which could well find a place within traditional IS conferences. Further, only 11 papers (of 170) involved shared authorship involving government practitioners.

On the positive side we found contributions from a number of disciplines, both social science ones and technically oriented, and international outreach beyond the North Atlantic shores was good with contributions from some 30 countries.

In this paper we repeat the 2004 study, however so far only with paper from the (DEXA) EGOV 05 conference, a total of 80 papers, which were classified by the organizers in two categories published in two different proceedings 30 papers were research papers" and 50 "workshop papers".

## 2 Research Questions

Just like in the 2004 study, the basic question asked in this paper is, what is the eGov field like in terms of what constitutes a scientific fields? This is operationalized by questions concerning rigor and relevance, with an emphasis on the former.

*Relevance:* To what extent is the eGov field distinct from other fields? This could be assessed by investigating what are the questions asked what (kind of) theories are used, or sought in an inductive manner? If eGov is indeed a specific field, at least some of these issues and theories would be different.
*Rigor:* Depending on the maturity of the field, the balance among methods used would likely change over time from case stories to more of methodologically sound examination of relevant issues, be they related to technological quality, user understanding, extent and qualities of use, or other. A mature eGov field would also involve many disciplines, certainly public administration and other fields specializing in government, not only IT-related disciplines by example from e g the HCI field. This time we compare the results with the 2004 study to find out whether there have been changes of any kind. We measure maturity according to the following rather intuitive model, which is based on the assumption that research fields mature over time passing through (but never completely leaving!) roughly the following phases:
*Philosophical* ("What will the world be like when everyone has a computer?"). As there are no or few theories in the field and empirical data is uncertain as the object of study is changing rapidly, studies will at this stage be mainly speculation based on philosophy, properties of technology, world view, etc.
*Anecdotal case stories* ("Ma, look what I found"). At this stage there is an increasing amount of data, but there are still no clear focus in the field so studies focus on "emerging" features, which may be anything but are usually grounded in factors like the researchers field of origin, personal interest, and commercial focus of the IT development. Focus is still on exploration, finding new exciting traits of the development. The researcher is an Amerigo Vespucci finding new land.
*Clustering* (grouping according to similarities among cases). At this stage cases abound and people start looking for similarities. The new continent is found physically, now we try to understand life on it.

*Theory creating* (similarities more strictly modelled). When similarities are found, people start looking for more stable relationships, models and theories so as to more credibly inform further research, product development and organizational remodelling.
*Theory testing* (using theories found by inductive methods or borrowed from other fields pertinent to government and/or IT). This stage would generally be expected to appear slightly after stage 4, as theory creating is usually qualitative and builds on smaller but richer data sets than theory testing and hence is more suitable to early stages of development where radical changes are about), but thereafter they continue in parallel.

Although vitality in a field probably requires that even mature fields contain some component of each of the above "stages", we propose that a new, immature, field would contain more of the early stages while a mature field would contain more of the latter ones.

## 3 Method

eGov related papers are beginning to appear in journals [2]. This is itself a quality mark of the field, as journals employ stricter criteria for rigor, whereas conferences tend to be very relevance-oriented, in particular so in field with an expanding practice, such as eGov. However, conferences also mirror the general views of the field, so increased calls for rigor should make a difference also in conference papers. There are several conferences in the field, even more now than in 2003, but for the purpose of comparison we stuck to those we studied in 2004. These were EGOV (set in the DEXA conference cluster; [2], HICSS [3], and ECEG [4]. This paper includes findings from EGOV 05 only. There are mainly two reasons for this limitation. First, EGOV 03 was the worst performer on rigor in our earlier study. Second, EGOV organizers have since made an effort to improve paper quality by improving the review process and by distinguishing between a "conference" for "full" research papers and a "workshop" for research in progress, case studies and the like. As no such major change effort had taken place at the other two conferences, we expected that if there would be significant changes, EGOV would be the place to look.
To assess rigor and relevance, the following categories were used:

*Rigor:* Research type, Method, Claim, Number of pages, Number of references.
*Relevance:* Focus unit, Target audience, Institution, Discipline, Collaborative, Country.

The categories were designed so as to involve a minimum of interpretation. Both category definitions and interpretation were "generous". As my hypothesis was that the eGov field is indeed immature, I wanted to avoid this bias to guide my interpretation, and so a generous approach was necessary. To check my coding, 25 randomly selected papers were coded by five independent reviewers (five papers each). In all cases but one where there were discrepancies (15 %), the control coders were harsher they required more data or more stringent use of theory than I did. Category definitions:

**Table 1.** Research type

| Category | Description |
|---|---|
| Descriptive | Describes a phenomenon in its appearance without any use of theory |
| Philosophical | Reflects upon a phenomenon without data or reference to any theory |
| Theoretical | Reflects upon a phenomenon based on some theory but without empirical data or with only anecdotal and particular such |
| Theory generating | Attempts to analyse/interpret quantitative or qualitative data in a systematic manner for the purpose of model building. |
| Theory testing | Attempts to test a theory using quantitative or qualitative data in a systematic manner, i.e. not just strict theory testing |

*Method.* The categories used are a mix of the whish to keep the number as low as possible, to include any quantitative and qualitative method while being specific enough to not hide the fact that sometimes very specific methods are used.

The latter is the reason for including GT as a separate item. The former motivates including both quantitative and qualitative methods under the category "interpretative". "Product description" was not preconceived but emerged as necessary.

**Table 2.** Method

| Category | Description |
|---|---|
| Argument | Logical argument but not based on any particular theory or relating explicitly or by clear implication to any theory |
| Case story | Tells about a case but as opposed to a case study there is no strict data collection method. Usually own experiences or anecdotal evidence |
| Etnography | Any attempt to understand actions by systematic observation and interpretation |
| Experiment | Field experiments included |
| GT | Grounded theory |
| Interpretative | Any kind of more strictly performed data collection than "case story" but not necessarily strictly explained or spelled-out method for interpretation. A case study belongs here, but also more limited studies where qualitative or quantitative data is analysed. |
| Literature study | Only documents used, be they scientific, policy documents or other. Not necessarily strict method or even explicitly labelled as literature study |
| Product description | IT product, method, or similar, described by the manufacturer |
| Survey | This covers also qualitative overviews of several documents or cases |
| Unclear | Not even the widely defined categories above fail to capture the method |

*Focus unit* employed largely categories used to define other fields, such as HCI, CSCW, and IS: Individual, Group, Method, and Organization. We added "Society", as government is not just any organization, and eGov research should consider not just internal efficiency but also societal role.
*Target audience* was a category we used in the 2004 study, but we dropped it this time because in the previous study we found it impossible to measure this reasonably well.
*Claim* concerns what validity authors claim for their results. A *Normative* papers claims generality beyond case, a *descriptive* paper claims validity but not generality. *Lessons* only claims anecdotal value, e.g. "we learned that we need a champion and we weren't prepared for that" and *ongoing* research is not completed and the paper does not make any claim as to the validity or scope of the findings, not even in principle. In cases when the claim was not explicitly stated, it was often very clearly implied by the way findings were formulated. When the claims were not possible to discern, the paper was classified as ongoing.

## 4 Findings

In the following, we compare data from EGOV 2003 and EGOV 2005. For comparison with the field more generally, we also display 2003 results from HICSS and ECEG. "EGOV 2005" refers to the "conference" (Wimmer et al, 2005), "EGOV workshop refers to the "workshop proceedings [5] *Research type.*

As shown in Tables 3 and 4.

- The share of descriptive research has increased, most so at the workshop, but the difference between the workshop and the conferences is very small.
- Theory generating has increased at EGOV compared to 2003 EGOV total
- Theory generating has decreased slightly at EGOV workshop compared to 2003 EGOV total
- Theoretical research has decreased to the point of extinction only 1 paper 2005 as compared to 12 in 2003.
- Philosophical research has decreased, but from a low level

To support our maturity model, philosophical and theoretical research has largely disappeared. We predicted a more mature field would include more of

**Table 3.** Research type 2003

| | EGOV 03 | | HICSS 03 | | ECEG 03 | | Total | |
|---|---|---|---|---|---|---|---|---|
| Descriptive | 57 | 61% | 6 | 24% | 27 | 53% | 90 | 53% |
| Philosophical | 3 | 3% | 0 | 0% | 2 | 4% | 5 | 3% |
| Theoretical | 12 | 13% | 5 | 20% | 9 | 18% | 26 | 15% |
| Theory generating | 12 | 13% | 12 | 48% | 7 | 14% | 31 | 18% |
| Theory testing | 10 | 11% | 2 | 8% | 6 | 12% | 18 | 11% |

**Table 4.** Research type 2005

| | EGOV 05 | | EGOV workshop 05 | | Total | |
|---|---|---|---|---|---|---|
| Descriptive | 20 | 67% | 34 | 68% | 54 | 68% |
| Philosophical | | 0% | | 0% | 0 | 0% |
| Theoretical | 1 | 3% | | 0% | 1 | 1% |
| Theory generating | 5 | 17% | 9 | 18% | 14 | 18% |
| Theory testing | 4 | 13% | 7 | 14% | 11 | 14% |
| Total | 30 | 100% | 50 | 100% | 80 | 100% |

theory testing and creation, and indeed theory generating and theory testing research has increased, but not much. We predicted less of description, but this category has instead increased from 61 to 68 %.

**Method.** As shown in Tables 5 and 6, "Argument" has in 2005 become almost extinct. Case stories are down from 34 % to 10 %, most so at the conference. Interpretative research has increased considerably, from 12 % (EGOV) or 14 % (total) to 35 %. It should be noted that Interpretative includes multi-method studies, for example a survey plus qualitative interviews. Hence some other categories show a lower number than the actually conducted studies. A finding that seems to contradict our maturity model is that "Product descriptions" have increased from 14 % to 31 % on the total. Literature studies have on the total increased slightly, but most remarkable (as for product descriptions) is the differentiation increase to 23 % at the conference and decrease to 3 % at the workshop.

In all, this still supports our maturity model, provided a modification concerning the object of study. This time we find more rigorous descriptions and less of stories, which is a quality improvement. We find a clear differentiation between the conference and the workshop, which is expected given the conference redesign. But we find product descriptions being increasingly common. Our interpretation is that this has to do with the current ways of funding "research",

**Table 5.** Method 2003

| | EGOV 03 | | HICSS 03 | | ECEG 03 | | Total | |
|---|---|---|---|---|---|---|---|---|
| Argument | 19 | 20% | 6 | 24% | 11 | 22% | 36 | 21% |
| Case story | 32 | 34% | 2 | 8% | 8 | 16% | 42 | 25% |
| ethnography | 0 | 0% | 1 | 4% | 0 | 0% | 1 | 1% |
| Experiment | 4 | 4% | 1 | 4% | 2 | 4% | 7 | 4% |
| GT | 0 | 0% | 2 | 8% | 0 | 0% | 2 | 1% |
| Interpretative | 11 | 12% | 8 | 32% | 5 | 10% | 24 | 14% |
| Literature study | 10 | 11% | 1 | 4% | 13 | 25% | 24 | 14% |
| Product description | 13 | 14% | 3 | 12% | 6 | 12% | 22 | 13% |
| Survey | 5 | 5% | 1 | 4% | 6 | 12% | 12 | 7% |

**Table 6.** Method 2005

| | EGOV 05 | | EGOV workshop 05 | | Total | |
|---|---|---|---|---|---|---|
| Argument | 1 | 3% | 4 | 8% | 5 | 6% |
| Case story | 1 | 3% | 5 | 10% | 6 | 8% |
| ethnography | | 0% | 1 | 2% | 1 | 1% |
| Experiment | 1 | 3% | | 0% | 1 | 1% |
| GT | | 0% | | 0% | 0 | 0% |
| Interpretative | 10 | 33% | 18 | 36% | 28 | 35% |
| Literature study | 7 | 23% | 3 | 6% | 10 | 13% |
| Product description | 9 | 30% | 16 | 32% | 25 | 31% |
| Survey | 1 | 3% | 3 | 6% | 4 | 5% |
| Total | 30 | 100% | 50 | 100% | 80 | 100% |

in particular in Europe, where participation in development projects is mandatory. For example, the (only) Swedish government agency funding eGov research states in their 2005 call that "Researcher(s) in the project shall take part in developing the e-service, not just evaluate it" [6] (p 4; authors translation). Could it be that what we see here is a logical outcome of this funding principle, a huge amount of papers describing products typically methods and IT artefacts, sometimes architectures and conceptual frameworks with little of comparison and critical analysis? If so, eGov is not a research field but one concerned with product development, and the maturity model does not really apply. We will return to this issue in the concluding discussion.

**Focus Unit.** As shown in Tables 7 and 8, the strong focus on IT has increased, from 33 % (EGOV) or 26 % (total) in 2003 to no less than 60 % in 2005. This is not only due to the workshop, also the conference has a high score (43 %). "Society" scores marginally higher, while "Method" and "Organization" score only about half what they did in 2003 on the total; however, at the conference they have all increased. "Individual" is dropping even more relatively, but from a low number. This is definitely not in line with our maturity model. If the field were about to mature in the direction of creating a distinct set of theories, we

**Table 7.** Focus unit 2003

| | EGOV 03 | | HICSS 03 | | ECEG 03 | | Total | |
|---|---|---|---|---|---|---|---|---|
| Individual | 6 | 6% | 7 | 28% | 3 | 6% | 16 | 9% |
| Group | 0 | 0% | | 0% | | 0% | 0 | 0% |
| Organization | 20 | 21% | 8 | 32% | 20 | 39% | 48 | 28% |
| Society | 12 | 13% | 2 | 8% | 6 | 12% | 20 | 12% |
| Method | 25 | 27% | | 0% | 16 | 31% | 41 | 24% |
| IT | 31 | 33% | 8 | 32% | 6 | 12% | 45 | 26% |

**Table 8.** Focus unit 2005

| | EGOV 05 | | EGOV workshop 05 | | Total | |
|---|---|---|---|---|---|---|
| Individual | 1 | 3% | 1 | 2% | 2 | 3% |
| Group | | 0% | | 0% | 0 | 0% |
| Organization | 5 | 17% | 3 | 6% | 8 | 10% |
| Society | 8 | 27% | 3 | 6% | 11 | 14% |
| Method | 3 | 10% | 8 | 16% | 11 | 14% |
| IT | 13 | 43% | 35 | 70% | 48 | 60% |
| Total | 30 | 100% | 50 | 100% | 80 | 100% |

should see more focus on all these points. Is it the model that is wrong, or is eGov turning away from research and into, again, becoming more a practitioner field concerned with practical applications of IT in government? One potential interpretation is the research funding one we applied to the previous tables. Another interpretation could be that the focus of the field is narrowing to matters more closely related to IT and less to organizational change and methods for that.

To investigate the last interpretations we counted the number of references. A low number would indicate a practitioner focus, a high would indicate more focus on research. As Tables 9 and 10 show, the number of references has grown enormously.

**Table 9.** Number of references 2003

| **References** | | | | | | | |
|---|---|---|---|---|---|---|---|
| No of refs | | EGOV 03 | | HICSS-03 | | ECEG-03 | |
| | 0-5 | 33 | 35 % | 1 | 4 % | 5 | 10 % |
| | 6-8 | 25 | 27 % | 2 | 8 % | 5 | 10 % |
| | 9+ | 36 | 38 % | 22 | 88 % | 41 | 80 % |
| Number of papers | | 94 | | 25 | | 51 | |

**Table 10.** Number of references 2005

| **References** | EGOV 05 | | EGOV workshop 05 | | Total | |
|---|---|---|---|---|---|---|
| <=5 | 1 | 3% | 3 | 6% | 4 | 5% |
| 6 to 8 | 1 | 3% | 5 | 10% | 6 | 8% |
| >=9 | 28 | 93% | 45 | 90% | 73 | 91% |
| (>=20) | 13 | 43% | 10 | 20% | 23 | 29% |
| (>=30) | 2 | 7% | 3 | 6% | 5 | 6% |
| (>=40) | 2 | 7% | 1 | 2% | 3 | 4% |

While in 2003, 62 % of the DEXA papers had less than 9 references, in 2005 93 % at the conference and 90 % at the workshop have 9 or more. 43 % of the conference papers have more than 20 references.

**Research Origin.** The affiliation of the first author is overwhelmingly a university at all conferences. In 2003, the figure for all conferences were 83 %, in 2005 the figure for EGOV conference is 97 % and for the workshop 94 % – in total only three papers had a first author from a company, one from government.

**Collaboration.** In 2003, around 1/5 of the papers were collaborative (involving more than one institution), and many of these involved no practitioners but researchers from more than one university or more than one discipline within the same university. In fact, only 11 papers involved at least one practitioner and one researcher (6 at EGOV, 2 at ECEG, and 3 at HICSS). In 2005, collaboration has increased at both the conference and the workshop to 39 % in total, with a slightly higher figure for the workshop (Table 11). Still, collaboration with practice is low, only 8 papers (as one is double-counted).

**Table 11.** Collaborations

| | EGOV 05 | | EGOV workshop 05 | | Total | |
|---|---|---|---|---|---|---|
| Non-collab | 20 | 67% | 29 | 58% | 49 | 61% |
| uni-gov | 1 | 3% | 4* | 8% | 5 | 6% |
| uni-biz | | 0% | 4* | 8% | 4 | 5% |
| uni-uni | 9 | 30% | 14 | 28% | 23 | 29% |
| Total papers | 30 | | 50 | | 80 | |

* One paper included gov-biz-uni and is here counted in both categories

**Claim.** A final factor indicating rigor is the credibility of the claims. To investigate this, we matched the categories "research type", "method" and "claim". A reasonable combination would be, for instance that a "descriptive" type implemented by an "argument" would result in modest claims. In 2003, we found no less that 49 dubious claims, equivalent to 29 % of the papers. There were several combinations, the largest being descriptive case story resulting in normative claims (11 cases) and theoretical argument ending by normative claims. At EGOV 2005 we found a completely different picture. The number of dubious claims was only 5 (6 %), 2 at the conference and 3 at the workshop. This seems a huge improvement. Even though we were a bit disappointed in the increased amount of descriptive research and product descriptions, at least this time authors do not make unwarranted claims. We were wondering here whether our 2004 paper scared people a bit and made them determined not to overstate their findings. One indication of that might be that perhaps instead this time papers were underclaiming. This time we found a very high number of "ongoing/no claim", 46 papers (58 %). Many of these were theory testing (6) and theory generating (6), or interpretative (7) making a total of 19 papers where given the method used, not necessarily the actual content of the paper claims could well have been stronger. In some cases the reason is that research is ongoing, but in many cases the research was indeed complete, however the author(s) made disclaimers of various kinds, typically including "More research is needed".

**Geographical Distribution.** It appears eGovernment conferences reach an increasing audience in a geographical perspective. EGOV 2003 gathered researchers from 30 countries, for 2005 the figure is 35 (17 for the conference and 27 for the workshop).

# 5 Conclusions

We set out to assess the maturity of the eGov field as a research area, and we did so by comparing 2005 papers to a study of 2003 papers. The results can be described as mixed. We find that authors efforts to comply with research publications standards have increased. The number of references has increased greatly, indicating better involvement with previous research. The number of dubious claims has been reduced from 29 % to 6 %. "Arguments" and "philosophical research" lacking empirical observations, theory or both have been virtually eradicated. What remains is a more strict research where empirical data is described and interpreted using sometimes a theory but almost always at least some structured method and where claims match the methods used.

On the disappointment side we find that descriptive research is increasing from 61 % to 69 %, and theory testing and creating is increasing only little. However, as also the descriptive papers are more integrated in the research literature , both as measured by number of references and by the agreement between method and claims, we conclude that the field has indeed matured as papers are now more rigorous. It should be noted here, that while this method allows us to tell what kind of research is done, and whether conclusions are drawn that are in principle reasonable given the research method, it does not help us understand whether papers are in fact good or bad. Clearly, descriptive papers can be just as interesting, relevant and rigorous as theory testing and theory generating ones. And clearly theory generating and theory testing papers can be poorly conceived and poorly written. While investigating this would be a much more time-consuming endeavour, we believe the method chosen at least gives us support in saying that there has been a change in a positive direction over the two years that have passed between measurements. Beyond the measurements made, our impressions from reading all the papers are that in fact, several "product descriptions" are well argued methods often based on realistic arguments; however, they are not theory based or empirically founded but rather based on arguments often heard in the eGov debate.

There is reason to discuss the findings in view of our maturity model, however. While we have seen a change towards less philosophical and argumentative research, we should also have seen a change towards more theory testing and theory building, which we did not really. As a final point for discussion we now propose a reason for that, open to confirmation or rejection by further research. Our proposition is that the basis of research the funding principles has changed so dramatically that our model, which was based on our view of traditional academic discipline development, does not fit anymore simply because research is no longer research. Today, research funding in Europe is increasingly hard to find without joining up with business and some development project. Some would say it is impossible in a field such as ICT. Looking at the papers presented in the examined conferences, they are to a large extent reports from EU funded projects. The principle underlying this funding mechanism is not to study and analyze the development to device better ways of doing things but to provide government support to industry in development projects decided by other mechanisms. This is sometimes explicit, as in the above quote from VINNOVA, sometimes implicit, but what it means in practice is that researchers are tied up to contribute to developing methods, software, architectures etc., not to critically examine them and discuss alternatives. Given also the funding administration delay where funding is often finally decided months *after* a project period has started, project time is often cut short and hence the race to complete artefacts is on already from the outset, and so the time for analysis is reduced even if it originally was part of the plan. There might be other reasons. One might be the "publish or perish" demand on researchers which is increasingly a reality also in Europe (it has long been in the US). Another could be the increasing volume and de-academization of higher education, parts of which includes research being increasingly project funded and competitive, and education being increasingly instrumentally job preparation-oriented and less academically intellectual. Clearly this study does not provide evidence to make conclusions on this issue, but we strongly believe it is worth further research. Independent science is historically a highly valued force in society, similar to the idea of an independent press, and if the current development is detrimental to this independence it should at least be discussed.

In this respect, the findings presented here should trigger some discussion about eGov as a research field. Our production has become more rigorous since last measure two years ago. But are we doing good research? As we have seen above, the eGov field

- increasingly descriptive,
- increasingly containing product descriptions, and
- increasingly focusing on IT.

Following our research maturity model, an eGov research field should rather focus on the *role* of ICT in contexts of society, government organization, method and individuals/citizens, and it should increasingly analyze rather than describe, hence creating and testing theories.

## References

1. Grönlund, Å. State of the art in e-Gov research - a survey. in Third International Conference, EGOV 2004. 2004. Zaragoza, Spain: Springer.
2. Traunmüller, R. Electronic Government. in Second International Conference, EGOV 2003. 2003. Prague, Czech Republic: Springer.

3. IEEE. Proceedings of the 36th Hawaii International Conference on System Sciences 2003. in 36th Hawaii International Conference on System Sciences 2003. 2003. Hawaii: IEEE.
4. Bannister, F. and D. Remenyi. ECEG 03 Proceedings. in 3rd European Conference on e-Government. 2003. Dublin, Ireland.
5. Andersen, K.V., et al. Electronic Government. in Fourth International EGOV Conference 2005. 2005. Copenhagen, Denmark: Springer.
6. Vinnova, Cross-departmental public e-services for businesses (Gränsöverskridande offentliga e-tjänster för företag), in Call 2 within the programme E-services in public sector, Vinnova, Editor. 2005: Stockholm.

# Is E-Government Research a Flash in the Pan or Here for the Long Shot?

Hans Jochen Scholl

University of Washington, Box 352840, Seattle, WA 98195-2840, USA
jscholl@u.washington.edu

**Abstract.** It has been questioned whether or not Electronic Government Research (EGR) qualifies as a legitimate discipline. This paper proposes that EGR might even want to avoid developing into a traditional discipline and restricting itself to a narrow set of accepted procedures. Rather EGR might best be served by drawing upon multiple disciplines spanning the whole spectrum of hard-pure, hard-applied, soft-pure, and soft-applied sciences. In so doing, EGR might best thrive as a multi-, inter-, or even as a transdiscipline.

## 1 Introduction

Like its siblings "e-Business" and "e-Commerce" the once "electrifying" acronym "e-Government" is seemingly losing its magic. This paper asserts that the fading appeal of the terms "e-Government" and "digital government" is not coincidental but may rather indicate a certain intellectual weakness in EGR concepts and a growing need for reassessing the EGR agenda. More importantly, EGR's scientific foundations, shared perspectives, and expectable prospects need clarification. This paper is intended to contribute to and advance a recently launched discussion on the subject (Cushing & Pardo, 2005; Delcambre & Giuliano, 2005; Grönlund, 2004, 2005).

EGR studies "the use of information and technology to support and improve public policies and government operations, engage citizens, and provide comprehensive and timely government services" (Anonymous, 2005b). This widely accepted academic definition of e-Government and EGR, however, defines a field or a domain of study, which spans across the boundaries of quite a number of existing disciplines including public administration, political sciences, organizational sciences, information science, computer science, information systems research, sociology, library science, statistics, law and ethics, and a host of other disciplinary sciences. According to Grönlund, a common study object alone does not establish a discipline or a field; rather a set of distinguishing theories and accepted methodologies are needed for defining a "classical" discipline in its own right (Grönlund, 2004, 2005). Hence, the question arises what, if any, is the disciplinary home turf of EGR in terms of theory, method, study object, and research community? Or, if EGR systematically goes beyond the scope of any one discipline, what are the characteristics and acceptable standards of this multi-, inter-, or transdisciplinary science?

M.A. Wimmer et al. (Eds.): EGOV 2006, LNCS 4084, pp. 13–24, 2006.

The paper is organized as follows: First, it discusses whether EGR is (or, at least, can be expected to become) a discipline. Then, it exemplarily looks at traditional disciplines involved with aspects of EGR including public administration, information systems research, and computer science. Third, the paper discusses the challenges and opportunities of cross-disciplinary EGR. Finally, the paper ponders the idea of defining and establishing EGR as a multi-, inter-, or transdiscipline rather than a discipline.

## 2 Would EGR Pass as a "Legitimate" Discipline?

To information scientists the discussion of "discipline versus field versus domain versus interdisciplinary science" provides the experience of déja-vu, since information science (InfSci), although some half century old with well-established and fully-fledged colleges, schools, departments, journals, conferences, societies, and research methods, has only recently gone through that debate (again). For the purpose of our discussion on the foundations of EGR it is insightful to draw upon that InfSci debate, which was rather charged at times. It surfaced several important indicators and dimensions of what defines a discipline: (1) a formal definition of the discipline/field, (2) a common base of knowledge, (3) a unique cluster of research problems, (4) unifying theories, (5) an accepted set of procedures and methods of inquiry, and (6) a shared vision of the discipline/field's impact (Becher & Trowler, 2001; Grönlund, 2004, 2005; Heilprin, 1991; Kuhn, 1970; Saracevic, 1999; Webber, 2003). These indicators, although not exhaustive, provide a basis for an initial assessment of the disciplinary nature of EGR and show that EGR satisfies a number of these criteria, while it falls short on several others.

*Formal Definition.* As shown above, a widely accepted formal definition of EGR exists.
*Knowledge Base.* Also, the accumulated knowledge on the subjects of EGR is rapidly growing. A recent survey of published peer-reviewed academic work shows a growing swell of literature in established and new journals and conferences. The current worldwide English-language literature base is estimated at 49 monographs, over 200 articles in established journals, over 60 articles in new journals, and over 500 articles at conferences. NSF has funded some 150 major EGR projects between 1999 and 2006. The European Union has likewise sponsored several dozens of EGR projects. With an estimated current annual going rate of some 120 peer-reviewed publications based on the number of recurring conferences, journal issues, and monographs, the knowledge base of EGR is rapidly expanding.
*Unique Cluster of Research Problems.* EGR uniquely intersects advanced IS- and IT- and government-related research problems, which have gone widely unattended and unaddressed in, for example, both the academic public-administration and information-systems literatures. Papers dedicated to and based on EGR were found 16 times in the top-five journals of Public Administration between 1999

and early 2006, while no single EGR-based publication was found in the top-two IS journals in the US for the same period of time.

*Unifying Theories.* (Grönlund, 2004, 2005) empirically analyzes the academic contributions at three major conferences and finds EGR immature and under-theorized. (Delcambre & Giuliano, 2005) identify two main clusters of EGR, one centering on developing IT tools in response to practical government problems and the other one revolving around government processes researched from a socio technical perspective. Certain EGR theory development, for example, has been dedicated to the integration, change, and transformational impacts of e-Government (Klischewski, 2004; Kubicek et al., 2003; Layne & Lee, 2001; Scholl, 2003, 2004a, 2005a, 2005b, 2005c). However, those theoretical contributions certainly have neither created a grand or unifying theory, nor a set of major competing theories (for example, like transaction-cost theory versus resource-based theory in economics).

*Procedures and Methods of Inquiry.* EGR has been found using almost the full spectrum of methodological and procedural approaches ranging from anecdotal accounts (Grönlund, 2004, 2005) over action research (Scholl, 2004b) and traditional survey-based research (Moon, 2002; Moon et al., 2005) to computational modeling (Hovy, 2003; Pantel et al., 2005) and simulation (Black et al., 2003; Cresswell et al., 2002). Such large range of procedures and methods representing very different fields and epistemic paradigms makes it difficult to assess the nature and quality of contribution (Delcambre & Giuliano, 2005), that is, neither an accepted set of methodologies and procedures nor a shared definition of rigor in EGR exists reminiscent of Feyerabend's provocative ideal of "anything goes" (Feyerabend, 1975).

*Shared Vision of Impact.* The long-range vision and impact of EGR has moved onto center stage of the discussion among members of the researcher and practitioner community only recently. It is fostered by the formation of a global Digital Government Society and also sponsored via research projects both in the EU and the US (Anonymous, 2005a, 2005b, 2006). A shared vision of the impact still needs to emerge.

Several monographs have been dedicated to special topics (for example, (Fountain, 2001; Huang et al., 2004)). In absence of established rules, procedures, or promotional pathways, no disciplinary allegiance has been found. Likewise absent is EGR-specific terminology, most prominently evident in the lack of an accepted term for the area of study itself (Digital Government, eGovernment, e-Government, e-Gov, etc.). However, compared with other areas of study, the *interaction between practitioners and scholars* seems to be relatively strong in EGR (Grönlund, 2001, 2004, 2005).

In summary, while EGR passes on the first three primary indicators of what constitutes a "classical," "legitimate" discipline, it fails the test on the other three primary indicators: There is no unifying theory or competing theories; no accepted standards of methods and procedures of inquiry have been established, and no shared vision of EGR's long-term impact has emerged. Also, when referring to collateral indicators, EGR would not fully qualify as a discipline, either, and fail the test for at least four indicators. So, in the classical and narrow sense EGR does not pass as a "legitimate:" discipline in its own right.

Hence, three questions arise (cf., also (Delcambre & Giuliano, 2005)): (1) what are the prospects for EGR to ultimately develop into a fully-fledged "legitimate" discipline? (2) Does it matter if EGR never assumes the status of a "legitimate" discipline in academia? And, (3) what are the alternatives, if any? The remainder of the article discusses these three questions from various angles.

## 3 Neighboring "Incumbent" Disciplines: Pub Admin and ISR/CS

In part and at the very least, EGR shares study objects with two neighboring disciplines, Public Administration (Pub Admin) as well as Information Systems Research (ISR) and Computer Science (CS). Pub Admin research itself would have trouble with satisfying all seventeen disciplinary indicators presented above. Unlike EGR, Pub Admin is solidly established on university level with colleges and departments, and it has developed a century-long tradition of scholarship and teaching. Like Business Administration it heavily draws upon other disciplines, for example, from administrative theory and organization science including human resource management research and also finance theory. Some authors label it an interdisciplinary applied science emphasizing its close relationship to the practice of government and not-for-profit organizations.

Although the study of IT and IT-based information in government undoubtedly falls within and not outside its realm, Pub Admin has hardly directed its efforts towards this increasingly important area. For example, unlike business schools, Pub Admin schools rarely have the equivalent to MIS departments, if any, let alone EGR units, that is, IS/IT topics are hardly researched nor taught at Pub Admin departments. This surfaces also in the top-five (Forrester & Watson, 1994) academic research outlets in Pub Admin research ("Public Administration Review (PAR)," "Administration & Society (A&S)," "American Review of Public Administration (ARPA)," "Journal of Public Administration Research and Theory (JPART)," "Public Administration Quarterly, (PAQ)"). Those journals combined a total of 1,252 research articles between 1999 and early 2006, only 41 of which were dedicated to information technology in the widest possible definition, including16 articles on EGR, representing just 1.3 percent of all articles published. Greatly missing, for example, are micro- and mezzo-level studies on immediate organizational outcomes of IT implementation, the IT artifact in its specific Pub Admin context, and the respective informational challenges and opportunities. EGR as it has been advanced via Pub Admin scholarship resembles traditional public management information systems research (cf., (Bozeman & Bretschneider, 1986; Bretschneider, 1990; Donald F. Norris & Kraemer, 1996)) in its remoteness from technology and practice and its unvarnished skepticism towards the concepts and efficacy of e-Government (for two examples, see (Bretschneider, 2003; D. F. Norris, 2003)). To the established Pub Admin departments and the scholarly publishing outlets IT-related research is peripheral.

Hence, they grossly under-represent the rapidly growing importance and quantity of EGR. Due to long-term scholarly commitments and emphases directed elsewhere, this under-representation of EGR is unlikely to end any time soon.

EGR also shares study objects with ISR and CS. While ISR widely overlaps with CS in research and teaching of IS foundations, programming, analysis and design, data management, data communications, it also extends into the analysis of IS policy and strategy as well as enterprise-level interoperation. CS, on the other hand, besides a focus on engineering and practical tool development also aims at the algorithmic formalization of problem solutions (Delcambre & Giuliano, 2005). ISR has its home in the IS departments of business schools, while CS research is conducted in departments and schools of its own. By disciplinary boundary definition, CS research is unambiguous about its orientation towards the technical engineering and computational side of a problem. In contrast in ISR, this boundary is not as sharply drawn. ISR deliberately considers task, structure, and context parameters of the organizational environment when researching the IS artifact (Benbasat & Zmud, 2003). However, it stops short of inquiring the rippling effects and impacts of the IS artifact in the formal and informal organization (ibid). Neither in CS departments nor in B-school IS departments, EGR occupies central focus. To CS researchers, EGR is another area for the application of computational tools with some potential for theoretical generalization and formalization. The application area itself is of no particular concern or interest. Also, to IS scholars, EGR is mostly beyond the scope of the B-school agenda. Likewise, CS scholars are interested in providing the CS tools for tackling a government problem, however, the implementation, use, and usefulness of the tool in its context is beyond the scope of CS (Delcambre & Giuliano, 2005) leaving open a critical feedback loop. More importantly, the specifics of the government task, structure, and context only occur as an input to research around the IT artifact but certainly not as a worthwhile study focus in its own right, in which the unique embeddedness of the IT artifact would be of central interest. Needless to say that a search on EGR literature in, for example, the leading ISR journals *MIS Quarterly* and *Information Systems Research* yielded no result. Hence, like in the traditional Pub Admin sphere, so in the ISR and CS disciplinary areas, EGR is unable to establish a home for itself as, for example, a recognized or "legitimate" sub-discipline.

This discussion also delivers partial answers to the first and the third question posed above: EGR draws upon both Pub Admin and ISR/CS connecting the objects of study as well as using procedures and methods of inquiry also found in both fields. However, like Bioscience with the natural sciences, EGR spans across disciplines by studying unique clusters of research problems, which tend to fall outside the boundaries of a single discipline. Further, EGR is not limited in its reach to Pub Admin and ISR/CS but rather includes relevant study objects, procedures and methods of inquiry as well as research questions shared with other disciplines such as information science, statistics, sociology, political science, geography, and the natural sciences among quite a few others. EGR, hence, appears to belong to the class of integrative interdisciplinary sciences addressing evolving clusters of research problems systematically underserved and understudied within the boundaries of established disciplines.

## 4 Challenges and Opportunities for Cross-Disciplinary EGR

Whether disciplinary or non-disciplinary, among the foremost challenges for any new endeavor in academia ranks gaining peer recognition and the status of legitimacy. Particularly for any non-single-disciplinary science, this has always proven an arduous undertaking, since disciplinary structures along with ruling paradigms have deeply shaped and pervaded the administrative, financial, and promotional framework of academia powerfully reinforcing its disciplinary and paradigmatic composition (Bailey, 2005; Kuhn, 1970; Lattuca, 2001; Lélé & Norgaard, 2005; Mervis, 2004; National Academies (U.S.). Committee on Facilitating Interdisciplinary Research. et al., 2005). One coping mechanism when dealing with such peer and system pressure has been to defensively draw the boundaries of an emerging new (sub-)discipline rather narrow and design it after the image of an existing legitimate discipline. ISR would be a case in point, which in its phase of inception defined its boundaries rather narrow and the criteria of rigor in a way acceptable to the established departments in B-schools (cf., (Benbasat & Zmud, 2003),), however, greatly at the expense of relevance to practice (Applegate & King, 1999; Davenport & Markus, 1999; Klein & Myers, 1999; Lee, 1999; Lyytinen, 1999; Markus & Lee, 1999). In other words, the initial fit into the system has helped send the sub-discipline into maintaining self-defeating standards leading to a serious identity crisis (Benbasat & Zmud, 2003) and a fight for survival (Dennis et al., 2006) at a later stage. EGR might want to avoid that trap.

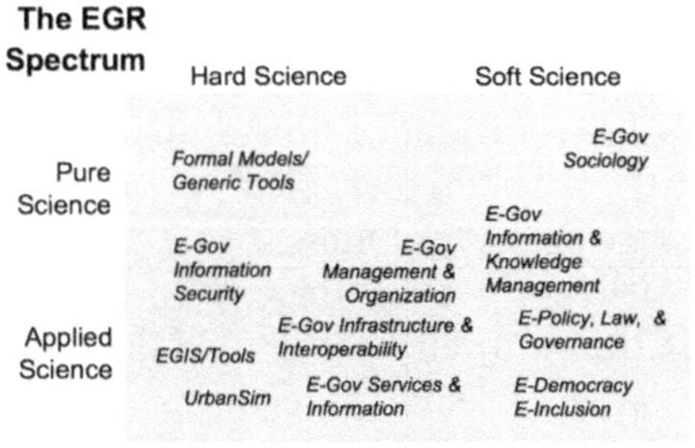


**Fig. 1.** Exemplary Research Orientations

Besides structural and self-imposed impediments, when crossing intra- and interdisciplinary boundaries other profound obstacles have confronted EGR and will continue to thwart it (Delcambre & Giuliano, 2005). When using Biglan's classification system of academic disciplines, four distinct categories emerge (Biglan, 1973): (1) hard science (that is, an epistemic stance, which relies on measurable facts, quantification, repeatability, generalizability, closely coupled concepts and principles, which are hierarchically arranged representing the world "as it really is"); (2) soft science (that is, an epistemic stance, which incorporates inter-subjective concepts of reality with open and loosely coupled concepts and principles, including qualitative accounts, with no claim regarding an objective reality; (3) pure science (examples include theoretical physics, mathematics, etc; applicability is circumstantial at best); and (4) applied science (examples include mechanical and electrical engineering, psychotherapy, pedagogy, etc; applicability is the mainstay).

The four pairs of hard-pure, hard-applied, soft-pure, and soft-applied help distinguish disciplines further: Examples for hard-pure can be found in the natural and computer sciences, for hard-applied in engineering and medicine, for soft-pure in history, sociology, and geography, and for soft-applied in law, education, and fine arts.

EGR, as depicted in figure 1, covers the entire Biglan spectrum. In CS, formal models and generic tools have been developed, which were transferred into practical e-Government Information Systems (EGIS) and other computer-/ network-aided tools, that is, the pure-applied boundary crossing can be observed, at least on the hard science side. When mapping the HICSS40 topical orientations into the grid, it also becomes obvious that EGR is all over the place. However, epistemic boundary crossing (hard/soft) has not been observed and might become the real challenge ahead for EGR (Delcambre & Giuliano, 2005).

Finally, traditional PMIS or MIS scholars both in Pub Admin and ISR might denounce EGR as a home turf intruder, or as overrated and a fad soon to disappear (Bretschneider, 2003). However, the first wave of EGR contributions has already outnumbered traditional PMIS research manifold and has most probably had a far higher impact on government practice than PMIS over the past two decades.

*Fragmentation of a discipline.* The explosive growth of disciplinary knowledge (Lattuca, 2001) brings about increasing degrees of specialization, which is also in part the result of reduction in the process of inquiry; however, in its wake the body of knowledge within a discipline begins to scatter (Despres et al., 2004). Such fragmentation has empirically been documented to most frequently occur in applied disciplines such as engineering- and technology-related research (Morillo et al., 2003). Thus, with the increasing complexity resulting from growth, reduction, and fragmentation, a need and a tendency to re-integrate the pieces emerge, which do not necessarily halt at disciplinary boundaries (Despres et al., 2004).

*Practical application and relevance.* A strong driver for integration has traditionally been found in applied research and in practice itself (Epton et al., 1983), which for all practical purposes (for example, the military) defies disciplinary straitjackets.

*Funding.* In both the European Union and the US, funding agencies (see, for example, www.esf.org, www.europa.eu.int, or www.nsf.gov) have repeatedly emphasized the need for cross- and interdisciplinary research (IDR) in program announcements and proposal solicitations. While some critics dismiss this emphasis as lip service (Bailey, 2005), the problem might be more subtle, since evaluation criteria for IDR cannot be preconfigured (Epton et al., 1983), predetermined bridges between inter-working disciplines (particularly, if situated in antipodal epistemic frames) do not exist (Lélé & Norgaard, 2005), and, for the lack of personnel alternatives, proposal reviews are performed by disciplinary-oriented referees (Bailey, 2005). Despite those potential shortcomings, funding agencies have supported EGR touching all four quadrants of the Biglan spectrum.

In summary, while the challenges to cross-disciplinary EGR are formidable, it has already established itself as a multi-discipline endeavor spanning the full spectrum of hard and soft as well as pure and applied sciences. The three strong drivers, complexity, relevance, and external funding, favor cross- and interdisciplinary EGR, which has already produced a sizeable body of knowledge. This again partially answers the first and second question above. While EGR might remain a co-hosted or spread-across-discipline science for some time, its legitimacy will rise the more it demonstrably copes with the complexity inherent in EGR producing high impact and relevant results in practice (cf., (Saracevic, 1999)).

## 5 Concluding Remarks: EGR on the Continuum Between Discipline and Transdiscipline

Truly interdisciplinary studies have not yet emerged in EGR, at least, when analyzing NSF-funded projects, which cluster around tool-development studies in a CS sense and socio-technical systems research with a social science orientation (Delcambre & Giuliano, 2005). If multiple disciplines are involved in a project, the research designs are of multi-disciplinary nature at best (ibid). At this point, it seems appropriate to recall the differences between disciplinary, multi-disciplinary, inter-disciplinary, and trans-disciplinary research.

While a disciplinary community researches a problem or phenomenon based on its particular worldview (Bruce et al., 2004) including accepted methods and procedures of inquiry, multi-disciplinary efforts obviously involve multiple disciplinary communities, and hence realities, and attempt to approach the phenomenon from the perspectives of the each discipline. However, each contribution remains within its disciplinary boundaries. Cross-discipline interaction, if any, is minimal (ibid). Results of such parallel studies are either not integrated or merely synoptically presented (Ramadier, 2004). However, this approach "highlights the different dimensions of the studied object and respects the plurality of points of view" (p. 433).

In contrast, interdisciplinary research strives to develop a shared model of understanding of a given problem/phenomenon by engaging the participating disciplinary scholars in a dialog with the goal of reaching synthesis (Bruce et al., 2004; Gibbons, 1994; Lattuca, 2001; Ramadier, 2004). Two approaches towards that end have been observed in practice, a hierarchical integration via models and tools, where participating researchers agree that one discipline takes the lead and specifies rules and procedures, to which the other disciplines adhere and submit

(Bruce et al., 2004; Lattuca, 2001; Ramadier, 2004). In the other approach, a non-hierarchical relationship between the participating disciplines is negotiated and established through adopting and translating each discipline' s concepts into the other disciplines (Balsiger, 2004; Ramadier, 2004). Disciplinary perspectives are fully maintained also in interdisciplinary integration, even though it requires each participating discipline to reinterpret the knowledge of another discipline within its own boundaries.

Transdisciplinary research has been suggested as an alternative to disciplinary approaches including multi- and interdisciplinary arrangements. It challenges fragmentation in science by emphasizing the hybrid nature of all knowledge, its inter-subjectivity, reflexivity, and context-dependency as well as its dependence on and grounding in practice (Balsiger, 2004; Bruce et al., 2004; Despres et al., 2004; Horlick-Jones & Sime, 2004; Ramadier, 2004; Thompson Klein, 2004).

Essentially, transdisciplinarity combines multidisciplinarity and interdisciplinarity to the extent that, while different levels of reality are explicitly accounted for (as in multi-disciplinary approaches), "it has adopted the effort to reinterpret knowledge in order to readjust the different levels of reality" (Ramadier, 2004) from interdisciplinary approaches.

EGR problems have been researched from fairly different disciplinary perspectives. In addition, EGR covers the entire spectrum of hard-pure, hard-applied, soft-pure, and soft-applied sciences making it unlikely to ever develop into a traditional "legitimate" discipline. However, little cross-pollination between those single-discipline approaches has been found. Yet the current intra- and interdisciplinary fragmentation prevents both EGR and e-Government practice from tapping its full potential of understanding and impact. EGR, this paper suggests, might be most effective when established as a multi-, inter-, and transdiscipline representing a more integrative understanding of knowing. By assuming such an integrative and transdisciplinary understanding and through extending Wilson's definition (Wilson, 1886), one could characterize EGR's "aboutness" (Hjorland, 2001) as "first, what government can properly and successfully do *with information and information technology*, and, secondly, how it can do these proper things with the utmost possible efficiency and at the least possible cost either of money or of energy."

## References


1. Anonymous. (2005a). Calls on eGovernment. Retrieved 1/27, 2006, from http://europa.eu.int/information_society/activities/egovernment_research/calls/index_en.htm
2. Anonymous. (2005b, 1/26). Digital government society mission statement. Retrieved 1/27, 2006, from `http://faculty.washington.edu/jscholl/DGS/DGS_Mission_Final.html`
3. Anonymous. (2006). The National Science Foundation Digital Government Research Program: Linking it research with government mission and studying its impact on democracy and governance. Retrieved 1/27, 2006, from http://www.diggov.org/

4. Applegate, L. M., & King, J. L. (1999). Rigor and relevance: Careers on the line. MIS Quarterly, 23(1), 17-18.
5. Bailey, K. D. (2005). Fifty years of systems science: Further reflections. Systems Research and Behavioral Science, 22(5), 355-361.
6. Balsiger, P. W. (2004). Supradisciplinary research practices: History, objectives and rationale. Futures, 36(4), 407-421.
7. Becher, T., & Trowler, P. (2001). Academic tribes and territories: Intellectual enquiry and the culture of disciplines (2nd ed.). Philadelphia, PA: Open University Press.
8. Benbasat, I., & Zmud, R. W. (2003). The identity crisis within the is discipline: Defining and communicating the discipline's core properties1. MIS Quarterly, 27(2), 183-194.
9. Biglan, A. (1973). The characteristics of subject matter in different academic fields. Journal of Applied Psychology, 57(3), 195-203.
10. Black, L. J., Cresswell, A. M., Luna, L. F., Pardo, T. A., Martinez, I. J., Thompson, F., et al. (2003). A dynamic theory of collaboration: A structural approach to facilitating intergovernmental use of information technology.
11. Bozeman, B., & Bretschneider, S. (1986). Public management information systems: Theory and prescriptions. Public Administration Review, 46(November (special issue)), 475-489.
12. Bretschneider, S. (1990). Management information systems in public and private organization: An empirical test. Public Administration Review, 50(September/October), 536-545.
13. Bretschneider, S. (2003). Information technology, e-government, and institutional change. Public Administration Review, 63(6), 738-741.
14. Bruce, A., Lyall, C., Tait, J., & Williams, R. (2004). Interdisciplinary integration in Europe: The case of the fifth framework programme. Futures, 36(4), 457-470.
15. Cresswell, A. M., Pardo, T. A., Thompson, F., Canestraro, D. S., Cook, M., Black, L. J., et al. (2002). Modeling intergovernmental collaboration: A system dynamics approach.
16. Cushing, J., & Pardo, T. (2005). Guest editors' introduction: Research in the digital government realm. Computer, 38(12), 26-32.
17. Davenport, T. H., & Markus, M. L. (1999). Rigor vs. Relevance revisited: Response to benbasat and zmud. MIS Quarterly, 23(1), 19-23.
18. Delcambre, L., & Giuliano, G. (2005). Digital government research in academia. Computer, 38(12), 33-39.
19. Dennis, A. R., Valacich, J. S., Fuller, M. A., & Schneider, C. (2006). Research standards for promotion and tenure in information systems. MIS Quarterly, 30(1), 1-12.
20. Despres, C., Brais, N., & Avellan, S. (2004). Collaborative planning for retrofitting suburbs: Transdisciplinarity and intersubjectivity in action. Futures, 36(4), 471-486.
21. Epton, S. R., Payne, R., & Pearson, A. W. (1983). Managing interdisciplinary research. Chichester [West Sussex]; New York: Wiley.
22. Feyerabend, P. K. (1975). Against method: Outline of an anarchistic theory of knowledge. Atlantic Highlands, N.J.: Humanities Press.
23. Forrester, J. P., & Watson, S. S. (1994). An assessment of public administration journals: The perspective of editors and editorial board members. Public Administration Review, 54(5), 474-482.
24. Fountain, J. E. (2001). Building the virtual state: Information technology and institutional change. Washington, D.C.: Brookings Institution Press.

25. Gibbons, M. (1994). The new production of knowledge: The dynamics of science and research in contemporary societies. London; Thousand Oaks, Calif.: SAGE Publications.
26. Golembiewski, R. T. (1977). Public administration as a developing discipline. New York: M. Dekker.
27. Grönlund, A. (2001, January). Democracy in an it-framed society. Communications of the ACM, 44, 23-26.
28. Grönlund, A. (2004, Aug 30 to Sep 3). State of the art in e-Gov research: A survey. Paper presented at the Third International Conference, EGOV 2004, Zaragoza, Spain.
29. Grönlund, A. (2005). State of the art in e-Gov research: Surveying conference publications. International Journal of Electronic Government Research, 1(4), 1-25.
30. Heilprin, L. B. (1991). The library community at a technological and philosophical crossroads: Necessary and sufficient conditions for survival. Journal of the American Society for Information Science (1986-1998), 42(8), 566.
31. Hjorland, B. (2001). Towards a theory of aboutness, subject, topicality, theme, domain,field, content. And relevance. Journal of the American Society for Information Science and Technology, 52(9), 774-778.
32. Horlick-Jones, T., & Sime, J. (2004). Living on the border: Knowledge, risk and transdisciplinarity. Futures, 36(4), 441-456.
33. Hovy, E. (2003). Using an ontology to simplify data access. Communications of the Acm, 46(1), 47-49.
34. Huang, W., Siau, K., & Wei, K. K. (2004). Electronic government strategies and implementation. Hershey PA.: Idea Group Pub.
35. Klein, H. K., & Myers, M. D. (1999). A set of principles for conducting and evaluating interpretive field studies in information systems. MIS Quarterly, 23(1), 67-88.
36. Klischewski, R. (2004). Information integration or process integration? How to achieve interoperability in administration. In R. Traunmüller (Ed.), Electronic government: Third international conference, egov 2004, Zaragoza, Spain, August 30-September 3, 2004. Proceedings (Vol. 3183, Lecture notes in computer science, pp. 57-65). New York, NY: Springer.
37. Kubicek, H., Millard, J., & Westholm, H. (2003). Methodology for analysing the relationship between the reorganisation of the back office and better electronic public services. In R. Traunmüller (Ed.), Electronic government: Second international conference, egov 2003, Prague, Czech Republic, September 2003: Proceedings (Vol. 2739, Lecture notes in computer science, pp. 199-206). New York, N.Y.: Springer.
38. Kuhn, T. S. (1970). The structure of scientific revolutions ([2d, enl. ed.). Chicago: University of Chicago Press.
39. Lattuca, L. R. (2001). Creating interdisciplinarity: Interdisciplinary research and teaching among college and university faculty (1st ed.). Nashville: Vanderbilt University Press.
40. Layne, K., & Lee, J. (2001). Developing fully functional e-government: A four stage model. Government Information Quarterly, 18(2), 122-136.
41. Lee, A. S. (1999). Rigor and relevance in mis research: Beyond the approach of positivism alone. MIS Quarterly, 23(1), 29-27.
42. Lyytinen, K. (1999). Empirical research in information systems: On the relevance of practice in thinking of is research. MIS Quarterly, 23(1), 25-27.
43. Lélé, S., & Norgaard, R. B. (2005). Practicing interdisciplinarity. Bioscience, 55(11), 967.

44. Markus, M. L., & Lee, A. S. (1999). Special issue on intensive research in information systems: Using qualitative, interpretive, and case methods to study information technology–foreward. MIS Quarterly, 23(1), 35-38.
45. Mervis, J. (2004). Risky business. Science, 306(5694), 220-221.
46. Morillo, F., Bordons, M., & Gomez, I. (2003). Interdisciplinarity in science: A tentative typology of disciplines and research areas. Journal of the American Society for Information Science and Technology, 54(13), 1237-1249.
47. National Academies (U.S.). Committee on Facilitating Interdisciplinary Research., Committee on Science Engineering and Public Policy (U.S.), National Academy of Sciences (U.S.), National Academy of Engineering., & Institute of Medicine (U.S.). (2005). Facilitating interdisciplinary research. Washington, D.C.: The National Academies Press.
48. Norris, D. F. (2003). Building the virtual state. Or not? A critical appraisal. Social Science Computer Review, 21(4), 417-424.
49. Norris, D. F., & Kraemer, K. L. (1996). Mainframe and pc computing in American cities: Myths and realities. Public Administration Review, 56(6), 568-576.
50. Pantel, P., Philpot, A., & Hovy, E. (2005). Data alignment and integration [US government]. Computer, 38(12), 43-50.
51. Rabin, J., Hildreth, W. B., & Miller, G. (1998). Handbook of public administration (2nd ed.). New York: Marcel Dekker.
52. Ramadier, T. (2004). Transdisciplinarity and its challenges: The case of urban studies. Futures, 36(4), 423-439.
53. Saracevic, T. (1999). Information science. Journal of the American Society for Information Science, 50(12), 1051-1063.
54. Scholl, H. J. (2003, 1/6 to 1/10). E-Government: A special case of business process change. Paper presented at the 36th Hawaii International Conference on System Sciences (HICSS36), Waikoloa, HI.
55. Scholl, H. J. (2004a). The dimensions of business process change in electronic government. In W. Huang, K. Siau & K. K. Wei (Eds.), Electronic government strategies and implementation (pp. 44-67). Hershey PA.: Idea Group Pub.
56. Scholl, H. J. (2004b). Involving salient stakeholders: Beyond the technocratic view on change. Action Research, 2(3), 281-308.
57. Scholl, H. J. (2005a). E-government-induced business process change (BPC): An empirical study of current practices. International Journal of Electronic Government Research, 1(2), 25-47.
58. Scholl, H. J. (2005b). Motives, strategic approach, objectives & focal areas in e-Gov-induced change. International Journal of Electronic Government Research, 1(1), 58-77.
59. Scholl, H. J. (2005c, August 22 to 26). Organizational transformation through e-Government: Myth or reality? Paper presented at the 4th International Conference EGOV05, Copenhagen, Denmark.
60. Thompson Klein, J. (2004). Prospects for transdisciplinarity. Futures, 36(4), 515-526.
61. Webber, S. (2003). Information science in 2003: A critique. Journal of Information Science, 29(4), 311-330.
62. Wilson, W. (1886). The study of administration. Retrieved 2/14, 2006, from http://teachingamericanhistory.org/library/index.asp?document=465

# The E-Government Melting Pot: Lacking New Public Management and Innovation Flavor?

Møyfrid Kårstad Sannarnes[1],
Helle Zinner Henriksen[2], and Kim Viborg Andersen[2]

[1] Department of Information Systems,
Agder University College, Service box 422, 4604 Kristiansand, Norway
moyfriks@hia.no
[2] Department of Informatics, Copenhagen Business School,
Howitzvej 60, 2000 Fredriksberg, Denmark
{hzh.inf, kva.inf}@cbs.dk

**Abstract.** The paper argues that e-government literature has by large not infused New Public Management (NPM) literature or innovation studies on e-government. Rather, e-government literature has used relative simple frameworks and observations from the NPM and innovation studies and applied them in studies of e-government implementation. Based on a literature review of 60 peer and double blind reviewed scientific studies, this paper argues that the domain has only been subject to research for about half a decade and that the domain is still unexplored in many aspects. One major absence is a lack of cross referencing of studies and limited number of cumulative studies on whether e-government can aid NPM or fuel innovation. However, the good news is that the literature review demonstrates that researchers entering the domain mainly base their research on empirical studies.

## 1 Introduction

Infusion is in the chemical field the process of extracting certain active properties by steeping or soaking. Although one should be careful applying laboratory techniques to the e-government research field, or other fields in social science research, this type of techniques serve as an excellent analogy and a good tool for studying and highlighting phenomena. Widespread examples are the terms "diffusion" and "critical mass" which origin from chemistry and physics respectively and have acquired a good foothold in social science research.

Since the 1980's there has been a growing trend of adopting private sector management practice to improve the efficiency of public administration. This trend is often labeled "New Public Management" in the literature [1], [2]. According to Hood [1] some important characteristics of NPM are that public managers are given more managerial autonomy and held accountable for results. Furthermore, more emphasis is put on definition and evaluation of targets, and a pressure is laid on greater discipline in resource allocation to ensure more efficient use of public resources. In the literature we find advocates of NPM arguing

M.A. Wimmer et al. (Eds.): EGOV 2006, LNCS 4084, pp. 25–36, 2006.

that it represents a shift to a new paradigm [17]. Others are critical and argue that NPM encompasses too many concept and practices [18] and that key parts of the NPM reform ideas have been reversed or stalled in several "leading-edge" countries [19].

One of the visions of successful e-government is a transformation from traditional bureaucratic government to an emphasis on effective client and citizen services, and internal and external collaboration [22]. Even though e-government is a prioritized activity in many countries [4] research shows, however, that the potential of e-government to transform public sector has remained largely unfulfilled [5]. There has been a key assumption underpinning NPM and many e-government initiatives that models and theories from private sector can be transferred and applied directly to the public sector domain. However, several authors acknowledge important differences between private and public sector, for example transparency and participation as requirements in public services [6], [7].

Osborne and Gaebler [3] argue that the reforms for innovation of public sector have been beneficial when coupled with information and communication technologies (ICT). Several e-government strategy documents emphasize the importance of modernizing and innovating public sector, with arguments like "eGovernment is a catalyst for change in organization, work processes, mindsets, and for innovation" [8]. Margetts et al. [7] describe the relationship between e-government and innovation as hypothetical and argue that more research is needed to assess innovation and change processes in e-government, especially whether models developed in one context is valid and could be adopted to other technically and culturally diverse contexts (ibid). The innovation literature is large and diverse (see [9], [10]). Focus has tended to shift from specific innovations towards analysis of innovation systems, which emphasizes that innovations are created, diffused and implemented within an interconnected and evolving social world [11]. It is often assumed that the public sector is less innovative than the private sector, lacking the incentives provided by market competition. Furthermore, there is a great variation in how innovation is defined and used within public sector. One of the challenges of addressing innovation in public sector is to decide for whom and for what the focal areas of the innovation are. In this paper, the variations and richness in use of the term innovation within public sector will be emphasized rather than focusing on a narrow definition.

Traditionally, there has been a different focus in NPM/innovation literature and e-government. Whereas the former usually has been political and organizational driven [1], the focus in the latter has to a large extent been on technological factors [13]. The objective of this paper is to scan the research literature to explore how the relations between NPM, innovation and e-government are addressed in research. No particular emphasis is laid on either the political/ organizational focus or the technological focus. Instead, the aim is to explore whether, on one hand, NPM and innovation is on the agenda in e-government research, and, on the other hand, whether e-government is a research theme within NPM and innovation research literature.

## 2 Methodology

Literature review is a source for getting solid grounds for further research and for suggesting areas that are in need for particular attention. Within interdisciplinary areas as e-government, there clearly is a need for being much more aware on the borders for e-government, how theories can be build and what we can learn from the past. There are several guidebooks/ research papers on how to make literature reviews (e.g. [34], [35], [33]). In our view, there are less studies that use systematic approaches on identifying previous research before conducting their own research. Often we find statements as: "there has been done limited research in this area" or "the area is fragmented". Yet, authors of such statements often fail to state the area they investigate and how they came to the conclusion that there is limited amount of research.

This literature review applies the methodology which has been used in similar literature reviews [13], [14]. A search was conducted during February 2006 in three online journal databases; Web of Science (SSCI), ProQuest (PQ), and Emerald Fulltext (EMF). The search included research published during the period 1990-2005. The reason for choosing this time span is that the beginning of the 1990s commences the discussion of the NPM discourse.

The following keywords were used as search parameters: New Public Management, including the abbreviation NPM, innovation and e-government, including variations of this term (egovernment, e-governance, egovernance, online government, digital government, e-gov and egov). Literature in this area frequently distinguishes between e-government and e-governance. E-government can be understood as what is happening within government organizations, whereas e-governance also includes activities involving citizens, companies and voluntary organizations taking part in managing society, including processes and flows of governance [4, p. 719]. For the purpose of this paper, we have used e-government as the common entry. In order to analyze the research questions the following combinations of search parameters were used;

- NPM and e-government and innovation
- NPM and e-government
- e-government and innovation

Using the term "innovation" as a generic term clearly holds the danger being too generic and covers totally different research disciplines. In our search we include only studies that combined innovation and e-government and innovation in combination with e-government and NPM. This prevents us from getting a too broad base of research.

The search procedure was restricted with filters that limited the search to articles where the combination of keywords occurred in the title, abstract or keywords. A further filter was added in the PQ database limiting the search to scholarly journals and peer-reviewed articles, and exclude book reviews and newspapers. The search resulted in 66 unique articles. From an initial screen of the articles editorials to special issues, speeches and contributions from non-academic magazines, and articles with peripheral reference to the three search entries were excluded, leaving us with 60 articles as basis for our review.

The research method applied has several limitations. Relevant research may not be included due to lack of categorizing and indexing in the online databases approached in our review. Other valid sources could be book chapters, conference papers, online media, and so forth. As Grönlund [15] points out, the greater part of e-government related papers appear in conference proceedings. Furthermore, the search is limited to three literature databases which are only accepting English-language publications, which puts limitation on countries studied. There are no quality assessments made regarding research methods in the studies or reported findings. However, it is our expectation that editors and reviewers are guardians of the quality assurance. Finally, one could question whether research in this area should be based exclusively on published articles and papers. Most innovative processes may be found in areas and projects which have not yet been explored. It is, however, beyond our aim and scope of this paper to pursue this path. Instead, the aim of this paper is to illuminate the relations from a research based stand.

## 3 Classification of the Contributions Included in the Review

As stated by Webster and Watson [33] "An effective review creates a firm foundation for advancing knowledge. It facilitates theory development, closes areas where a plethora of research exists, and uncovers areas where research is needed." (p. xiii). One of the challenges with respect to making a literature review is the classification of the materials included in a review. Analysis across different studies can be challenging especially in cross disciplinary fields where no common paradigms or models and theories are taken considered to be the core. The definition of the key variables which should guide the literature review [33] therefore becomes more ad hoc than driven by models and theories. It is our assumption that in emerging fields such as e-government and its combination with NPM and innovation a more explorative approach is a more feasible path. To assess the relations between the terms NPM, innovation and e-government in the research literature, a classification model was used consisting of three dimensions; Research category, Research type, and Origin of study.

The first dimension, *Research category*, defines the research area and focal themes of the paper. Research category goes into the core of our research question namely whether NPM and innovation is on the agenda in e-government research or whether e-government is a research theme within NPM and innovation research literature. Based on the three themes NPM, Innovation, and E-government the dimension research category is defined as shown in table 1.

The second dimension included in the analysis, *Research type*, refers to how the researcher(s) have approached the field. The research type dimension has overlapping characteristics of the research methodologies identified by Chen and Hirschheim [16] though we do not stick strictly to the positivist/ interpretivist

**Table 1.** Definition of Research categories

| Research category | Description |
|---|---|
| EGOV- NPM | E-government literature addressing NPM themes |
| EGOV-INN | E-government literature addressing innovation themes |
| NPM-EGOV | NPM literature addressing e-government themes |
| INN-EGOV | Innovation literature addressing e-government themes |

and the cross-sectional/ longitudinal dichotomies. The rationale behind the applied parameter in this study is that it is our assumption that access to and deployment of empirical data influences the way a phenomenon is studied. Ceteris paribus the more conceptual a study is the more is there room for dissolute suggestions to possible directions of government and its application of NPM, innovation or e-government. Inspired by the categories suggested by Chen and Hirschheim [16], we applied the following three main categories of research type; Empirical study, Conceptual study, and Descriptive/ secondary data study in our classification of studies published during the period 1990-2005.

**Table 2.** Definition of Research type

| Research type | Description |
|---|---|
| Empirical study | Studies with analysis/ interpretation of first-hand qualitative or qualitative data are located in this category. Includes research designs as survey, case study, laboratory/ field experiments and action research [16]. |
| Conceptual study | Studies that describe concepts, theory-testing and/or theoretical models fall into this category. |
| Descriptive/ secondary data study | Includes articles that describe a phenomenon with no or little use of theory (e.g. system description, e-government design, documents/reports). Research studies based on secondary data like statistics or existing data datasets are also included in this category. |

The third dimension included in the analysis, *Origin of the study*, is related to in which country the study was conducted. Some countries are generally perceived as being more innovative and up-front with respect to e-government and NPM-reforms. That is for example the case with the US. To examine if that is reflected in the published academic literature the dimension related to origin of the study was included.

# 4 Discussion of Findings

In this section, the findings from our literature analysis of literature that address e-government, NPM and innovation themes are discussed.

## 4.1 Distribution of Articles During the Search Period Span

Our literature search led to 60 unique entries where combinations of the defined search criteria were met. Our assumption was that the time span 1990 to 2005 was a good starting point for the retrieval of contributions covering our research theme given that NPM was on the agenda from the beginning of 1990s. The distribution of the 60 publications over time demonstrates, however, that it is rather the end of the 1990s than the beginning of the decade that can muster academic publications meeting our search criteria (see figure 1). As one of our reviewers rightfully pointed out one reason for this outcome could be that it was not until the mid 1990s that the term e-government found its way to the vocabulary of researchers and practitioners. If terms such as IT in government had been included in the search it would probably have led to a different outcome.

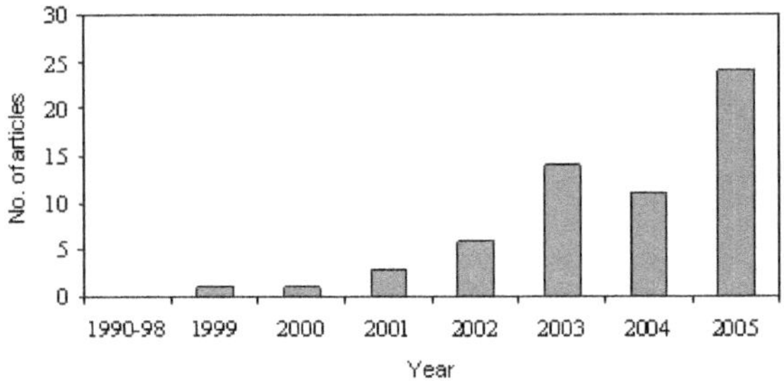


**Fig. 1.** Distribution of contributions during the period 1990-2005

### 4.2 E-Government and Innovation Themes

Of the 60 articles in our analysis, most of them were e-government related articles addressing Innovation themes. There have been an increasing number of articles the last three years in this category (see table 3). The largest numbers of articles were identified in the category e-government studies addressing innovation (32 articles) while the opposite innovation related literature addressing e-government was the least often found theme (2 articles).

The themes of the articles in these categories reflect the fact that the innovation research literature is large and diverse. The articles on innovation cover several themes from those based on innovation and organizational change, technology adoption to those more specifically contextual oriented. *Organizational themes* cover learning, organizational change, knowledge management and technology management themes related to innovation [e.g. 22]. Other themes are *intra-organizational* by nature, focusing on cross-boarder collaboration, co-operation and virtual networks related to innovation. One dominant theme is the *technology innovation* theme covering diffusion theory, adaptation of innovation, demand for innovation and barriers to citizen adoption [e.g. 25]. Findings from Carter and Belanger's study [26] suggest that perceived relative advantage, perceived image, and perceived compatibility are significant elements of e-Government adoption. They argue that an understanding of these factors is critical as e-government grows in importance worldwide. There are a lesser amount of articles combining organizational and technology themes. Finally, there are articles covering contextual e-government themes, debating needs in

**Table 3.** Articles per Category

| | NPM (I) | E-GOV Innovation (II) | NPM EGOV (III) | Innovation EGOV (IV) |
|---|---|---|---|---|
| | 2002: 3<br>2003: 4<br>2004: 2<br>2005: 8 | 1999: 1<br>2001: 2<br>2002: 2<br>2003: 8<br>2004: 7<br>2005: 12 | 2000: 1<br>2001: 1<br>2002: 1<br>2003: 1<br>2004: 1<br>2005: 4 | 2003: 1<br>2004: 1 |
| Total | 17 (28%) | 32 (54%) | 9 (15%) | 2 (3%) |

e-government for improved legislations, competition and a framework to drive e-government change [e.g. 23].

Even if the articles typically ask for a more innovative government, we also find critical voices like Hazlett's and Hill's [21]. They point out that the two central aims of e-government; high quality service and value-for-money, may be in conflict and conclude their paper by proposing the question whether e-government can produce truly innovative, responsive public services. Similar arguments are put forward in the study by McNeal et al. [23] analysing three UK cases using process reengineering method for transformational change. The authors ask why none of the cases seeds a process of ongoing innovation and question the radical vision of e-government's potential of transforming public organizations.

### 4.3 E-Government and NPM Themes

The analysis shows that more articles are found in the category "E-government articles addressing NPM themes" (17 articles) compared to "NPM articles addressing e-government themes" (9 articles). In the former category there has been an increasing focus in 2005 compared to previous years, while in the latter there has been no significant change. It should be noted, however, that some of the articles are discussable to which category they belong.

NPM, described as a complex set of ideas about the political, economic and organizational bases of modernisation of public sector [27] has been adopted by several of the government organisations discussed in the articles. In his essay Tupper [12] argues that the Canadian government has confronted continuous pressure for change, which has resulted in a transformation of the government over the last decade. The administrative reform has been driven by the management ideas of NPM. In his view, the impact of e-government and debate of the role of government will generate demands for continuing administrative reform.

Some of the authors see NPM as an external force pushing for transformation and an important reform that has laid the groundwork for e-government (e.g. [29], [30]). Saxena [27] argues that e-government builds on NPM but goes further and aims to transform processes in which public services are generated and delivered. Others are critical to the applicability of private sector's practices and management tools in the NPM agenda [31], [28]. Collins and Butler [32], for example, state that e-government relies heavily upon NPM principles of efficiency and measurement. In their article potential dangers of an uncritical transfer of e-commerce models from business to public sector are raised. The diversity of public sector must be understood, and consideration of the special aspects of public sector product, organizations and "marketplaces" must precede the adaptation of management frameworks, tools and techniques (ibid).

However, the majority of the articles in this group address e-government and NPM as separate themes. No systematic and comparative analysis is made on what impact the two reforms have on each other.

### 4.4 Major Research Types Applied in the Sample

Empirical studies dominate the articles included in our sample (see table 4). The empirical research methodologies are case studies, surveys, or observations. The dominating research designs found were case studies and surveys (13 articles of each). Our findings suggest that there is willingness in public sector to provide access to data and support collaboration with academia. Furthermore, it means that the researchers are interested in getting first-hand experience of e-government initiatives. The rest of the empirical studies were content analysis based on observation of public sector web sites. The domination of empirical studies is found both in e-government articles addressing innovation themes and NPM themes.

Several papers are descriptive, typically describing e-government initiatives, technologies or policies. Two of the articles in this category are research based on secondary data from existing datasets and statistics.

**Table 4.** Articles per Research type

| Research type | Articles |
|---|---|
| Empirical study | 29 (48%) |
| Conceptual study | 11 (18%) |
| Descriptive/secondary data study | 20 (33%) |
| Total | 60 (100%) |

Finally, the minorities of the papers in our review are categorized as conceptual or theoretical, suggesting frameworks and theories based on e-government, NPM or innovation literature. Most of the conceptual articles are found in the category e-government addressing innovation themes.

### 4.5 Origins of the Reviewed Articles

North America and Europe have an approximate equal share of articles (24/25 articles per continent). As mentioned earlier, an important limitation is that only English-language publications are included in the review. Those articles which have their origin in the US are dominated by empirical studies reporting from surveys of e-government initiatives. We also find some conceptual and descriptive studies from the US. In the European studies most of the articles originate from UK, followed by Italy. The Italian e-government studies in our sample are typically empirical, addressing innovation themes. Specific characteristic for the UK studies compared to other European countries is that about half of articles focus on NPM issues. In the Australian, New Zealand and Canadian e-government studies we also find that NPM issues are addressed. Thus, our finding suggests that it is in regions that traditionally were adopters of NPM ideas [17] that relations between NPM and e-government are on the research agenda.

Generally the Asian continent is not well represented. The Asian studies have similar to the US often Innovation on the agenda. However, based on the count described in Table 5, we have not reason to conclude that US is a forerunner with respect to e-government, NPM or innovation. No studies from African countries were found based on the search criteria.

**Table 5.** Focal issues in articles grouped by country and continent

| Origin | EGOV/NPM | EGOV/INN | Total per Continent |
|---|---|---|---|
| North America | | | 24 |
| USA | 7 | 13 | |
| Canada | 3 | 1 | |
| Europe | 1 | 4 | 25 |
| UK | 3 | 4 | |
| Italy | | 4 | |
| Switzerland | 1 | 1 | |
| Austria | 1 | | |
| Germany | | 1 | |
| Ireland | 1 | | |
| Northern Ireland | | 1 | |
| Slovenia | 1 | | |
| Spain | 1 | | |
| (Russia*) | | 1 | |
| Asia | | | 5 |
| Singapore | | 2 | |
| India | 1 | | |
| Jordan | 1 | | |
| South Korea | | 1 | |
| Australia/Oceania | | | 3 |
| Australia | 2 | | |
| New Zealand | 1 | | |
| General study | 2 | 1 | 3 |
| Total | 26 | 34 | 60 |

* Note: Russia is included in the European continent. We have no intentions of disturb any political or ideological discourse by this categorization.

## 5 Conclusions

The review of the 60 peer-reviewed articles meeting our criteria indicates that the process where extracts of NPM and innovation are infused in e-government research has not really started. One observation from the review is that the combination of the three search entries (e-government, NPM and innovation) is still in its infancy. Articles are registered in the chosen databases from 1999 and onwards. The term e-Government emerged in the late 1990s, but research originally labeled IT in the public sector emerged from the 1970s [4]. Given that also innovation in organizations is an old research area, whereas NPM is a bit younger but still at least a decade old it appears that there is an unexplored area, which deserves attention in future research. From this perspective our literature review was successful given that one of the objectives of literature reviews is to uncover areas where research is needed [33]. This is also supported in articles from our literature search. Criado and Ramilo, for example, argue that "NPM implies an intriguing and unstudied relationship with ICTs enhancement within public organizations" [20, p. 196].

As stated in the introduction the objective of this paper is "to scan the literature to explore whether on one hand, NPM and innovation is on the agenda in e-government research, and on the other hand, whether e-government is a research theme within NPM and innovation research literature." Our analysis of 60 peer-reviewed academic journal articles suggests that the e-government literature addresses NPM and innovation rather than the other way round. Most prevalent is e-government literature addressing innovation themes. About 50% of our cases fall into this category whereas only a few cases address e-government from an innovation perspective. The distribution between e-government studies addressing NPM themes and NPM studies addressing e-government is more even. The majority of the articles in this group, however, addresses the themes separately and makes no systematic and comparative analysis on the impacts of NPM on e-government and visa versa.

Our findings give rise to speculations with respect to whether research within the domain of e-government, NPM and innovation is on the right track. As suggested by Andersen and Henriksen [13] and Grönlund [4] there are good reasons to strengthen the theoretical foundation of e-government research. One way would be to borrow theoretical frameworks from the domains of NPM and innovation. The good news from our review is that approximately half of the reviewed studies report from field experience by using empirical studies. First of all it means that there are many e-government activities taking place. Secondly, it indicates that there is willingness in the respective governments to provide access to data and to support collaboration with academia. Thirdly, it suggests that academia is interested in getting first-hand experience of what is going on in the public sector. The review suggests that most research activity in the area is taking place in North America and Europe. From the few reported studies it is, however, evident that e-government plays a central role in the Pacific as well as in Asia.

Our findings call for further investigation of innovation within the core areas of government. Based on our scan of the research we propose that most e-government research when being innovative, deals about innovation with the administrative domain. Innovation in the core activities appears to be less covered. However, this shortcoming might be due to that such projects have only recently emerged and therefore not made into the scientific journals yet. Also, the dynamic interchange between public administration and IT have at least in Europe a language bias in the sense that there could be a rich literature on NPM and e-government published in European national and perhaps more practitioner journals without making it to the research outlets included in our search.

## References


1. Hood, C.: Explaining Economic Policy Reversals. Open University Press, Buckingham (1994)
2. Page, S.: What's New about the New Public Management? Administrative Change in the Human Services. Public Administration Review, Vol. 65, No. 6 (2005) 713-727
3. Osborne, D. and Gaebler, T.: Reinventing government. Addison-Wesley, Reading Mass. (1992)
4. Grönlund, Å.: Introducing e-Gov: History, Definitions, and Issues. Communications of the Association for Information Systems, Vol. 15 (2004) 713-729
5. West, D. M.: E-Government and the Transformation of service Delivery and Citizen Attitudes. Public Administration Review, Vol. 64, No. 1 (2004) 15-27
6. Lenk, K. and Traunmüller, R.: Broadening the Concept of Electronic Government. In: Prins, J.E.J. (ed.): Designing E-Government. On the Crossroad of Technological Innovation and Institutional Change. Kluwer, The Hague (2001) 63-74
7. Margetts, H., Dunleavy, P., Bastow, S. and Tinkler, J.: Leaders and Followers: E-government, Policy Innovation and Policy Transfer in the European Union. Paper presented at the EUSA Conference, Nashville, Tennessee, 27th March 2003
8. CoBrA: eGovernment Beyond 2005. Modern and Innovative Public Administrations in the 2010 horizon. `http://europa.eu.int/information_society/activities/egovernment_research` (2005) (Accessed January 20th 2006)
9. Scott Poole, M. and Van de Ven, A.: Handbook of Organizational Change and Innovation. Oxford University Press, Oxford (2004)
10. Fagerberg, J., Mowery, D. and Nelson, R.: The Oxford Handbook of Innovation. Oxford University Press, Oxford (2005)
11. Lundvall, B-Å.: Innovation, Growth and Social Cohesion. The Danish Model. Edward Elgar, Cheltenham (2002)
12. Tupper, A.: The contested terrain of Canadian public administration in Canada's third century. Journal of Canadian Studies, Vol. 35, No. 4 (2001) 142-160
13. Andersen, K. V. and Henriksen, H. Z.: E-government research: Domains and Application Areas 1998-2003. International Journal of Electronic Government Research, Vol. 1, No. 4 (2005) 26-44
14. Swan, J., Scarbrough, H. and Preston, J.: Knowledge Management: The next fad to forget people? In: Proceedings of ECIS '99, Copenhagen, Denmark (1999) 668-678
15. Grönlund, Å.: State of the Art in e-Gov Research – A Survey. In: Proceedings at the Third International Conference. EGOV 2004, Zaragoza, Spain, Aug,/Sept. 2004, Springer (2004), 178-185
16. Chen, W. and Hirschheim, R.: A Paradigmatic and Methodological Examination of Information Systems Research from 1991 to 2001. Information Systems Journal, Vol. 14 (2004) 197-235
17. Kettl, D.: The Global Public Management Revolution. Brookings Institution, Washington (2000)
18. Lynn, L.: A Critical analysis of the New Public Management. International Public Management Journal. Vol. 1, No. 1 (1998) 107-123
19. Dunleavy, P., Margetts, H, Bastow, S. and Tinkler, J.: New Public Management Is Dead-Long Live Digital-Era Governance. Journal of Public Administration Research and Theory. September 8 (2005) 1-28
20. Criado, J. I. and M. C. Ramilo.: E-government in practice: An analysis of Web site orientation to the citizens in Spanish municipalities. The International Journal of Public Sector Management, Vol. 16, No. 3 (2003) 191-218

21. Hazlett, S-A. and Hill, F.: E-government: the realities of using IT to transform the public sector. Managing Service Quality, Vol. 13, No. 6 (2003) 445-452
22. Archer, N. P.: An overview of the change management process in eGovernment. International Journal of Electronic Business, Vol. 3, No. 1 (2005) 68-87
23. McNeal, R.S., Tolbert, C.J., Mossberger, K. and Dotterweich, L.J.: Innovating in digital government in the American states. Social Science Quarterly, Vol. 84, No. 1 (2003), 52-70
24. Scherlis, W. L. and Eisenberg, J.: IT research, innovation, and e-government. Communications of the ACM, Vol. 46, No. 1 (2003) 67-68
25. Hinnant, C. C. and O'Looney, J.A.: Examining Pre-Adoption Interest in Online Innovations: An Exploratory Study of E-Service Personalization in the Public Sector. IEEE Transactions on Engineering Management, Vol. 50, No. 4 (2003) 436-447
26. Carter, L. and Belanger, F.: The utilization of e-government services: citizen trust, innovation and acceptance factors. Information Systems Journal, Vol. 15, No. 1 (2005) 5-25
27. Saxena, K.B.C. Towards excellence in e-governance. International Journal of Public Sector Management, Vol. 18, No. 6 (2005) 498-513
28. Teicher, J., Hughes, O. and Dow, N.: E-government: a new route to public sector quality. Managing Service Quality, Vol. 12, No. 6 (2002) 384-393
29. Hughes, V. and Love, P.E.D.: Toward cyber-centric management of policing: back to the future with information and communication technology. Industrial Management & Data Systems, Vol. 104, No. 7 (2004) 604-612
30. Davison, R.M., Wagner, C. and Ma, L.C.K.: From government to e-government: a transition model. Information Technology & People, Vol. 18, No. 3 (2005) 280-299
31. Griffin, D. and Halpin, E.: An Exploratory Evaluation of UK Local e-Government. From an Accountability Perspective. The Electronic Journal of e-Government, Vol. 3, No. 1 (2005) 13-28
32. Collins, N. and Butler, P.: The marketplace, E-government and E-democracy. Irish Marketing Review, Vol. 15, No. 2 (2002) 86-93
33. Webster, J. and Watson, R.T.: Analyzing the Past to Prepare for the Future: Writing a Literature Review. MIS Quarterly, Vol. 26, No. 2 (2002) xiii-xxiii
34. Lewis, M.W. and Grimes, A.J.: Metatriangulation: Building theory from multiple paradigms. Academy of Management Review, Vol. 24, No. 4 (1999) 672-690
35. Cooper H.M.: Synthesizing Research: A Guide for Literature Reviews, (3rd ed.) Sage Publications, Thousand Oaks, CA (1998)

# The Organisation and Coordination of European e-Government Research for the EU in 2010

Jaro Berce[1], Annaflavia Bianchi[1], Clara Centeno[1], David Osimo[1], Jeremy Millard[2], and Jamal Shahin[3]

[1] Institute for Prospective Technological Studies, Sevilla, Spain (DG JRC, European Commission)*
[2] Danish Technological Institute, Denmark
[3] European Institute of Public Administration, The Netherlands

**Abstract.** The objective of this study – the first of its kind – was to validate and further analyze the specific e-Government research challenges and opportunities for the enlarged European Union that had been identified in previous research. The study reveals some important indications for future EU organisation and coordination of e-Government research activities.

The study outlined the fact that the organisation of EU e-Government research should be better linked along the value chain of research (between basic/theoretical, applied, development and review research). The results of the study also indicate that links between eGovernment research and policy should be made more explicit. E-Government research innovations are positioned in a political environment, where research results could bring innovative eGovernment implementation which would support public value as its ultimate goal, through increased efficiency and effectiveness.

In addition, the results of the study highlight a number of organisational research challenges such as: the need for more cooperation, collaboration and networking between stakeholders; the opportunity to build synergies in research across public sectors in a truly interdisciplinary way and between different public stakeholders (i.e. along with e-Health, e-Learning, etc.) and the private sector.

## 1 Introduction

This paper is based on the results of the study contracted by the Institute for Prospective Technological Studies (IPTS[1]) to the Danish Technological Institute (DTI) and the European Institute of Public Administration (EIPA) on "Towards the eGovernment vision for EU in 2010: Research Policy Challenges".[2]

* The views expressed in this publication are the sole responsibility of the authors and do not necessarily reflect the views of the European Commission.

[1] The IPTS is the Institute for Prospective Technological Studies and one of the seven institutes of the Joint Research Centre (JRC) of the European Commission (http://www.jrc.es). Its main mission is to provide prospective analyses in support of the EU's policy making-process.

[2] The draft report can be downloaded from http://fiste.jrc.es/pages/egovernment.htm

M.A. Wimmer et al. (Eds.): EGOV 2006, LNCS 4084, pp. 37–46, 2006.

This study is informed by the awareness that the present paradigm on the use of Information and Communication Technologies (ICT) in e-Government, focusing mainly on delivering existing services through cheaper ICT-based distribution channels or by complementing existing services with added e-Features, should be renewed and enlarged. For example, over the next decade, the EU will undergo a number of social and economic transitions such as increasing cultural and religious diversity, population ageing and changing living, working and consumption patterns, which will require public services to be rethought and even recreated. Technological advances in ICT miniaturisation and portability suggest that, in the future, e-Government will form part of an Ambient Intelligence environment, where issues such as surveillance, identity management, and the distinction between public and private spheres will arise.

The vision that emerged from prior research into the future prospects for e-Government research (Centeno et al, 2004) defines e-Government in the EU in the next decade as a tool for better government in its broadest sense. It places e-Government at the core of public management modernisation and reform, where technology is used as a strategic tool to modernise structures, processes, regulatory frameworks, human resources and the culture of public administrations to provide better government, and ultimately, increased *public value.*

However, in order to take full advantage of the opportunities promised by the envisaged future for e-Government, a number of research issues must be addressed. Several research areas which contain specific research challenges had been identified by experts, based on their knowledge in current state-of-the-art research (as described in the report by Centeno et al, 2004).

## 1.1 The Objectives of the Study

Building on the vision and challenges developed with the experts' input, the main objective of this study has been to identify the key e-Government research areas, challenges and opportunities that need policy attention in order to achieve the e-Government vision and contribute to the Lisbon economic and societal objectives. The study aims, among other things, to contribute to the definition of the European Commission 7th Framework Programme for Research.

In particular three objectives were determined for the study:

1. to validate the policy relevance of each of the initially identified research areas and to provide an assessment of priority,
2. to identify the major research challenges and opportunities ahead and,
3. to identify potential research policy options and provide an assessment of their priority.

In the following chapters, we present selected outcomes of the study, which has investigated research challenges in key areas for the implementation of the *e-Government* vision, as opposed to generic challenges to the development of the Information Society. The purpose was not to conduct research on these areas, but about these areas. While the overall study explored all the e-government research challenges, this paper focuses mainly on the specific issues relating to organisation and operation of e-government research. What are the organisational challenges for e-government research to fully support the contribution of e-government to public value? Which type of research should be carried out? How should the actors be involved? How should research be organised?

Chapter 2 describes the methodology used and the taxonomy developed prior to the research effort. Chapter 3 presents some conclusions on the overview of the status of e-Government recent (up to the end of 2005) research in Europe. Chapter 4 presents selected major organization and coordination challenges of e-Government research in Europe, and Chapter 5 examines some of the conclusions that could be drawn from the research work done in the field.

## 2 Methodology and Taxonomy

In order to meet the stated objectives, data has been collected using three main methods: a questionnaire-based survey, content analysis of e-Government research literature, and interviews with experts. Data collection for this study was quite difficult, and relied upon several diverse sources of information, which had no coherent semantic interoperability. Therefore, specific efforts were made to validate a taxonomy of e-government research challenges, building on the results of previous work (Centeno et al 2004). As the following table shows, research challenges were categorized according to whether they were inward (back office) or outward (user orientation) facing, and by the policy level they were related to (from operational to general).

With regard to the methods, first, a questionnaire was completed by 200 e-Government research stakeholders (academics, consultants, and representatives of the public sector, the ICT industry, users and media, and the European Commission). While there was no prior basis for determining the representation of the stakeholder sample, balanced participation was obtained by looking at the types and numbers of stakeholders contributing to conference publications and participating in EU research. Thus, 21% of the questionnaires were sought and obtained from academics, 16% from consultants, 26% from the public sector, 18% from the ICT industry, 13% from users and the media, and 6% from the European Commission. Of these 200 stakeholders, 66% were European and 34% from elsewhere. The questionnaire addressed questions related to the three research objectives stated above. In particular, there were questions on which areas the respondent had carried out recent (in the last 2 years) research, which research areas she/he recommended for future research, and what they considered to be the main research policy options for e-government research.

Second, an assessment of recent research was carried out, through a content analysis of e-Government research literature, mainly (but not exclusively) focussing on the proceedings of the DEXA e-Government Conferences in 2004 and 2005, and on EU-funded e-Government research projects. This choice, limited by resources and time constraints, was based on the fact that the DEXA Conference has wide stakeholder and geographical coverage (Grnlund, 2005), and on the purpose of the research, mainly designed to support EU policy-making. Overall, the study reviewed nearly 400 sources, authored by 829 stakeholders. This method aimed to identify which areas have been recently, or are currently being, addressed by research and their status in terms of deployment (theoretical research, applied research, development research and review research).

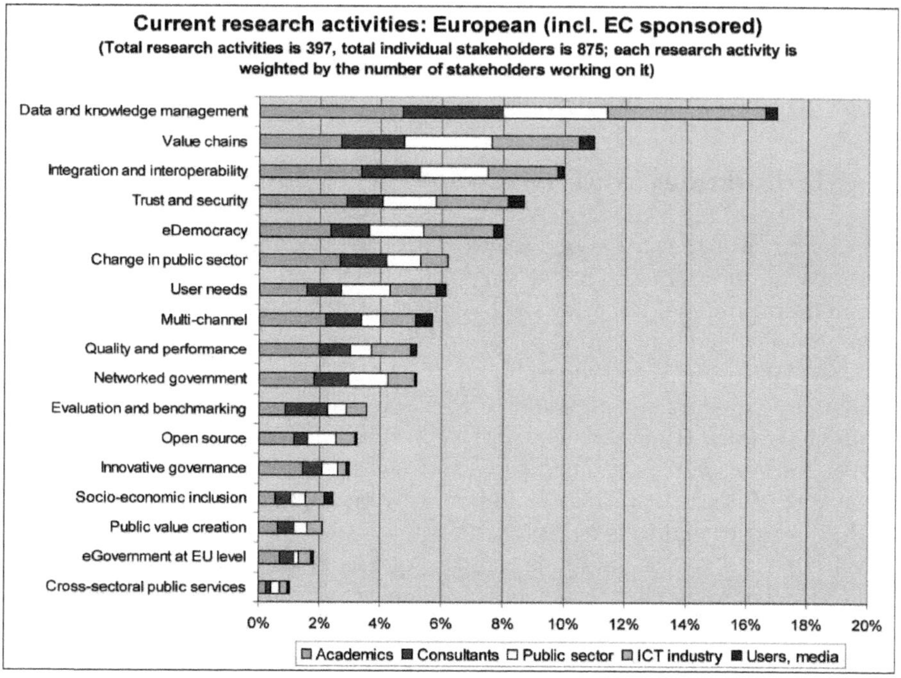


**Fig. 1.** Key areas of e-Government-specific research challenges

In order to support a quantitative analysis of recent research (see Chapter 3), results from the above mentioned two methods have been integrated by giving a weighting to each research activity according to the number of stakeholders working on it. A "research activity" is a generic term that included a paper, an article or a research project on e-government. Due to the exploratory nature of this study, which address a research area which is not yet well defined such as e-Government, it has not been the intention to collect statistically significant samples, but rather to collect information to be used and analysed qualitatively and heuristically.

Third, interviews were carried out with 58 e-Government experts worldwide, to validate the quantitative results and provide additional insight into existing research policy challenges. In addition, results were also extensively discussed and validated by around 20 experts, who had not previously participated in the research, in two dedicated one-day workshops.

# 3 Recent e-Government Research in the EU

The first results presented in this chapter are based on the questionnaires and the content analysis and provide a map of recent research areas with policy relevance. For each area of recent research, the deployment status – from theoretical, applied, up to development – was also analyzed.

## 3.1 Areas of Recent Research in Europe

The chart on the next page (Figure 2) shows the relative ranking of recent European e-Government research activities across the 17 research areas of Table 1. Research effort is measured by the number of research activities covering each research area, where each research activity is given a weighting according to the number of stakeholders working on it. This chart shows a distinct research focus on areas heavily oriented towards direct technology use and implementation, such as "Data and knowledge management", "Value chains" and "Integration and interoperability". The focus of recent research activities is therefore very much oriented towards inward-facing and design issues, related to the daily activities and operational objectives of e-Government. On the other hand, areas like "Public value creation", "Innovative governance" and "Cross-sectoral public services" have very low relative focus. User orientation of e-Government is emerging as a research field, with "e-Democracy", "User needs" and "Trust and security" being relatively well represented.

"Data and knowledge management" appears as the most researched area by far, being addressed by all stakeholders. Data and knowledge management is a fundamental aspect of many research projects in terms of ICT-based development. These are integrated into applied research initiatives as the building blocks of many e-Government projects.

When positioning EU research with the rest of the world, questionnaire respondents indicated that Europe is relatively strong in research on "e-Democracy" and "Change in the public sector". However, they indicated that European research is comparatively weak in areas such as "Multi-channel delivery", "Value chains", "Quality and performance", and "User needs". They stated that, best practice in these last four research areas can be found in North America and Australasia.

## 3.2 Deployment Status of the Research Areas

When looking at the deployment status of analyzed literature in each research area, the main conclusion for European research is that the first two inward facing e-Government objective areas: "Data and knowledge management" and "Integration and interoperability" appear to be well advanced along the path to deployment. However, the third of these areas, "Change in the Public Sector", in spite of the significant research activities identified (see Figure 1), has progressed less in deployment. The analysis concludes that research activity is more concentrated at national and regional level than at EU level, and is carried out mainly by academics, rather than industry and/or public sector. This might

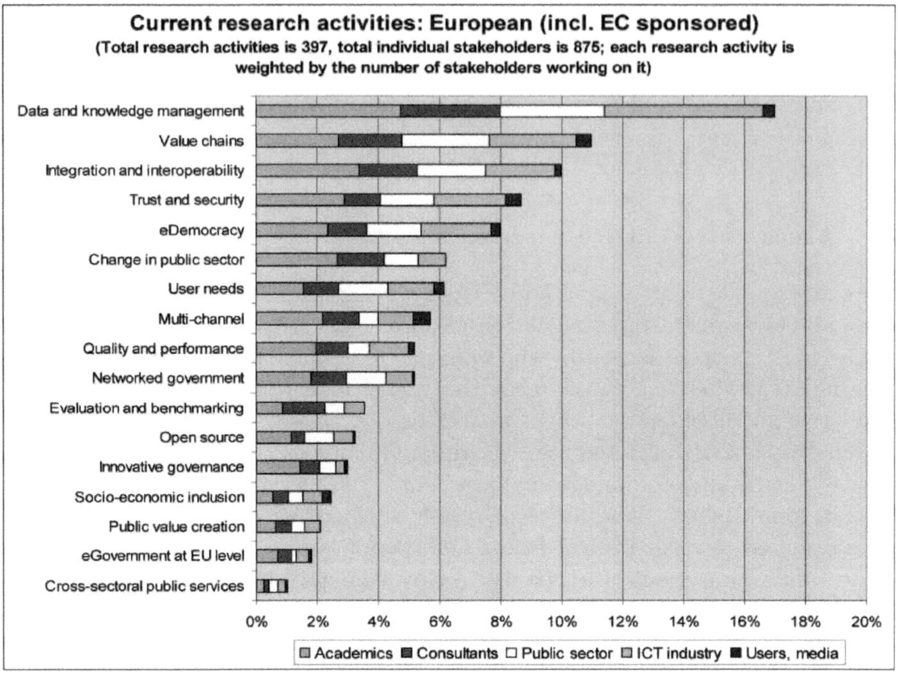


**Fig. 2.** Recent research in Europe

partly explain the low degree of deployment, which may also be due to political and bureaucratic resistance and the long time scale needed for change.

Service design/delivery areas have a few applications in place, but generally they are still areas where deployment is some way off. This may be due to the practical difficulties of designing and delivering e-Government services in collaboration with the private and voluntary sectors or with other public agencies at different levels, and in getting the high levels of coordination needed for multi-channel rollout to be successful.

The research area "Users needs" is quite varied in terms of deployment, as it includes theoretical discussion on the importance of designing systems to meet user needs, simple user and customer satisfaction surveys, and development of systems to allow the user to participate in the actual design of the delivery mechanism or service. The development implications of inclusive and universal access to e-Government services are being addressed more extensively in Europe.

Furthermore, the analysis shows that EC-sponsored research activities are generally closer to deployment and thus more likely to have a direct impact on EU policy. Moreover, EC-sponsored research involves a higher number of different stakeholders (i.e. is more multi-stakeholder), including a larger proportion of public sector and ICT industry stakeholders, and covers a larger number of disciplines (i.e. is more multi-disciplinary) than the other research activities examined in this study.

## 4 Organisation, Coordination and Operation of European e-Government Research

In this chapter, we present the most relevant results on identified challenges to organization, coordination and operation of European e-Government research. This chapter is based on the input received from the questionnaire and interviews.

Interviewed stakeholders focussed their observations on the type of research to be carried out and on the coordination and funding of this research. While this input was very diverse, it pointed out strongly to the problem of fragmentation and the need for increased collaboration.

First and foremost, there was wide agreement on the fragmented status of e-Government research, seen as a key weakness which hinders the possibility to take full advantage of the research effort. This is not a new theme, but the consensus around it was very significant. Though the role of the Commission in stimulating the coordination of research was widely recognized as very important and effective, it was also largely agreed that this role should be further strengthened. Also, the generic problem was further described in relation to specific aspects: between researchers, between researchers and practitioners, between different stages of research, between different parts of government, and others, illustrated in more detail below.

With regard to the quality of the research, fragmentation leads to lower quality because of duplication and wasted effort. New research does not build on existing research and a tendency to "re-invent the wheel" arises. When looking at conference papers, for example, few references appear to other papers on the same subject, and literature reviews are often partial. This lack of integration was indirectly reflected in this study, which has had to look for e-government research activities from a wide range of sources and create a single taxonomy in order to consolidate very different research activities, which use various approaches and terms.

Also, the fact that e-government research is by nature multidisciplinary reinforces this risk, as dialogue and cross-fertilisation across disciplines is obviously more difficult. The fact that e-government is a rather new research area is at the same time a cause of fragmentation but also an urgent reason for better coordination, in order to consolidate and accelerate the learning processes.

Respondents pointed to an additional element of division, between the different parts of the public sector. As we have seen above, research on e-government across different public sector domains is not very common in Europe, while the US appear to be more advanced in this sense. Indeed, stakeholders pointed to the need for a wider approach to e-government, integrating research activities on different functions of government, which share similar problems, like, for example, the administration of social security and of health services.

Last but not least, fragmentation along the value chain of research hinders the impact of e-government research. At the technological level, respondents pointed out that better linking is needed between basic/theoretical, applied, development and review research. For example, in order to stimulate the transfer of research, more focus should be placed on the use of laboratories, pilots, trials, test beds in real life situations, and prototyping. At the policy level, explicit and strong links should be made between e-government research and policy priorities, as the ultimate justification of e-government research is promoting innovation in government that delivers public value. This is further confirmed in other parts of the study, not reported here, which indicate a strong predicted increase in relevance of research on public value. Not only should e-government research be assessed by the positive impact it has on e-government itself, but also by how it helps to translate e-government into increased public value for the citizens.

In view of these observations, it comes as little surprise that recommendations for research organisation concentrate on the need for consolidation, communication and collaboration.

At the policy level, e-Government is not yet widely recognized as an important field of research. Apart from European funded research, very few countries have dedicated research programmes, even though e-government deployment is a national competence. Also, because of the absence of this strategic framework, e-government research often appears to be carried out autonomously, and in isolation, in universities, industry and the public sector. Dedicated research programmes are important not only because they stimulate research, but also because they aggregate it around similar topics, thereby reducing fragmentation.

In terms of priority-setting, stakeholders suggest the need for further strategic prioritising of eGovernment research. This would allow EU resources to be focused largely on more top-down strategic priorities, whilst leaving a healthy growth of bottom-up, decentralised research to academia, the ICT industry, and the public sector.

Better communication of research is also a very frequent recommendation from interviewees. This would involve communication between researchers themselves and between researchers and practitioners. In the research community, there is a perceived need to share positive and also negative research results better, in order to facilitate mutual learning. Some sort of pooling of European e-government research resources was seen as necessary, so that all involved in e-government could come together to share knowledge and avoid the duplication of research efforts. Collaboration in global e-government research, seen as insufficient at the moment, should also be increased to reinforce knowledge exchange. As we have seen in Chapter 3, some non-EU countries present very interesting developments in e-government research and collaboration could help the learning process in the EU. Some respondents even suggested that a specific budget should be dedicated to networking and communication between research activities, within Europe and at the global level.

Communication with e-government practitioners should be seen as a two-way exchange of information. It should aim to transfer research results and also to achieve a better understanding of the research needs in e-government implementation. Thinking along the same line, many respondents insisted that e-government research should devote particular attention to involving as far as possible the full spectrum of different stakeholders, perhaps at different stages of the research.

## 5 Conclusions

This paper elaborates on a part of the study on e-government challenges in Europe by providing an overview of current research areas in e-government, and of the organisational challenges that have to be addressed in order to maximize its impact. Firstly, it shows that e-government research areas are addressed with very different intensity, and that the current focus is very much on ICT applications that favour integration within government, such as data and knowledge management, and interoperability. There is evidence of some research activity on the user orientation of e-Government, with "e-Democracy", "User needs" and "Trust and security" being relatively well represented.

Less attention is currently devoted to the impact of e-government on delivering public value, although interest is expected to grow in the future. In fact, the more stringent linking of e-government research with overarching policy goals is one of the main recommendations expressed by interviewed stakeholders. Research should be more focussed and oriented toward policy goals. Also, closer integration between different disciplines and different government sectors is seen as important for future organisation of e-government research.

However, the most urgent claim was certainly for overcoming the current fragmentation of e-government research in Europe. A serious and widespread concern was that fragmentation and lack of coordination are leading to inefficient outcomes, especially in terms of risks of duplication of efforts, lower quality of the results and less relevance and impact of the research. There is evidence of perceived important opportunities, especially for the EC, for further promoting the integration of European research in this field: not only in order to reinforce links between research carried out in different countries, but also between research activities and centres, between academic disciplines, and between policy areas. Some stakeholders indicated the opportunity to set up a virtual European centre for e-government in order to promote knowledge sharing and dissemination. While it is not within the remit of this research to discuss this idea, it is certainly a sign that demand for bringing together European e-government research exists.

It is true to say that these are not new ideas: in 2006, for example, the Commission (DG INFSO) has launched three projects aimed precisely at promoting integration of European research in this field.[3] A call for tender was launched for a study on bringing together and accelerating eGovernment research in EU. Two research projects were launched under the 4th call of the IST programme, eGOVERNET and eGOVRTD2020, which aim, respectively, to create a common framework of national eGovernment research programmes, and a common roadmap for e-government research in Europe, both of which are important steps towards building a European Research Area on e-government. This research spells out some of the fragmentation elements to be addressed, and that this type of action strongly meets the demand of European stakeholders.

[3] For further information, see http://europa.eu.int/information_society/activities/egovern ment_research/index_en.htm

One of the clearest needs indicated by the study, with regard to organisational challenges, is to ensure the communication of research and research results. Sharing of research data and results is paramount. The EC's research funding initiatives could clearly help in this regard at the European level, but considerable work needs to be done to ensure that research carried out at the national and local levels is integrated into this perspective. This is crucial as it would help researchers to increase the quality and relevance of their work, practitioners to design and implement more effective ICT solutions, and policy-makers to better understand the significance of e-government research, in order to design appropriate e-government deployment and research strategies. This study, and the results of the part presented here, aimed to provide a basis for the formulation of e-government research policies, by promoting a better and common understanding of how e-government research is carried out, and the key challenges it is facing in Europe.

## References

1. Centeno, C. et al. (2004) e-Government in the EU in the next decade: the vision and key challenges, IPTS Technical Report, [online], `http://fiste.jrc.es/download/eur21376en.pdf`.
2. Grönlund, Å. (2005) State of the art in e-gov research: surveying conferences publications, Idea Group Inc.
3. Millard, J, Shahin, J. Leitner, C, Warren, R. (2006 forthcoming) "Towards the eGovernment vision for EU in 2010: research policy challenges", for the Institute of Prospective Technological Studies, Seville, Spain, European Commission, DG JRC.

# What Role Has Scandinavian IS Tradition in eGovernment Implementations

Arild Jansen

Section for eGovernment Studies, University of Oslo, Norway
arildj@jus.uio.no

**Abstract.** The aim of this paper is to take part in the discussions on how the Scandinavian IS research tradition in information system research may contribute to eGovernment developments and implementations. Although this tradition does not represent a coherent set of principles and methods for system development, they share some common ideas and goals related to user involvement, participatory design and democracy at the work place. Even if some of the most basic ideas are inherent in our understanding of the IS field to day, many of the lessons from the past may have been forgotten. Some do also claim that the dominant understanding of eGovernment is primarily based on efficiency, customer orientation and competition. I will argue that advanced development and use of ICT also can support ideals and goals similar to those of the Scandinavian approaches to IS; we should not least have a greater focus on studying the consequences of various approaches to system design, implementation and use.

## 1 Introduction

The Information Systems Research in Scandinavia seminars (IRIS) is celebrating its 30$^{th}$ anniversary next year, and it gathers every year up to 150 participants, including a number of international researchers. The journal (Scandinavian Journal of Information Systems) will publish its 23. edition this year. A number of books have been written, and this research community has had significant influence on the IS field in general.

Scandinavian research projects[1] in system development have traditionally put a strong emphasis on user participation and support for different interests as a strategy for increased work life democracy, and also for the society at large. However, as important goals have been to develop well-functioning, user-friendly and high-quality system. The basic assumption is that one only can achieve long-term benefits by combining these different goals and by managing the clashes of interests and contradictions that necessary will appear in system development projects.

[1] The intention is not to attribute these views on system development work to the Scandinavian IS research only; this tradition has to day supporters in a number of countries, see e.g. the PDC (Participatory Design Conference) community, http://www.pdc2006.org/

M.A. Wimmer et al. (Eds.): EGOV 2006, LNCS 4084, pp. 47–57, 2006.

There have in recent years been great achievements and progress in eGovernment developments and implementations. We have also seen a number of failures. To what extent are the experiences and knowledge gained from the research in the past relevant to day? And what have the influence of new managerial paradigms been, in its focus on market orientation, service provision to customers and high performance through competition?

This paper does not aim at answering all these questions, but may hopefully stimulate to a debate on how the knowledge and experiences gained in past Scandinavian IS research effort can contribute to further progress in this new field.

The structure of the paper is as follows. Chapter 2 summarizes the basic ideas of the Scandinavian school(s) of IS research. Chapter 3 visits the debate on the relation between eGovernment and New Public Management, followed by a discussion of the role that Scandinavian IS approaches may have in the eGovernment era.

## 2 Scandinavian Traditions in System Development Research

System developments has, from the outset been an expert-dominated and top-down oriented activity from problem description to implementation, use and maintenance, frequently referred to as "phase-driven" or the "Waterfall" development method. This approach is characterized by system-theoretical thinking, often based a functional analysis of the system to be modeled and designed and implemented. However, it became early clear that this approach had a number of weaknesses.

The Scandinavian tradition in information system research has its roots the early action-oriented research projects and efforts in late 60thies and 70thies. Important inspirations came from the socio-technical research by the Norwegian Industrial Democracy project that started in 1960 as cooperation between the Norwegian Federation of Trade Unions (LO) and the Employers organization (NAF, later renamed NHO). But first of all this tradition is linked to the NJMF-project (Norwegian Iron and Metal Workers), in cooperation with Kristen Nygaard and Olav Terje Bergo (Nygaard og Bergo 1974), followed by the Swedish Demos-project and the Due-project in Denmark (se e.g. Ehn og Sandberg 1979, Bansler 1987, 1989, Bjerknes, Ehn og Kyng (1987), Nurminen, M. (1987), Bjerknes, Dahlbom et al 1990, Iivari 1991, Bjerknes and Bratteteig 1995). Although these projects had partly different goals and perspectives, they can be characterized as action research, having a socio-technical orientation and strong user- involvement in all phases, and aiming at democratization at the workplace.

These and other projects were the inspiration and empirical background for the textbook "*Professional System development*" by Andersen et al (1986), in which they emphasizes the relation between development work and management, between process and product and between planning and evaluation, and the need for communication at all levels in the system development processes.

Another important and very interesting contribution is textbook "*Computer and controversy. The philosophy and Practice of Systems Design*"[2], written by Bo Dahlbom and Lars Mathiassen, in which they reflect over the profession of system development and its essential ideas, and not least, discuss some of the fundamental contradictions that is inherent in the practical work. Starting out by addressing our understanding of systems, information and the use of computers as tool for problem solving, and by drawing on various philosophers, they spell out three different frameworks for system development work in distinguishing between *hard, soft, and dialectical* system thinking. Following from that, they outlined three corresponding paradigms for system development. The first one, *construction*, suggests a rational and analytical strategy, while the *evolution* approach focuses on uncertainty and suggests an experimental strategy for problem solving. In the third approach, *intervention* the problem is no longer given, and development cannot be seen as some thing isolated from the life of the organization, and accordingly, system development must be seen as an integral part of organizational change. Furthermore and perhaps the most pioneering, they discuss the many dimensions of quality of technical artifacts, as e.g. functional, aesthetic and symbolic quality, and points to the power, politics and ethics in defining quality.

Many of these and other ideas and experiences have been integrated into a comprehensive method: *Object-Oriented Analysis* and Design (Mathiassen et al 2000), thus offering common framework with a coherent set of principles, concepts and way of thinking, that is based on knowledge and experience collected outside Scandinavia[3]. The footprints from the pioneering research efforts in Scandinavia in this field is easy identifiable. Another original thinker in this field is Claudia Ciborra. His contributions include among others theory and concepts as improvisation, bricolage and tinkering, drifting, Krisis, etc, see e.g. (Ciborra 1996, 2002). In this way, I believe it is fair to say that the basic ideas of this tradition are different from what is found in mainstream system development methods.

## 3 E-Government – More Than the Emperor's New Clothing?

It has not always been obvious that computers could be used for administrative applications. Howard Aiken, designer of one of the very first computers, stated in 1956: "*If it should ever turn out that the basic logic of a machine designed for the numerical solutions of differential equations coincide with the logics of*

[2] In the preface to this book, the Scandinavian IS tradition is not explicitly mentioned, but many of the ideas are inherent in this tradition.

[3] In these projects and other activities, the Scandinavian IS researchers have drawn heavily on international IS research, as e.g. Thorsrud and Emery (1970), Checkland (1981), Mumford (1975, 1983), Borland and Hirschheim (1987), Boehm (1976, 1988), Klein and Hirscheim (1989), Parnas and Clements (1985), Ciborra (1996, 2000, 2002), Grudin (1988), Greenbaum (1995), and many others.

*a machine intended to make bills for a department store, I would regard this as the most amazing coincide that I have ever encountered*"

Aiken was, as we all know, terrible mistaken, and even in Norway, computers were used for governmental tasks already in 1957. During the next decades to come, computers and later on ICT including Internet have being used in a large range of tasks; thought the concept of EGovernment was not used until Internet was in use. EGovernment is today becoming a global phenomenon that is consuming the attention of politicians, policy makers as well as ordinary citizens.

There exits a number of different definitions of eGovernment in the literature. Some are rather narrow, focusing on using ICT, particularly the Internet, as e.g. "the use of technology to enhance the access to and delivery of government services to citizens, business partners and employees" (Deloitte Research 2000, p4.) Others view eGovernment more broadly as efforts to transform government. Such examples can be: "*The use by the government of Web-based Internet applications and other ICTs, combined with processes that implement these technologies, to a) enhance the access to and delivery of government information and services to the public, other agencies, and to government entities; or b) bring about improvements in government to operations that may include effectiveness, efficiencies, service quality, or transformation*" (US government 2002)

EGovernment is thus far more than a technological phenomenon. It is transformative in nature, affecting the management of human, technological, and organizational resources processes. Consequently, the implementation of eGovernment systems will be monumental change effort, which clearly shows that eGovernment to day is qualitatively different from the more isolated ICT-system in the past. The emphasis of eGovernment as a transformational endeavor has inspired some commentators to ask if there is a close a link between eGovernment and the New Public Management paradigm (NPM). New Public Management is a management philosophy used by governments since the 1980's to modernize their public sector. Based on public choice and managerial schools of thought, NPM seeks to enhance the efficiency of the public sector and the control the government has over it.

NPM can among others be characterized by: i) a customer rather than citizen orientation focusing on high quality services that serve narrow interest of the citizens, ii) performance orientation, iii) lean and highly decentralized structures, iv) emphasis on accountability upwards, v)use of divisional structures breaking down former unitary bureaucracies (Bruening 2001). He claims that this type of reform has a techno-optimistic, analytic flavor which seems to reinforce the effects NPM is having on the organizations throughout the industrialized world.

Homburg (2005) has analyzed the use of modern ICTs and especially Internet technologies; from its focus on improving and reengineering internal processes to aiming at the redesign of external relationships in order to improve public administration's accessibility and quality of service provision. He identified 4 different patters: i) markets government, ii) participatory government, iii) flexible government (e.g. virtual organizations) and iv) deregulated government. He thus claims that "underlying to all patterns of practices, is a notion of departure from the classic public administration paradigm". Especially, the notion of decentralization conflicts with public management of strict hierarchy and rules, and centralization by integration. However, he continues, the means used to achieve this may vary from different contact with citizens, market mechanisms and more organic relationships. His analysis seems to indicate that eGovernment services in practice, in its focus on transformation of the public sector, mark a deviation from the classical public administration paradigm. It shows thus no unambiguous relationship between eGovernment and a specific form of public management, rather that there are many different scenarios or trajectories.

More recent research studies point to that while the NPM wave in public sector organizational change was founded on themes of disaggregation, competition, and incentivization, we now see ICT-centered changes based on reintegration, needs-based holism and digitization (Dunleavy et al 2005). They argue that these new shifts are towards a "digital-era governance", offering perhaps a unique opportunity to create self-sustained change, in a broad range of closely connected technological, organizational, cultural and social effects. Without subscribing to all their claims, it seems highly relevant to discuss how to involve the various groups of citizens in these change processes.

## 4 EGovernment and the Scandinavian Tradition: Is There Any Relation?

It thus seems to be evidence for claiming that EGovernment is far more than realizing NPM. If we look at the work on eGovernment in the EU Commission, they focus on these overall objectives for eEurope (Com 2003):

- A public sector as e.g. open and transparent, that is understandable and accountable to the citizens, open to democratic involvement and scrutiny.
- A public sector that is at the service of all, being inclusive and exclude no one from its services
- A productive public sector that delivers maximum value for taxpayers money

These goals may, at a general level conform to the ideas and thinking of Scandinavian IS traditions. However, that is not to say that all eGovernment solutions have consequences we may support from a work life democracy perspective. There are powerful pressure groups, not least from the consulting industry that are pushing strongly for implementing their solutions in rather standardized ways, similar to what we see in the private sector. The strong emphasis on evaluations, benchmarking and ranking (e.g. Com 2003, Capgemini 2005 etc) does not necessarily encourage user involvement and participatory design. The question is then: what role can the Scandinavian IS approaches have in such processes?

Greenbaum (1995) summarizes the main motivations for conducting participatory design as *pragmatic* (improving system design), *theoretical* (e.g. for communication benefits of the involved parties) and *political* (e.g. further workplace democracy). On a more concrete level, these reasons for stronger user involvement are normally given as: i) improving the knowledge upon which systems are build, ii)allowing for experimenting and learning before the solutions are finally implemented and put into use, iii) enabling people to develop realistic expectations and reducing resistance to change, and iv) increasing workplace democracy by giving the member of an organization the right to participate in decisions that are likely to affect their work

However, the way IS systems are being developed and used have been changed during the last 15-20 years, and many will maintain that the above arguments are no longer valid, e.g. because modern system development methods are different from those used in the past, in providing various opportunities for involvement. Internet and Web-based systems tools have changed the way systems are developed. Furthermore, we have a much more knowledgeable and skilled work force related to IT than in the past. There has been a move from internal systems aiming at rationalization to external (customer-oriented) systems aiming at improving the quality of public services, which implies that the users to a large extent are not as employees, but as citizens. One can also argue that new legislation, such as the Working environment act in Norway, provide means for involvement and participation at various levels.

On the contrary, it can also be argued that greater involvement and participation in all phases of development and deployment are even more necessary now, e.g. because:

- We see greater changes in organization than before; the traditional organizational patterns are being challenged in that the borders between private and public sector is continuously being challenged.
- What differs from the past is the change of focus from stand-alone system to large-scale integration of various systems and restructuring, and a shift from focus on the users to consumers and citizens. Systems are getting more and more complex through closer interaction and integration, as basis for radical restructuring of the public sector at large
- There is an increasingly tendency to outsourcing and globalization. We thus see new types of conflicts and contradictions, which best can be handled through participation on various levels.
- The different threats related to digital divide calls for professionals that can support the various groups of citizens that do not have a strong voice on their own.

I am not arguing that we should return to the ideology-driven debates and actions of the "good old days". But we should critically assess the experiences from the past and use them as inspiration and a knowledge base for new thinking and initiatives.

### 4.1 User Participation, Where and How?

User participation is not a panacea in the context of eGovernment. It is not obvious how and where participation best may take place. Marginalization and cultural bias are favoring dominant groups in access and decisions were the important topics in the participatory design activities. And who are the real users? This simple framework may illustrate that there are many different constellation and stakeholders when new ICT-solution are to be implemented:

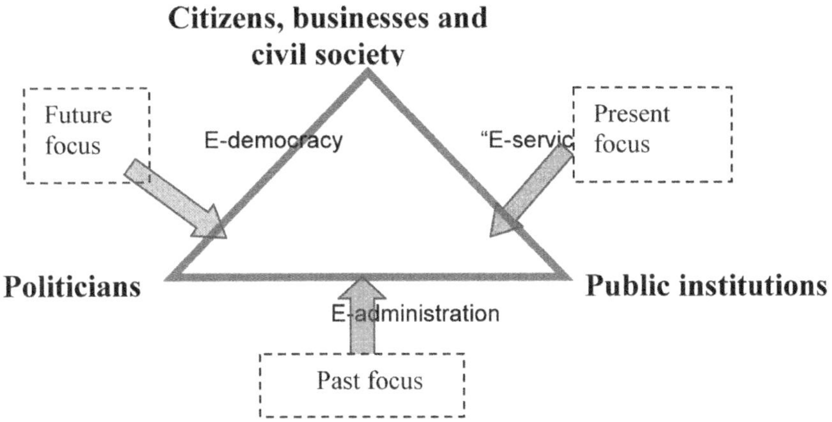


**Fig. 1.** A framework for eGovernment

The above figure aims at illustrating that while one in the pioneering period mostly worked along the horizontal line, and the users were mostly the employees, the focus to day are most related to service provision, and the users are outside the organization, primarily as customers). We are now gradually seeing more efforts toward the "e-democracy" dimension, though mostly as small scale experiments, involving various groups of citizens. It is rather obvious that this wide range of projects types require quite different system development strategies, depending on the goals and perspectives. Thus, in the individual projects, we will have to organize projects such that all involved parties will have their voice heard.

Følstad, Jørgensen et al (2005) have studied user involvement in eGovernment development projects in Norway. They found that there seems to be a broad agreement on the importance of user involvement, at least among the project leaders. However, actual user involvement is often conducted according to the participant practice of the industrial democracy, emphasizing formal procedures rather than the processes and methods advocated within the traditions of HCI. The most frequently deployed user involvement is user representation in project teams, rather than e.g. usability tests and user group analysis. One conclusion from the study is that there seem to be an explicit need of more structured processes for user involvement activities for eGovernment projects.

Oostveen and van den Besselaar (2005) discusses different methods for engaging users in systems design, and ask: To what extent can we use lessons and methods from participatory design, as e.g. being active in the specification and design process, to include a variety of political views and social interests in the social-technical shaping of future trajectories of large-scale of large-scale eGovernment systems. They claim, based on experiences from to large projects, that such traditional methods does not apply for various reasons: i) the models and methods are based on small scale projects, ii) the number and variation of user groups are quite different, and iii) it involves not (only) users as citizens and civil servants, but also politicians on various levels. Their conclusion is that a combination of methods from technology assessment approaches with participatory design practice can be successful, but is not yet practiced enough.

### 4.2 Different Levels of Participation

Bjerknes and Bratteteig (1995) point to that there are many different arenas of participation and democracy, and they describe these three:

1. The *work situation level*, in which the use of technology depends on the nature of work tasks, and the ICT systems are viewed basically as concrete tools. It is possible to influence through participation in the individual development projects, which used to be the traditional type of involvement.
2. The *workplace or organization level*, which depends on how different activities are coordinated and integrated in the organization. Focus is not only on individual systems, but their interlinkage and integration, where the information (technology) architecture and infrastructure are designed, including choices of standards and type of software. Important issues will be the degree of (de)centralization (as e.g. in the national wide systems in public sectors as Tax administration, National Health Insurance offices, etc.) To ensure the employees influence on their work organization, it is necessary to address the whole organization.
3. The *interorganizational level*, in which the focus is on the relation between an organization and its environment, as e.g. the external users (customers), cooperating agencies, private businesses. Important issues are how to design technical and organizational infrastructure, and how changes in the environment can and will affect the internal structure of the organization. In Norway, such examples are cross-sectoral ICT initiatives as common solutions for businesses, collaborative use of registers, (including a common meta database), the reorganization of National Insurance Administration, Directorate of Labor and social welfare into one unit, the PKI (public Key Infrastructure) initiatives, etc. At this level, user involvement and participation are complicated issues, involving many stakeholders and interests.

## 5 Are Other Strategies More Adequate?

Should we choose a political or an ethical road to more democracy in system development work?

The ACM (Association for Computer Machinery) has its Code of Ethics and Professional Conduct[4], in which a commitment to ethical professional conduct

[4] ACM home page: http://www.acm.org/constitution/code.html

is expected of every member. E.g. 2.5 reads: "Give comprehensive and thorough evaluations of computer systems and their impacts, including analysis of possible risks". Another approach is chosen by the North America[5] based organization Computer Professional for Social Responsibility, which through individual participating members have been able to provide substantial contribution to important areas within the field. Is this the way to go?

Bjerknes and Bratteteig (op. cit.) expressed in their article a concern about a shift in locus from being seen as the realm of systems design as such to a notion of responsibility testing on individual ethics. They see the danger that user participation in system development activities is a mean or the only mean. They argue that the political dimension should be reintroduced. The change of power structures in society during the last decades is an important challenge for system developments research that cannot be dealt without discussing the political dimension, on various levels.

Eevi Beck (2001), in her provocative article in SJIS claim that "in a world made global by ICT, political concerns remain on the minds of many, PD (participatory design) must encompass work motivated political conscience which is expressed through of approaches and conducted at multiple points throughout the processes of computer development and adoption, not only participatory design". She calls for a community of professionals that develops a stronger demand for analysis of societal and ethical consequences of ICT developments, adoption and use.

## 5.1 Conclusions – A Value-Laden Research Agenda Is Still Needed

My intention with this paper has been to take part in a discussion on how the Scandinavian tradition in information system research may contribute to eGovernment developments and implementations. It is not argued that the Scandinavian IS tradition represents a coherent set of principle and methods for system development, but that it shares some common ideas and goals related to socio-technical thinking, user involvement and democracy at the work place. Without aiming at raising the whole debate of the emancipatory dimension of user involvement or digital divide in general, I will argue for a greater focus on studying the consequences of various approaches to system design, implementations and use. We accordingly need to study how user involvement is practiced in various types of eGovernment projects and what impact different approaches have had.

I believe that specific challenges are related to outsourcing strategies, where top-down, specification-driven projects are dominating. Referring to Dahlbom and Mathiassen (1993), I will maintain that we also need experimental and evolutionary approaches, allowing for "failures" without dramatic consequences. Not least, we need a better understanding of the problems associated with defining quality as an objective and measurable entity, as well as the efforts it takes to change the culture in an organization.

---

[5] CPSR do also have chapter outside US, e.g. in Europe, see http://www.cpsr.org/

## References

1. Andersen, N.E. et al (1986) Professionel systemutvikling Teknisk forlag, a.s. Kbenhavn.
2. Bansler, J. (1987) Systemutvikling. Teori og historie i et skandinavisk perspektiv. Studentlitteratur, Lund.
3. Bansler, J. (1989) System Development Research in Scandinavia. Three Theoretical schools. I New Technology, Work and Employment Vol 4, NO 2, 1989.
4. Bjerknes, G. og T. Bratteteig (1995) User Participation and Democracy: A Discussion of Scandinavian Research on System Development. I Scandinavian Journal of Information System, Vol 7(1),
5. Bjerknes, G., B. Dalhlbom et al., red. (1990) Organisational Competence in System development . Studentlitteratur, Lund.
6. Bjerknes, G., P. Ehn, M. Kyng red. (1987) Computers and Democracy. Aldershot, England Avebury.
7. Boehm, B. (1976) Software Engineering. IEEE Transactions on Computers, Vol. C-25 (12), Dec. 1976.
8. Boehm, B. (1988) A Spiral Model for Software Development and Enhancement. IEEE Computer. May 1988.
9. Borland, R.J. and R.J.Hirschheim (1987) Critical Issues in Information Research John Wiley & Sons
10. Broening, G. (2001) Origin and theoretical basis of New Public Management. International Public Management Journal 2001 4(1): p 1-25
11. Capgemini (2005) Online Availability of public services: How is Europe Progressing? European Commission DG Information Society, Bruxelles.
12. Checkland, P. (1981) Systems Thinking, Systems Practice. Chichester. New York Basic Books
13. Ciborra, C. eds. (1996) Groupware and Teamwork. Chichester, UK: John Wiley.
14. Claudio Ciborra (2002): The Labyrinths of Information: Challenging the Wisdom of Systems. Oxford: Oxford University Press
15. COM (2003) The Role of eGovernment for Europe's Future. Communication from the Commission to the Council, COM (2003) 567 Final. Brussels 26.9.2003
16. Dahlbom, B. and L. Mathiassen (1993) Computers in Context. Basil Blackwell
17. Deloitte Research Public Sector Institute (2004) At the dawn of e-government. The citizens as customer. http://www.deloitte.com/dtt/article/0,1002,sid
18. Ehn, P. og Å. Sandberg (1979) Fretaksstyrning og Lntagermakt. Prisma, Falkøping. Emery, M (1993) Participative Design for Participative Democracy. Centre for Continuing Education, Australian National University.
19. Greenbaum, J. (1995) Windows at the workplace. Monthly ReviewPress, N.Y.
20. Greenbaum, J., & M- Kyng, eds. (1991) Design at Work . Hillsdale, N.J. Lawrence Erlbaum Ass
21. Grønlund, Å og A. Ranerup eds (2001) Elektronisk frvaltning, elektronisk demokrati. Studentlitteratur, Lund.
22. Grønlund, Å. Eds. (2002) Electronic Government: Design Visions and Management. Idea Group Publishing. 2002
23. Grudin, J. (1988) Why CSCW fails: Problems in the design and evaluation of organisational interfaces: Proceeedings of the CSCW'88 Conference on Computer Supported Cooperative Work, 85-93. New York. ACM
24. Gustavsen, B. (1992) Dialogue and Development. Arbeidslivscetrum & Van Gorcum. Assen/Matricht

25. Hirschheim, R., & Klein. H-K. (1989) Four Paradigms of Information Systems Developments. Communications of ACM 32, no 10, 1199-1216
26. Heeks, R. (1999) Reinventing government in the information age. London and New York Routledge,p 9-12.
27. Homburg, V.(2005) E-government and NPM: A perfect Marriage?. Proceedings of the 6th international conference on Electronic commerce. Pages: 547 - 555, Year of Publication: 2004, ISBN:1-58113-930-6 In ACM Int. Conference Proceeding Series; Vol. 60 archive, http://portal.acm.org/citation.cfm?id=1052289
28. Iivari, J. (1991) A paradigmatic analysis of contemporary schools of IS development. I European Journal of Information Systems Vol 1, No 4, pp249-272
29. Mathiassen, L. (1982) Systemutvikling og Systemutviklingsmetode. DIAMI PB 136, Mat. Inst. Århus.
30. Mumford, E. (1975) Industrial Democracy and Systems design. I Mumford og Sackman (1975) Human Choice and Computers . North Holland
31. Mumford, E. (1983) Designing Human Systems. Manchester Business School, Manchester ,England
32. Nilsson A. & A. Ranerup (2001) Improvisatorisk frendringsarbete - nye arbeidsett med gruppeprogramvara In Grnlund og Randerup (red): Elektronisk frvaltning og elektronisk demokrati, 2001. Studentlitteratur, Lund.
33. Nurminen, M. (1987). Different Perspectives. What are they and How can they be used. Dockerty et al. (red.1987) Systems design for Human Development and Productivity. IFIP 1987, North Holland.
34. Parnas, D.L. og Clements, P.C. (1985) A Rational Design Process: How and Why to Fake It. I H Ehrig et al. (red. 1985) Formal Methods and Software development Springer-Verlag.
35. Dunleavy Patrick , Helen Margetts, Simon Bastow and Jane Tinkler (2005) New Public Management Is Dead–Long Live Digital-Era Governance. In Journal of Public Administration Research and Theory,
36. Schuler, D. and A. Namioka (red.) Participatory Design. Principles and Practices Lawrence Erbaum Ass. Publ. New Jersey. 1993
37. Thorsrud, E. og F. Emery (1970) Mot en ny bedriftsorganisasjon. Universitetsforlaget, Oslo
38. US government (2002) The e-government act of 2002. HR 2458. http://csrc.nist.gov/policies/HR2458-final.pdf
39. Wikipedia (2005) http://en.wikipedia.org/wiki/Public_Sector

# Maximizing Knowledge for Program Evaluation: Critical Issues and Practical Challenges of ICT Strategies

Sharon S. Dawes and Theresa A. Pardo

Center for Technology in Government, University at Albany, SUNY, USA
{sdawes, tpardo}@ctg.albany.edu

**Abstract.** Policy makers and public managers want and need to know how well government programs perform, but few have the information to accurately and continuously evaluate them. Performance measurement and performance-based decisions can be improved by more sophisticated information systems designed to support analysis and decision making. However, such systems demand close and continuing involvement of program staff, attention to programmatic context, and much better understanding of business processes and the data they generate. Through the example of the prototype Homeless Information Management System, this paper highlights how challenging these issues are and how attention to them can lead to useful and usable performance analysis and evaluation systems.

## 1 Introduction

Traditional program evaluations, program audits, and performance measurement programs are all formal, information-based attempts to answer the question "How well are we doing?" Most audit and evaluation approaches rely on external reviewers collecting their own data, sometimes supplemented with standard statistical reports and administrative data from the programs under review. Performance measurement activities are usually conducted by people internal to the agency, but separate from those who manage the programs. They typically use existing administrative data or collect separate information specifically for performance reporting. Intended to be "objective," these traditional approaches are designed to be independent of day-to-day program operations. As a consequence, however, the people with the program knowledge and the ability to act quickly on many findings  program managers and staff  are generally not involved or enthusiastic about program evaluation.

At the same time, the detailed databases and information systems that support program operations are seldom used routinely or to best advantage for program and policy assessments. Ironically, recent developments in IT can enable unprecedented access to this information for ongoing program assessment, decision making, and planning. These two factors – uninvolved program staff and unexploited program information – mean that program performance is assessed only periodically or sporadically and without making the most effective

M.A. Wimmer et al. (Eds.): EGOV 2006, LNCS 4084, pp. 58–69, 2006.

use of either expert knowledge or existing expensive data sources. Consequently, performance information produced by these traditional means is seldom actually used by managers to improve program designs or operations [1]. This is not to say that formal, independent program evaluation is not needed or valuable, but that alone it is inadequate to the goal of improving program performance.

## 2 Evaluating Government Performance

In its strict definition, the term policy analysis is used to describe the process of developing and evaluating alternative courses of action before policy decisions are made, although the term is often applied to the evaluation of alternatives to existing policies. *Program evaluation* is the process of after-the-fact review of implemented policies. *Program audits* similarly look at the effects of policy implementation in terms of the cost and effectiveness of program operations. *Performance measurement* focuses on a few key factors that are believed to be the most important indicators of quality and effectiveness. In practice, however, all these terms tend to be used to denote an effort to determine how or how well a government program or policy is working. In short, they are all forms of evaluation.

Newcomber [2] classifies formal evaluation efforts into three basic strategies: problem-based investigations, performance assessments, and impact evaluations. Each of these strategies has its own implications regarding focus, evaluator, data requirements, time, resources, tools, and the reaction of program staff. For example, a problem-based investigation may focus on immediate issues in program operations. It may be conducted over a period of weeks by state auditors using agency records and generating a performance audit report which is received without enthusiasm or with outright hostility by program managers. Performance audits have grown out of the financial audit tradition and tend to be conducted with a strong emphasis on financial factors and with a focus on finding explanations for documented or alleged poor performance. Given their usually negative connotations, agency leaders and program managers seldom welcome them. By contrast, an impact evaluation conducted by an agencys own research staff might go beyond agency records to gather information from clients and other external sources. It might take a year or longer and investigate questions that cannot be addressed in other ways. Depending on the questions asked and the evaluation and reporting methods used, program staff reaction can range from resistance to enthusiasm. Regardless of differences in method or data type, all three strategies rely on professional evaluators (i.e., research professionals, auditors, or other trained observers). None of these strategies makes extensive use of advanced information technology for data collection, analysis, or presentation.

Performance measurement as a strategy relies less on formal research programs than on organizational self-assessment. As a management concept, performance measurement has the merits of focus on clear objectives, standards for their accomplishment, and regular feedback about performance into decisions about strategies and practices [3]. Essentially a performance-driven government is expected to deliver more effective programs and make more efficient use of public funds. It is further expected to improve accountability of elected officials and administrators while giving them the information they need to improve operations and outcomes [4].

Despite the benefits usually associated with performance measurement, the practice has also generated controversial and unintended effects. These include a bias toward quantifiable elements of performance and inadequate attention to qualitative aspects. In addition, successive aggregations of data for oversight at higher organizational levels reduces its operational relevance. The result can be over-reliance on simplified, symbolic numbers divorced from their context and from the processes of management [4].

Based on a study of state and local government employees, de Lancer Julnes and Holzer [1] found that the actual use of measurement systems is shaped by political and cultural factors including the participation of internal stakeholders and external interest groups as well as the support of elected officials and the public. Successful performance measurement programs involve more than choosing and promoting measuresthey also require organizational "readiness," involvement of stakeholders and unions, patience, and emphasis on a culture of improvement.

## 3 Information Technology Tools for Analysis and Decision Making

The focus on performance measurement in the public sector [5] and customer-focused marketing in the private sector [6] have provided the impetus for organizations to invest in technologies that support these new assessment and management models. Mass storage devices, growth in processing capability, ubiquitous access to the Web, and new software designed to integrate data from multiple disparate sources are just some of the innovations that can enable organizations to draw on vast data resources for virtually "real-time" use in decision making [7].

The fundamental characteristics of decision support have been incorporated into a variety of specific tools to support managerial decision in the last decade. New data management technologies such as multi-dimensional data warehouses, data marts, and Web servers enable large volumes of data to be stored, organized and made accessible for more efficient use. New analytical technologies enable managers to use onlineanalytical processing and visualization tools such as geographic information systems to explore data. New delivery mechanisms such as Web portals allow them to integrate the readily available operational data into decision making and planning activities [8], [7], [9].

A well-designed Decision Support System (DSS) is useful to an organization as it provides the means to use operational data, managerial expertise, and powerful analytical tools to understand ongoing performance and to make decisions about how to continuously improve it. The basic concepts underlying DSS grew out of managers dissatisfaction with the limitations of earlier MIS systems with their focus on transactions, pre-defined reports, rigidity, and reliance on computer professionals for access to information. One of the key design principles of a DSS is that neither the DSS nor the decision maker alone is as effective as the two combined. A DSS should improve decision making by merging human intuition-judgment and computer systems [10]. According to Keen and Scott Morton [11] the merger of intuition and data is required in a decision for which managerial judgment alone would not be adequate and one for which the model or data alone are also inadequate because the solution involves judgment and subjective analysis. One definition that emerged from research on strategic policy making in the public sector characterizes DSS as an electronic aid to improve governance outcomes by facilitating more systematic and accurate identification and analysis of different policy problems, resources, objectives, solutions, costs, benefits, risks, probabilities, priorities, processes, outputs, and outcomes [8].

## 4 Alternative Performance Assessment Strategies

The foregoing overview of research literature on performance evaluation and the technologies that can support it suggests a framework for comparing different public sector evaluation approaches. Table 1 compares formal program evaluations, performance audits, performance reporting systems, and what we call "self-assessment systems" that are based on the principles of DSS. These four types are compared on the motivation for assessment; their frequency, scope and focus, the kind and quality of information typically used, their cost implications, the nature of program staff involvement, and the usability of findings for program management.

All of these approaches are costly and resource intensive, and they are designed to generate information for different audiences and purposes. However, self assessment systems offer some advantages that the other methods lack. They take full advantage of the expert knowledge of program staff and engage them fully in the process of building the system, selecting and defining data, and using it for performance monitoring and improvement. Because these systems can deliver continuous information and ongoing opportunities to identify problems and act on them, they offer more frequent opportunities to assess performance and make needed changes.

Making technology investments to support performance assessment and decision making is difficult in the public sector due to the need to identify and work within multiple, sometimes competing, agendas. As a result, they have no clearly defined bottom line, but instead need to balance a variety of demands and expectations about performance. These multiple agendas represent the influence of multiple stakeholders both within and outside government. In addition, most government programs rely on interagency or intergovernmental processes or may cross the boundaries of public and private sector organizations, making accountability both more important and more difficult to demonstrate. In the section below, we recount the experience of one government program that designed such a system. We use this case to illustrate these difficulties and the strategies that can be used to address them.

**Table 1.** Comparison of Selected Evaluation Approaches

| | Evaluation Approach | | | |
|---|---|---|---|---|
| **Characteristic** | **Formal program evaluation** | **Performance audit** | **Performance reporting systems** | **Self-Assessment Systems** |
| **Motivation** | Planned review or to address a problem, external accountability | To address a problem, external accountability | Response to monitoring & reporting requirements, external accountability, internal management | Continuous performance improvement, internal management |
| **Frequency** | Infrequent | Situational | Periodic, usually semi-annual or annual | Ongoing |
| **Scope and focus of evaluation questions** | Flexible | Determined by nature of the problem | Fixed by formal rules or directives | Flexible |
| **Kind of information available** | Detailed data in context | Detailed data in context | Aggregated, pre-defined data removed from context | Detailed data in context plus expert knowledge |
| **Data Quality** | Depends on quality of data sources and understanding of evaluator | Depends quality of data sources and understanding of evaluator | Generally low | Generally high |
| **Cost** | Medium to High depending on scope | Medium to High, depending on nature of the problem | High to initiate, low to maintain | High to initiate, medium to sustain |
| **Nature of program staff involvement** | Reactive, sometimes defensive | Reactive, often defensive | Little to none after initiation | Fully engaged |
| **Potential usability in program operations** | Indirect, delayed | Indirect, delayed | Indirect if at all, delayed | Direct and continuous |
| **Typical IT tools** | none | none | Standard reports, statistical packages. | Full range of DSS technologies |

## 5 Case: The Homeless Information Management System (HIMS) Prototype

Each night in New York State (NYS) nearly 29,000 homeless people receive emergency shelter and support services. The 6,400 families and 10,000 single adults require assistance in dealing with their immediate incidence of homelessness as well as assistance in dealing with a variety of other problems including domestic violence, alcoholism or substance abuse, poor parenting skills, mental illness, and a lack of education or employment skills. Many lack the skills to maintain their own housing.

New York State and its localities spend $350 million annually and devote substantial effort in providing both housing and services to these homeless single adults and families. The NYS Bureau of Shelter Services (BSS) manages the temporary housing services programs. The program determines eligibility and need for services, provides case management, direct services, and referrals to outside service providers.

Professionals in the homeless services field believe the various service programs they provide to homeless people reduce public assistance costs by helping people achieve independence. But there is little evidence to either support or challenge this belief. Program managers do have quarterly aggregated statistical reports from shelter and service providers regarding the numbers of people being served for payment purposes. However, information about service effectiveness is mostly anecdotal. Detailed data about individuals, programs and services resides in various separate systems or in paper records that are not integrated. As a result, it is unclear whether self-sufficiency, reduced recidivism, reduced dependence on public assistance, and improved overall life skills are being systematically achieved. Consequently, BSS began to consider the feasibility of a new information resource which they called the Homeless Information Management System (HIMS), to help them assess effectiveness across programs, services, and population groups. The new system was intended to fill an important gap in program management by continuously linking and comparing information on services to information about client outcomes.

The project was a departure from traditional regulatory relationships among the participants in that it attempted to create both a community of practice and a jointly defined, shared data resource for the voluntary internal use of all the participating organizations. It required that these organizations agree on some key performance criteria, jointly define key data elements, understand each others business processes, and look more deeply into the information policies that would govern the use of the data. The HIMS prototype drew its data from multiple existing case management systems and financial systems already in use in the participating organizations. Overall, the project sought to determine whether it was feasible to develop an integrated database from such a wide variety of data sources, possible to accurately match individual client information across multiple systems, reasonable to create a system that would allow for the integration of external data sources, and if it was realistic to think that effective partnerships could be formed to support the necessary collaborations to ensure HIMS included the necessary data BSS faced many challenges in achieving this objective including engaging stakeholders and securing their collaboration, developing service evaluation models that respond to the varied service populations and programs, testing existing information policy frameworks, and wrestling with serious data issues. Each of these is discussed below.

## 5.1 Stakeholders and Their Motivations

Shelter providers were the key stakeholder group to be engaged. These organizations provide shelter and services to homeless people under the regulatory supervision of BSS. They vary greatly in size, specialization, and scope of service. Some are singlesite facilities, others are part of a large corporate nonprofit organization. Some have extensive case management systems, others less sophisticated systems, and still others only manual paper records. Each provider has its naming conventions for specific data elements. And, each has individualized business rules that dictate how work is done and what types of data are collected.

About half of the nonprofit homeless service providers are members of an informal Technology Committee which was formed in 1997 to respond to a new information system for case reporting that was being mandated for use in NYC-based shelters by the NYC Department of Homeless Services (DHS). The Technology Committee strongly opposed that system for several reasons. It was a canned commercial system selected by DHS without consulting with the shelter providers. The system did not assist providers in case management, but added a new system and reporting responsibility to their existing operations. The system would collect not only demographic information about clients, but also case notes, the highly personal information that case workers collect for purposes of working with clients on their individual problems and needs. The Committee successfully brought pressure on the City agency to abandon the effort.

Given the experience with the Citys case reporting system, BSS staff recognized that the success of any new state system would rest heavily on the extent to which providers supported it. Although BSS has the authority to mandate compliance with any program it sponsors, the staff decided to pursue a collaborative approach. Consequently, BSS made significant investments in building relationships and trust in the early stages of the project. The BSS Director made a personal and organizational commitment to the provider community that "if they don't see value in the system as a tool to support individual providers as well as the community as a whole, then it wont be built." Despite these assurances, and their commitment to high quality service, the Technology Committee members were very guarded in their early participation.

However, the providers did recognize that HIMS could offer them important benefits. They would be able to assess their own programs against their peers. And, the ability to compare programs and outcomes across the whole system would identify the best performers which would probably signal best practices that everyone could share. Through meetings, presentations, conference calls, and one-on-one discussions with providers, BSS generated growing trust that information the providers shared with the state would not be used to threaten the well-being of clients or used against specific providers or program managers. In this more trusting atmosphere, the group was able to turn its focus to the practical questions of the design, usability, and value of HIMS.

## 5.2 Agreeing on How to Define and Measure Performance

A fundamental issue was whether BSS and the homeless shelter providers could agree on a service evaluation model that would satisfy their various assessment needs. In a series of meetings devoted to this question, the group explored the possibility of developing standard service definitions and evaluation measures.

They tackled the difficult questions of performance measurement and tried to define, for example, what kind of behavior, or outcome constitutes "success" for a deeply troubled individual compared to a relatively stable family. The group began to specify how HIMS might identify what services lead to good outcomes for different types of clients.

They first focused on simply identifying the various services provided to homeless individuals and families. A list of 66 distinct services was generated. Participants then began to work toward standard definitions of those services provided by the broadest array of shelters. This exercise demonstrated that it would be possible to develop a manageable, usable set of standard categories and types of services.

Following identification of the services, the group identified the attributes of specific services so they could be compared. Some services were straightforward with few attributes that vary from one place or client type to another; others had many variables. An attribute such as location of service could be applied to all services and was considered useful for comparing the outcomes of similar service programs offered in different locations. But temporary housing, for example, varied considerably across the providers programs. The discussions identified 26 different forms of temporary housing, described through types of beds, family or single units, or special population characteristics. For each attribute, a decision had to be made about how to define and capture the data for future analysis.

After determining that services and their attributes could be standardized, the focus moved to identifying an explicit set of prioritized outcome goals. The providers were surprised to find that their desired outcomes were very similar to each other and to those identified by BSS: a decrease in recidivism, completion of service programs, and self-sufficiency were the most desired outcomes for homeless clients. Several other outcomes were also rated highly including placements in permanent housing, reducing lengths of stay, and increasing sobriety.

Recognizing that professional judgment is critical to the correct interpretation and use of the data, the group then explored factors that are important for interpreting outcome data. Although HIMS would provide access to more robust data than previously available, it would still not tell the whole story. For example, HIMS would allow a user to determine the recidivism rates. However, recidivism rate is not an absolute measure, but must be assessed in the context of different demographic profiles. The profile of one segment of the homeless population might cause them to be less resilient or more likely to be recidivists. For example: a 50% drop in recidivism would be an unrealistic outcome for chronically mentally ill, unemployable single women, but should be regularly expected of employable, single women.

The group then sought to determine if there was sufficient consistency across their programs and their program implementation and assessment models to move forward with a technology investment. At first glance they appeared to be too different for any standard assessment model to be applicable however, after many meetings where they talked through their service environments, their implicit and explicit assessment models, and their desired outcomes, they began to see that they did have a core set of services and goals and that sufficient benefit would be achieved from jointly investing in assessment tools.

### 5.3 Information Policy Concerns

Shelter providers are in the human services business. Their staff interact daily with people who have a variety of personal problems and needs. Many are trained social workers and a strong ethic of client confidentiality pervades the provider community. This concern dominated early discussions.

In this context, several specific concerns emerged. One had to do with unique populations. For the majority of providers, sharing data meant the release and use of client demographics such as name, social security number, age, and address. The Domestic Violence shelter providers had quite different concerns than the rest. Since their clients are in danger of being assaulted or otherwise harmed by people who know them, their most confidential information had not to do with their identity, but with their physical location. Sharing information that linked a particular client to a particular shelter was therefore of great concern to these providers. The group came to understand that different kinds and levels of data security would be necessary to account for these differences among programs. In this case, all agreed that the facility information and address had to be masked to protect the location of the client.

The Director of BSS compiled these policies and sent them to the committee with a cover letter of assurance from the Commissioner of the agency. The material cited specific statutes, regulations, guidelines, and procedures that addressed this threshold concern for providers. The combination of formal documentation with a strong legal basis and the assurance of the agencys top executive allowed the group to move forward to operationalize these policies.

### 5.4 Data Challenges

Data issues in particular presented significant challenges to the team. These included data quality, data context, data definitions, and data usability.

*Data quality.* One common source of data errors is the stressful situation of the client at the point of entry to a shelter. The decision to go to a shelter is frequently a last resort for a client. In some cases, clients may deliberately provide false information in order to protect their anonymity. More commonly, the stress associated with the situation causes clients to forget or have no record of dates, social security numbers, and past histories. Thus the information provided to the case manager at intake can be fraught with gaps and errors. In many cases data for a client remains incomplete in some respects.

*Data in context and the importance of expert knowledge.* The design team was intentionally made up of program staff as well as technology experts. It was imperative to have both kinds of professionals involved. At different phases of the project, different skills were needed, and different team members were added to the mix. The provider communitys practical perspective gave the team the ability to address operational and policy issues as soon as they were identified. As technologists or business analysts were needed they were brought in. As their roles were completed, their activity diminished. The one consistent facet of the project team was the involvement of the BSS staff. They provided both managerial and program focus including the continuous, consistent communication that was so important in building and maintaining provider trust.

*Harmonizing data definitions and the value of meta data.* A major challenge was finding commonality among the data elements as used by the different organizations. The design team needed to understand how the data was collected, what similarities existed among the data sources, and how the data was going to be aggregated in the new system and to document all this with meta data. This required business rules and standards for the new integrated system. Each question had to be considered from the program and business perspectives as well as the technical perspective. For each data element, the team had to agree on common definitions and consider how these definitions would affect the inclusion or exclusion of data elements into the integrated system. Many decisions needed to be revisited with each additional data source. This iterative process helped define the business rules that shaped the system.

*Data usability for different purposes and users.* Each data code for the integrated system needed to be reviewed in the context of related programmatic issues. In some cases, data was collected based on unique policies or business rules specific to a provider. For example, each system contained information regarding a clients ethnicity. Usually ethnicity had five categories, but one provider used 12 categories because they were tied to federal regulations and funding requirements for its programs. Therefore, the system design needed to incorporate a translation table that would feed data to HIMS while retaining the ability to provide data back to that provider in the original categories.

## 6 Discussion

The HIMS prototype represented a new information resource. In the process of designing it, representatives from all stakeholder groups came to have a much more detailed and nuanced understanding of their clients, programs, processes, and relationships. The system allowed them to answer questions about performance that could not be answered before. They developed a deep appreciation for the power of information to help them design and operate effective programs and a similar appreciation for how difficult and time-consuming it is to assure that the data quality was sufficient for their purposes.

Systems like HIMS can fill an important gap in performance information. Because they are the result of deep involvement by program managers and staff, they are much more likely to be used to make decisions about processes and performance. They allow mangers and line staff to assess their own programs frequently and to act on the data with confidence in its quality and relevance. As shown in the figure below, selfassessment systems like these offer the opportunity for continuous intelligence about program performance and frequent

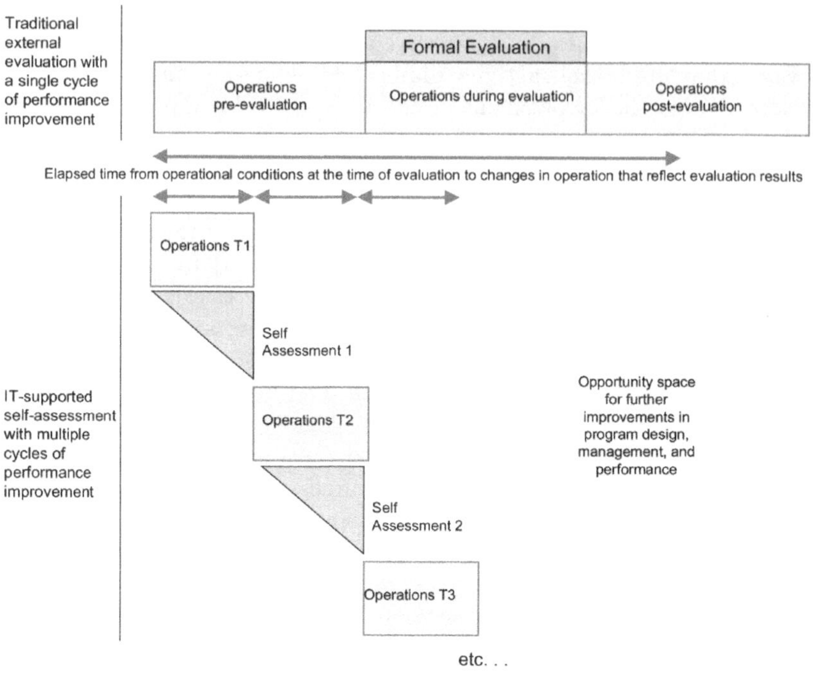


**Fig. 1.** A Continuous Intelligence Model of Program Evaluation

opportunities adjust design or operations. However, such systems are not easy or inexpensive to create and should therefore be approached with a clear understanding of their costs, benefits, and limitations.

The cost of the program staff time, especially in the early stages of problem definition and relationship building are often hidden costs that do not go into investment calculations, yet are essential, substantial, and continuous. Building and maintaining trust also consumes large amounts of time and managerial attention. In addition, as the case amply demonstrates, choosing relevant performance measures and selecting data to support them demands expert knowledge sharing and putting data in context as well as careful process analysis, harmonizing data definitions across programs and organizations, improving quality data, and acquiring or sharpening analytical skills.

Despite its benefits, this approach has limitations. Self-assessment systems are beneficial for ongoing monitoring and frequent adjustments to the factors that managers have some discretion to change. However, because they are internal, they are not likely to be effective for fostering major, highly visible changes in program policies or design. Those kinds of changes need the financial and political resources that come from legislative or public support – they demand the political credibility that internal actions cannot command. For this reason, traditional external evaluation approaches with their public accountability benefits are also needed. Self-assessment systems should take a place along side formal external evaluation methods as a complementary investment in better government performance.

## References

1. De Lancer Julnes, P. D, and Holzer, M. (2001). Promoting the utilization of performance measures in public organizations: an empirical study of factors affecting adoption and implementation. Public Administration Review 61(6): 693-709.
2. Newcomber, K. E. (1998). Evaluating public programs, in Perry J.L., ed. Handbook of Public Administration (2nd edition). San Francisco: Jossey-Bass.
3. Drucker, P. (1973). Management: tasks, responsibilities, practices. New York: Harper & Row.
4. Thompson, J. R. (2000). The dual potentialities of performance measurement: the case of the Social Security Administration. Public Productivity and Management Review, 23(3): 267-281.
5. Nyhan, R.C. and Martin, L.L. (1999) Comparative Performance Measurement: A Primer on Data Envelopment Analysis. Public Performance and Management Review 22(3): 348-364.
6. Flynn, P., Curran, K., and Lunne, T. (2002). A decision support system for telecommunications. International Journal of Network Management. 12:69- 80.
7. Liang, L.Y. and Miranda, R. (2001) Dashboards and Scorecards: Executive Information systems for the Public Sector. Government Finance Review.
8. Cloete, F. (2003). Assessing governance with electronic policy management tools. Public Performance and Management Review, 26(3): 276-290.
9. Goddard, Steve, Sherri K. Harms, Stephen E. Reichenbach, Tsegaye Tadesse, and William J. Waltman. (2003). Geospatial Decision Support for Drought Risk Management. Communications of the ACM 46(1): 35-37.
10. Lee, S.M., and Eom, H.B. (1990). "Multiple Criteria Decision Support Systems: The Powerful Tool for Attacking Complex, Unstructured Decisions," Systems Practice (3:1) pp 51-65.
11. Keen, P. and Scott Morton, M.S. (1978) Decision Support Systems: An Organizational Perspective. Addison Wesley.

# The Citizens in E-Participation

Henning Sten Hansen and Kristian Hegner Reinau

Aalborg University & National Environmental Research Institute
Fibigerstrde 11, DK-9220 Aalborg, Denmark

**Abstract.** Recent advances in GIS and the Internet have improved the technical possibilities for supporting the public participation through e-Participation systems – e.g. Public Participation GIS. On the other hand there has been too much focus on many technical aspects of public participation with reduced focus on the citizens. Equal opportunities to express their opinions and an open debate between people are the basic foundation for democracy. Therefore the design of participatory processes must take outset in the citizens and their knowledge and commitment concerning the issue to be debated. The current paper presents the results of a survey among actively involved citizens in Northern Jutland County. Our analysis shows a high degree of involvement among *middle-age well-educated males* with a *higher education* and *income above average*. It seems that contrary to the planner's vision of an open debate among all citizens, the result of a PPGIS service is a debate among a rather limited group.

## 1 Introduction

The issue of public participation goes back to the late sixties and early seventies. Local and regional authorities made brochures and posters and arranged meetings to involve the citizens. However, in these processes, the common method for citizen involvement was through public meetings in which the project and potential impact were presented and discussed. This form of public participation was carried out according to the judgements from various 'experts' and decision makers, whereas a real interaction between the authorities and the citizens were rather limited. Only few people were really involved unless there was a strong opposition against for example a controversial new motorway in their neighbourhood.

Until the nineties public participation continued much in the same manner. At that time three important events took place [1]. First, there was a growing awareness of the environment and the importance of making the citizens accountable for a sustainable future. The Conference on Environment and Development (Earth Summit) in Rio de Janeiro in 1992 [2] and Agenda 21 [3] called for increased public participation in environmental decision-making and led to the adoption in Europe of the Aarhus Convention [4]. This development is enhanced by the appearance of "symbolic politics" and growing popularity and acceptance of non-Governmental organisations like Greenpeace and World Wildlife Fund [5]. Second, the emergence of the Internet and its rapid expansion

M.A. Wimmer et al. (Eds.): EGOV 2006, LNCS 4084, pp. 70–82, 2006.

to millions of users facilitates the spread of information at a rate without any counterpart in history – and opposed to for example television – it supports bi-directional communication. The Internet has the potential to advance in one of several different directions. Since most new media technologies are developed with the fuel of commercially gained income, much of the newest technology will not be designed to promote democracy, but will more likely promote commercially driven activities such as Internet gambling and e-commerce [6]. However, if the users want to embrace the Internet as a tool for democracy then it will happen – but only if the users will see positive results from their actions. This requires a pro-active approach from the relevant public authorities. Third, GIS became a mature technology to be used outside the very technical environments, and not at least the recent advances in Internet GIS have facilitated the use of GIS in public participation. Many opportunities for public participation are laid down in the environmental legal framework and Internet GIS can support and facilitate citizen involvement in environmental planning and decision-making. But simply designating a GIS effort as PPGIS because a non-technical citizen is involved is unfair to the many efforts of non-GIS public participation that seek to enhance the democratic process. On the other hand, being explicit about the domain within which a particular PPGIS effort falls can enhance the credibility, efficacy, and theoretical foundation of such a project [7].

All in all, the Internet has the potential of being a strong medium for involving the citizens in decision-making, but in order to design on-line participatory systems, more research about participatory systems is needed. Much of the research until now has focused on technical issues of advanced Internet based participatory systems like PPGIS. Although we should not neglect the importance of more research within this field, very little has been done in the analysis of the public. There is some general ideas concerning the so-called digital divide, but until now there has been no detailed analysis of the citizen's background.

The background for the current study has been the requirements of public participation in the new river basin management plans according to the EU Water Framework Directive. The Watersketch project (www.watersketch.net) aims at setting up guidelines for this complicated participatory process, where environmental and socio-economic factors have to be balanced against each other. The aim of the current study has been to make an analysis of the current theories about the public in participatory processes and present the results of a detailed analysis of the citizens actively involved in e-participation in a given case. The paper will be divided into 4 parts. After the introduction we will in the second section give short overview of theories and taxonomies on public participation including e-participation. The section will focus on the citizens and their role in public participation. The third section presents in detail the analyses of the citizens and their backgrounds from two case studies in the Northern Jutland. Finally, we have some concluding remarks and present for you some ideas for following up activities.

# 2 Public Participation

Public participation is a growing part of spatial and environmental planning. The main purpose of environmental decision-making and thus the main purpose of public participation in this matter are to achieve protection, conservation, and wise management of the environment. This can only be achieved if the proponent properly collects (and acts upon) evidence, opinions and perspectives from all the interested or affected citizens. The level at which the public is involved varies with the relevant legislation, and the attitude of the other stakeholders. Often public participation just means informing the public of a previously, made decision and asking for comments, which may or may not be heeded. Sometimes it means informed consultation, but for public participation to be effective at any level, it requires the public to be well informed and kept aware of the possibility of participation. This requires a pro-active approach from the relevant public authorities.

## 2.1 The Public

In its purest form, citizens are all of us. We live our lives; we vote in elections; and we form special interest groups to influence decisions. In this way, the role of government is to create a society that presents for the individual citizen a possibility to live this kind of life. Therefore communication between government and the individual member of society is necessary, because this communication is the only way to develop a society that gives the individual citizens a basis on which to live out their dreams. Furthermore it is the role of government to deal with the flaws that arise from those values: excessive travel, poor housing, the provision of services, and accommodation of regional infrastructure needs.

Achieving a balanced representation of the citizens in the decision making process depends on many factors. However, most agree that those citizens who have a legitimate interest should be included in decision-making, but who this would be for a given process is unclear. Sanoff states that those who are most affected by a decision should have the greatest voice in the decision [8]. Despite the fact that the general public should be informed about opportunities to participate, the people who have the most at stake should have the greatest level of involvement. Besides this group the participating public should also include those with technical knowledge offering assistance in data collection or contribute essential information if the process has technical components [8]. This is often the case in many spatial planning processes – e.g. in environmental impact assessment. Although the citizens possessing power do not necessarily have a legitimate interest in a particular case they might have the ability to support – or impede – a decision, and therefore they should be considered for involvement.

The identification of potential stakeholders is an essential first step in getting stakeholders to participate. The principles stated above can be reformulated into more operational terms. Creighton developed a set of ways to identify the affected publics by considering the following items [9]:

- *Proximity:* Citizens living near where a project or plan is implemented is more vulnerable than people living in at longer distances from the new project
- *Economic:* Some citizens may experience financial gain or lose dependent on their relationship to the new project
- *Use:* A new regional plan implying the construction of a motorway may limit some people's use of a resource or facility due to for example barrier effects.
- *Social:* A project or policy may threaten a tradition or culture, or it may significantly alter a demographic structure of a community.
- *Values:* A group may be affected only in terms of how an action relates to its values.

Often the term stakeholder is used when discussing participatory processes. A widely accepted, broad definition of a stakeholder is given by Freeman, who considers "any group or individual who can affect or is affected by the achievement of the organisation's objectives" to be a stakeholder [10]. The stakeholder concept emerged in the 1960s where it was suggested that, instead of focusing exclusively on shareholders, a firm also should be responsible to a variety of stakeholders without whose support the organisation would collapse. The expansion of the original concept by Freeman resulted in widening the view of the firm from a strictly economic view to a political view, and nowadays the term is used everywhere when dealing with participatory processes.

Mitchell et al. distinguish three variables in the stakeholder-firm relationship that determine stakeholder salience [11]. The first is power, which they describe as the ability of one actor to make another actor do something he would not otherwise have done. Power is usually unevenly distributed among actors in a relationship. The stakeholder can have power over the authority, or the authority can have power over the stakeholder. The second variable is legitimacy: the degree to which the authority and the stakeholder find each other's actions desirable, proper, or appropriate. The third variable is urgency: The degree to which stakeholder claims call for immediate attention. Based on these three variables, Mitchell et al. define eight types of stakeholders, which can be grouped into 3 main categories (Fig. 1).

Latent stakeholders:

- *Dormant stakeholder* (P) – has power to affect the decision making process, but its participation is not considered legitimate and neither from the stakeholder nor from the authority the need is felt to participate.
- *Discretionary stakeholder* (L) – do not have the resources to affect the planning process, and feel no urgent need to participate, although they do have a legitimate role in the process.
- *Demanding stakeholder* (U) – without power and legitimacy, but with urgency towards the issue. They will normally not receive more than a passing attention from authority.

Expectant stakeholders:

- *Dominant stakeholder* (P, L) – does not see any immediate interest in participating, while his or her participation is considered desirable from the perspective of the planning process.
- *Dangerous stakeholder* (P, U) – have power and urgency but no legitimacy, will in general take unlawful and sometimes violent action to achieve their objectives.
- *Dependent stakeholders* (L, U) – are important for the general support of a new plan and they see the need to participate in the planning process, and in general, little effort will be needed to involve these stakeholders in the process, provided that the dependent stakeholders are aware of the process taking place.

Definitive stakeholders:

- *Those stakeholders* (P, L, U) – have the power to affect the planning process, and their involvement is indisputable. Little effort is needed to involve these stakeholders, and in some cases, efforts should be directed to preventing these stakeholders to become too dominant in the process.

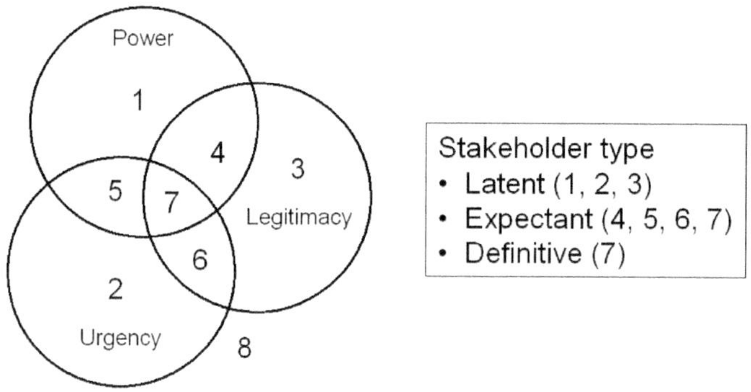


**Fig. 1.** Mitchell's (1997) Stakeholder Typology

When setting up a public participation process, the authority has to consider how to involve the various kinds of stakeholders. Will there be an open discussion with the whole public or will only selected groups of stakeholders be involved. An open discussion seems superficially to be most democratic, but this presupposes that the actively involved public really represent the most affected citizens. When the authority decides actively to select stakeholders the authority must decide on the criteria for selecting stakeholders.

## 2.2 Participation

After having identified "the public" we need to determine the objective with the participatory process. Arnstein claims, that the involvement of the public in decision-making represents a redistribution of power from the authority to the citizens [12]. She describes the public participation by a 'ladder' with 8 rungs each representing the level of citizen participation. This so-called ladder of public participation has 8 rungs divided into three main groups. The uppermost ladder representing 'citizen power', involves public-authority partnerships in which citizens are in control, or can veto agency decisions.

Based on the Arnstein ladder, Weideman and Femers [13] developed a revised ladder of public participation, where the involvement increases with the level of access to information as well as the citizen's rights in the decision-making process. According to Weideman and Femers, the public involvement increases as the authority grant the citizens rights higher in the ladder, which can only be reached by full filling all the requirements of the lower steps in the ladder. In most cases, the public participation is limited to the right to object, but the current and future information and communication technologies will provide opportunities to helping the degree of involvement to move further up in the public participation ladder. Considering the current advances in ICT (Information and Communication Technology), Smyth has updated the traditional ladder concepts [14] [15]. Climbing up this so-called e-participation ladder enhances the degree of interactivity and participation. The lower rungs of this e-participation ladder represent online delivery of public services such as payment of rates and services. This kind of self-service has recently received a high degree of attention among politicians and public administrators. At the upper rungs of the e-participation ladder, the communication becomes more bi-directional facilitating a more interactive participation through the sharing of information, proposals and feedback.

However, we should not forget the users when a public participation process is designed. Although we may have high ambitions for the level of participation, we cannot expect that every citizen should be able to evaluate various scenarios or even set up their own alternatives. According to Jackson the following questions are important before setting up the level of participation: a) what is the level of knowledge of a particular issue among stakeholders? and b) what is their degree of commitment? [16] He describes the various stages of public involvement by taking outset in the citizen's knowledge and commitment. For uninformed people a one-way information process is appropriate. For other people with awareness of the issue but with insufficient "technical" knowledge an educational effort is needed. Citizens with more knowledge may be called upon for consultation or even discussing alternatives. The ultimate level of public participation is collaborative, shared decision-making. This requires first of all an informed and educated public, and next an authority that is ready to delegate or share the power with the community. Besides being a good guideline for identifying appropriate levels of involvement Jackson's description can be used to explain the numerous unsuccessful implementations of the participatory process.

## 2.3 Internet Use, the Digital Divide and Inequality

Nowadays, it is generally accepted that participatory on-line systems will become a useful means of informing the public and to allow access to data and planning tools (on-line GIS) as an additional means of public participation. These will provide mechanisms for the exploration, experimentation and formulation of decision alternatives by the public in future spatial planning processes and have the potential to move the public further up the participatory ladder, although we must be aware of adapting the participation to the knowledge and commitment among the public.

The open structure and architecture of the Internet provide a rather simple mechanism by which information can be released to the public at relatively low cost for as well provider (the public authority) as the consumer (the citizens). Generally the Nordic countries have been in the forefront concerning penetration and use of ICT. The statistical offices in the Nordic countries have made a survey in 2002 of the use of ICT in the Nordic countries [17]. Despite the general spread of information and communication technologies, large parts of the world remain technologically disconnected. This so-called "digital divide", threatens to cut off populations from good jobs and the chance to participate in the affairs of the broader society. Among the Nordic countries the digital divide exists but perhaps less pronounced than in other countries. Thus, gender does not have any significant effect on the use of the Internet, but age has more remarkable effects on the use. For example in Denmark, 68 % of citizens aged 16-29 have access to the Internet, whereas the corresponding figure for senior citizens (over 60 years) is 33 % [17]. A similar inequality is related to education. Nordic persons with only primary education have Internet user rate between 44 % (Finland) and 50 % (Sweden) while academic and advanced professionals have user rates between 69 % and 82 % (Sweden). One important finding in the report from the Nordic Council of Ministers are that if a person lives in a household with children he or she will be more likely to have access to computer and the Internet than those living in households without children. Thus children can be considered as the key to close the digital divide. However, solely relying on Internet based system for public participation may have to potential to strengthen the voice of younger, male, higher-income people who have more frequent access to the Internet, and thus possibly overriding the voice of the poor which we will show later.

## 3 Case Study

The county administration in Northern Jutland (Denmark) have just finalised a major spatial planning effort with associated public participation. The Northernmost part of Jutland called Vendsyssel is separated from the mainland Jutland by a long fjord called Limfjorden. The current Aalborg City Bridge across Limfjorden was opened in 1933 and in 1986 a new motorway tunnel under Limfjorden more than doubled the transport capacity. However, since then there has been a debate on the necessity of a new third connection in the Aalborg area and where it eventually should be located. In February 2002 the County Administration decided to launch the work on a supplement to the regional plan concerning the third Limfjorden connection. The Northern Jutland County administration was quite aware of the fact that the decision concerning the new Limfjorden connection was very sensitive for as well citizens as politicians. Many people have already taken their decision based without detailed knowledge about the various alternatives. All descriptions and assessments of the project were published on the Internet in order to give all the citizens the best possible background for being involved in the decision-making process. The county administration also decided to utilise the Internet for advanced geo-visualisation, interactive maps and a priority game to support making up the citizen's mind about the alternatives [18].

The first step in the public involvement was a traditional public hearing with 184 participants of whom 37 came from various authorities, 20 participants were from the County Administration, 13 from local authorities, and 4 form state authorities. The remaining 147 represented NGOs, citizens and citizens groups.

The county administration sat up an Internet based communication system for easy adding comments from the citizens. All comments from the citizens were stored in a database, facilitating searching and querying, and the information was organised into a report, which was added to the project home page. The database contains 151 comments from a wide spectrum of respondents. Remark, that there is no direct stakeholder identification procedure, and that the system is open to all citizens. First the citizens were divided into various categories and generally the ordinary citizens or groups of citizens made up two thirds of the objections or comments. 29 were from other government bodies (mainly municipalities within the County), 20 comments were from NGO's and 101 were from citizens (91) or groups of citizens (10). The involved Non-Governmental Organisations were divided into the following categories: a) Nature & Leisure (7), b) House owners' Associations (6), c) Business (5) and d) Others (2). The numbers in brackets refer to the number of respondents within each category. The dominating role of nature conservation organisations is not surprising at all, considering the fact that a new motorway will inevitably affect the surrounding nature and environment. Moreover it is expected that the house owners living adjacent to the proposed new connections will argue against a new motorway in their own neighbourhood. First, it is obvious that nobody really wants to have heavy traffic generating noise and air pollution in his or her backyard. Additionally, the construction of a new motorway may have negative economic consequences for house owners living close to the new road. This is not an unusual situation.

Next we focused more deeply on the citizens, group of citizens and private companies. Based on the address information in the database we added a geographic location to each citizen. Hereby we could analyse the geographic pattern of the respondents. It was clear that the involvement in the plan concerning the new tunnel or bridge across Limfjorden showed a rather clustered geographic pattern with high spatial density in the neighbourhood to the new connection (fig. 2). This finding is also in accordance with the above mentioned proximity principle formulated by Creighton [9].

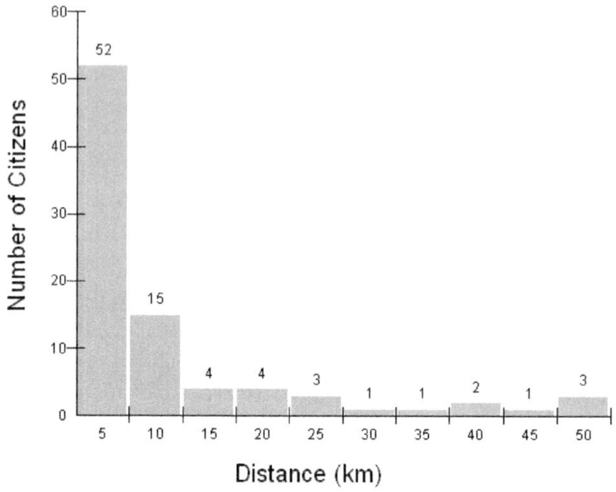


**Fig. 2.** Relationship between active involvement and distance from the proposed connections

The primary aim with the current study has been to achieve a deeper insight in the involved citizens and their background. Accordingly, we performed a questionnaire among the citizens involved in the participatory phase related to the new connection across Limfjorden. The questionnaire contained 22 questions focusing on the ordinary citizens in order to analyse their background concerning age, gender, income, and educational background. Behind the 91 comments from citizens were 49 individuals, and 39 citizens answered the questionnaire, which was made by telephone interviews in September 2005. The number of answers are absolutely satisfactory – not at least when we recognise the sensitive nature of some of the questions. Below we present the results of the questionnaire survey.

**Demography.** The most remarkable result is that 82% of the active involved citizens are men, leaving less than one fifth for the female participation. At first sight these figures might surprise because women are generally more concerned about the environment, which was the main concern from most respondents. However, we must not forget that some of the proposals for the new connection across Limfjorden will go through the most prosperous neighbourhood in Aalborg, and might have negative influence on the house prices in that neighbourhood. Perhaps this could explain the remarkable high percentage of male participation. The age distribution of the involved citizens is bell shaped with a peak between 50 and 60 year and a little skewness towards the more mature people (figure 3). This distribution is not surprising because these age classes have generally more time for being involved in such spatial planning issues than younger families with smaller children and their own carrier to take care of. This does not mean that they do not participate in the local democracy, but they will normally focus their efforts in steering boards for kindergarten and schools.

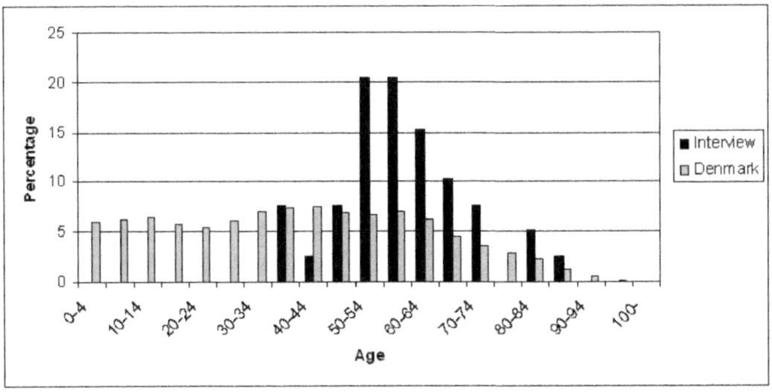


**Fig. 3.** Age distribution for the involved citizens

**Socio-economy.** Concerning basic education 6 out of 10 of the respondents have an Upper Secondary Education and this fits well with the fact that 59 % of the respondents have a medium-length higher education (college) or a university degree (table 1). These figures are significantly higher than national average figures, which are less than 20 % for medium-length higher education (college) or a university degree taken together. However, this result is not surprising because citizens with an academic background are generally more active in public participation than others.

**Political Activity.** At first we were a bit surprised when we analysed the respondent's relationships to the political parties and other Non-governmental organisations. Nearly half (46 %) of the respondents were member of a political party, whereas the same figure for Denmark, as a hole is less than 5 % according to Denmark Statistics. On the other hand it is a fact that politically active people has a strong interest in owing influence on the general development of

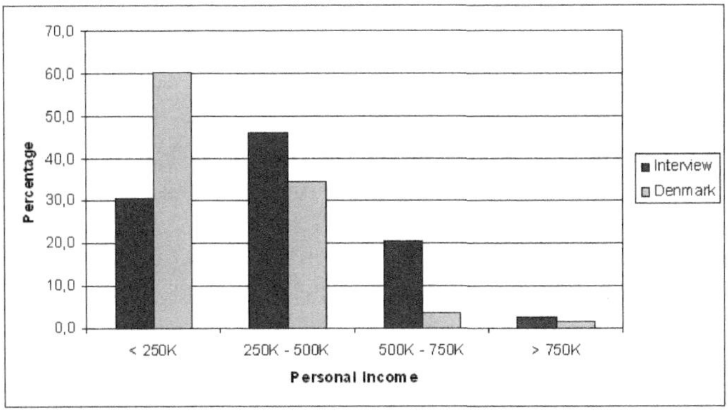


**Fig. 4.** Personal income among involved citizens

the society. Another way of being "politically" active can be membership of some grass-root organisation, and the survey showed that 11 out the 39 respondents were member of such an organisation. Seven respondents were member of as well a political party as a grass-root organisation.

**Internet Experiences.** The last parameter to be discussed in the current paper is the Internet experience among the involved citizens. The survey showed that 59 % of the active citizens had an Internet experience of more than 5 years, and 28 % had Internet experiences of between 3 and 5 years. This means that 13 % of the involved citizens can be considered as novice users, but obviously they have already recognised the possibilities of using the Internet, as a platform for the involvement in a public consultation phase – and this is a rather positive finding. According to the survey mentioned above, 35 out of 39 respondents agreed that the Internet is a suitable platform for involving the public in decision-making, but 56 % of the active citizens would have sent their comments to the County administration even if there had been no Web-site supporting the discussion among the citizens. However, 38 % of the respondents wouldn't have done this without the tailor-made Web page. Thus the Internet seems to play an important role for a broader participation compared with the traditional public meetings

**Summarising the result of the survey.** First we can conclude that in the current case, the active citizens can be described as: a) male; b) middle age – or above; c) higher education; d) above average income; e) political active; and f) experienced Internet user. Perhaps this is not surprising, but at least the strong male dominance is not appropriate for a modern society. Furthermore, the high level of participation among the more mature people can be criticised – we are planning mainly for the future and therefore the younger generations, but they are nearly absent in the participatory process. Therefore the county administration must consider these findings to make the participation tools more targeted in the future.

## 4 Concluding Remarks

Improved decision-making is perhaps the most promising element in e-Government, and the central idea in all decision-making is how to make the optimum solution and how to get acceptance by the citizens. Public participation has been an answer to this challenge since the late sixties, and recent advances in GIS and the Internet have improved the technical possibilities for supporting the public participation through PPGIS systems. On the other hand we should not be too fascinated of the technological possibilities and forget the digital divide as well as the value of face-to-face discussions between the citizens. Equal opportunities to express their opinions and an open debate between people are the basic foundation for democracy. Therefore the design of participatory processes must take outset in the citizens and their knowledge and commitment concerning the issue to be debated. The current paper has presented the results of a survey among actively involved citizens in Northern Jutland. Our analysis showed a high degree of involvement among *middle-age well-educated males* with a *higher education* and *income above average*. Additionally, the analysis shows that *he* is *political active* and *familiar with the Internet*. This group represents perhaps less than 5 % of the adult population, but is not surprising at all. It seems that contrary to the planner's vision of an open debate among all citizens, the result is a debate among a rather limited group. Perhaps, it would be better to actively identify stakeholders among a broader group of citizens, and ask for their opinion. Especially women and younger generations are much more needed in the participatory process. Therefore the authorities must consider these findings to make the participation tools more targeted in the future – e.g. making the project web sit more appealing to those groups. We are fully aware that our findings are based on only one study, although the current case is dealing with a major topic, which has been debated much among the public in Northern Jutland. Accordingly, the involvement of the citizens has also been stronger than for a traditional regional plan. We will continue our work, and we have just started an analysis of the citizens involved in the latest regional planning process, and here we focus on the involvement among younger people and particularly women. Besides interview among the active involved, we will also make a survey among not active citizens. Hopefully, this will give us more insight in why they are reluctant to the process and thus how to redesign the participatory process.

## References


1. Hansen, H.S. & Prosperi, D.; Citizen Participation and Internet GIS – some recent advances (Editorial). Computers Environment and Urban Systems, Vol. 29, pp. 617-629., (2005)
2. United Nations: The Rio Declaration on Environment and Development. United Nations, Rio de Janeiro, Brazil, (1992)
3. United Nations: Agenda 21. United Nations, Rio de Janeiro, Brazil. (1992)
4. UN ECE: Convention on Access to Information, Public Participation in decision-making and access to justice in environmental matters. ECE Committee on Environmental Policy, Aarhus, Denmark, (1998)
5. Castells, M.: The Power of Identity. Blackwell Publishers, Great Britain, (1997)
6. Castells M.: The Rise of the Network Society. Blackwell Publishers, Great Britain, (1996)
7. Schlossberg, M. & Shuford, E.: Delineating "Public" and "Participation" in PPGIS. URISA Journal, vol. 16. pp. 15-26., (2005)
8. Sanoff, H.: Community participation methods in design and planning. J. Wiley Sons., (2000)
9. Creighton, J. L.: Identifying publics/staff identification techniques. The Institute for Water Resources. U.S. Army Corps of Engineers, (1983)
10. Freeman, R. E.: Strategic management: A stakeholder approach. Boston: Pitman Publishing, (1984)
11. Mitchell, R. K., Agle, B. R. and Wood, D. J.: Toward a theory of stakeholder identification and salience: defining the principle of who and what really counts. The Academy of Management Review. vol. 22, pp. 34., (1997)
12. Arnstein, S.R.: A ladder of citizen participation. American Institute of Planners Journal, vol. 35, pp. 216-224., (1969)

13. Weidemann, I. and Femers, S.: (1993) Public participation in waste management decision-making: analysis and management of conflicts. Journal of Hazardous Materials, Vol. 33 pp.355-368, (1993).
14. Smyth, E.: Would the Internet widen public participation? Unpublished M.Sc. Thesis, University of Leeds, (2001)
15. Carver, S.: Participation and geographic information: A position paper. ESF-NSF Workshop on Access to geographic information and participatory approaches using geographic information, Spoleto, (2001)
16. Jackson, L. S.: Contemporary Public Involvement: Toward a Strategic Approach. Local Environment, Vol. 6, pp. 135-147, (2001)
17. Nordic Council of Ministers: Nordic Information Society Statistics 2002. Helsinki, (2002)
18. Hansen, H.S. & Kristensen, P.N. (2006). Applying Internet Based 3D Visualisation and Priority-game in Public Consultation. Proceedings 25th Urban Data Management Symposium, Aalborg, 14.-17. May 2006. pp. 10.89-10.98.

# From Market Squares to Homepages: A Survey of Swiss MPs' Interactivity

Jean-Loup Chappelet and Kristian Pierre Kilchenmann

IDHEAP Swiss Graduate School of Public Administration
associated to the University of Lausanne
21 Route de la Maladière
CH-1022 Chavannes-Lausanne, Switzerland
http://www.idheap.ch
{Jean-Loup.Chappelet, Pierre.Kilchenmann}@idheap.unil.ch

**Abstract.** As is the case in many democratic countries, MPs in Switzerland are close to their constituencies and have adapted to the various new means of mass communication as these emerged over the last century: from newspapers to the Internet, via radio and television. Today, a large majority of Swiss MPs have both an e-mail address and a homepage. This paper explores the use of the Internet by the Swiss MPs for their relationship with citizens almost two years prior to the next national elections for the Federal Parliament (2007). It is based on a quantitative and qualitative survey of all the personal homepages of the members of the lower and upper houses conducted in 2005. Particular attention is paid to interactive means of communication (such as e-mail, forums, blogs, online polls, chats, etc.) that are made available in order to foster online dialogue between politicians and citizens. Based on this data, on a few European comparisons, and on some focused observations of particular sites, the paper identifies the new challenges and opportunities that Swiss MPs must face to better interact with their electorate.

## 1 Introduction

The use of information and communication technology (ICT) by parliamentarians is not new. Many MPs have progressively harnessed the functionalities of mobile phones, desktop PCs, handheld organisers (PDAs) and the Internet to better carry out their roles of representatives, legislators and party members as these technologies became widely available. In this paper, we shall concentrate on the use of e-mail and homepages by Swiss members of the Federal Parliament (hereinafter MPs) in their capacity as representatives of the People. The broad aim is to see whether this usage changes their relationship with the electorate. We shall not discuss the MPs' use of electronic mail and the Internet in their roles of legislators and party members.

We concentrate on e-mails and homepages since these two related technologies allow for asynchronous interaction with the citizens who the MPs are supposed to represent. All those MPs who have a homepage also have an e-mail address,

M.A. Wimmer et al. (Eds.): EGOV 2006, LNCS 4084, pp. 83–95, 2006.

although one that is at times unpublished. Inversely, those who have an e-mail address do not always have a homepage.

As far back as 1999, the IBM Institute for electronic government published a survey of the emerging digital democracy in Europe (Caldow 1999). The sample was drawn from among "wired legislators", i.e. those who already had an e-mail address. Some 4,506 legislators in fourteen countries were invited by e-mail to participate in the survey and 426 responded (about 9.5 %). The survey showed that 39 % had a personal website, although most of these homepages had not yet evolved beyond a "brochure"-type content. Those who had homepages were twice as likely to use e-mail in campaigns as those who did not. Moreover, national legislators were more likely to have a homepage than their peers at regional and municipal levels.

Switzerland was included in this sample and its MPs represented 28 % of the respondents: by far the largest number of all the countries surveyed. This revealed that the use of e-mail by Swiss MPs was already widespread. In the same year – 1999, a national election year – only 5 % of all MPs had their own website (Wuthrich 1998); two years after the elections, however, 24 % had a website (Galland & Chappelet 2001) and in 2003 – another election year –, this percentage had risen to about 30 % (Chappelet 2004). In 2005, the present survey shows that more than half (57 %) of Swiss MPs have a website dedicated to their political activities.

The aim of this paper is to explore this growing phenomenon in Switzerland on a quantitative and qualitative level in order to inform all stakeholders. In particular, it investigates the degree of interactivity between Swiss MPs and citizens that is made possible by various tools available on these websites. It explores the potential new relationships between the Swiss electorate and its representatives in a so-called direct democracy system whereby one hundred thousand citizens can quite easily disagree with their representatives by means of a referendum to oppose a law passed by Parliament. The paper should thus be very relevent for politicians and their parties.

This survey complements a recent study of ICT awareness, understanding and activity levels on the part of parliamentarians in the 25 member states of the European Union (Coleman & Nathanson 2005). Switzerland is not a member of the EU, but shares a similar linguistic and cultural background as its neighbouring countries that are members (i.e. Germany, Austria, France, and Italy). It will thus be interesting to compare the results of this recent study with those of the present article, although the latter is based on a complete survey of all Swiss MPs and the former on only 42 in-depth interviews of European MPs.

The paper is organised as follows: Section 1 gives a quantitative analysis of Swiss MPs' use of e-mail and homepages. The two following sections provide a qualitative analysis. Section 2 examines the responsiveness of Swiss MPs to e-mails. Section 3 then compares the content and degree of interactivity of the Swiss MPs' personal homepages by concentrating on the twenty best and twenty worst sites. The conclusion shows that despite a few encouraging cases, there is no great cause for optimism regarding parliamentarians developing their interaction with Swiss citizens via the electronic means provided by the Internet, at least given the situation two years before the next Federal election in 2007.

Due to page restriction, we invite you to visit www.idheap.ch/MPSI ¿ "Publications" for a full presentation of the methodology which was used and of the exhaustive results of the survey.

## 2 Quantitative Analysis

The Swiss Parliament is composed of two chambers: the National Council, with 200 members (National Councillors) and the Council of States, with 46 members (State Councillors). Following the 2003 Federal elections, the 246 MPs include 59 women (or 24%); 178 native speakers of German (72%), 58 of French (24%) and 10 of Italian (4%). Six main parties are represented in the Swiss Parliament: The People's Party (64 members or 26%), the Socialist Party (61 members or about 25%), the Radical Democrat (& Liberal) Party (54 members or 22%), the Christian Democrat Party (43 members or 17%), the Green Party (14 members or 6%), the Evangelical Party (5 members or 2%) and five non-aligned members (2%).

**Table 1.** MPs' homepages and e-mail addresses

| | N | Percentage | EU MPs (EPRI Study) |
|---|---|---|---|
| Swiss MPs | 246 | 100% | - |
| MPs with an e-mail address | 234 | 95% | 37% |
| MPs with a homepage | 158 | 64% | 26% |

The following survey is based on information provided in each MP's official short biography published on the Swiss Parliament website. At the end of February 2005, 95% of the MPs had an officially published e-mail address, although the parliament's services department offered all MPs a generic address with the formula FirstName.LastName@parl.ch. (We tested these addresses for the MPs without published addresses, but received neither responses nor error messages.) Moreover, 64% of the MPs had a listed personal homepage (see Table 1). These figures compare very favourably with the figures obtained in the study mentioned above concerning a sample of MPs from the 25 European Union member states (Coleman & Nathanson 2005, EPRI long report p. 20).

### 2.1 Council

There is no significant difference between the proportions of MPs with e-mail depending on the council to which they belong. 95 to 96% of the members of each of the two councils have a published e-mail address. Members of the National Council, however, are more likely to have a homepage (66% versus 57%). They are also younger on average: this factor is explored in the next paragraph.

## 2.2 Age

The fact that Table 2 shows that the younger MPs are more likely to have a homepage and an e-mail address than older ones is, of course, not surprising: All MPs between 26 to 35 years of age have an e-mail address and 91% have a homepage.

What is surprising, however, is the fact that above the age of 35, the older an MP is, the more likely he or she is to have a homepage. The reason for this could be that the MP in question has more time available to maintain such a homepage because he or she is virtually a full-time politician.

For e-mail, the picture is more confused: the possession of an e-mail address varies from 91-92% (from ages 36-45 and 56-65) to 99-100% at both ends and the middle (ages 46-55) of the age range. This situation might be due to the fact that many professionally active MPs do not publish their professional (and political) e-mail addresses in order to avoid spam.

**Table 2.** Homepage and e-mail addresses according to MPs' ages

| | | *Homepage* | | *E-mail* | |
|---|---|---|---|---|---|
| *Age* | | *Total* | *in %* | *Total* | *in %* |
| 66 - 75 years | no | 4 | 36% | 0 | 0% |
| | yes | 7 | 64% | 11 | 100% |
| 56 - 65 years | no | 37 | 36% | 9 | 9% |
| | yes | 65 | 64% | 93 | 91% |
| 46 - 55 years | no | 36 | 37% | 1 | 1% |
| | yes | 61 | 63% | 96 | 99% |
| 36 - 45 years | no | 10 | 40% | 2 | 8% |
| | yes | 15 | 60% | 23 | 92% |
| 26 - 35 years | no | 1 | 9% | 0 | 0% |
| | yes | 10 | 91% | 11 | 100% |
| Total MPs | | 246 | | 246 | |

## 2.3 Gender

Female MPs appear a little more oriented towards ICT than their male colleagues, especially regarding homepages (69% compared with 63% – see Table 4). This confirms Hoff's findings that female parliamentarians have a much stronger belief in ICT than their male counterparts (Hoff 2004).

## 2.4 Mother Tongue

German-speaking MPs are more likely to have a homepage than those whose mother tongue is French or Italian (see Table 3). More than two-thirds (70%) of German-speakers have such a page, while only half (50%) of those speaking the two other main Swiss national languages have one. Almost all (95 to 98%) of German- and French-speaking MPs have an e-mail address, while only 80%

of their Italian-speaking colleagues have one. This lag might, however, be explained by the small number of MPs from Ticino, the Italian-speaking Canton.

Table 4 shows that German-speaking Swiss MPs are slightly behind their German colleagues regarding their use of websites, but well ahead of Austrian parliamentarians, while French- and Italian-speaking Swiss MPs are far ahead of their counterparts in France and Italy. Language (and culture) are, of course, not the only factors influencing the maintenance of a homepage. One should note that most Swiss MPs are not full-time politicians, unlike their colleagues in Austria, France, Germany and Italy, who moreover enjoy strong administrative support.

**Table 3.** Homepages and e-mail addresses according to MPs' mother tongues

| | | *Homepage* | | *E-mail* | |
|---|---|---|---|---|---|
| *Language* | | *Total* | *in %* | *Total* | *in %* |
| German | no | 54 | 30% | 9 | 5% |
| | yes | 124 | 70% | 169 | 95% |
| French | no | 29 | 50% | 1 | 2% |
| | yes | 29 | 50% | 57 | 98% |
| Italian | no | 5 | 50% | 2 | 20% |
| | yes | 5 | 50% | 8 | 80% |
| Total MPs | | 246 | | 246 | |

**Table 4.** MPs' homepages in neighbouring countries

| Countries | MPs | With websites | Precent | Swiss MPs with same language |
|---|---|---|---|---|
| Germany | 601 | 538 | 90% | 70 % (German mother tongue) |
| Austria | 245 | 77 | 31% | 70 % (German mother tongue) |
| France | 331 | 34 | 10% | 50% (French mother tongue) |
| Italy | 639 | 70 | 11% | 50% (Italian mother tongue) |

## 2.5 Party

Table 5 clearly demonstrates a significant difference between the left-wing parties (Greens, Socialists, Evangelicals), in which 100% of MPs have an e-mail address and 70 to 80% maintain a homepage, and the right-wing parties (Radical Democrats & Liberals, Christian Democrats, Swiss People's Party), in which 89% to 95% of MPs have an e-mail address and only 48 to 67% have homepages. These figures could be linked to the intensity of usage of e-mail and the internet within each party: further investigation would be needed there. It is also evident that the small parties (Greens and Evangelicals) reveal higher figures than the larger ones.

**Table 5.** Homepages and e-mail addresses according to MPs' parties

| | | *Homepage* | | *E-mail* | |
|---|---|---|---|---|---|
| *Party* | | *Total* | *in %* | *Total* | *in %* |
| Christian Democrats | no | 14 | 33% | 2 | 5% |
| | yes | 29 | 67% | 41 | 95% |
| Evangelicals | no | 1 | 20% | 0 | 0% |
| | yes | 4 | 80% | 5 | 100% |
| Greens | no | 4 | 29% | 0 | 0% |
| | yes | 10 | 71% | 14 | 100% |
| Non-aligned | no | 2 | 40% | 0 | 0% |
| | yes | 3 | 60% | 5 | 100% |
| Radical Democrats and Liberals | no | 16 | 30% | 3 | 6% |
| | yes | 38 | 70% | 51 | 94% |
| Socialists | no | 18 | 30% | 0 | 0% |
| | yes | 43 | 70% | 61 | 100% |
| Swiss People's Party | no | 33 | 52% | 7 | 11% |
| | yes | 31 | 48% | 57 | 89% |
| Total MPs | | 246 | | 246 | |

## 3 Analysis of MPs' Reactivity to e-Mail

In order to test MPs' reactivity to e-mails, we sent them two e-mails. The first one resembled a mail from an unknown citizen asking a current political question ("citizen's e-mail"). The second e-mail was sent one week later, and asked three questions relative to this survey ("academic survey e-mail"). Both sets of e-mails were sent at the same time of day, in the mother tongue of the MP concerned.

In both cases we carried out an automatic measurement of the response time using the following scale: 5 points for answering within one day (24 hours), 4 points for answering within 2 days, 3 points for answering within 3 days, 2 points for answering within 5 days, 1 point for answering within 7 days (one week) and 0 point for taking more than 7 days or no answer at all (we had one response more than five months after our e-mail!).

In both cases, 28% of MPs responded within 24 hours, although not exactly the same MPs answered the two e-mails. The results of the "citizen's e-mail" and "academic survey e-mail" are presented in the two following sections.

### 3.1 "Citizen's e-mail" Reactivity

On 28 November 2005 at noon, all MPs received an e-mail containing a simple question about a current political subject ("Are you in favour of the liberalisation of the "last/first mile" in telecommunication services?"). The e-mail was not anonymous, but signed with a very common name. Figure 1 shows the breakdown of the 28% of responses by number of days and political parties. More than half of all responses arrived within one day. The right-wing parties (People's Party, Radical Democrats and Christian Democrats) are all under-represented by more than 6%.

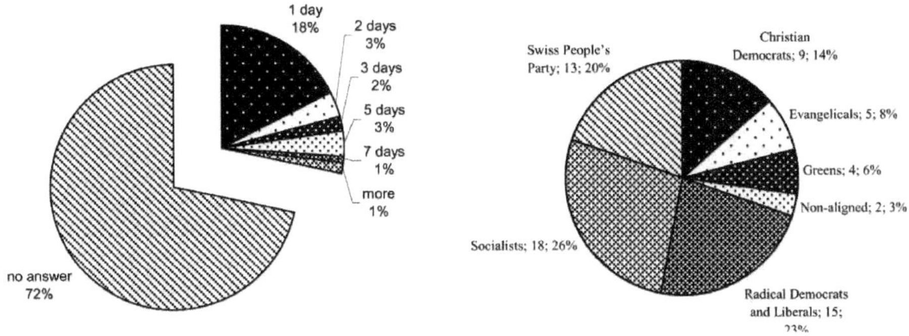


**Fig. 1.** MPs' reactivity to a "citizen's e-mail"

The detailed content of the MPs' answers has not been analysed, but can be broken down into three categories: a short answer to the question: for instance "yes" or "no" (79% of responding MPs); link to a website for more information: for example "please refer to my homepage" (6%); request for more information about the person asking the question (15%).

Despite the 28% response rate, it is notable that the large majority of MPs did not answer. This shows that most Swiss MPs are not particularly fond of using e-mail, and in particular for interacting with unknown persons even if they are potential electors. This might be due to MPs' fear of being overwhelmed by huge volumes of e-mails from the public if they started to answer such questions systematically and/or be the result of the Swiss election system, which builds on party rather than personal voting as shown by Zittel (2004) for other countries.

### 3.2 "Academic Survey e-mail" Reactivity

On 29th November 2005 at noon, all MPs received an e-mail with four questions:

Do you have a homepage? If yes: a) since when? b) Do you find it useful? (5 possibilities from very useful to useless) c) How many visitors do you have on average per month? This e-mail was signed with the name and details of one of the authors.

Figure 2 shows the breakdown of the 28% of responses received by number of days and political parties. Unlike the "citizen's e-mail", less than half of all responses arrived within one day. This probably means that MPs considered this e-mail important enough to take time to answer it but required some time for reflection.

Unfortunately, a technical problem has resulted in the data received in reply to the four questions being unsuitable for meaningful analysis. It is already known,

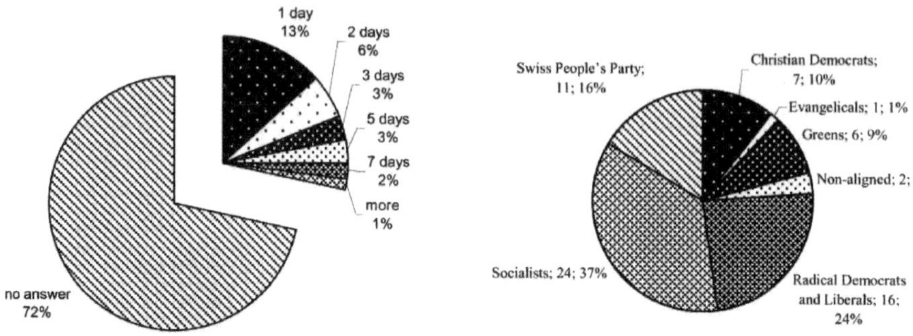


**Fig. 2.** MPs' reactivity to an "academic survey e-mail"

however, that most of the MPs' websites were opened a few months before the Federal elections in 1999 and in 2003 (Chappelet 2004). Although at least one MP closed his website (www.arthur-loepfe.ch) immediately following the last election, most MPs maintained them, sometime without updating them at all (for instance www.daguet.ch).

## 4 Qualitative Analysis of MPs' Homepages

Beyond the mere existence of MPs' homepages, it is important to evaluate their quality in order to see whether this could be of use in fostering the MPs' relationship with the electorate. Some Swiss newspapers have recently explored this topic (see for instance Jeanneret 2005, Zimmer 2005), but not in a systematic way.

Of the 158 MPs' homepages listed in the Swiss Parliament website, only 140 will now be considered for the purposes of this paper. The 18 websites not included were unavailable at the time of the survey, or were not related to political activities but only presented an MP's professional activity. (Most Swiss MPs are only part-time politicians and therefore have a professional activity that could be presented on their professional website).

The following qualitative appraisal of the remaining 140 MPs' political homepages is based on criteria used for the eCandidates survey at the time of the Federal elections in Germany (Neymanns 2002), i.e.:

- Appearance: layout, design and illustrations.
- Navigation: ease of orientation for the user, navigation bar, site map and loading time of the homepage.
- Content: global quality of information and how frequently the content is updated
- Interactivity: tools for interactivity and time taken to answer an e-mail. For each of the four dimensions, the following scale of points was applied: 5 points = excellent, 4 points = good, 3 points = average, 2 points = sufficient, 1 point = poor, 0 points = very poor.

The evaluation of the 140 homepages was carried out by one of the authors at the beginning of December 2005. While the grading of the first three dimensions (appearance, navigation and content) was subjective (dependant on one of the author's opinions), the grading of the interactivity dimension was based on the grades obtained for answering our e-mails (see section 2) and on the presence or absence of a number of supporting tools (see section 4.1).

### 4.1 Potential Interactivity of MPs

In order to evaluate the MPs' potential interactivity with their electorate, we looked for the presence in their homepages of tools such as chats, e-mails, forums, guestbooks, links, news or newsletters, online polls, and web logs ("blogs").

Of the 140 homepages analysed (N=140), a first intriguing fact is that 3 MPs do not publish their e-mail address on their website despite having one (see figure 3). About 84% of the homepages have links to other information sources such as the MP's party website or various interest groups. Less than half (61) of the MPs post news related to current political discussions or publish a regular newsletter. Only 16 MPs (11%) have a guestbook and 10 (7%) use a forum or a blog (for example one of the youngest MP: www.christa-markwalder.ch/weblog) to communicate with their electorate. The potential abuse of these last two tools by pranksters (for example on Walter Donze's homepage at www.wdonze.ch in August 2005) might explain their rather low use.

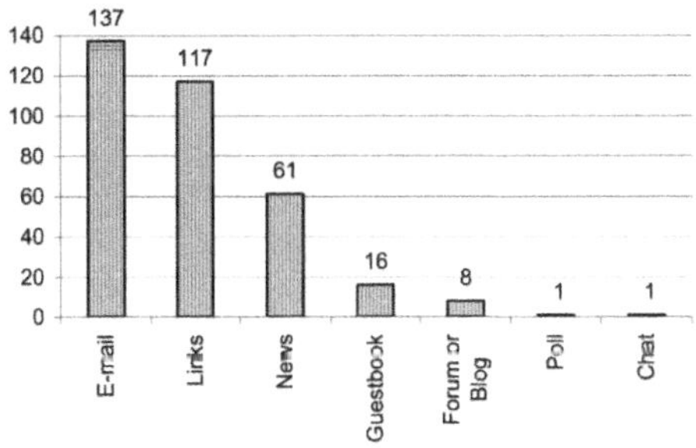


**Fig. 3.** MPs' interactivity tools available on their homepage

Only one MP (Claude Janiak from the Socialist Party who is the National Council President in 2006) proposes online chats during the Parliament sessions (four times a year) through his homepage (www.janiak.ch). Another MP (Hans Fehr from the Swiss People's Party) uses a poll on his homepage to obtain the electorate's opinion on several current topics (www.hans-fehr.ch). He also provides a video portrait. These features remain exceptional.

Apart from e-mail, almost all the other MPs rely on what amounts to a very small number of genuinely interactive tools such as forums, blogs and guestbooks.

Moreover, unlike in the United States, no Swiss MP attempts to enrol supporters or to raise funds through his/her homepage. It should be noted that an experimental forum was run by the Swiss Parliament itself in 2001 and 2002 but that this was discontinued for lack of interest (Schaffner 2002). No online consultation experiments at parliamentary level have been carried out in Switzerland, unlike for instance in the United Kingdom (Coleman 2004).

Based on the observation of each homepage, the following scale of points was applied: 5 points = at least 5 interactive tools available on the homepage, 4 points = 4 tools, 3 points = 3 tools, 2 points = 2 tools, 1 point = 1 tool, 0 points = no tools at all. These grades were added to the ones obtained for the response times to our e-mails (see section 2).

### 4.2 Overall Results

The overall ranking follows a normal Gauss curve. The "zero" ranked websites have been left aside since they are simply not active or do not concern an MP's political activities. See figure 4.

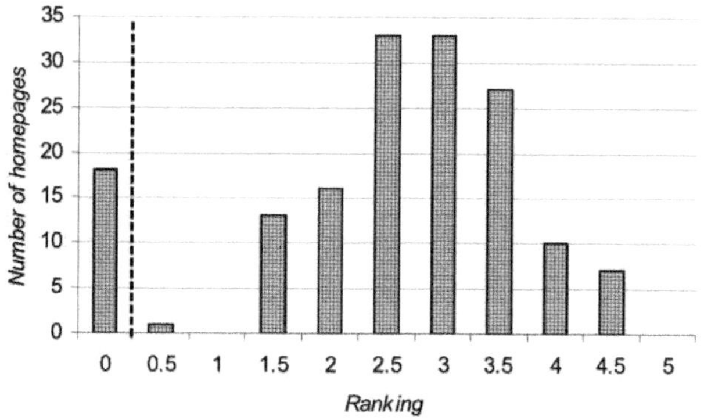


**Fig. 4.** Ranking overview of the 158 MPs' homepages

Out of these results, we selected the twenty "best" (grades 4.5 to 3.75) and twenty "worst" (grades 0.5 to 1.75) homepages to analyse their MPs' party, linguistic region and age.

## 5 The Top Twenty Homepages

75% of the top twenty homepages belong to MPs affiliated to left-wing parties (Socialists, Greens and Evangelicals). 85% of these homepages belong to German-speaking MPs. See figure 5.

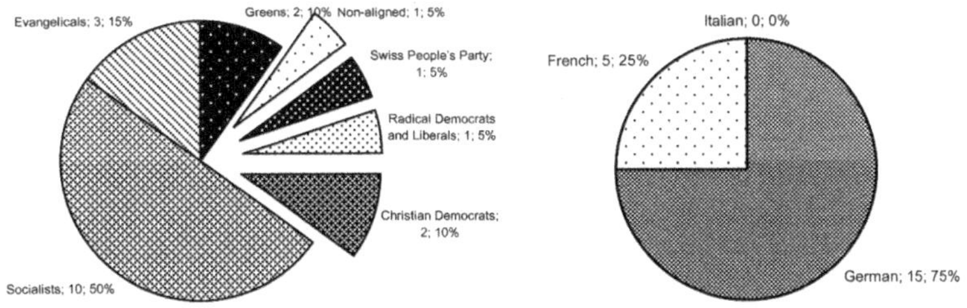


**Fig. 5.** The 20 best MPs' homepages sorted by political parties and by language

Although none of the top twenty homepages come from a MP aged over 65, more than half of them are owned by MPs aged over 45. See figure 6.

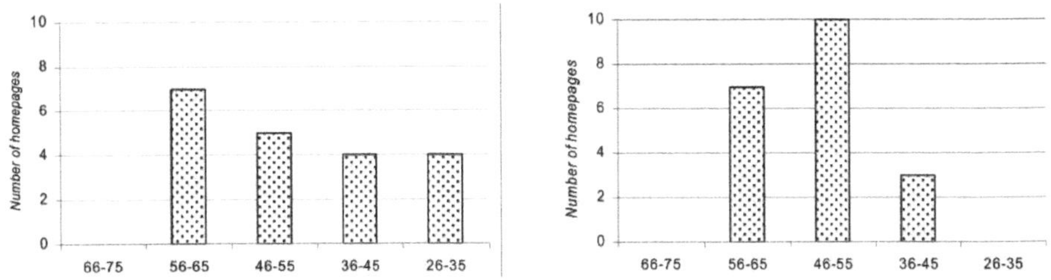


**Fig. 6.** The 20 best (left) and 20 worst (right) homepages sorted by MPs' age

## 5.1 The Bottom Twenty Homepages

The twenty worst homepages are better distributed among all parties than the twenty best of them (although none of the bottom twenty comes from the Green and Evangelical Parties).

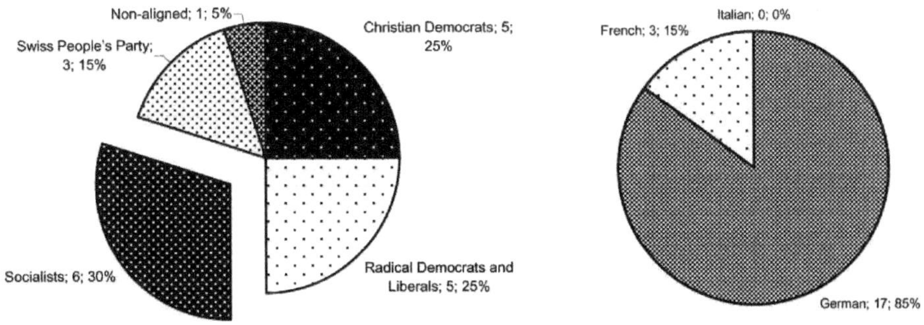


**Fig. 7.** The 20 worst MPs' websites sorted by political parties and by language

Despite this more equal distribution, 70% of the homepages belong to MPs from the right-wing parties with the Socialist MPs providing the remaining 30%. Figure 7 is almost the reverse picture of figure 6, which showed a score of 25% for the right-wing and 75% for the left-wing MPs among the twenty best homepages. Three-quarters of the bottom twenty homepages comes from the German-speaking MPs and the remaining quarter comes from the French-speaking MPs. None come from Italian-speaking MPs, as is also the case for the top twenty.

It is interesting to observe (figure 7) that the worst homepages are not those of either the youngest or oldest Swiss MPs. Half of them belong to the age 46-55 category, who probably have little time to devote to their personal website and/or do not consider it important to delegate this task to an assistant.

## 6 Conclusion

This article is a snapshot of the situation in Switzerland at the end of 2005. From it, the lack of online interactivity between MPs and their electorate is clear, although Swiss parliamentarians are slightly ahead of their counterparts in neighbouring countries. Swiss MPs seem to prefer personal contacts or radio and television appearances. These findings confirm similar studies in Australia (Chen 2002) and Canada (Kernaghan et al 2003).

Only a little more than one-quarter (28%) of Swiss MPs respond to e-mails within a week and very few (10 of them, i.e. less than 5%) make real use of interactive tools such as blogs, forums and chats on their homepages. Most of them do have a homepage but they do not really spend the time and effort necessary to make it interactive or even attractive to read. One reason for this situation might be the lack of interest on the part of the Swiss electorate. A recent survey in the UK showed that fewer than 2% of Internet users had visited the personal website of their MPs (Ward et al, 2005). It would thus appear that most Swiss MPs have a website in order not to appear out of touch with the new media, yet they do not use it in order to interact with citizens and/or to differentiate themselves from other MPs.

There is, however, a handful of MPs (5%) have embraced the Internet with a view to better fulfilling their role as elected representatives. They see the opportunities that this new media offers them to be more efficient, accountable and positioned vis-à-vis their electors. These early-adopter MPs might set a trend for others, especially as the 2007 Federal elections are approaching. This will be worth observing closely, especially as political parties also seem to enter the fray (Graffenried 2006).

Further research, over a certain period of time, would also be needed to investigate the real benefits for MPs of having a website. A barometer of Swiss MPs' eParticipation could be established. It can nevertheless already be stated with assurance that it is not tomorrow that homepages will replace the marketplace or radio and TV talk shows as a way for Swiss MPs to interact with their electorate. Although the new technologies should not be written off as far as their political use is concerned, the well-established media and personal contacts will remain the main means of interaction between Swiss citizens and their parliamentarians for the foreseeable future.

## References


1. Caldow, J. (1999). The Virtual Ballot Box: A Survey of Digital Democracy in Europe. IBM Institute for Electronic Government. 13 May 2005 ¡www.ieg.ibm.com¿.
2. Chappelet, J.-L. (2004). The appropriation of e-mail and the Internet by members of the Swiss Parliament. Information Polity, 9(1-2), pp. 89-102.
3. Chen, P. (2002). Australian Elected Representatives use of New Media Technologies. Research Report, Center for Public Policy, University of Melbourne. 17 June.
4. Coleman, S. (2004). Connecting parliament to the public via the Internet: Two case studies of online consultations. Information, Communication & Society, March, 1-17.
5. Coleman, S. & Nathanson, B. (2005). Learning to live with the Internet: How are European parliamentarians adapting to the digital age? January. Brussels: EPRI Knowledge.
6. Galland, B. & Chappelet, J.-L. (2001). Cyberparlementaires : l'appropriation de l'Internet par les parlementaires fédéraux. Lausanne: cahier de l'IDHEAP.
7. Graffenried, V. de (2006). Le blog, nouvelle arme électorale des partis. Le Temps, Geneva, 1st May 2006.
8. Hoff, J. (2004). The democratic potentials of Information Technology: Attitudes of European MPs towards new technology. Information Polity, 9(1-2), p. 55-66.
9. Jeanneret, M. (2005). Les politiciens, ces cyberlosers! Le Matin, Lausanne, 15 May 2005, p. 21.
10. Kernaghan, K. et al (2003). Politicians' use of ICTs: A Survey of Federal Parliamentarians. November. ¡www.publicsectorit.ca/publications/CBStudy.pdf¿.
11. Neymanns, H. (2002). eCandidates 2002 – der King lebt. Berlin: PolitikDigital. 15 May 2005. ¡www.politik-digital.de¿
12. Norris, P. (2000). Virtuous Circle: Political Communication in Post-Industrial Democracies. Cambridge: CUP.
13. Schaffner, D. (2002). Trotz positiver Erfahrung sollen auf der Website des eidgenössischen Parlaments in Zukunft nur selten Diskussionen stattfinden. Tagesanzeiger, 3 Sept.
14. Ward, S., Gibson, G. and Lusoli, W. (2005). Old Politics, New Media: Parliament, the Public and the Internet. 13 May 2005 ¡www.ipop.org.uk¿.
15. Wuthrich, B. (1999). Internet débarque dans l'arsenal électoral des parlementaires. Le Temps, Geneva, 15 May.
16. Zittel, T. (2004). MPs and the Internet: Between the Rock of Technology and the Hard Place of Politics. Proceedings of the EPRI Conference, Stockholm, 27-28 October.
17. Zimmer, C. (2005). Bitte kommen Sie später wieder. Facts, Zürich, 16 June 2005, pp. 24-26.

# 'Mind the Gap': e-Government and e-Democracy

Ailsa Kolsaker and Liz Lee-Kelley

School of Management, University of Surrey, Guildford,UK
{A.Kolsaker, L.Lee-Kelley}@surrey.ac.uk

**Abstract.** It is claimed that Internet technology offers governments the opportunity to engage citizens online and bridge the growing gap between citizens and the state. In the current climate of citizen disengagement this is a potentially important prospect. Academic studies into e-government tend to follow a well-trodden path of technology acceptance, citizens' willingness and ability to use public services online and the digital divide. Where issues of e-democracy are considered, studies generally highlight opportunities rather than measuring any actual changes in citizen behaviour. This study examines citizens' perceptions, attitudes and behaviour, seeking specifically to expose whether citizens feel that e-government enhances democratic participation and brings them closer to government and the machinery of the state. In this paper we present the results of the pilot study which suggest that citizens perceive some moderate value in using e-government as a means of keeping themselves informed and communicating with the state, but little value in e-government as a tool of democratic participation.

## 1 Introduction

Since 1999 much has been written about the potential of e-government in terms of enhancing both back-end and front-end systems. Back-end processes can be re-engineered and joined up to enhance information sharing, knowledge transfer and cost-effectiveness, whilst joined-up, front-end processing can enhance government-citizen communications, improve the delivery of public services and engage citizens in the processes of democracy [1] [2] [3] [4]. In relation to e-democracy, recent reports suggest increasing participation across Europe [5] [6] [7]. Whilst the reports actually provide supply-side metrics such as 'e-government readiness' and 'e-participation potential' [6], they are commonly interpreted as evidence that citizens are engaging with government online. There is little evidence to suggest that this 'engagement' entails much beyond using online versions of public services; a far cry from engagement in political dialogue with decision-makers. Yet, driven by a desire to address citizen disengagement and improve the quality and legitimacy of decisions, Western European governments are striving to increase active public participation [8]. To be successful, this requires real dialogue between the government and the governed; a dialogue that e-government appears well placed to facilitate.

For interactive, collaborative decision-making between citizens and politicians, two key elements are required. Firstly, citizens must be prepared to become

M.A. Wimmer et al. (Eds.): EGOV 2006, LNCS 4084, pp. 96–106, 2006.

knowledgeable about current issues and to express opinions (particularly on new initiatives) in order to bring clarity to the decision-making processes of elected representatives [9]. Secondly, the state must be prepared to provide timely, comprehensive information as well as channels of communication through which citizens can express their opinions and engage in debate. In a study of parliamentarians [10], it is suggested that the success of online consultations depends upon politicians and citizens acquiring new types of communication skills and new ways of operating. In addition, however, for representative democracy to work, decision-makers must take citizens' views into account, thus there needs to be some way of tracking how decisions have been reached, who has had an input, what that input has been, and so on. In an ideal model electronically-enabled engagement would be based upon a continuous, mutually beneficial 'transmit' and 'receive' cycle in which the e-government platform is exploited to transmit and receive information, acquire knowledge, express opinions, make (joint) decisions – and to track this progress. What is emerging however, is a much more bounded model of e-government with a limited pattern of usage in which citizens are using the Web to access public services in preference to more traditional offline modes. There is little sign of the Web being used to invite citizens to become more proactive partners in the processes of democracy, or to promote transparency of decision-making – both of which are important in an increasingly sceptical, post-modern era. Observing that much of the interest in e-government currently focuses on technology, Cavanagh [11] predicts that narrow technical solutions will have little impact upon the quality of democratic governance and that until ideas of citizenship and democratic governance are revised, modern ICT will make no contribution to democracy. Thus, whilst acknowledging the importance of technology, it is argued here that the lens must be broader. Focusing purely upon improving public service delivery whilst ignoring the potential of e-government for collaborative dialogue and communitarian decision-making underplays the potential scope and relevance of e-government in an era of citizen disengagement.

Currently, although governments like to think that connecting state and citizens through the Web will bring both parties together, this is supported by only patchy empirical evidence. Whilst some local initiatives may have enhanced citizens' feelings of being part of a community (see EU reports citing local e-government projects), overall there is little to suggest that the ability to access public services electronically has any impact upon citizens' feelings of closeness to government or sense of proactive engagement in democratic processes. On the contrary it might be argued that the electronic medium may well increase feelings of remoteness and disengagement by a further reduction in contact between bureaucrats and the citizenry. Against this background this study seeks to clarify citizens' perceptions of e-government in terms of their usage patterns and citizen-government relations to ascertain whether UK e-government's strategic mission of bringing government closer to the people is anywhere near becoming a reality.

## 2 e-Democracy

E-government has been identified as a means of enhancing democracy by increasing representative participation in political decision-making [12] [13] [5]. The concept of e-democracy is ill-defined however, and the field poorly theorised and relatively under-researched. Such theory as exists reflects the ambiguities and over-simplifications of traditional theories of democracy. In the classic models of democracy derived from ancient Greece, elected representatives act in the best interests of the people on behalf of the people. The power, credibility and authority of government emanate from citizens and are rooted in trust, so governments are sustained only as long as citizens are minded to sustain them. It is this trust which has gradually been eroding in the post-modern era of professional politicians and citizen disengagement. In Touraine's [14] analysis, representative democracy takes place when there is a democratic will to enable those who are subordinate and dependent to act freely and to discuss rights and guarantees on equal terms with those who possess economic, political and cultural resources. But this idealised model of democracy ignores a number of uncomfortable realities, for example, that politicians may lose touch with the electorate, and governments may cling to power long after they have lost popular support. Theoretically at least, the Web may offer new opportunities to prevent this from happening by facilitating on-going contact and dialogue between citizens and politicians.

Emergent theories of e-democracy are based on a number of assumptions about citizens' interests and abilities, for example, the consumerist model identified in Hoff et al's [15] typology assumes that citizens are well informed and eager to acquire knowledge, demanding freedom of choice and insisting upon the right to have a voice and be listened to via an electronic platform that is widely accessible and easy to use. This is a highly idealised scenario. It is also undermined by a number of factors, for example, it may be unrealistic to assume technological competence or the ability to recognise prejudice and misinformation [16]; or the possession of an ability to interpret, navigate and shape the landscape of virtual democracy [17]; or that all citizens will have the possibility or ability to engage online [18]; or that people will wish to use the Web to participate in democratic decision-making rather than private communication or entertainment.

Additionally, according to Barnes et al [8] the constitution of 'the public' in public participation is not always straightforward and needs to be explored within the context of power relations operating within any particular initiative. Thus far there has been little detailed consideration of the purpose and form of new, participative relations between citizens and state and indeed whether truly egalitarian relations are possible between governors and the governed. It is suggested [19] that when citizens and politicians interact online in public debate, despite the dialogic nature of the interaction politicians tended to dominate. This supports Young's [20] stance that the concept of deliberative democracy masks very real inequalities in access and power and that the notion of an 'active citizen' engaged as an equal in democratic debate may be somewhat idealised. A recent study [21] of why so many countries fail to involve the public in electronically-enabled decision-making concludes that politicians fear that e-democracy may result in a loss of power. Paradoxically, the very people who would be responsible for introducing new forms of citizen participation in political decision- making are those who both explicitly and implicitly oppose it. Consequently, as things stand, there is little empirical evidence that e-government enhances state/citizen relations and citizen engagement, since although theoretically the Web is well positioned to enhance democracy by providing new forms of mediation between citizens and state, it is unlikely to do so if based upon over-simplified assumptions of responsibilised, participating citizens, ignoring issues of exclusion, access, motivation, legitimacy and so on. Since there is a paucity of research in this area however, to conclude that this is the case would be premature. It is timely, therefore, to explore more closely the concept of e-democracy and examine citizens' perceptions of e-government, in particular whether there exists any relationship at all between the availability of e-government and citizens' feelings of closeness to government and engagement in the processes of democracy.

## 3 Citizens' Perceptions of e-Government

There is a growing body of literature on consumers' propensity to buy online, but relatively little on citizens' attitudes towards and use of e-government. At the most basic level of service delivery it is anticipated here that many of the issues uncovered in relation to e-commerce may apply to citizens' use of online public services. For example, a study of Internet users' perceptions [22] identifies trustworthiness and effective communication, site design and content as key determinants of perceived service quality for browsers and browsers/buyers alike. Piccoli et al [23] propose that site design and functionality are key to usage, as browsers make judgements about perceived value and utility. In Piccoli et al's analysis, currently a number of sites fail to offer sufficient personalisation, support and explanation to browsers, resulting in disappointment and sub-optimal usage. In an earlier paper we identify vendor benevolence, credibility and competence as antecedents of online shopping [24]. Echoing these findings, a recent study [25] of online shoppers' acceptance of a virtual store suggests that they are influenced by intangible as well as tangible elements, including the nature and quality of the offering, information richness, usability of storefront, perceived trust and perceived service quality, including prompt, reliable delivery. Chen and Tan's findings suggest that although browsers are becoming more familiar and confident with the Web environment, their intention to transact online remain highly influenced by perceptions of the features of the store and the more intangible dimensions of quality and trust. Similarly, it may be anticipated that if e-government sites are perceived to be an ineffective means of communication or offer little of value, then citizens will not use them.

Regarding intention to continue to use online services, it is suggested [26] that the user's ability and confidence as well as the quality of the site are important – Internet self-efficacy and satisfaction with the online experience emerge as key determinants. Another potentially relevant study [27] reaffirms the importance of high quality e-service delivery. Defining e-service operations as 'hard': right place, right time, right price, right condition, and 'soft': site design, information readiness, smooth transactions, the study identifies a number of barriers erected not by the technology, but by the inability of the provider to offer services of an appropriate quality. These studies imply that providers have the potential to influence perceived value and that over time (if online service provision is good) one might expect an increase in the user's perceptions of value and propensity to continue to use online services. In the current context a study of service quality amongst members of a Web community [28] is of interest. Extrapolating these findings, which, employing Kano's two-way quality model reaffirms the importance of customer perceptions in service delivery and the influence of perceptions upon customer satisfaction, it is suggested here that if citizens are to be encouraged to use e-government services, it is of paramount importance that such services offer overt and unambiguous added value over and above that provided by the offline alternative and a satisfactory service experience. Further studies [29] [30] suggest that consumers, quite naturally, compare novel technology-enabled delivery with traditional alternatives – there is no reason to anticipate that citizens will judge e-government services any differently.

In sum, the existing body of knowledge suggests that citizens' use of electronically-enabled public services may be influenced by a portal's content, features, functionality and usability as well as intangibles such as satisfaction and trust. It is apparent that perceptions play a critical role in usage intentions. But engaging citizens in new, networked relations, encouraging participation in consultation and a proactive role in the democratic process rather than simply using the Web to receive public services requires a significant and coordinated effort. The OECD publication, 'Citizens as Partners' [31] urges 'greater transparency, more consultation and more participation' through: i) providing easy access to information which is complete, objective, reliable, relevant, easy to find and to understand; ii) ensuring that consultation has clear goals and rules defining the limits of the exercise and accounting for the use of citizens' input, and iii) ensuring that participation allows sufficient time and flexibility to allow for the emergence of new ideas [31]. The OECD regards 'information as a basic precondition, consultation as central policy-making and participation as a new frontier' [31]. Whilst the existing literature provides some pointers as to how citizens may perceive e-government services, the lack of empirical data means it is difficult to draw any meaningful conclusions and misguided to make assumptions.

In an attempt to add to the existing, limited body of knowledge the issues touched upon above are explored further in this study. For non-users in the research population, the starting-point is to assume that they perceive no added value in using e-government, whilst e-government users are assumed to perceive some benefits and to be knowledgeable enough to form perceptions of site characteristics and of whether e-government affects their feelings of engagement in the processes of democracy. Non-users' perceptions are examined using descriptive statistics and open ended questions, and thereafter the following research questions are posed for e-government users:

- Is usage intensity related to perceptions of benefits (availability, time savings, money savings, useful information etc)?
- Is usage intensity related to perceptions of site characteristics (support, personalisation, confidentiality, trustworthiness etc)?
- Is usage intensity related to feelings of engagement in democracy?

## 4 Methodology

This study departs from the positivistic approach found in many earlier studies to explore not the objective rationality of e-government but the subjective interpretations of those in whose name it is being introduced. It seeks to investigate how citizens perceive e-government in terms of closeness to government and the machinery of the state. This is potentially of enormous importance to government against a background of increasing voter apathy and a widening gap between government and the people. Governments have continually expressed a great belief in e-government as a driver of citizen engagement, but in order to gauge the true potential of the medium in this regard citizens' perceptions and intentions must be afforded higher priority than government rhetoric.

The full study will be conducted in the UK, since the UK is ranked first in the latest United Nations e-participation index [5]. For the purpose of having easy access to the research population, the study will be conducted in a medium-sized county town in a relatively affluent region of South-East England. The population is defined as citizens who have access to the Web. Since the sampling frame (directory of postal addresses) includes both those with and without Web access, membership of the research population is to be determined by way of an opening yes/no question in the instrument. Streets are selected using simple random sampling, facilitated by SPSS. This initial pilot study was conducted with 1,000 envelopes being distributed and 110 returned, representing an 11 percent response rate.

## 5 Initial Findings

Of the 108 usable questionnaires, 74 (68.5%) used e-government sites and 37 (31.5%) did not. Of the 34 who did not use e-government, 32% did not have Internet access at home, with the remainder having Internet access but expressing a preference to communicate in other ways such as the telephone, mail or visiting government offices. Analysis of the descriptives suggest overwhelmingly that non-users perceive some potential value in information provision, aiding understanding of services available to them, and of local issues, having their say and as a means of communicating with the council (means > 3.00 in each case), but the perceived value is not great enough to entice them online. These are the traditional information provision and communication aspects of e-government.

Those variables relating to e-democracy were not perceived as offering much added value either in terms of increasing trust, helping citizens to feel closer to government or being more engaged and better represented (means $< 3.00$).

Citizens who use e-government services were surveyed about their motivations for usage. Initial analysis using descriptive statistics and ANOVA testing provides the following overview:

- *'Perceived benefits'*
  Echoing earlier studies, '24/7' availability was identified as the most obvious benefit (mean = 4.12). Thereafter, e-government was perceived as offering useful information, time savings and saving money (all means $> 3.50$).
  Three categories of usage intensity were identified regarding the use of the Web to contact local or central government departments; whenever possible, sometimes and rarely. Using ANOVA to look for differences between usage intensity, the results indicate no significant difference in perceptions between groups on any of the items. f was greatest ($f = 2.408$, $p > .05$) for 'time savings' and 'money savings ($f = 1.610$, $p > .05$) and smallest for 'useful information'($f = .310$, $p > .05$) and '24/7 availability' ($f = .184$, $p > .05$). Because there is no significant difference between groups, the results of the analysis of means may be interpreted uniformly.
- *'Site characteristics'*
  Descriptives for ease of use, good design and reliable technology produced only slight variance in means (3.36; 3.33 and 3.48 respectively). The results suggest that e-government sites are perceived as moderately trustworthy (mean =3.33), moderately protective of confidentiality (mean =3.29) and reasonably able to allow citizens to achieve his/her aims of using e-government (mean =3.25). Means for personalised service, support if citizens get stuck and looking after the visitor's interests were below 3.00 in each case.

  Using ANOVA to look for differences according to usage intensity, the results indicate no significant difference in perceptions. The greatest differences were in perceived trustworthiness ($f = 1.372$, $p > .05$) and good support ($f = 1.134$, $p > .05$) and the smallest in confidentiality ($f = .385$, $p > .05$) and personalised service ($f = .335$, $p > 0.5$). Again, none of the differences was statistically significant, and therefore the results can be interpreted uniformly.
- *'Engagement in democracy'*
  Firstly, respondents were asked whether they thought that their opinion was valued by i) local government, and ii) central government and iii) whether there was enough public consultation. The results indicate strongly that respondents feel disenfranchised (means = 3.01; 2.55; and 2.30 respectively), reflecting the citizen disenchantment cited in the literature and the widening between citizens and state.

Then, respondents were asked about whether using e-government made them feel that they were playing a greater role in democracy. Descriptives indicate that respondents feel that e-government may be of some help in acquiring knowledge and expertise about issues that are important to them (means > 3.28). Regarding involvement in democracy, however, all the results suggest a minimal effect. The highest values were recorded for 'have my say' (mean = 2.71) and 'communicate effectively with decision-makers' (mean =2.56) and the lowest for e-government makes respondents feel closer to the state (mean = 2.21) and that they are working in partnership with the state (mean =2.29).

Once again, looking for differences between groups, there was no significant difference based upon level of usage intensity. The greatest differences were in relation to 'feeling that decision-makers listen' ($f = 1.477$, $p > .05$) followed by 'enables me to build up expertise' ($f = .945$, $p > .05$), the lowest being 'communicate with decision-makers ($f = .130$, $p > .05$) and 'enables me to have my say' ($f = .120$, $p > .05$).

Overall, there was some agreement that e-government portals had value to citizens (mean =3.57), local councils (mean =3.79) and central government (mean =3.65) and overall respondents appeared moderately satisfied (mean = 3.18).

Measuring differences in perceptions between groups according to usage intensity, the only significant difference was in relation to the variable 'value to government', with $f = 3.227$ and $p = .047$. Neither 'value to local councils' ($f = 1.762$, $p > .05$), nor 'value to me' ($f = .285$, $p > .05$) recorded significant differences between groups, suggesting that as usage increases, perceived value to the individual is unaffected. There were no significant differences in satisfaction levels between high, medium and low-intensity users.

## 6 Discussion of Findings

Although at this pilot stage the results should be considered tentative, they provide an interesting insight into the subjective evaluations by respondents of the three key components of use: perceived benefits, site characteristics and democratic participation. It is intended that the findings will inform for a follow-up, more comprehensive study.

Review of the literature suggests that citizens may well have to be convinced of the benefits of engaging online in new forms of political dialogue. The current study suggests that for citizens to want to access and continue to use e-government websites, 'perceived benefits' must be very evident; in particular 24/7 availability. This may well be related to the consumerist tradition of individual choice and control. Respondents also rated usefulness of information and time savings as important. 21st century life-style is busy, hectic and constantly bombarded with a host of possibilities for leisure and work, hence individuals will want to know that accessing and using government websites can either help them to become better informed, more able to have their say and lead to some tangible outcome.

Respondents' evaluations of 'site characteristics' such as ease of use, design and reliability continue the focus on convenience and further emphasises the need for control, choice and payoff. In terms of 'possible barriers', trust and confidentiality emerge as the two most important variables, echoing the e-commerce literature. Interestingly, the third possible barrier was revealed to be in matching personal aims, which should not be ignored by e-government implementers as this indicator extends beyond the sheer convenience emphasis to a psychological match of wants, needs and offerings. This may provide a pointer to active participation; say for example citizens feel strongly about a particular local issue (such as a new road cutting through countryside) if they feel that the e-government platform allows them to have their say, be listened to and receive some response then this potentially could be the springboard for engagement and dialogue. To engage citizens in political dialogue online there needs to be a forum for exchange, a mechanism for convincing citizens that their opinions are welcomed, valued and acted upon, and a means of tracking decision-making. It may be that it is the lack of these elements that underlies respondents' view that going online helps them acquire or increase their knowledge and understanding of current issues, but has little impact on their feelings of democratic involvement.

## 7 Conclusion

As intimated, conclusions from the pilot study must be regarded as tentative. That stated, in relation to the research objectives the results offer some interesting, initial indications. Taken holistically, the results appear to suggest that citizens perceive some moderate value in using e-government to access information, increase their knowledge and understanding of available services and to communicate with the state. The greatest value is perceived to be in relation to 'round the clock' availability, echoing earlier studies of online retailing. Overall, perceived value of using the Web to access government services is not as great as earlier research would suggest. In relation to engagement in democratic processes and feeling involved as an active citizen, the results suggest very little perceived value. Respondents appeared overwhelmingly ambivalent about using the e-government platform as a way of engaging in closer relations with the state – although, they could see some moderate value to central government, local councils and themselves in using e-government as an interface between citizens and state. Overall, the results appear to support the view that if citizens are to be encouraged to use e-government services, it is of paramount importance that such services offer overt and unambiguous added value over and above those provided by the offline alternative. As anticipated, there is no reason to expect citizens to judge e-government portals using different criteria to those employed by consumers judging e-commerce sites. If government wishes to engage citizens pro-actively in the process of e-democracy then our initial findings suggest that the fundamental issues of trust and responsiveness must be addressed within a broader shift to a more communitarian style of governance.

## References

1. Fang, Z. (2002) E-Government in the Digital Era: Concept, Practice and Development, International Journal of the Computer, the Internet and Management, Vol. 10 (2): 1-22.
2. Ling, T. (2002) Delivering Joined-up Government in the UK: Dimensions, Issues and Problems, Public Administration, Vol. 80 (4): 615-642.

3. Coleman, S. (2004) Connecting Parliament to the Public via the Internet, Information, Communication and Society, Vol. 7 (1): 1-22
4. Gerald, G. (2004) Realizing the Promise of Electronic Government, Journal of Global Information Management, Vol. 13 (1), pp. 1-5.
5. United Nations (2005) Global e-Government Readiness Report, New York. Available from http//: unpan1.un.org.
6. European Commission Directorate General for Information Society and Media (2005) Online Availability of Public Services: How is Europe Progressing?, Fifth Measurement, Capgemini. Available from http://europa.eu.int.
7. Office of the Deputy Prime Minister (2005) Two Years On: Realising the benefits from our investment in e-government, London, ODPM Publications.
8. Barnes, M., Newman, J., Knops, A. and Sullivan, H. (2003) Constituting the 'public' in public participation, Public Administration, Vol. 81 (2): 379-399
9. Biasiott, M. and Nannucci R. (2004) Learning to Become an E-citizen: The European and Italian Policies in (M. Wimmer, Ed.): Knowledge Management in Electronic Government, Lecture Notes in Computer Science 3035, Springer.
10. Coleman, S. (2004) Connecting Parliament to the Public via the Internet, Information, Communication and Society, Vol. 7 (1): 1-22.
11. Cavanaugh, J. (2000) E-Democracy: Thinking About the Impact of Technology on Civic Life, National Civic Review, Vol. 89 (3) 229-234.
12. International Council for Information Technology in Government Administration (ICA) (2001) e-Government in the Service of Democracy, ICA Information No. 74. Available from www.ica-it.org.
13. Lenihan, D. (2002) Realigning Governance: from e-Government to e-Democracy, OECD Centre for Collaborative Government. Available from www.collaborativegovernment.com.
14. Touraine, A. (1997) What is Democracy? (tr. by D. Macey), Colorado, Westview Press.
15. Hoff, J., Lofgren, K. and Torpe, L. (2003) The state we are in: e-democracy in Denmark, Information Polity, Vol. 8 (1/2): 44-69.
16. Line, M. (2005) Democracy and information: transmitters and receivers, Library Management, Vol. 24 (8/9): 386-392.
17. Joint, N. (2003) Democracy, eLiteracy and the internet, Library Review, Vol. 54 (2): 80-85.
18. Lee-Kelley, L. and James, T. (2003) e-Government and Social Exclusion, Journal of Electronic Commerce in Organisations, Vol. 1 (4) pp 1-16.
19. Jensen, J. (2003) Virtual democratic dialogue? Bringing together citizens and politicians, Information Polity, Vol. 8 (1/2): 29-48.
20. Young, I.M. (1990) Justice and the politics of difference, Princetown, NJ, Princetown University Press.
21. Mahrer, H. and Krimmer, R. (2005) Towards the enhancement of e-democracy: identifying the notion of the middleman paradox, Journal of Information Systems, Vol. 15 (1) : 27-42.
22. Shaohan, C. and Minjoon, J. (2003) Internet users' perceptions of online service quality: a comparison of online buyers and information searchers, Managing Service Quality, Vol. 13 (6): 504-520.
23. Piccoli, G., Brohman, M. K., Watson, R. and Parasuraman, A. (2004) Net-Based Customer Service Systems: Evolution and Revolution in Web Site Functionalities, Decision Sciences, Vol. 35 (3): 423-456.

24. Kolsaker, A., Lee-Kelley E. and Choy, P.C. (2004) 'The Reluctant Hong Kong Consumer: Purchasing Travel Online, International Journal of Consumer Studies, Vol. 28 (3), pp. 295-305.
25. Chen, L-D. and Tan, J. (2004) Technology Adaptation in E-commerce:: Key Determinants of Virtual Stores Acceptance, European Management Journal, Vol. 22 (1): 74-87.
26. Meng-Hsiang, H. and Chiu, C-M. (2004) Internet self-efficacy and electronic service acceptance, Decision Support Systems, Vol. 38 (3): 369-382.
27. Douglas, A., Muir, L. and Meehan, K. (2003) E-quality in the e-services provision of legal practices, Managing Service Quality, Vol. 13 (6) pp 483-491.
28. Kuo, Y-F. (2003) Integrating Kano's Model into Web-community Service Quality, Quality Management and Business Excellence, Vol. 15 (7): 925-940.
29. Meuter, M.L., Ostrom, A.L., Roundtree, R. and Bitner, M.J. (2000) Self-Service Technologies: Understanding Customer Satisfaction with Technology-Based Service Encounters , Journal of Marketing, Vol. 64 (3): 50-65.
30. Szymanski, D.H. and Hise, R. T. (2000) e-Satisfaction: An Initial Examination, Journal of Retailing, Vol. 76 (3): 309-323.
31. OECD Public Administration Group (PUMA) (2001) Citizens as Partners: Information, Consultation and Public Participation in Policy-Making, Paris, OECD.

# To Be or Not to Be Active: Exploring Practices of e-Participation

Annelie Ekelin

Department of Interaction and System Design Blekinge
Institute of Technology, Box 520, SE-372 25 Ronneby, Sweden
http://www.bth.se
annelie.ekelin@bth.se

**Abstract.** This paper discusses the interplay of participation and non-participation within institutional and public practices of electronically mediated policy-making in the local public sector. The aim is to contribute to practice-centred development of situated theoretical conceptualisation in the research domain. Applying a dialectical analysis, including also examples and processes of dissociation detected in ethnographic studies of actual use and design of these technologies, suggests a re-specification of the conceptual basis of e-participation.

## 1 Introduction

Key themes in e-democracy development have more and more emerged as various forms of electronic participation in different stages of democratic processes. Concrete examples of experiments of participatory e-democracy in Scandinavia as well as in other parts of Europe, could be described mostly as strivings towards improvement of information and communication by ICT, rather than achievements of direct involvement of citizens in decision-making within the existing and established forms of representative government. [5] [10] [13] The primary attention has lately focused upon the potential to stimulate new forms of deliberative processes, and visions of improving communication between citizens and decision-makers, as well as ensuring access for all (inclusion) which is also highlighted through the new directions in the e-government development, presented i.e. in the Communications of the European Commission [2] [6] However, these changes in policy put a lot of pressure on all involved parties, i.e. citizens, politicians and practitioners to be constantly active and engaged.

### 1.1 Need for Situated Evaluations

Recently there have been several demands on comparisons, evaluations and guidance of ongoing governmental pilots and projects of electronically mediated participation within the context of policy-making. [10] Electronic participation (e-participation) has hitherto been almost uncritically promoted and emphasised as having great potential of transforming relations between local administration and the public, and expected to help reform the classical model of democratic involvement.

M.A. Wimmer et al. (Eds.): EGOV 2006, LNCS 4084, pp. 107–118, 2006.

The issue of developing methods aiming at evaluating and steering these new forms of participation, especially concerning e-consultations and other kinds of public engagement, which are intended to inform or even transform policy-making, [9] is increasing in importance. However, there is a risk that evaluations even though they are well intended and thoroughly organised, scratch only at the surface of the phenomenon, if the interest for these activities mainly concentrates on what could be labelled "conversations at the interfaces" [17] Experiences from local research and development (R&D) pilots concerning either general development of relations between citizens and local administration or specific e-democracy pilots in Scandinavia [3] described in this paper, accentuate the need of including inquiries into work practices and use-situations as bases for developing methods in this area. Those are often neglected dimensions in mainstream management studies, which ought to be added to the ongoing strivings of picturing e-participation conceptually. The context of the local activity of setting up for instance e-consultations must be better accounted for in future evaluations and discussions, not solely the abstracted knowledge and the *outcome* of the mediated participation. Strivings of characterising e-participation must not get stuck on analysing what is ultimately displayed and visible on the web, they should also include the local work practice of *preparing, supporting and maintaining e-participation*, since these activities also influence the conduct of e-participation. The experiences from these local cases, further described and discussed in this paper, show that denial to take responsibility for the contextual issues and work practices of these activities seriously affects the outcome of mediated participation.

### 1.2 Interplay of Dissociation and Commitment

Secondly, the activities of promoting e-participation could also, if using an incisive wording, be summarised as concentrating mainly on how to entice people to become more active and how to convince them to stay active forever. Again practice-based evidences suggests that more emphasise must be put on *exploring the interplay of dissociation and commitment*, not necessarily with the prior intention to come up with the right formula on how to minimise non-participation, rather acknowledge that there are different modes and degrees of non-participation also *within* participation and vice versa and that this is an essential part of the dynamics in e-participation. These variations of participation and non-participation must be explored in a dialectic way in order to generate practice-based conceptualisation, which is of great relevance when coping with the dilemma of handling e-participation in every-day situations.

## 2 Theoretical and Empirical Basis

This paper draws primarily on systematisation and analysis of experiences derived from practice [15], basically described as a situated research approach, coupled with a social theory on learning, as elaborated by Lave and Wenger [7] and further discussed in Wenger [18] and Smith [14]. Greenbaum and Kyng [4] explained the implication of a situated approach towards development of computer systems as deriving mainly out of a social constructionist view, i.e. that the computer systems, often comprehended as purely technical, is mainly generated through and by interactions among people who are engaged in a particular design process, in a specific situation and under certain circumstances. They label this situated design. Those views on learning and design processes as contextual and particular social interactions is also useful when discussing the issue of e-participation both as an activity of mutual learning (among all involved parties) and as several processes of participation, rather than strivings to implement fixed frameworks based on general assumptions about how e-participation might come true. This fluid nature of e-participation needs to be taken into account in examinations and evaluations of activities and goals. E-participation must be seen as relational (i.e. taking place as an evolving set of relations which develops over time). It have to be constructed as an activity that is not cut loose from a workplace context, even though it is a mediated activity, since the activity itself is depending on the concept of full participation, not only by the engaged citizens, but also by the staff and politicians who are intended to get involved in preparing, supporting and maintaining the event as such. Methods supporting e-participation must therefore support a system of relations, including also the work situation, and not solely focusing on support of the single activity of citizen's participation.

Greenbaum and Kyng [4] stressed the point that computerisation often is aiming towards rationalisation of work, rather than enhancing work locally, which might not always be the most economic alternative in the long run. In a similar way the ultimate goal of promoting e-participation must be aiming at enhancing the quality of local attempts of mediated participation, and not take its starting point in the intention to rationalise or formalise e-participation with the ultimate purpose to quantify or transfer generalisations and abstractions out of local contexts. The strong intention to transfer good practices of e-participation, emphasised by for instance the European Commission is in some ways conducted out of the wish to *increase the production* of e-participation, that is enable a greater amount of activities labelled e-participation, but a grounded perspective suggests that the elaboration of e-participation frameworks must be done in order to gain quality rather than quantity of those activities. The social anthropologist Lucy Suchman [16] showed by her research that the local activities of human beings is not as much steered by plans, as based on specific conditions and situations. That is also an argument for emphasising that conceptualisation of e-participation must be rooted in experiences, not just generalised rules, also explaining why it is so important to include work practices and real use- and design situations in evaluations of e-participation and relate those contextual dimensions to future development of concepts in the emerging field. E-participation is thus dependent on the complex situations where the realisation of e-participation actually takes place.

## 3 Description of Cases

The empirical basis for this paper is ethnographically based work-oriented interviews, and participatory observations [1] of specific situations. The fieldwork took place during two local municipally driven projects, which ran in Scandinavia 2002 and 2004-05. The projects are here called the *Invitation-project* and the *Election-project*, both aiming at furthering e-participation among local inhabitants. These projects could basically be described as attempts to vitalise a public debate on future development of the local society and stimulation of dialogue between citizens to citizens (CÔC), between citizens and civil servants (CÔ CS), and citizens and politicians (CP), by asking "What's your opinion on future living?" and "What do you want to know about the local society?" respectively "What do you want to know about local politics and the process of voting?" The *Invitation-project* was divided into two parts, each part aiming at developing web support for extended dialogue with citizens. The *Vision Site* was built on the idea of involving citizens in planning the future local society and was in that sense extending what the Swedish law command in formal consultations on spatial planning.

The project members were municipal officers from the information office and the spatial planning unit, researchers, a small software company and a marketing company. The task was to jointly design an interactive web site describing future development plans for the city. In the periphery of the actual design-process there were also citizens and politicians taking part. They were either invited as participants in what was called focus groups interviews within the project, more correctly described as sessions of user-evaluations involving primarily citizens and municipal officers, or in another realm of the periphery; members in the political steering group (the politicians). The concrete examples of participation and non-participation is primarily taken from those events or peripheral actions, based on the claim earlier described in this paper that work practices and design-in use events also matters for basic stimulation of developing e-participation. A common dilemma, which seems to be troubling the involved parties in developing e-participation (the citizens, the politicians and the civil servants) in this local context was, formulated on empirical basis: 1) the problem of motivating and engaging other people, coupled with 2) the necessity and difficulty of motivating oneself. My aim is to elaborate on these dilemmas from the basis of 3) how to find ways of motivating each other, instead of regarding the lack of motivation as separated problems, which by coincidence seems to occur simultaneously in separate domains?

## 4 Analysis

Lave and Wenger [7] describes in their presentation of a social theory on learning a process, which they call legitimate peripheral participation. This could in a simple way be described as a form of apprenticeship, but is according to the authors a much more complex activity. It is "*a description of the particular mode of engagement of a learner who participates in the actual practice of an expert, but only to a limited degree and with limited responsibility for the ultimate product as a whole.*" [7] They claim that learning is fundamentally a social process and not solely happening in the learner's head. The authors maintain that learning viewed as situated activity has as its central defining characteristic a process they call legitimate peripheral participation. Learners participate in communities of practitioners, moving toward full participation in the sociocultural practices of a community. Translated into an e-participation context this means that cooperating constellations of local politicians, civil servants and citizens, jointly taking part in for instance an evaluation activity of an e-consultation could be described as participants in a community of practice, enabling learning and full participation. User-evaluations, focus group interviews taking place within these projects were all sharing the specificity of a community of practice, which is; *shared domain of interest, a shared repertoire of resources and mutual engagement* [16], involving also citizens' as equal practitioners due to their characteristic as active citizens'.

In this regard it is appropriate to look upon e-participation in communities of practice as learning in situated activities where it is of importance to focus on the relations as such, in order to detect those moments of balance and integral participation and in what way they relate to imbalance and non-participation. Then e-participation might occur in different kinds of communities of practice, rather than in the prepared places where it is designated to take place, i.e. in the fixed discussion forums presented on the *Vision Site* dealing with spatial planning, or in the pre-defined activities on the web where politicians turned out to be very reluctant to participate actively, with reference to the unpleasant experiences of individual exposure. There did however occur several examples of democratic activity in the somewhat informal space or terrain of the public evaluation meetings where the suggested prototype was tested, where the citizens could combine their own personal interest with acting in co-operation as a group who where in the mode of learning to move from being ordinary citizens to experts on their own use of e-consultation tools.

### 4.1 The Dilemma of Exposing Inactivity and Incompleteness

During the Election-project the issue of politicians reluctance to take part in debate in public web-forums came up in the public evaluation and in the media. Different actors constantly highlighted the issue in different contexts. One of the politicians (P1) reflected upon his role as "worn-out dialoguing politician", in one of these follow-up interviews: "*The experiences with the Election-site made me think about this. I am not sceptical to the website, but ... there are different expectations on different politicians, but still it is expected that you have to be fully engaged, that you are accountable and being able to answer all kind of questions. I am now talking out of my personal experience here, I am expected to take part in ordinary meetings since I am involved in political committees, internal political meetings in the evenings and then it is expected that I, when I am back at home nine o' clock in the evening I have to go online and check if there are any questions for me [in the debate forum]. At that time I have to be intellectually clear, and sit down and compose answers. / ... / It requires much more intellectual strain, and this is often during the evenings, if you are a spare time politician and not a professional politician. / ... /*"

This particular volunteer politician highlights an important aspect of non-participation in his reflection. He indirectly points out that politics in a debate-forum becomes more of an individual performance than a teamwork, which is not always favoured by all sorts of politicians, because all politicians are not expected to have the same position in the political group which could be said form a certain community of practice. The politician experiences demands that he has to be a competent representative which, in his interpretation means; intellectually clear and focused, able to write and answer all sorts of questions as well as being up-dated about the local and national political agenda as well as current debate on different subjects. He also experiences high demands on his performance of participation. He has to be fully engaged in all activities (off-line as well as on-line), he is held accountable for all sorts of actions, and he is also expected to be active on multiple levels in the organisational structure. This indicates that there are several degrees and levels of participation asked for. A crucial issue also seems to occur in connection to experiences of lacking competence. What is at stake here? Is the role of politicians as "in formed representatives" threatened by the possibility to be questioned by the public? Are politicians safeguarding their legitimacy and superiority as "competent representatives"? Is it concern for old traditions in political practice or is it fear for change of political structures? It may very well be all of this, and earlier research in Europe, conducted by Mahrer and Krimmer has suggested a notion called "the middle-man paradox" [12], in order to identify politicians as inhibiting factors in the general transformation of e-democracy. This notion makes it possible to highlight the fact that those who are responsible for introducing new democratic forms in fact also might be afraid of loosing their gained position as political represents. This is also part of the trajectory in the process of legitimate peripheral participation, which not always is harmonious. It could also be suggested that this particular politician expresses his need for having a possibility to move slowly into the centre of full participation, and that he expresses a need to manage his own non-participation?

A web designer in the municipality who took part in the Election-project describes the demands on the politicians: "*We told them what we expected them to do; [they had] to be active in the debate forum, to write information in the module for candidate presentation... participate in political cafs that were supposed to be conducted in real-time and simultaneously webcasted, lead by a moderator from the local radio station. We expected active politicians. They had to answer questions; after all it is in their interest. They have got a free marketing channel here, but they were reluctant. They said, "it is too close to the election, people haven't got the time to participate" and so on. But a couple of the politicians said; go ahead and arrange it, and we will assure that someone [politicians] shows up.*"

The web designer presents a picture that easily could be understood as a requirement of the active politician. But from the politicians point of view it meant that they had to cope with multi-channel broadcasting, and be prepared to interact with many receivers. Some of them were reluctant but a couple of them said that they were prepared to take on the workload of getting things running. However, the interactive cafs were finally cut out of the activity program and the debate in the forums were later on criticised for being dominated by a few talkative politicians, debating mostly with each other.

The politician pointed out that *fear of exposure* is a natural part of everyday experience of a volunteer politician, which one has to cope with. However, his experience of debating on the *Election-site* was a frustrating experience, manifested as an anxiety of exposing himself as inactive and incapable instead of being active and accountable and constantly prepared and open to public evaluation. And for the web designer it was of course a disappointment when the thoroughly developed website and the additional implementation activities turned out to be rejected by those who eventually could benefit the most of the planned arrangement, and for the civil servants who had done everything right according to the action plan on transforming public administrations by inviting citizens to take part in discussions and to inform themselves in time for the election, was it of course a disappointment with low degrees of participation.

In the debate forum about the future development of the city there where also comments made by the citizens asking why politicians did not take part in the debate. The head of the information office (HIO) commented the lack of politician's contributions in the following way: "*Why have not local politicians been active in this debate forum, presenting their opinions, commenting other opinions or discuss with each other? My guess is that the channel still feels a bit unfamiliar and strange for some of the politicians, but not for everyone. Several of the politicians are frequent Internet users. Some politicians probably comprehend the Invitation-site as a "listening ear" rather than a forum for debate, as with the debate on spatial planning and the discussion about future living. Maybe some of them are afraid that the time will not be enough if they start to use the debate forum. One who says A has to proceed with B, and since many politicians are volunteer politicians they find it difficult to manage. We remind them about the existence of the debate forum, then it is up to them to participate or not.*"

## 4.2 The Dilemma of Cross-Over Dialogue

The issue of politicians' and civil servants' unwillingness to take active part in an electronic dialogue with citizens was also brought up for discussion in another context and in relation to another project, during a focus group interview (FGI) in the *Invitation*-project, which indicates that this political non-participation runs the risk of becoming an established contradiction in the municipality. Eight citizens took part in the discussion along with municipal officers and researchers. The aim with the session was to conduct a user-evaluation of the website "*Vision Site*" and provide the municipal and the software firm with viewpoints for adjustment of the application. This discussion was circulating around the issue of avoiding exposure of inactivity. From statements made by the civil servants, one could draw the conclusion that there were uncertainties in the distribution of responsibility concerning who was supposed to run the discussion on the site, and that this was largely depending on under-staffing and changes in work-organisation. This organisational issue also had effects on the interaction with the citizens and was also contributing to the effect of causing a one-way communication, along with the consequences of absent politicians. The joint meeting with the citizens taking part in a focus group interview did provide the involved parties with opportunities to understand the motives behind the choices made, and find out that the unwillingness to respond on the public opinions were more complicated than the simple dichotomisation between opposing parts such as non-participation and participation. In the vision of a functioning e-government world the politicians and local administration must be prepared to open up for participation also in decision-making, and not avoid taking responsibility. But what to do if the work practice puts constraints on or even work against the new demands on implementing a new culture of interaction and the new openness also means vulnerability for the decision-makers and the civil servants?

The potential of online discussions and deliberation is envisioned both as bridging and bounding in rhetorical claims, but the politicians and civil servants who where active in the Election-site described another experience. P2: "*Politicians in general do not communicate with their voters, that is a myth. If I really examine myself, I talk to my party members, my working team but I will not talk to people on the street, I do not cross the categories in which I normally circulate.*"

### 4.3 Another Item in the Program or a Part of the Decision-Making Process?

During an interview with a politician concerning the running consultation in the Invitation-project the question whether the role of online-discussions were considered an essential part of the total comprehensive planning process in the *Invitation*-project came up. The discussion between the politician and the researchers made clear that the *mix of representative (i.e. involvement in the parliamentary steering group) and full participation (public evaluation of website*) was causing complexity and misunderstanding concerning what role e-participation really should play.

The differences referred to here could be visualised as examples of "formal" and "informal" processes of political participation. There had been a traditional consultation period (formal participation) before the writing of the proposed spatial plan, where the parliamentary group had been involved, according to general procedure. The *Invitation-project* (including also preparation of the *Vision-site*) was in relation to this considered to be an informal part of the traditional spatial planning, since it was not properly adjusted to the formal timeline of the consultation period, and it was also informal in that sense that it was an e-participation initiative, which had not yet gained enough legitimacy among local politicians. However, the issue here is not that distinction, but the issue of *who should really* take part, making clear a predefined division of labour, some politicians' steer and plan, others make the plans come true. The duties had not only to be negotiated between the practitioners and the politicians, it had also to be negotiated within the group of politicians and it was also made clear that the actual e-participation had several functions as an event, i.e. as a showcase, a training-dialogue, a marketing effort and so on.

The interviews revealed several difficulties to separate *the immediate or representative role of e-participation in relation to formal participation.* Then there was the issue of "who should really take part in these different types of e-participation", indicating that participation has to be negotiated within the political community of practice. This distribution of tasks had to be discussed along with the need to form a new, *shared community of practice* together with the citizens who participate in the discussion, the need to transform the dialogue from a one-way communication into a two-way communication and truly interactive space. A professional politician (P3) turned out to be reluctant to define himself as a full participant, because he had a leading political role and therefore also was afraid of putting the lid on the discussion, because he were suspected to take on the leading role. These experiences *and the prior expectations on his participation* were literally hindering him to take active part in the discussion. But he seemed more willing to re-negotiate his motives for non-participation when he became aware of the need of establishing a shared goal and meaning and that the participants had to define a common repertoire, in order to reach any effect with the e-consultation.

There was an obvious mismatch between traditional political practice and the practice of the new dialogue arenas, and also a lack of strategy on how to feed in the outcome of what could be considered an "informal dialogue" on the website into the "formal" or established process of decision-making. An asynchronous discussion forum visualise and reveals both the posted answers but also the shortages in responses, which easily could be interpreted as irresponsibility by the politician, in fact it makes non-activity visible and traceable. The practice described here shows that there could be several explanations to this lack of responding politicians, for instance obscurity about the division of labor within the political group or community of practice, rather than unwillingness to take part. The debate on the website required that the politicians took responsibility also for the process of situating the meaning of e-participation, besides the actual debate about the future society. This is in practice normally is handed over to the civil servants.

### 4.4 The Dilemma of Multi-level e-Participation

During the work with the Vision Site which was basically run as an online e-consultation and planning of the future development of the municipality, several focus groups-interviews were held in order to introduce the new online consultation about the spatial plan, to evaluate the functionality of the consultation-site and also to gather opinions about the proposed formulation of the spatial plan. During the discussion in the group, it became obvious that there were ambiguities concerning the multiple ways to hand in opinions. Several levels of communication and engagement were requested from the citizens: they were supposed to have their say about the selected themes of the future such as: what about "*the plans on the new residential area between the railway station and the stream*"? Or "*What about the small places in the municipality, how is it possible to sustain public services there*"? The citizens were also asked to evaluate the functionality of the site, and take part in an ongoing evaluation of the project, which was also initiated by the researchers and presented on the site. The citizens were asked to answer an online questionnaire or announce if they were willing to take part in a face-to-face interview.

One of the politicians, also a member of the political steering group for the comprehensive planning process, raised the participatory aspects of the Invitation project and the use of the Vision Site during a project meeting where politicians also were invited: P4: "*In my opinion there has been great confusion concerning the role of the politicians in this process. The former spatial plans were either products of consultants, or a civil servant product where the political committees were called in as expert advice. The city architect and the local government committee chaired jointly the public face-to-face consultation meeting, which took part on several occasions. In my opinion does this open up for [referring to the Vision-site] a more thorough process and a possibility to keep a continuous dialogue with citizens. This will of course have consequences for the formal representative system, emphasising more direct democratic features in the process.*"

Another politician made the following comment about the decision to extend the traditional consultation period by opening up for individual citizens to present their opinion: P2: "*We can't meet every separate, contribution, what we want is to include the opinions in the process. This is a first throw-in in order to get a reaction, invite to discussion and a way to put forward the strategic vision 2010. This does not compensate other forms of communication. It is one way of discussing, valuing opinions and to broaden the basic data. Democracy has always been criticised, for example when discussing universal right to vote, and there is contempt for elected representatives, and thereby also the citizens who has voted for these specific candidates. There is a gap between the elected and the voters, the general society has developed in that way. I think it is important to see the municipality as an association, not as a company and the citizens as customers. The representative, democratic system in society includes elected, that is a better word than politicians. I think that it is an inclination in society to look upon e-democracy as something that has to go on beside the ordinary democracy development, and elected representatives as something that has to be pushed aside.*"

What he really is (even though unintentionally) putting his finger on is the need of establishing new communities of practice involving all parties; citizens, civil servants and politicians where legitimate peripheral participation allows also multiple forms of legitimate non-participation within established forms of participation.

## 5 Conclusions

What to say finally about the division of these described conditions or activities of participation, based on experiences within practice? First of all these activities seem to happen at the same time, they are not unconditionally following upon another or compensating one another, they could all be seen not primarily as frozen contradictions, rather they could be interpreted as descriptions of different positions in a field of participation, where the citizens, the practitioners and the politicians gradually are entering processes of learning e-participation by conducting legitimate peripheral participation. However, their trajectory, moving from the periphery to the centre, may look different and may also cause dilemmas of participation and even breakdowns and effects of non-participation. In that sense it was of course a misconduct that debate forums were put up without clear respondents, but there were as practice shows several explanations to that besides for unwillingness to take part; i.e. the issue of exposing incompleteness as inactivity, the difficulties in creating cross-over communication and interplay with formal practices of consultations as well as the fact that the expected role of for instance a participant got in the way for the situated participation. The citizens also expressed difficulties in handling demands on multi-level e-participation. A first step towards legitimising the participation was however taken by the fact that all parties acknowledged, "it has to be taken care of in some sense".

Non-participation could of course be experienced as an example of conscious manipulation of another person's possibility to act, or even seen as a token activity, but non-participation could also be consciously chosen and a legitimate position in order to await the next move, to avoid taking responsibility for the mutual learning that might occur in these activities, such as in the case with the reluctant politicians who did not want to be active participants and motivated their choice with practical reasons. They were not interested of changes in their political practice, since they experienced a heavier workload due to increased demands on taking individual responsibility, but very little response from the citizens in taking on their share of society-building. However, the effects of non-participation among politicians is also to be understood as an act of excluding themselves not only from developing new forms of democratic activities, but also from the possibility to conduct legitimate peripheral participation in the overall transformation processes of government. At the same time the citizens, who demand them to take their share and responsibility for dialoguing and decision-making, also exclude them. This causes a circle of reproduction of those regimes of practices or frozen relations concerning exclusion from both sides, and this is in the long run causing no development of e-participation at all, hindering a more inclusive approach to develop in order to make progress.

The practical examples also reveal that the issue of motivating others, while avoiding to motivate oneself, got in the way of upholding a debate, both among politicians and municipal officers. They were more concerned of what the other parts were doing or not doing, than seeing the possibility of e-participation as a way to motivate each other in learning by participation.

## References


1. Blomberg, J M.Burrell and G Guest: An ethnographic Approach to Design, in Jacko, J and sears. (eds.) Handbook of Human-Computer Interaction in Interaction Systems. Lawrence Erlbaum Associaties, Inc. New Jersey, (2002).
2. Communications of the Commission, available at: http://europa.eu.int/information_society/activities/egovernment_research/doc/highlights/egov_action_plan_en.pdf [Accessed 060528].
3. Ekelin, A, P. Elovaara, S. Eriksén, C. Hansson, S Landén, A. Larsson, I. Olén and J. Winter: "A Small Project about Big Issues". Short paper. Proceedings of the Participatory Design Conference PDC2004, Toronto, Canada, July 27-31, (2004)
4. Greenbaum, J and Kyng, M (eds.) Design at work: Cooperative Design of Computer Systems, Lawrence Erlbaum, Hillsdale, NJ. (1991).
5. Hague, Barry N and Brian D. Loader [eds.]: Digital Democracy: discourse and decision making in the information age Routledge, London (1999).
6. i2010, European Information Society for growth and employment http://europa.eu.int/information_society/eeurope/i2010/index_en.htm [Accessed 060315].
7. Lave, J., & Wenger, E. Situated Learning: Legitimate Peripheral Participation. Cambridge, UK: Cambridge University Press, (1990).
8. Lave, J and Chaiklin, S (eds.) Understanding Practice: Perspectives on Activity and Context, Cambridge: University of Cambridge Press, USA, (1993)
9. Macintosh, A: "Characterising E-participation in Policy-Making", in Proceedings of the 37th Hawaii International Conference on System Sciences, (2004) 1-10.
10. Macintosh, A: eParticipation: How and what to evaluate? Available at: http://bibliothek.fh-burgenland.at/macintosh_abstract.pdf [Accessed 060315].
11. Macintosh, A, Davenport, E, Malina A and A. Whyte: "Technology to support Participatory Democracy". In Electronic Government: Design, Applications and Management, (2002) 226-248
12. Mahrer, H Krimmer, R: Towards the enhancement of e-democracy: identifying the notion of the "middleman paradox" in Info Systems Journal, 15 (2005) 27-42.
13. Mälkiä, M (ed.) eTransformation in Governance: New Directions in Government and Politics. Hershey, PÅ, USA:Idea Group Inc. (2003).
14. Smith, M. K "Communities of practice", The Encyclopedia of Informal Education, www.infed.org/biblio/communities_of_practice.htm , (2003) [Accessed 060209] (14).
15. Strauss, A L., and Corbin, J. Basics of Qualitative Research: Techniques and Procedures for Developing Grounded Theory, 2nd Edition, (1998).
16. Suchman, L. Plans and Situated Actions: the Problem of Human-Machine Communication. Cambridge University Press, New York, (1987).
17. Suchman, L. "Writing and Reading: A Response to Comments on Plans and Situated Actions", in Journal of the Learning Sciences Vol. 12, No. 2, (2003 )299-306.
18. Wenger, E: Communities of practice. Learning, Meaning and Identity. Cambridge:Cambridge University Press , USA, (1998).

# e-Participation Behind Closed Doors: Online Evaluation of Teaching Performance

Kim Viborg Andersen

Department of Informatics, Copenhagen Business School,
Howitzvej 60, 2000 Fredriksberg
kva.inf@cbs.dk

**Abstract.** Student involvement in the governance processes has in the case analyzed in this paper incorporated the internet for facilitating qualitative and quantitative evaluation of the teachers' performances in class. The asynchrony evaluation ensures access, transparency, and accountability at the IT University challenging neo-institutional hypothesis on isomorphism.

## 1 Introduction

According to a neo-institutional approach, one would expect public institutions to enforce e-participation by ineffective isomorphism mechanisms [1, 2] adopting IT-applications tested and reported to have positive impacts on participation within conventional participation forums. The isomorphic behavior could be reinforced benchmarking the participation level and publish studies on best practices.

The neo-institutional hypothesis is contrasted by the case presented in this paper on e-participation in teaching evaluation at a Danish university. Since 1999 the university has carried out teaching evaluations by inviting enrolled students to assess the quality, etc., of the teaching. The evaluations are made public using internet technology. The online and transparent evaluation process has enabled bottom-up and top-down participation and an informal and formal communication style to flourish, thus facilitating e-participation in the evaluation process.

We define the e-component in e-participation in line with our earlier work on IT in the Political World as "...those mechanical, conceptual, human and organizational components whose function is to transmit or store data and information using digital devices." [3]. The particular domain of our inquiry is the uses of e-participation in the public administration, which includes those structures, processes, actors and policies that determine or implement the allocation of public values in the collectivity [4].

E-government is by and large building on previous decades of adoption of computing in government seeking to solve data interoperability and also to face integration challenges that existed previously but only became apparent and critical due to implementation of, for example, web based one-stop services for citizens. The front-end user interfaces for the users of the public sector services have made substantial progress on the supply side. There is a growing consensus

M.A. Wimmer et al. (Eds.): EGOV 2006, LNCS 4084, pp. 119–127, 2006.

that the provision of front-end services has followed a path not attached to preferences at the demand side.

The evolvement of using IT to assess, take part in and depart from formal and informal decision-making forums are all part of what we refer to as e-participation in this paper. Paradoxically, public sector management has close to no formal experience in this field and is only starting to use digital components within this area due to the emergence of the Internet. We have reviewed the research literature on IT in government in three rounds (1987-1992, 1992-2000 and 2000-2004) and each time concluded that first-hand empirical studies reporting on the use of IT for strengthening democratic channels are rare [3, 5, 6]. We label it as a paradox since participation in the public sector is a cornerstone of the corporatist and public governance models.

## 2 Institutional Control Versus Customer Control

The e-government wave with extensive use of URLs, virtual workspaces, e-mail, instant messaging, SMS and blogging might not bring about any fundamental new mechanisms in government [7, 8]. Yet, it is our proposition that management is challenged to move away from a transactional view of IT to a more strategic view of IT adoption in government [9, 10]. One of the areas where this will be most apparent is within e-participation. Although strategic challenges for e-participation share many challenges with the diverse set of e-participation challenges facing the private sector, there are at least two reasons to be concerned with e-government per se.

First, IT in government follows essentially a budget driven approach and is generally facing demands of a much faster pay-back time than the private sector. Government departments will often have to finance their spending on IT on current accounts and not be able to argue that investment in IT will lead to reductions in transaction costs, etc., on the longer term.

The second reason to address e-government management challenges is the societal importance and the policy context of e-participation in government. Direct customer involvement in governmental service areas is part of an overall democratic debate in government on what, how, and when to involve customers. The challenge with studying IT from a democracy point of view is that " ...both democracy and good governance remain 'essentially contested concepts' [11], since there is not now, nor will there likely be, a final consensus on their definition or content" [12]. This stance applies equally well to the e-participation perspective.

Regardless of ideological platforms on viewing government as a business or as part of a democratic platform, there is a cost of involvement of what we here label the customers. Managers of the public sector are challenged by balancing fully transparent processes, facilitating the gathering of disparate information, and running a cost-effective organization.

This might explain why government tends to use conventional technologies when aiming for e-participation. E-participation occurs in a variety of technological settings and situations rather than in a stereotyped and unified pattern.

In some instances, participation requires high levels of security technologies, as in the case of elections. In other cases, there is less demand on security and more emphasis on flow of information and open dialogue, as in the case of public hearings. Most of the participation and involvement media that has been implemented is text based, rather than speech and video enabled, and, in general, is not an active part of the dynamics of multimedia. Instead, government lags behind in the uptake of media that supports involvement based on audio-visual media and synchronous dialogue, such as chat.

Also, most of the applications designed for involvement are done half-heartedly in the sense that critical parameters, such as scalability, logs, and software transparency/updates, are left unattended at the time of the first round of implementation of the application. Instead, government often implements applications for very small numbers on behalf of front-end and back-office/ politicians. For example, local government in Denmark develop chat forums for involvement and user surveys for examining various policy issues, but neglect to allocate bureaucrats or politicians to be involved in these.

Further, most applications for user involvement seem to be top-down driven, supporting formal communication following the traditional administrative-bureaucratic procedures and standards, where traditional technologies are used, and institutional values are applied as measures. Few applications are situated at the left side of the user involvement flow (depicted in Figure 1) enabling informal communication and non-institutional values using experimental technologies. While the top-down approach might be useful in various settings, it falls short in understanding the gate-keepings mechanisms deployed by the street-level-bureaucrats that are interacting with the customers and managers [13]. The gate-keeping perspective does not assume that policy strategy on increasing e-participation is an issue of straight forward top-down implementation. Rather, understanding the means of gate-keeping, such as psychological issues, time, and budget allocation mechanisms, holds the key to successful implementation of e-participation.

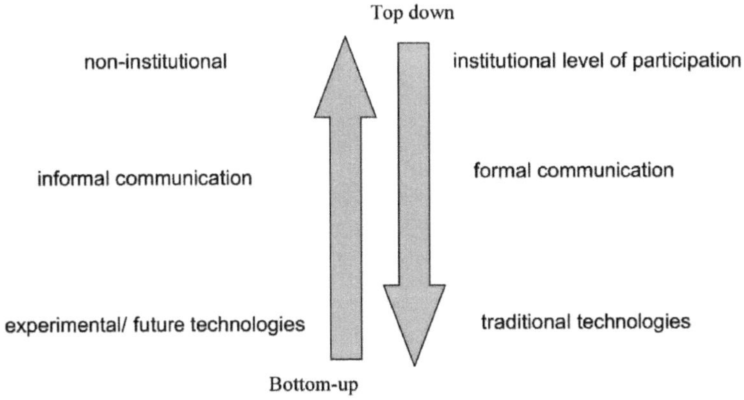


**Fig. 1.** Top-down and bottom-up approaches to e-participation

The more informal the communication where the IT applications invite the customers to take part in the debate, the less is the requirement for structured involvement. The second component technology refers to the sophistication of the applications, ranging from the well-known current or conventional technologies to the experimental. Finally, the third component focuses on the degree of institutional level of participation, ranging from institutional to non-institutional participation.

# 3 A Case Study on e-Participation

## 3.1 Rankings on e-Participation

According to the UN-poll of e-participation, Denmark ranks sixth in their 2005 report [14]. In Europe, only Britain ranks higher. The UN rankings on e-participation measure e-consultation, e-information, and e-decision making at primarily national sites. Clearly, there are problems in using the UN rankings for government in countries with very decentralized structures, as is the case for Scandinavian countries. The national policy perception on the rankings has been very ambitious in the general e-government field. The Deputy Chief on IT, Mr. Mikkel Hemmingsen, stated at the DEXA 2005 conference:

"Denmark's ambition is to be number one at all rankings. The Eurostat, the OECD, the UN and Economists rankings.we want to be number one in all rankings."

The commitment to advance on e-government is not supplemented by equally explicit ambitions to advance on e-participation or e-voting. Although involvement of citizens in various decision making bodies in the public administration has showed a serious deficit in magnitude of involvement by the number of people involved and the degree of involvement [15], the commitment to use technology for increasing involvement has been sparse. Part of the argument that has been put forward is that the lack or diverse pattern of uptake of e-participation is that the existing democracy and involvement channels work well; hence, the need and urgency to pursue e-participation is less apparent. The urgency of increasing e-participation is far from being a uni-directional issue where more is equal to better [16, 17].

**Table 1.** UN e-participation index 2005

| Country | Index |
|---|---|
| United Kingdom | 1.0000 |
| Singapore | 0.9841 |
| United States | 0.9048 |
| Canada | 0.8730 |
| Republic of Korea | 0.8730 |
| New Zealand | 0.7937 |
| Denmark | 0.7619 |

### 3.2 Student Evaluations at the IT University

The institutional challenges become very apparent with online evaluations of teaching that is designed to improve quality where involvement by the end users comprises very formal language, standard scales, and having the evaluations filtered through traditional physical meetings and formal policy channels.

Prior to the Internet, evaluation of teaching in Denmark was often undertaken by teachers at the end of lectures, that is, with an oral evaluation and/or physical distribution of a questionnaire. After completing the questionnaire, the teacher collected them, summarized them and made a report to the study board. In other cases, a separate evaluation unit undertook the evaluation and provided the evaluation data to the study board and Dean of the school.

The students perceived the evaluation system as being non-transparent and raised concerns whether their evaluation of teaching performances were taken into account in (re-)designing curriculum and allocation of teachers. Also, it gave rise to concerns whether unqualified teachers kept their teaching positions regardless of continuously receiving negative evaluations from students. Further, the individual student feed-back appeared to reach the decision-making bodies too late in order to be taken into account for the design of curriculum and teaching methods for the coming semester. In Figure 2 we have illustrated what we label the conventional evaluation process.

The IT University (ITU) of Copenhagen was founded in 1999 to provide technological education at the Master's and Ph.D. level. The University is a graduate school with fewer than 1,500 students. The evaluation system has gone through a series of iterations where the rector and the study directors have identified parameters for evaluation of teaching performance provided by the classes, each parameter containing qualitative and quantitative components. The quantitative scale has a span from 1 to 6, six being the highest.

The evaluation is carried out in the middle of the semester, comprising of four phases. In the first phase students receive an e-mail from the rector asking them to access the evaluation system and to enter their evaluation. Students who do not reply receive two reminders. Students can, however, choose to remain anonymous, i.e., not to have their identity (name and id number) displayed to the teacher.

In the second phase, each teacher (external and internal faculty) receives an e-mail from the rector asking them to comment on each of the qualitative comments given by the students. A teacher running a class with, for example, 40 students could easily receive 100 qualitative comments. The teacher is required to answer each of the qualitative comments. If the teacher fails to respond, (s)he will receive automatic reminders until each comment is answered.

In the third phase, each study director reviews the comments and evaluation. The director can decide whether some of the evaluations should be withheld from public access and kept confidential. An example of this could be where clearly offensive language is used in the qualitative comments. The evaluations that are withheld are used in very few instances. Teachers with performance less than the performance criteria are called for an interview at the rector's office in this phase.

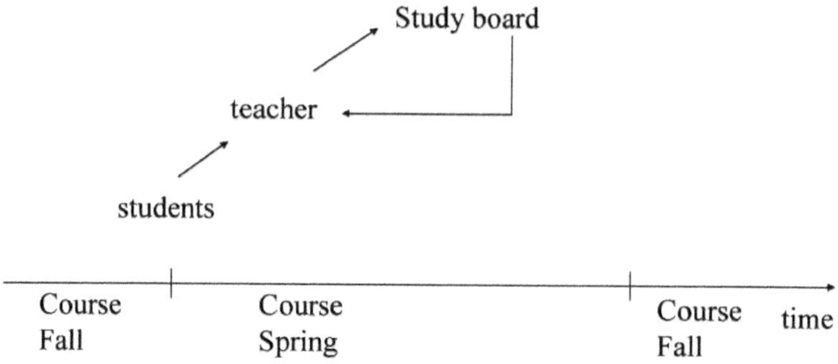


**Fig. 2.** The conventional teaching evaluation process

In the fourth phase, the evaluation rankings and comments are made public for all students enrolled at the University. Thus, all students can access previous evaluations of classes prior to selecting classes for the coming semester. The data are kept online and not erased from the records. Thus, students are able to trace possible progress on evaluations and assess whether a teacher has improved on critical issues pointed to by students.

The evaluation system has raised concerns from several of the involved teachers and the study boards although students were much more supportive of participation. The institutional power was at stake and the communication style could erode serious evaluation of the teaching. The reaction from teachers employed in places other than the ITU was much more negative. The argument put forward was that public evaluations of teaching would lower the standards since teachers would opt for pleasing students and easing their burden in order to get good evaluations of their performance.

This argument draws on the classical discussion on the role of citizens as users or customers of the public sector. The public sector reforms on new public management (NPM) have at the rhetorical level aimed for more transparency, transferring the client role to a customer role. In the education sector, the EU Bologna process is an example of this. However, with regards to the evaluation of the performance, the evaluation systems in general have been kept behind closed doors.

Those arguing for evaluation being mediated through bureaucratic channels base their support on concerns for the employees: how would the filtering process be able to adjust for employees' sickness and low performance in teaching due to competing, legitimate tasks in administration and research projects. The instrumentation of the evaluation process could lead to non-emergence of arguments difficult to express in formal language [18].

The evaluation system at the University had the advantage of being implemented at a new institution from day one. Thus, there was not an issue of abandoning an existing physical evaluation system or eroding existing participation bodies. This possibly was the key to the successful implementation. Also,

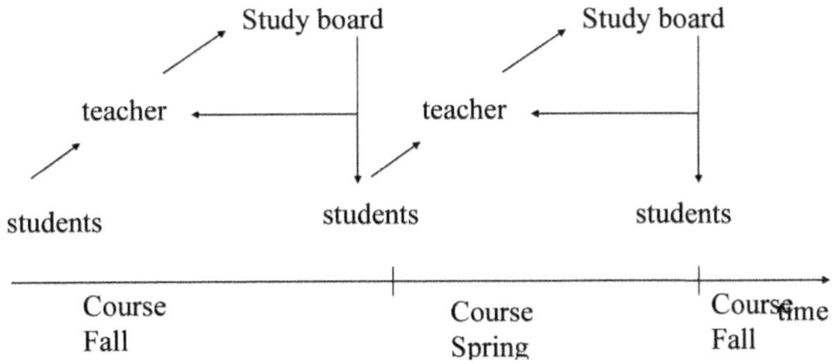


**Fig. 3.** The online teaching evaluation at the ITU

the issue of small scale and the need to create visibility in order to attract new students were key drivers. Additionally, firm top management during the implementation of the evaluation system and the eagerness to meet the challenges up front may have been key factors in the rapid implementation.

## 4 Discussion and Conclusion

Students' evaluation of teaching performance is a key component in getting feedback for continuous improvement of educational programs. A key decision making body at Danish universities is the study board which has partial representation by students and faculty. The chairman is a faculty member but the vice-chairman has to be a student.

The evaluation processes introduced at the IT university case analyzed in this paper have de-institutionalized the flow of information and made the decision process more transparent. Also, the communication style has become more informal. Teachers' responses to the comments provided by the students are written in an informal style. The dynamics introduced by the bottom-up mechanisms for e-participation have, however, not decreased the power of overall management. By contrast, it can be argued that top management power has been increased due to the more transparent user feedback.

The institutional challenges become very apparent when online evaluations of teaching designed to improve quality through involvement by the end users wind up using very formal language, standard scales, and filtering the evaluations through traditional physical meetings and formal policy channels.

One normative implication of the managerial challenges put forward by the case study presented in this paper is to examine whether decision-makers and customers could be perceived as digital entities with a physical presence, rather than the reverse. In an executive training session for executives in the social welfare service area taught by the author of this paper, the participants had substantial objections to the proposed digital view of users. Their view was that certain groups of society (the disadvantaged) and certain public services were not suitable for digitalization and would in the end do more harm than good to the policy objectives of the area. Clearly this argument has political merit and has been addressed in several national policy plans as well as in the international debate forums such as the World Submit of Information Society.

## Acknowledgements

This paper is a result of the efforts of integrating the research on e-participation in the European Network of Excellence DEMO-net (http://www.demo-net.org). Previous versions of the paper have been discussed with partners from the network. The author of this paper is indebted to partners who provided their comments.

## References

1. Scott, R.W., Organizations: Rational, Natural, and Open Systems. 1997, Englewood Cliffs, NJ: Prentice Hall.
2. DiMaggio, P. and W.W. Powell, The Iron Cage Revisited: Institutional Isomorphism and Collective Rationality in Organizational Fields, in The New Institutionalism in Organizational Analysis, P. DiMaggio and W.W. Powell, Editors. 1991, Chicago University Press: Chicago.
3. Danziger, J.N. and K.V. Andersen, "Impacts of IT on Politics and the Public Sector: Methodological, Epistemological, and Substantive Evidence from the "Golden Age" of Transformation". International Journal of Public Administration, 2002. 25(5), 591-627.
4. Easton, D., A Systems Analysis of Political Life. 1965, New York: John Wiley & Sons.
5. Andersen, K.V. and J.N. Danziger, "Information Technology and the Political World: The Impacts of IT on Capabilities, Interactions, Orientations and Values". International Journal of Public Administration, 1995. 18(11), 1693-1724.
6. Andersen, K.V. and H.Z. Henriksen, "The First Leg of E-government Research: Domain and Application Areas 1998-2003". International Journal of Electronic Government Research, 2005. 1(4), 26-44.
7. Bretschneider, S., "Information technology, e-government, and institutional change". Public Administration Review, 2003. 63(6), 738-744.
8. King, J.L. and K.L. Kraemer. E-government: Will the Time after Be Any Different? 2003 [cited 2005 May 5]; Available from: http://www.crito.uci.edu.
9. Stamoulis, D., et al., "Revisiting public information management for effective e-government services". Information Management & Computer Security, 2001. 9(4), 146.
10. Affisco, J.F. and K.S. Soliman, "E-government: A Strategic Operations Management Framework for Service Delivery". Business Process Management Journal, 2006. 12(1), 13-21.
11. Gallie, W.B., "Essentially Contested Concepts". Proceedings of the Aristotelian Society, 1956. 51, 167-198.
12. Landman, T. Map-Making and Analysis of the Main International Initiatives on Developing Indicators on Democracy and Good Governance. 2002 [cited 2003 December 7]; Available from: http://www.oecd.org/dataoecd/0/28/20755719.pdf.
13. Lipsky, M., Street Level Bureaucracy: Dilemmas and the Individual in Public Services. 1980, New York: Russel Stage Foundation.

14. UNPAN. UN Global E-government Readiness Report 2005. 2005 [cited; Available from: http://www.unpan.org.
15. Srensen, E., "Brugeren og demokratiet". GRUS, 1997(53), 81-96.
16. Hoff, J., I. Horrocks, and P. Tops, eds. Democratic Governance and New Technology. 1999, Routledge: London.
17. Rose, J. and Ø. Sæbø, "Democracy Squared". Scandinavian Journal of Information Systems, 2005. 17(2), 133-168.
18. Weizenbaum, J., Computer Power and Human Reason. 1976, Cambridge, MA: MIT Press.

# A Review of Quality Dimensions in e-Government Services

Xenia Papadomichelaki, Babis Magoutas, Christos Halaris, Dimitris Apostolou, and Gregoris Mentzas

Information Management Unit,
Institute of Communication and Computer Systems
School of Electrical & Computer Engineering,
National Technical University of Athens,
9 Iroon Polytechniou str. Zografou Campus, 157 80 Zografou Athens, Greece
xpg@central.ntua.gr,
{elbabmag, chala, dapost, gmentzas}@mail.ntua.gr
http://www.imu.iccs.gr/

**Abstract.** This paper presents a synthetic summary of the literature in the area of quality of e-government services, as a basis for the future construction of a relevant model and ontology. We include 18 different approaches concerning quality of service for public sector in general and e-government more specifically. Using as a criterion the focus of each approach on organizational issues or the front end of the service we classified them in introvert and extrovert ones. As a result of the review we were able to organize the main components influencing quality of e-government services in the following four key areas: service, content, system and organization.

## 1 Introduction

In the last years, quality of service in the public sector has become an issue of great concern. Many organizations try to self-assess and measure the quality of service delivered. An evidence of the above is the Quality Conference for public Administration in the European Union, started in 2000[1]. At the same time, significant progress has been made in the development of e-government services and e-participation systems. A variety of public services are now delivered online, with many benefits for e-citizens. Although various initiatives investigate the application of quality management principles to the delivery of electronic public services, manifold problems related to quality of public e-services still exist, according to Top of the Web survey [8]. Not being able to find the needed service/information, difficult use of e-services, the need for better help regarding the e-service provided on the website, the language understandability etc. are some of frequently reported usability problems. These together with issues like back office efficiency and system reliability create the need of a quality perspective in the development and provision of e-government services.

[1] See http://www.4qconference.org/en/ for more information.

M.A. Wimmer et al. (Eds.): EGOV 2006, LNCS 4084, pp. 128–138, 2006.

A quality model which allows the specification of quality of services' dimensions and the relations between them will have significant impact on the improvement of online public services and on the increase of e-citizens satisfaction. As part of the "Fostering self-adaptive e-government service improvement using semantic technologies" multinational research project, we intend to develop a quality model for e-government services, which will contribute to the qualitative improvement of the online available services. In order to develop such a model a critical literature survey at the field of quality of service for e-government services is necessary.

The purpose of this paper is to present a synthetic summary of the literature survey. The paper is structured in 5 sections. After this brief introduction, we present in sections 2, 3 and 4 the most appropriate methodologies and research initiatives that concern quality of service for public sector in general and e-government more specifically. Section 5 includes our conclusions about the presented models and our recommendations for future work.

## 2 Quality of e-Government Services

The approaches that we examine and finally present in this paper are classified into categories and subcategories and for each category, a synthetic summary is conducted. For a common understanding of the names we use abbreviations for the presented models, as presented in table 1 that follows:

**Table 1.** Abbreviation table

| Approach | Reference |
|---|---|
| CAF | CAF Resource Center (2006), [4] |
| Balanced Scorecard | Kaplan and Norton (1992), [12] |
| Six Sigma | Motorola University (2006a), [15]<br>Motorola University (2006b), [16]<br>Process Quality Associates Inc. (2001), [18] |
| ISO | ISO (2006), [10] |
| Baldrige Criteria | Baldrige National Quality Program (2006), [3] |
| egov-ACSI | American Customer Satisfaction Index (2006), [1] |
| g-CSI | Kim et. al. (2005), [13] |
| EUSI | European Public Administration Network (2005), [9] |
| SITEQUAL | Webb and Webb (2004), [22] |
| Portal Usage Quality | Lin and Wu (2002), [14] |
| IP-Portals | Yang et. al. (2005), [23] |
| e-government inThai | Sukasame (2004), [19] |
| Norwegian Approach | Jansen and Ølnes (2004), [11] |
| IBM Approach | Anbazhagan and Nagarajan (2002), [2] |
| METEOR-S Approach | Cardoso et. al. (2002), [6] |
| QoS for WS-Best Practices | Sumra and Arulazi (2003), [20] |
| MAIS Approach | Cappiello et. al. (2004), [5] |

In the literature of quality of e-government services one can distinguish two main approaches: The first includes the models which view the issue of quality in a more 'introvert' approach. They regard quality as an issue that stems from within the organization and has an impact on the front office. This means that since quality of the delivered services is influenced by many aspects within an organization as back office procedures, leadership of the organization, management's dedication to quality etc. an assessment and continuous monitoring of the above will give inevitably a clue of the overall quality of services delivered. The field from which it borrows the elements to measure and assess is the organization itself. It includes all the levels of management in addition to the employees. (Some models of this category may include some dimensions of the outcome but they do not focus on the outcome).

The second approach is focused on the quality of the service delivered itself. It is a more 'extrovert' view since emphasis is put on the way the client receives the services from the front office-web site. It is a customer-oriented approach since it is motivated by the customer's needs. Quality dimensions of this approach are related to the delivered service (availability, usability, security etc. of the service) and/or input from the receivers of the service (customers' priorities and needs). The models of 'extrovert' approach can be divided into three sub-categories:

- The first one includes models that measure customer satisfaction with the public authorities. Customer satisfaction is affected both from perceived by citizens quality and from their expectations about the service. Many factors compose perceived quality and are taken into account for the satisfaction measurement.
- The second category pays attention at the portal's characteristics that influence the perceived quality. These models focus on interface issues that influence the final qualitative result, so their quality dimensions are appropriate for the front office.
- The third category includes models that focus on the Quality of Service (QoS) for web service. Quality dimensions derived from this category concern technical characteristics of web services that influence perceived quality of a service that is based on web services.

The described categorization of the approaches is illustrated in table 2 that follows:

**Table 2.** Categorization of existing approaches

| Introvert | Extrovert | | |
|---|---|---|---|
| | CSI | Portal/Site quality | Qos for WS |
| CAF | egov-ACSI | SITEQUAL | IBM Approach |
| Balanced Scorecard | g-CSI | Portal Usage Quality | METEOR-S Approach |
| Six Sigma | EUSI | IP-Portals | QoS for WS-Best Practices |
| ISO | | e-government in Thai | MAIS Approach |
| Baldrige Criteria | | Norwegian Approach | |

During the examination of the quality dimensions each approach suggests, an effort was made to analyze the meaning each author gives to each dimension, to find the overlaps and the areas that the different studies concur.

## 3 Introvert Approaches

The models of this category emphasize more on the internal attributes of the organization both for assessment and for improvement – although most of them have feedback from the results. CAF is a common European quality framework that can be used across the public sector as a tool for organizational self assessment. Through the Balanced scorecard, an organization monitors both its current performance and its efforts to improve processes, motivate and educate employees, and enhance information systems. Six Sigma uses quality tools in order to achieve performance improvements. On the other hand ISO's principles can be used by senior management as a framework to guide their organizations towards improved performance. Finally, the Baldrige Criteria is a framework that any organization can use to improve overall performance. In table 3 the criteria/perspectives/principles of each model are presented:

**Table 3.** Synthetic Table for Introvert Approaches

| CAF | Balanced Scorecard | Six Sigma | ISO | Baldrige Criteria |
|---|---|---|---|---|
| Leadership | | | Leadership | Leadership |
| | | Minimize variation in processes | Factual Approach to Decision Making | Measurement analysis and knowledge management |
| Strategy & Planning | | | | Strategic Planning |
| HRM | Learning & Growth Perspective | | Involvement of people | Human Resources Focus |
| Partnerships & Resources | | | Mutually Beneficial Supplier Relationships | |
| Process & Change Management | Business & Process Perspective | Driving rapid and sustainable improvement to business processes | Process Approach | Process Management |
| | | Aligning key business processes to achieve those requirements | System Approach to Management | |
| | Customer Perspective | Understanding and managing customer requirements | Customer Focus | Customer & Market Focus |
| People Results | | | Continual Improvement | Results |
| Customer Results | | | | |
| Society Results | | | | |
| Key Performance Results | Financial Perspective | | | |

The main conclusion is that Leadership, Human Resources, Process Management and Customer Focus are domains that almost all the models stress as very critical for the assessment and improvement of an organization. By comparing the different models, we notice that the Baldrige criteria focus on results and continuous improvement. Together with CAF, the Baldrige criteria are the main examples of organizational assessment tools. They provide a framework for designing, implementing, and assessing a process for managing all business operations. On the other hand, the ISO 9000 series of five international standards can be used by organizations to assist them determine what is needed to maintain an efficient quality conformance system. ISO 9000 registration determines whether an organization complies with its own quality system. Overall, ISO 9000 registration covers fewer criteria than Baldrige. So a quality management system established during ISO 9000 implementation efforts can easily be expanded to support the addition of key processes based on the Baldrige criteria.

As far as the balanced scorecard is concerned it offers an alternative to Six Sigma. Assessment of an organization's current status is the first step for building a Balanced Scorecard. The Balanced Scorecard uses assessment data to determine what improvements and breakthroughs in performance are most needed, so that strategies can be crafted to meet these needs. The Balanced Scorecard includes much more than assessment, but these tools are useful to get a full picture of the situation in an organization, and they are recommended as an initial step in strategic planning and management.

## 4 Extrovert Approaches

### 4.1 Customer Satisfaction Models

This category comprises of three models. The first two approaches that have many resemblances are the American egov-ACSI and the Korean g-CSI, whereas the third approach is the European EUSI still under development.

Indexes are constructs that try to capture a complex situation into a single figure. Well-known examples are the consumer price index, the inflation rate, the consumer confidence index, the stock market index, etc. Such an index is calculated by aggregating weighted factors that influence the final result. Satisfaction with a website is a complex equation with multiple elements determining how well the online experience meets the needs of site visitors. Customer Satisfaction Index methodologies identify key drivers of satisfaction and quantify their relationship to overall customer satisfaction, i.e. they calculate the impact of the different drivers of satisfaction based on direct "voice of the customer" feedback for each measured site.

The cause-and-effect nature of these methodologies enables an agency or department to predict the impact of website enhancements in a particular area, (e.g., navigation) on overall satisfaction. Going further, such a methodology predicts how increases in satisfaction affect desired future behaviors of site visitors, such as return visits and referrals to the site. Typically, an area with a low satisfaction score and a high impact score is considered high priority. The identification of high priority satisfaction drivers provides valuable insight into how an agency or department should prioritize website improvements based on where they will have the greatest impact on citizen satisfaction.

A key feature underlying all approaches of this category is that they are based on a 'model'. This model consists of a number of latent variables (such as 'quality') and the cause and effect relationships between them. Each of these latent variables includes several manifest variables that act as concrete proxies for the latent variable. Consumer satisfaction is the latent variable that is at the centre of the model; it is encased within a system of variables relating to causes and effects.

The future existence of such an index in America, Asia and Europe implies that both local and global comparisons can be realized, using a single number. The importance of such a comparison is very high, because it has as consequence improvement efforts between competitors. The final result of these efforts will be the improvement of customer satisfaction.

### 4.2 Portal/Site Quality

In this category five approaches have been included. SITEQUAL [22] provides us with guidelines and an instrument to measure the quality of a Web site over time. The approach of Lin and Wu [14] provides general hints on the construction of a portal in order to keep people continuing to visit the portal site and the aim of this work is to explore users' intention and behavior of the portal site. The five-dimension service quality model by Yang et. al. [23] focuses on Web portals that function as an information presenting (IP) and communication-enabling site for users. The overall aim of Sukasame's study [19] was to develop a conceptual framework and to elicit the factors affecting the e-Service provided on the Web portal of Thailand's government. Finally, the Western Norway Research Institute initiated a project to develop a set of quality criteria for evaluating public websites in Norway [11].

The models of this category are primarily focused on quality characteristics of the service delivered, on what kind of information is presented and on how it is presented and on some system characteristics. All the different dimensions these approaches use are presented in Table 4. In constructing the table an effort was made to correlate the meaning each researcher gives to each dimension with the corresponding dimensions of other models although not always strictly feasible.

A characteristic of this category of models is that most of the studies result from composition, adaptation and extension of existing models. The constitutive studies for the models presented here are SERVQUAL [17] from service quality literature and Wang and Strong's [21] study and TAM [7] from the data quality literature. SITEQUAL combines SERVQUAL with Wang's work, while Portal Usage Quality, SERVQUAL with TAM. Finally IP Portals is based on TAM model.

By reviewing the table, it is apparent that all models presented value mostly the quality of information presented on the site/portal and its characteristics as relevancy, accuracy, completeness, understandability, together with the way this information is presented i.e. appearance, navigability etc. Also four out of five models give a great importance to the service dimension of a site such as reliable delivery of service, personalized services etc.

**Table 4.** Synthetic Table for Extrovert Approaches/Portal-Site Quality

| | SITEQUAL | Portal usage quality | IP-Portals | e-government in Thai | MAIS |
|---|---|---|---|---|---|
| Service | Reliability | Reliability and Response | | Reliability (a) | Reliability |
| | Assured Empathy | Customization | Interaction (a) | | |
| | | | Interaction (b) | Self-Service | |
| Information | Relevant Representation | Information Content | Adequacy of information | Linkage | Availability Completeness Timeliness |
| | Accuracy | | Usefulness of content | Content | Reliability Accuracy |
| | | | Usability (a) | Ease of Use | Usability |
| | | | | | Traceability |
| System | Navigability | | Accessibility | Reliability (b) | |
| | Security | Security | Security and Privacy | | |
| | Tangibility | | Usability (b) | | |

The Norwegian Approach although dealing with the service provision does not follow the mentality of the rest of the models of the category so it is not included in the table 4. Its democratic dimension however, is a differentiation characteristic which is scarcely included in other models. Because of that distinct perspective, we have decided to include it to the set of presented models. Finally, although MAIS approach [5] is set in the next category, as it is related more with QoS for web services, than with portals quality, it has quality dimensions of both approaches, so a column is dedicated to it in the tables of both categories.

### 4.3 Quality of Service for Web Services

In the current category four different models have been included. IBM [2] addresses the subject of web services quality in seven aspects. Cardoso et. al. [6] present, as part of METEOR-S project, a comprehensive model for the specification of workflow QoS as well as methods to compute and predict QoS. Sumra and Arulazi [20] propose seven dimensions that contribute to service quality. Finally, MAIS project team has proposed a general framework for the definition of quality of service dimensions [5].

The elaborated models of this category point on the system characteristics. They deal with the probability that a service is available, with the degree it is capable of serving a request, whether it maintains the correctness of interaction, with the execution time, the degree it is capable of maintaining the service quality, the security of the system etc. They are all embraced in Table 5 with their corresponding dimensions.

**Table 5.** Synthetic Table for Extrovert Approaches/Quality of Service for Web-Services

| IBM approach | METEOR-S approach | QoS for WS-Best practices | MAIS approach |
|---|---|---|---|
| Availability | | Availability | Availability |
| Accessibility | | Accessibility | |
| Integrity | | Integrity | |
| Performance | Task Time | Web Services Performance | Response Time<br>Provisioning Time |
| Reliability | Task Reliability (a) | Reliability | |
| | Task Reliability (b) | | |
| Regulatory | | | |
| | | Interoperability | |
| Security | | Security | Security<br>Non Repudiation |
| | Task Cost | | Price |

It seems that the performance dimension (related with the response and provision time) is considered the most important one, since all the models of the category refer to it among the dimensions they propose for ensuring high quality of service. The availability dimension (whether the system is ready for immediate use) follow, together with reliability (the degree the system is capable of maintaining service quality) and security (confidentiality, non reputation, encrypting).

## 5 Recommendations and Future Work

Although internationally there is a noticeable shift of governmental service provision from traditional channels to web-based ones, restraints due to poor quality of service are apparent. In the literature there are studies and methods for assessing the efficiency and effectiveness of public organizations and on the other hand there are multiple studies and tools trying to measure the quality of the delivered e-service. We believe that in order to deliver a high quality of services we cannot draw close one of the two approaches disbounded one from the other. We need a more 'holistic' view of the subject which embraces the back office, the front office and the customers' needs in a unified model.

Nevertheless, work done on quality of services in e-government and the different points of view of the researchers provide us with an exhaustive list of aspects, criteria and dimensions concerning the issue. They cover the possible factors that may contribute to the delivery of high quality services from a governmental portal. Our effort was to explore the components and dimensions that influence the quality of the delivered service and in turn the satisfaction of the citizens. According to the literature review and our previous expertise we categorize all the respective components to four major key areas influencing quality of e-government service, as illustrated in Figure 1.

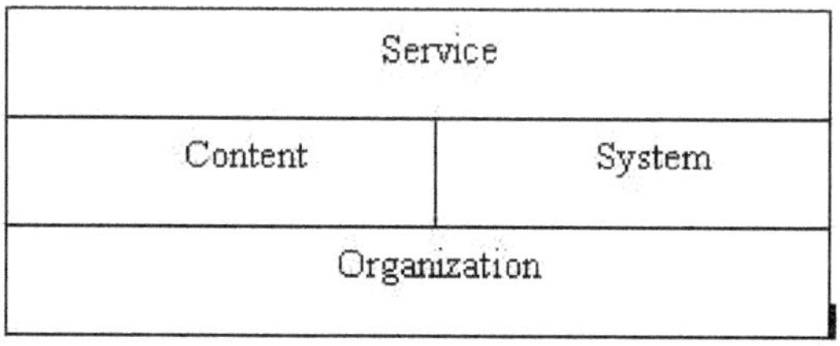


**Fig. 1.** Key Areas Influencing Quality of e-government Service

Each of these key areas is divided into other quality dimensions.

- The service key area involves not only the ability to perform the promised service accurately, consistently and in time but also the interaction between users and service providers' employees, users and the web site and among peer users. It is affected by the knowledge and courtesy of employees and their ability to convey trust and confidence. Moreover, it is also linked to the degree of personalization of the service and facilities such as message boards and chat rooms the site may provide.
- The content key area comprises quality dimensions relative to both information and presentation issues. The informational part includes the accuracy, correctness, reliability, timeliness, completeness, relevancy and ease of understanding of data and the number and quality of hyperlinks the site offers. On the other hand the presentation part consists of the web site's structure, design and appearance, search facilities, easiness of navigation and an easy to remember URL.
- The system key area contains quality dimensions such as availability, accessibility, system integrity, performance, reliability, interoperability, regulatory and last but not least security. Security can be furthermore analyzed into confidentiality, non-repudiation, encrypting messages and access control.
- The organization key area is comprised of quality dimensions like leadership, strategy and planning, human resources, measurement analysis and knowledge management, partnerships and resources, process management and customer focus.

We believe that in order for an organization to deliver quality services all of the above must be taken into account and put effort and resources to it. Of course, not all factors and components mentioned are equally important for the final citizen satisfaction so the respective organization has to weight and primarily invest to the most important ones.

Future work consists of the development of a quality of e-government services model and ontology to allow the specification of quality of services metrics and the relations between them. Also, specification of methods and development of tools to estimate and monitor the quality of e-government services will be attempted, by supporting the continuous computation of quality metrics.

## References


1. American Customer Satisfaction Index, (2006). The American Customer Satisfaction index - the voice of the nation's consumer. Retrieved February 10, 2006, from http://www.theacsi.org.
2. Anbazhagan, M. and A. Nagarajan (2002). Understanding quality of service for web services . Retrieved January 10, 2006, from IBM Developerworks Web site: http://www-128.ibm.com/developerworks/library/ws-quality.html.
3. Baldrige National Quality Program, (2006). Criteria for Performance Excellence. Retrieved February 10, 2006, from Baldrige National Quality Program Web site: http://www.quality.nist.gov/
4. CAF Resource Center, (2006). Common assessment framework - CAF. Retrieved January. 05, 2006, from COMMON ASSESSMENT FRAMEWORK Web site: http://www.eipa.nl/CAF/CAFmenu.htm
5. Cappiello, C., Missier, P., Pernici, B., Plebani, P., Batini, C. (2004). Qos in multichannel IS: the mais approach. Retrieved January 17, 2006, from http://www.elet.polimi.it/conferences/wq04/final/paper05.pdf.
6. Cardoso, J., Sheth, A., Miller, J., Arnold, J., Kochut, K. (2002). Modeling quality of service for workflows and web service processes. Journal of Web Semantics, Retrieved February 06, 2006, from http://lsdis.cs.uga.edu/lib/download/CSM+QoS-WebSemantics.pdf.
7. Davis, F.D. (1989). Perceived usefulness, perceived ease of use, and user acceptance of information technology. MIS Quarterly, 13. Retrieved Mar 10, 2006, from http://www.cba.hawaii.edu/chismar/ITM704/Davis-TAM1989.pdf.
8. eGovernment Unit, DG Information Society, European Commission, (2004). Top of the web: user satisfaction and usage survey of egovernment services. Retrieved January 18, 2006, from Europe's Information Society Thematic Portal Web site: http://europa.eu.int/information_society/activities/egovernment_research/doc/top_of_the_web_report_2004.pdf.
9. European Public Administration Network, (2005). The EPAN contribution to the success of the Lisbon strategy. Retrieved February. 10, 2006, from European Public Administration Network Web Site: http://www.eupan.org/cms/repository/document/14_LisbonAdHocGroup_ TheEPANcontributionToLisbon.pdf
10. ISO, (2006). Quality management principles. Retrieved January. 19, 2006, from International Organisazion for Standardization Web site: http://www.iso.org/iso/en/ iso9000-14000/understand/qmp.html.

11. Jansen, A. and S. lnes (2004). Quality assessment and benchmarking of Norwegian public web sites. Proceeding from European Conference on e-government, Retrieved February 10, 2006, from http://www.afin.uio.no/english/research/ arild/QualityAssessment.pdf.
12. Kaplan, R S and Norton, D. P. (1992). The balanced scorecard: measures that drive performance. Harvard Business Review.
13. Kim, T.H., Im, K.H., Park, S.C. (2005). Intelligent measuring and improving model for customer satisfaction level in e-government. Electronic Government: 4th International Conference, EGOV 2005, Copenhagen, Denmark, August 22-26, 2005. Proceedings, 3591. Retrieved February 10, 2006, from http://www.springerlink.com/index/2L3470XQW507C8DP.pdf.
14. Lin, C.S. and Wu, S. (2002). Exploring the Impact of Online Service Quality on Portal Site Usage. Proceeding of the 35 th Hawaii International Conference on Systems Science , Hawaii , USA, Retrieved January 10, 2006, from http://doi.ieeecomputersociety.org/10.1109/HICSS.2002.994223
15. Motorola University, (2006a). The inventors of six sigma. Retrieved February 10, 2006, from Motorola University Web site: http://www.motorola.com/content/ 0,,3079,00.html.
16. Motorola University, (2006b). What is Six Sigma. Retrieved February 10, 2006, from Motorola University Web site: http://www.motorola.com/content/ 0,,3088,00.html
17. Parasuraman, A., Zeithaml, V. A., Berry, L. L. (1988), "SERVQUAL: a multiple-item scale for measuring consumer perceptions of service quality", Journal of Retailing, 64.
18. Process Quality Associates Inc, (2001). How does six sigma work. Retrieved Mar. 10, 2006, from Process Quality Associates Web site: http://www.pqa.net/ ProdServices/sixsigma/W06002001.html.
19. Sukasame, N. (2004). The development of e-service in thai government. BU Academic Review, 3. Retrieved January 14, 2006, from http://www.bu.ac.th/ knowledgecenter/epaper/jan_june2004/nittana.pdf
20. Sumra R. and D. Arulazi, (2003). Quality of Service for Web Services-Demystification, Limitations, and Best Practices. Retrieved February 10, 2006, from Web Services Articles, Tutorials, Discussions, News and other Resources Web site: http://www.developer.com/services/article.php/2027911.
21. Wang, R. Y. and Strong, D. (1996). Beyond Accuracy: What Data Quality Means to Data Consumers. Journal of Management Information Systems, 12
22. Webb H. W. and L. A. Webb, (2004). Sitequal: an integrated measure of web site quality. Journal of Enterprise Information Management, 17.
23. Yang, Z., Cai, S., Zhou, Z., Zhou, N. (2005). Development and validation of an instrument to measure user perceived service quality of information presenting web portals. Information and Management, 42. Retrieved February 10, 2006, from http://www.sciencedirect.com.

# Is It Only About Internet Access? An Empirical Test of a Multi-dimensional Digital Divide

J. Ramon Gil-Garcia[1], Natalie C. Helbig[2], and Enrico Ferro[3]

[1] Center for Technology in Government, University at Albany, SUNY, 187 Wolf Road, Suite 301, Albany, NY 12205 USA
jgil-garcia@ctg.albany.edu

[2] Rockefeller College of Public Affairs and Policy, University at Albany, SUNY, 135 Western Avenue, Albany, NY 12222 USA
nhelbig@ctg.albany.edu

[3] Instituto Superiore Mario Boella (ISMB) Via P.C. Boggio 61, 10138 Torino, Italy
ferro@ismb.it

**Abstract.** Scholars from different disciplines have recently studied a phenomenon called "the digital divide". Since many of the new government information technology initiatives are based on Internet technologies and require the use of the Internet by citizens, understanding the digital divide (and consequently, the potential demand) is important for e-government scholars. For some researchers, the divide is not a problem and Internet access is the only relevant determinant of Internet use (access divide). For other researchers, the divide is rooted in more fundamental social differences and opportunities (multi-dimensional divide). Using data from the Piedmont region in Italy, this paper tests these two competing views of the digital divide. Overall, the models based on a multi-dimensional view have greater explanatory power and provide evidence about the relevance of multiple factors affecting both Internet access and Internet use. For instance, females use the Internet for a smaller number of activities than males. Individuals with more formal education and who can speak English use the Internet more. Finally, individuals with more experience using a PC and the Internet itself also use the Internet to perform a broader range of activities.

## 1 Introduction

In recent years, scholars and practitioners have recognized the importance of understanding how diverse social groups use information and communication technologies (ICTs) in their daily lives. The so-called digital divide has been conceptualized very differently, from access to computers and the Internet, to a much more complex social phenomenon with multiple dimensions and frames of reference. Since many of the newest government information technology initiatives are based on Internet technologies and required the use of the Internet by citizens, understanding the digital divide (and consequently, the potential demand) is important for e-government scholars.

M.A. Wimmer et al. (Eds.): EGOV 2006, LNCS 4084, pp. 139–149, 2006.

The term digital divide is difficult to define and carries broad social and political implications. Robinson, DiMaggio and Hargittai (2003) write, "[t]he digital divide implies that significant minorities of the population are effectively denied access to a technology that, like other public facilities like libraries and super highways, is thought to be open to anyone" (p. 2). The consequences of which, imply differing life chances and opportunities for those who are not technologically savvy (DiMaggio & Hargittai, 2001; Servon, 2002).

Using data from the Piedmont region in Italy, this paper explores the relationships between multiple factors, access to the Internet, and the extent of Internet use. We argue that computer and Internet access do not automatically lead to meaningful uses of the Internet, but that there are several other important determinants. The digital divide is not only about access, but also about other characteristics that define the social opportunities of an individual such as gender, education, employment status, IT skills, and an ability to speak foreign languages, among others. In addition, this paper operationalizes Internet access and Internet use using multiple variables and concepts instead of a dichotomous variable only.

The paper is divided in five sections, including these introductory comments. Based on a review of existing academic literature, the second section describes two of the most prominent approaches to study the digital divide: access divide and multi-dimensional divide. Relevant hypotheses are developed for each of the two views. Section three briefly presents the research design and method used in this paper, including the main characteristics of the respondents and the operationalization of the dependent variables. Using multiple and logistic regression, section four empirically tests the two views and discusses the results. Finally, section five provides some concluding remarks and suggests future areas for research in this topic.

## 2 Characterizing the Digital Divide: Approaches and Assumptions

The digital divide is often characterized as some type of relationship between information and communication technologies (ICTs) and groups of individuals, who are situated within a complex arrangement of social, environmental, political, and economic issues. ICTs include any communication device (such as a computer hooked up to the Internet, radio, satellite systems, cellular phones, etc.) used to communicate with and access information. The following section outlines the viewpoints and assumptions taken by different authors about the digital divide. While scholars investigate many different types of technology, connectivity and uses, the last fifteen years yielded two common approaches to understanding the digital divide: access divide and multi-dimensional digital divide (Helbig, Gil-Garcia & Ferro, 2005). In addition, scholars also often narrow the term ICT to mean either personal computers (e.g., hardware and software) or the Internet, in an attempt at a meaningful representation of the digital divide.

Several hypotheses are developed based on the factors and relationships relevant to each view.

### 2.1 Access Digital Divide: Simple Dichotomy

One of the first, and most simplistic accounts of the digital divide expresses a separation between the "haves" and "have nots." Scholars argue that a gap exists solely because of an 'access to technology problem' and tend to frame the access divide as an inherent delay in the diffusion of technology among different geographic areas and social groups (Adriani & Becchetti, 2003; Benjamin, 2001; Compaine, 2001). Accordingly, this view implies that once online, everyone has the same potential to use and benefit from the information society and it is also assumed everyone uses the Internet for the same purposes (Walsh et al., 2003). Based on these assumptions, access to the Internet and use of the Internet are often equated (DiMaggio & Hargittai, 2001). Solutions often promote market forces as being able to eventually close the "perceived" gap and public policy or government intervention is not necessary. If government intervention is suggested, from this view, public policies should foster only Internet access, since Internet use depends, and is derived almost exclusively from access.

Thus, one of the main assumptions of this approach is that only Internet access has a direct effect on Internet use. Therefore, the research endeavor is to identify and test how different factors affect Internet access and how access influences Internet use. In general terms, access to the Internet and computers is strongly correlated with socio-economic status (Bimber, 2000; Selwyn, 2002). Access divide scholars attempt to explain factors responsible for an individual having or not having access to computers and/or the Internet. Three main factors have been associated with access: income, age, and education (Hoffman, Novak, & Schlosser, 2000; Mossberger, Tolbert, & Stansbury, 2003; Robinson et al., 2003). Additional factors that have been examined are attitudes toward technology, race/ethnicity, geography (i.e., rural versus urban), and gender (Bimber, 2000; Ferro, 2005; Mossberger et al., 2003). Therefore, based on the access divide view, relevant hypotheses are:

- H1: Income has a positive effect on access to the Internet
- H2: Age has a negative effect on access to the Internet
- H3: Education has a positive effect on access to the Internet
- H4: Attitude about technology has a positive effect on access to the Internet
- H5: Race/ethnicity has a significant effect on access to the Internet
- H6: Geography has a significant effect on access to the Internet
- H7: Gender has a significant effect on access to the Internet
- H8: Access to the Internet has a positive effect on use of the Internet

### 2.2 A Multi-dimensional Digital Divide

A competing viewpoint has challenged the simple access dichotomy. Servon (2002) and Norris (2001) assume access to be a basic building block (i.e., almost a "given") and Internet use to be the real question. DiMaggio and Hargittai (2001) take this position also stating, "As the technology penetrates into every crevice of society, the pressing question will be not 'who can find a network connection at home, work, or in a library or community center from which to log on?' but instead, 'What are people doing, and what are they able to do, when they go on-line?". Therefore, from this view scholars do not automatically assume that once online people will wish to use the Internet or engage in meaningful uses. Generally this view advocates for public policy intervention and does not see the market as being able to close the gap over time with respect to access, information literacy, employment opportunities, and community redevelopment, among other factors (Chin & Fairlie, 2004; Cole, 2004; Mossberger et al., 2003).

This view understands access to the Internet and use of the Internet as two different constructs and their relationships are examined separately. Access is treated as one more dimension of the digital divide, equally as important as other factors such as race/ethnicity, income, skills, geography, cultural content, education, information literacy and training (Norris, 2001; Servon, 2002). There is no consensus among scholars concerning which factors predict Internet use; however, it is clear they agree there are many dimensions that do (Helbig, Gil-Garcia & Ferro, 2005). DiMaggio and Hargittai (2001) list five dimensions of digital inequality, including equipment, autonomy of use, skill, social support, and the purpose technology is employed that are important. Robinson et al. (2003) found education is more consistently associated with increases in Internet use (including types of sites visited, uses made of the Internet, and political engagement) and that the higher your education, the more likely you are to use the Internet. Hargittai (2002) argues that skill, defined as "the ability to efficiently and effectively find information on the Web," will determine the likelihood of using the medium to the person's maximum benefit (p. 3). Kennedy et al. (2003) suggest that people with children use the Internet less than people without children. Hollifield and Donnermeyer (2003) find that employment by a company has a positive relationship with an individual's adoption of technology. Bimber (2000) argues that gender is a very important factor, which affects not only Internet access but also Internet use. Mossberger (2003) found that use is not related to race when controlling for access. Therefore, hypotheses concerning use of and access to the Internet according to the multi-dimensional perspective are:

- H9: Income has a positive effect on use of the Internet
- H10: Age has a negative effect on use of the Internet
- H11: Education has a positive effect on use of the Internet
- H12: Attitude about technology has a positive effect on use of the Internet
- H13: Race/ethnicity does not have a significant effect on use of the Internet
- H14: Geography has a relationship to use of the Internet
- H15: Gender has a significant effect on use of the Internet
- H16: Speaking English has a positive effect on access to the Internet
- H17: Speaking English has a positive effect on use of the Internet
- H18: Having a PC at home has a positive effect on access to the Internet
- H19: Having a PC at home has a positive effect on use of the Internet

- H20: PC use has a positive effect on access to the Internet
- H21: PC use has a positive effect on use of the Internet
- H22: Information technology skills have a positive effect on access to the Internet
- H23: Information technology skills have a positive effect on use of the Internet
- H24: Size of household has a significant effect on access to the Internet
- H25: Size of household has a significant effect on use of the Internet
- H26: Employment status has a significant effect on access to the Internet
- H27: Employment status has a significant effect use of the Internet
- H28: Individual Internet experience has a positive effect on use of the Internet
- H29: Household Internet experience has a positive effect on use of the Internet

## 3 Research Methods and Design

This paper is based on a survey to 2206 Italians who live in the region of Piedmont. The sample used for the purpose of this paper was created from a database provided by the Italian National Statistical Institute (ISTAT) whose data refer to the last periodical census carried out in 2001. The entire data set was collected via Computer Aided Telephone Interviews (CATI). Thus people without a fixed line are not represented in the sample. The stratified sample was created using a differentiated probability approach in order to over-represent segments with a higher variance in terms of technology adoption and usage (i.e., young versus older people). The variables adopted for the stratification of the sample were: age, gender, and size of town of residence. Following the guidelines provided by the European Statistical Institute, people less than 16 years old were excluded from the sample. Respondents were asked questions about computer ownership, Internet access and Internet use. Relevant individual demographics and household characteristics were also collected.

### 3.1 Characteristics of the Respondents

The average age of participants is forty-eight years and the sample is almost equally split between men and women. Almost three-fifths of the population have dependent children, making the average household size slightly less than three persons. Approximately, eight out of ten have a primary and secondary education, while thirty-eight percent have an upper secondary education. Occupation among respondents varied, nearly one-third identified as employed. The majority of respondents live in either a town or village. Forty-four percent speak English. Over half of respondents have a personal computer (PC) at home, about half of them have Internet access and slightly less than half use the Internet.

### 3.2 Operationalization of Dependent Variables

Generally, Internet access and Internet use are studied as dependent variables and their operationalization varies from study to study (DiMaggio & Hargittai, 2001).

Internet access has many different meanings. For example, Mossberger et al., (2003) used various measures such as access to a computer at home, home access to the Internet, and an e-mail account to operationalize Internet access. Ferro et al. (2005) used specific access types (i.e., modem or broadband). This study uses three measures of Internet access: (1) the number of locations where an individual can access the Internet, (2) the number of devices an individual uses to access the Internet, and (3) a dichotomous variable representing whether the individual has access to the Internet (complete results available from authors).

Internet use also has different meanings. Generally, frequency of use and type of use are operationalized. Bimber (2000) looked at the frequency of Internet use ranging from never to daily. Kennedy, Wellman, and Klement (2003) looked at types of Internet uses (i.e., what people actually do when they were on line: meeting new people, searching for information, participating in recreation activities such as games, and engaging in commerce). This study uses two measures of Internet use: (1) a dichotomous variable representing whether an individual uses the Internet, and (2) the number of distinctive activities that an individual uses the Internet for (complete results available from authors).

## 4 Analysis and Main Findings

Based on multiple and logistic regression models, this section presents the results of testing the access divide and the multi-dimensional divide views. Overall, it seems clear that the additional variables suggested by the multi-dimensional view significantly improves the explanatory power of the models. Therefore, other factors such as gender, employment status, IT skills, PC use and ability to speak other languages, among others are important determinants of Internet access and Internet use. The following sections present and describe the results for several specifications of the models for Internet access and Internet use.

### 4.1 Determinants of Internet Access

Table 1 presents the results of an access divide model and a multi-dimensional divide model using the number of devices for Internet access as the dependent variable. Income is positively associated to Internet access. Age is significantly associated with Internet access, but in the access divide model the relationship is negative and in the multi-dimensional model it is positive. Education and attitude towards computers are positively associated with Internet access. Being female is negatively associated with Internet access measured as the number of devices to access the Internet.

Several variables related to the multi-dimensional divide were found to be important determinants. Speaking English is positively associated with Internet access. Having a PC at home and individual use of a PC are positively associated with Internet access. Information technology skills as represented by an IT training course is positively associated with Internet access. Finally, employment status is a significant determinant of Internet access. Overall, there was an improvement in adjusted R-square from 0.403 to 0.575.

**Table 1.** Determinants of Internet Access (Number of Devices)

| Independent Variables | Access Divide Model | Multi-Dimensional Divide Model |
|---|---|---|
| Constant | -0.343** (-2.232) | -0.217 (-1.537) |
| Income | <0.001*** (7.675) | <0.001*** (3.813) |
| Age | -0.009*** (-10.483) | 0.002* (1.776) |
| Education | 0.174*** (8.139) | 0.033* (1.700) |
| Attitude towards Computers | 0.093*** (9.705) | 0.038*** (4.450) |
| Nationality (Italian = 1) | 0.164 (1.603) | 0.028 (0.319) |
| Location (Town = 1) | 0.079 (1.290) | 0.031 (0.593) |
| Location (Village = 1) | 0.049 (0.803) | 0.013 (0.240) |
| Gender (Female = 1) | -0.109*** (-3.860) | -0.047* (-1.916) |
| Other Language (English) | | 0.120*** (3.966) |
| PC at Home | | 0.105*** (3.191) |
| PC Use | | 0.630*** (16.756) |
| IT Skills | | 0.083*** (2.685) |
| Household Size | | 0.003 (0.235) |
| Occupation (Employee = 1) | | -0.258*** (-4.744) |
| Occupation (Self Employed = 1) | | -0.264*** (-4.070) |
| Occupation (Unemployed = 1) | | -0.231*** (-3.101) |
| Occupation (Other = 1) | | -0.338*** (-5.132) |
| | | |
| R-square | 0.407 | 0.580 |
| Adjusted R-square | 0.403 | 0.575 |
| F-statistic | 115.712*** | 108.750*** |

Note: T-statistics are in parentheses under coefficient values. Those coefficients followed by * are significant at the 10 percent level, those followed by ** are significant at the 5 percent level, and those followed by *** are significant at the 1 percent level.

An access divide and a multi-dimensional divide logistic regression models, where access was measured as a dichotomous variable, were also calculated and the results are described next. Again, income is positively associated with Internet access. Age is negatively associated with Internet access in the access divide model and not statistically significant in the multi-dimensional divide model. Education is positively associated with Internet access in the access divide model, but not significant in the multi-dimensional divide model. Attitude towards computers was positively associated with Internet access. Location (city, town, or village) was a significant determinant of Internet access.

Similar to previous specifications, some variables related to the multi-dimensional view were also significant. For instance, PC use was positively associated with Internet access. IT skills were a significant determinant of Internet access, but the sign was negative. Finally, employment status seems to be an important variable, but significant differences were found only between students and self-employed and students and other. The Cox and Snell R-square improved from

0.328 to 0.601 and the Nagelkerke R-square went from 0.438 to 0.802 suggesting that the additional variables in the multi-dimensional model have an important impact on the percentage of variance explained.

### 4.2 Determinants of Internet Use

Following a similar logic as with Internet access, this section presents the results from several specifications of Internet use models. Overall, the multi-dimensional divide models have greater explanatory power and untangle the complex relationships in a more specific manner. Table 2 presents the results of three models using the extent of Internet use as the dependent variable. The extent of use is operationalized as the number of activities an individual performs using the Internet. The first regression model is based purely in the access divide view and therefore considers Internet access as the only relevant factor affecting Internet use directly. The second model includes the factors mentioned in the access divide view, but tests direct relationships from all of them to Internet use. Finally, the third model incorporates additional variables related to the multi-dimensional divide view.

Overall, there is an important improvement in adjusted R-square, which went from 0.371 in the access divide model to 0.528 in the extended access divide model, and then to 0.697 in the multi-dimensional divide model. Internet access is positively associated with Internet use in all specifications. Income is positively associated with Internet use in the extended access divide model, but becomes not statistically significant once controlling for other variables. Age is negatively associated with Internet use. Education and attitude towards computers are positively associated with Internet use. Being female is negatively associated with Internet use.

Similar to Internet access, there were several variables related to the multi-dimensional divide that were significantly associated to Internet use. For example, speaking English was positively associated with Internet use. Having a PC at home was negatively associated with Internet use, but individual use of a PC was positively associated with Internet use. Similarly, individual Internet experience was positively associated with the extent of Internet use, but household Internet experience was negatively associated with the extent of individual Internet use.

The same three models were run, but using a dichotomous variable to represent Internet use. Similar to the previous set of models, income is positively associated with Internet use in the extended access divide model, but is not significant in the muti-dimensional divide model. Age is negatively associated with Internet use in the extended access divide model, but is not significant once controlling for other factors. Education and attitude towards computers are positively associated with Internet use. Being female is negatively associated with Internet use.

Several variables related to the multi-dimensional view were also found as important determinants of Internet use. Speaking English is positively associated

**Table 2.** Determinants of Internet Use (Extent of Use)

| Independent Variables | Access Divide Model | Access Divide Model (Extended) | Multi-Dimensional Divide Model |
|---|---|---|---|
| Constant | 0.376***<br>(6.545) | -0.824*<br>(-1.650) | -0.117<br>(-0.265) |
| Internet Access | 2.929***<br>(35.882) | 1.842***<br>(16.408) | 1.488***<br>(9.426) |
| Income | | <0.001***<br>(2.881) | <0.001<br>(0.912) |
| Age | | -0.023***<br>(-7.644) | -0.007**<br>(-1.964) |
| Education | | 0.550***<br>(7.801) | 0.138**<br>(2.229) |
| Attitude towards Computers | | 0.253***<br>(7.906) | 0.099***<br>(3.706) |
| Nationality (Italian = 1) | | 0.276<br>(0.831) | -0.035<br>(-0.132) |
| Location (Town = 1) | | 0.050<br>(0.249) | 0.051<br>(0.315) |
| Location (Village = 1) | | -0.012<br>(-0.060) | 0.023<br>(0.140) |
| Gender (Female = 1) | | -0.554***<br>(-5.980) | -0.285***<br>(-3.737) |
| Other Language (English) | | | 0.201**<br>(2.120) |
| PC at Home | | | -0.484***<br>(-3.461) |
| PC Use | | | 1.160***<br>(9.275) |
| IT Skills | | | -0.099<br>(-1.023) |
| Household Size | | | -0.025<br>(-0.660) |
| Occupation (Employee = 1) | | | -0.083<br>(-0.489) |
| Occupation (Self Employed = 1) | | | -0.228<br>(-1.120) |
| Occupation (Unemployed = 1) | | | 0.133<br>(0.570) |
| Occupation (Other = 1) | | | -0.184<br>(-0.891) |
| Individual Internet Experience | | | 0.368***<br>(18.430) |
| Household Internet Experience | | | -0.089***<br>(-3.548) |
| | | | |
| R-square | 0.371 | 0.532 | 0.701 |
| Adjusted R-square | 0.371 | 0.528 | 0.697 |
| F-statistic | 1287.531*** | 168.124*** | 152.547*** |

Note: T-statistics are in parentheses under coefficient values. Those coefficients followed by * are significant at the 10 percent level, those followed by ** are significant at the 5 percent level, and those followed by *** are significant at the 1 percent level.

with Internet use. Individual PC use is positively associated with Internet use, but having a PC at home has a negative effect on Internet use. Employment status is an important determinant of Internet use. Three of the four dummy variables representing employment status were statistically significant. Finally, similar to the previous specifications, household Internet experience has a negative effect on individual Internet use.

Overall, the explanatory power of the different specifications improved from a Cox and Snell R-square of 0.381 in the access divide model to 0.544 in the extended access divide model, and then to 0.628 in the multi-dimensional divide model. Similar improvements can be observed in the Nagelkerke R-square, which values went from 0.511 to 0.728 and then to 0.841, respectively.

## 5 Final Comments

In general terms, the results of this paper provide evidence that multiple variables are important in explaining Internet access and use. For instance, income is an important determinant of Internet access (measured as a dichotomous variable and number of devices). Individuals need financial resources to buy the necessary equipment for accessing the Internet. However, income is not as important as a determinant of Internet use, at least it is not when controlling for Internet access, availability of equipment, and location. Similarly, IT skills is an important predictor of Internet access, but not of Internet use. However, education, which creates a broader set of capabilities, is very important for both Internet access and use. Attitude towards computers, employment status, gender, PC use experience, and the ability to speak English are important determinants of Internet access and Internet use. Finally, there seems to be a reinforcing dynamic regarding Internet use; the more experience an individual has with the Internet, the more activities this individual performs using it.

The results show that Internet access is the most important determinant of Internet use. However, other variables are also important and characterizing the digital divide as being only about access offers a limited understanding of this phenomenon. In fact, it seems clear from the results of this research that once online not everybody uses the Internet for the same reasons and performs the same activities. For instance, females use the Internet for a smaller number of activities than males. Individuals with more formal education and who can speak English use the Internet for a greater number of activities. Finally, individuals with more experience using a PC and the Internet itself also use the Internet to perform more activities.

An access divide view also limits the capability of governments to develop appropriate policies that address other interrelated inequalities. In fact, public policies regarding the digital divide need to be re-framed and re-examined given the changes over the last 15 years in technology and patterns of Internet use. These policies should also take into consideration that virtual inequalities are the result of other inequalities in terms of education, gender, income, ability to speak foreign languages, IT skills, employment status, etc. The complexity of the associated social problems (demand) and their implications to the success of e-government initiatives (supply) need to be fully understood and future research should explore these relationships.

Research is now questioning whether the concept of the digital divide provides an accurate portrayal of reality. Some scholars have begun re-theorizing technology's relationship with race, gender and culture (Castells, 2001; Kennedy et al., 2003). In this view, the multiple perspectives an individual holds are brought to the center of any discussion about technology and circumstances are evaluated based on how the intersections of their race, gender, class, worldview etc. come together (Kennedy et al., 2003; Servon, 2002; Helbig, Gil-Garcia & Ferro, 2005). Future research should explore how the relationships between Internet access, Internet use and their determinants are similar or different for different social groups.

## References


1. Adriani, F., & Becchetti, L. (2003). Does the Digital Divide Matter? The role of ICT in cross-country level and growth estimates: CEIS Tor Vergata.
2. Benjamin, M. (2001). Re-examining the Digital Divide: Internet and Telecom Consortium, MIT.
3. Bimber, B. (2000). Measuring the Gender Gap on the Internet. Social Science Quarterly, 81(3).
4. Castells, M. (2001). The Internet Galaxy. Reflections on the Internet, Business, and Society. New York: Oxford University Press.
5. Chin, M. D., & Fairlie, R. W. (2004). The determinants of the Global Digital Divide: A Cross-Country Analysis of Computer and Internet Penetration: Economic Growth Center Yale University.
6. Cole, J. I., et al. (2004). The Digital Future Report: USC Center for the Digital Future.
7. Compaine, B. M. (Ed.). (2001). The Digital Divide: Facing a Crisis or Creating a Myth? Cambridge, MA: MIT Press.
8. DiMaggio, P., & Hargittai, E. (2001). From the 'Digital Divide' to 'Digital Inequality': Studying Internet Use As Penetration Increases: Support from the Center for the Arts and Cultural Policy Studies, Woodrow Wilson School, Princeton University.
9. Ferro, E., et al. (2005). Urban vs. Regional Divide: Comparing and Classifying Digital Divide. In B. e. al. (Ed.) (pp. pp. 81-90, M.): TCGOV 2005, LNAI 3416.
10. Hargittai, E. (2002). Second-Level Digital Divide: Differences in People's Online Skills. First Monday, 7(4).
11. Helbig, N., Gil-Garcia, J. R. & Ferro, E. (2005). Understanding the Complexity of Electronic Government: Implications from the Digital Divide Literature. Paper presented at the Americas Conference of Information Systems 2005, organized by the Association for Information Systems, Omaha, NE, USA, August 11-14.
12. Hoffman, D. L., Novak, T. P., & Schlosser, A. (2000). The Evolution of the Digital Divide: How Gaps in Internet Access May Impact Electronic Commerce. Journal of Computer-Mediated Communication, 5(3).
13. Hollifield, A. C., & Donnermeyer, J. F. (2003). Creating demand: influencing information technology diffusion in rural communities. Government Information Quarterly, 20, 135-150.
14. Kennedy, T., Wellman, B., & Klement, K. (2003). Gendering the Digital Divide. IT & Society, 1(5), 72-96.
15. Mossberger, K., Tolbert, C. J., & Stansbury, M. (2003). Virtual Inequality: Beyond the Digital Divide. Washington, DC: Georgetown University Press.
16. Norris, P. (2001). Digital divide : civic engagement, information poverty, and the Internet worldwide. New York: Cambridge University Press.
17. Robinson, J. P., DiMaggio, P., & Hargittai, E. (2003). New Social Survey Perspectives on the Digital Divide. IT & Society, 1(5), 1-22.
18. Selwyn, N. (2002). Defining the 'Digital Divide': Developing a Theoretical Understanding of Inequalities in the Information Age. Cardiff University School of Social Sciences Occasional Paper 49, 330-967.
19. Servon, L. J. (2002). Bridging the Digital Divide: technology, community, and public policy. Oxford: Blackwell Publishers Ltd.
20. Warschauer, M. (2003). Technology and Social Inclusion: Rethinking the Digital Divide. Cambridge, MA: MIT Press.

# Hidden Negative Social Effects of Poor e-Government Services Design

Enrique Stanziola, Mauricio Minuto Espil, Luis Landoni, and Santiago Montoya

Subsecretariat of Public Income, Ministry of Economics
Government of the Province of Buenos Aires, Argentina
{estanziola, mminuto, llandoni, dar}@ec.gba.gov.ar

**Abstract.** Poor usability in e-government, preventing universal adoption, has social, economic and political effects. Some effects can be observed by analysts directly from the results produced by the system itself. However, there exists effects that may be hidden from the analyst direct view-point. One of those effects is the expert intermediation. This phenomenon is launched as a direct consequence of the system design, and originates a "new elite" within the society. It also generates negative externalities for citizens, and creates an artificial digital divide, which is far from the democratic and egalitarian goals of e-government. In this paper we faced the phenomenon, analyzing possible causes and solutions.

## 1 Introduction

E-government services must be universally accessible and usable in order to become a real benefit for people [6]. It is well known that interaction with users differs significatively within e-commerce and e-government contexts. The differences rely on purpose, characteristics and social effects [20]. Within e-commerce contexts, a negative economic impact may follow poor usable websites; If a potential customer cannot easily perform what she expects to do when visiting a company site, it is very easy for her to look for a competitor, and the company to lose that customer. Within e-government boundaries, however, the situation is very different. Poor usability in this context may have social and political effects in addition to economic ones. Many of the effects produced are somewhat known. The literature has extensibly studied the "digital divide" phenomenon [4,23,24], and the accessibility problem [1] when applied to e-government. Accessibility in e-government, for instance, has been specialized in two categories: availability or access to physical media, and approachability or understanding of abstract models and configuration of the user state of mind [1,2]. Those effect can be observed from the virtual point of view of the system. Despite designers and analysts do not actually know who is interacting with the website and whether the user is satisfied or not with the service, they can identify users and infer satisfaction indicators [10] from the results produced in the system itself (databases, logs). We define here those effects as *observable externalities.*

M.A. Wimmer et al. (Eds.): EGOV 2006, LNCS 4084, pp. 150–161, 2006.

Nonetheless, not all effects are directly observable. Some negative and undesirable effects may be not visible from direct inspection. They are hidden behind the barrier that separates citizens from designers and analysts, because the latter do not know who is behind the scenes. We define those effects as *hidden externalities*. In this paper, we focus our study on a type of hidden negative externalities [17] that consists in the artificial creation of a class of intermediaries, "expert" contractors that offer their expertise and knowledge of use as a value, and constitute a "new elite" within the society, due to methods imposed by government. They invert the costs problem, and transfer part of the cost reduction from government to citizens (the cost of contracting intermediaries). Expert intermediation is extremely undesirable; it prevents universal adoption, and creates an artificial digital divide, which is far from the democratic and egalitarian goals of e-government. This divide may be hidden by some time, or worst, it may remain unknown indefinitely. Furthermore, when the use of an electronic service is mandatory, and users are forced, by legal or practical reasons, to learn to use the system; a phenomenon of resistance and conflict appears as a consequence [5]. Some governmental agencies keep manual alternatives for people not used to computer interaction and the Internet. Thus, the government will not achieve its goal of being more efficient in its operation. Extra costs are added like system updates, user manuals and help desks.

We faced with this phenomenon when attempting the formulation of requirements for the redesign of the website of a provincial tax agency. A tax system website is particularly useful for the study of the social and political impact of usability because the services it implements are supposed to be universally available (In democracies nowadays, an adult citizen is always considered a potential taxpayer). In particular, the website in question had being used largely (almost 750,000 operations performed monthly), and revealed, after a simple inspection, severe usability problems. We were looking for a design that offer an accessible service for the whole base of users. The task shows many challenges to face; many of them difficult to assess. A user-centred design process should be employed, with an evaluation survey of actual and potential users as a first step. We needed to know how many of the intended users had adopted the website, and what were the differences between those who used the site and those who did not use it. We found out that many of the actual users behaved like experts of the website, and that they were using it on a daily or weekly basis, contradicting intuition. Given that in the province taxes have to be filed once a month at most, our assumption was that those frequent users were intermediaries. Meanwhile, a large group of users were being left behind and we needed to find out why. Although the website had been advertised thoroughly for more than a year, many taxpayers who did use the WWW had not adopted the site for interaction yet. We think adoption may be influenced by usability and accessibility drawbacks. In consequence, our first hypothesis was that many taxpayers were not using the website for one of these reasons: (1) they did not use computers or the WWW, or, (2) even if they regularly used the WWW, the website was not fit for their skills, knowledge or needs.

We hypothesized that intermediaries had a higher level of adoption than direct users, and the reasons behind that phenomenon. We guessed that intermediaries found the website more usable and useful than those who used it for their own affairs (direct users). That is, in general terms, intermediaries were generally more satisfied than direct users. Another hypothesis hinted that intermediaries had more skills and knowledge than direct users with respect to the site functionality, so they were better prepared to use it.

In order to prove or discard these hypotheses we did a survey of plain citizens in the agency's branches. From the survey's results we can conclude that usability is affecting the adoption of the website, since its users are significantly different in age, education, and computer skills from the whole population. In the process of developing a new website we are defining a method for user-centred design of e-government services, which takes into account the universality of them.

### 1.1 Paper Organisation

This paper contains: in section 2, a conceptual description of the paradigms and methodologies that underpin this research and development project; in section 3, an explanation of the problem; in section 4, a description of the method we used to test the hypotheses; in section 5, the results of the study; in section 6, a discussion on consequences and possible solutions for the problem and in section 7, conclusions and possible future lines of research.

## 2 Concepts of Citizen-Centred e-Government

Frequently, e-government projects are developed for achieving more efficiency and efficacy in the performance of services, bringing transparency to public administration, improving digital inclusion and Internet adoption, and increasing the citizen's participation. In order to fulfil these goals, e-government services have to be designed from the citizen's point of view [22], otherwise, citizens find it difficult to use and learn. This is not a trivial task, specially in the public sector. Human-computer interaction, user-centred design and usability engineering could be very useful to enable a citizen-centred e-government development process. We explain why here.

### 2.1 Human-Computer Interaction, User-Centred Design and Usability

"Human-computer interaction (HCI) is a discipline concerned with the design, evaluation and implementation of interactive computing systems for human use and with the study of major phenomena surrounding them" [8]. HCI methodologies are very useful for the development of e-government since they involve real users in all stages of the process. Among these, we choose: user-centred design, which subordinates technology and functionality to users' needs, and usability engineering, which enables to make informed design decisions in order to assure that the final product is usable by the intended users [16].

Human-computer interaction methods have been successfully applied to improve business systems' usability. Its benefits are well studied in terms of cost justification [15]. In the case of e-government services for citizens, the intended users are the whole adult population, regardless of age, sex, abilities, literacy, language, or culture.

Thus, we consider it is necessary to assure universal usability [21]. There are some literature examples of user or citizen-centred approaches to the development and evaluation of e-government systems [3, 7, 22]

### 2.2 User Roles: Intermediary and Direct Users

Within the context of this paper, we call "intermediary users" to those who access the website to make transactions on behalf of taxpayers. They perceive a monetary stipend for their services. "Direct users" are those who access the website to make transactions referred to their own obligations as taxpayers.

## 3 The Challenge: To Redesign a Live Tax Website

The province of Buenos Aires reached an estimated population of 10,148,270 over 20 years old in 2005 [9]. According to the local tax agency, the province has approximately 7,850,000 taxpayers, which have monthly, bimonthly or annual dues for income, real estate and automobile taxes. The tax agency decided to redesign its website because, although there were 744,949 operations per month on average during 2005, the agency was receiving too much calls from users that had problems trying to use it. Firstly, an expert's inspection (a heuristic evaluation) of the website yielded inconsistency in visual design, organization-centred information architecture, technical jargon, text on small characters and low contrast, and cumbersome navigation techniques.

In order to improve the website's performance, it was decided to redesign it, following the usability engineering methodology [11, 14]. The first need was to know who the users were. In order to have a broad vision of the users profiles, a survey was done. The survey was designed to find out the user's skills and experience. General skills and needs associated can be determined with demographic data (sex, age and education). Male-female proportion indicates the rate of colour-blind users we may have. It is important to know that if there is red text over a green background, 24% of male users and 1% of female users will not be able to read it. Age gives us information on vision accuracy. Users over 40 years old are very probable to need glasses for presbyopia [22]. Education determines the language we can use.

The first question we needed to answer is the level of adoption of website, that is, the percentage of taxpayers that are using the website. Some surveyed taxpayers may not be WWW users, due to educational, social or economical factors that are not relevant for our study, thus, they will not be taken into account in this calculation. However, those taxpayers that are WWW users but are not users of our website, are being influenced by other factors that are worth to be studied. If the website is a real benefit for the whole community, it should be used by almost every taxpayer that uses the WWW, at least once per year. A reasonable goal would be that at least 90% of those taxpayers that use the WWW, use the website as well. Therefore, our first hypothesis is: H1: Those taxpayers that use the WWW use the website.

As we said before, those users that did not adopt the website may have contracted intermediaries to fulfil their tax duties through the website. Therefore, we studied if there was a difference between the adoption level of intermediary and direct users. Our second hypothesis is: H2: The level of adoption among intermediary users is significantly higher than the level of adoption among direct users.

As we found usability problems in the website, we supposed it was specially difficult to use for direct users, since, by definition, they use the site less frequently. In order to find out if this was the case, we established the third hypothesis: H3: Intermediary users have a general satisfaction with the website significantly higher than direct users.

Another suspicion was that the website was more difficult to use for those with lower computational skills and level of education. Therefore, we think intermediaries may have more skills and education than direct users. Our fourth and fifth hypotheses state that: H4: Intermediary users have a general computational experience significantly higher than direct users. H5: Intermediary users have a general level of education significantly higher than direct users.

## 4 Method

### 4.1 Sample

A total of n=1832 subjects participated in the survey. They were sampled through random selection in 48 of the 175 branches of the agency. The branches were carefully chosen to cover uniformly the province, with geographical, and demographical criteria. These subjects received a paper questionnaire in-person while they were waiting to be attended. The response rate was 85% on average for all branches. The agency estimates that there are N=7,850,000 taxpayers in the province. In order to have a level of confidence of 95%, and an error margin of 0.03, the size of the sample should be 1022[1]. Summarizing, our sample of 1831 individuals gives us significant results.

### 4.2 Questionnaire

The questionnaire covered three areas: (1) demographic information (sex, age, education), (2) frequency of use of the agency's services and satisfaction with them, and (3) experience with computers and the World Wide Web.

[1] It was used the formula for large populations: n $= (z_{\alpha/2})^2 s^2$ / $e^2$, where $z_{\alpha/2}$ is the value for normal standardized distribution for probability $z_{\alpha/2}$; the standard deviation s was based on the estimated proportion as p(1-p); and e=0.003 [13].

# 5 Results

## 5.1 Level of Adoption of the Website

Level of adoption (LA) is the proportion of individuals that use the website. 535 respondents said they use the website. Calculated over the whole sample (n=1832), we have 31.66% of adopters. However, we know there is a large group of people that do not use the WWW[2], due to social and economical factors beyond our control. A more realistic estimation is to calculate LA over the number of WWW users (n=1083), which yields an LA of 49.40%. In consequence, H1 was rejected. Still, WWW users may be seen as potential users, since they do not have practical limitations to use the website. Our challenge is that at least 90% of WWW users become actual users of the new version of the website. In order to inform the redesign process, we investigated the probable factors of adoption. We compared the demographics (age, education, computer skills) and behaviour (frequency of visits to a branch and calls to the agency's phone) of actual and potential users in order to infer some reasons for the adoption.

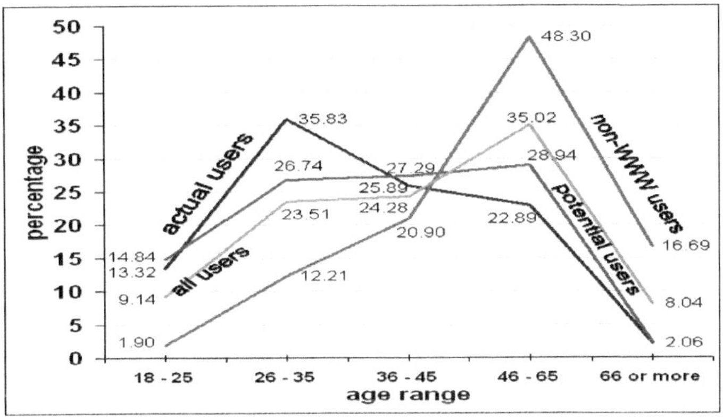


**Fig. 1.** Percentage of users per age range

We found higher levels of adoption for these subgroups: those whose age is between 26 and 35 years old, 56.68%; those with complete or some university or technical studies, 56.13%; those who go to an agency's branch more than once per month, 77.49%; those who call to the agency's phone more than once per month, 87.65%; those that use a computer daily, 55.56%.

The distribution of respondents per age range (Fig 1), for actual users, potential users, non-WWW users and all users, shows how the adoption is just above average for young users, clearly high for adults under 35, and lower than average for 46 or older.

[2] According to the national census in 2001, just 8.9% of households in this province have a computer with access to the Internet. [9]

Therefore, we infer that age is affecting adoption. One reason could be that the website is easier to use for people under 35 years old. We observed in previous inspections that the most text has a size of 10 points. Another reason could be that people older than 46 are less confident to make transactions on the WWW.

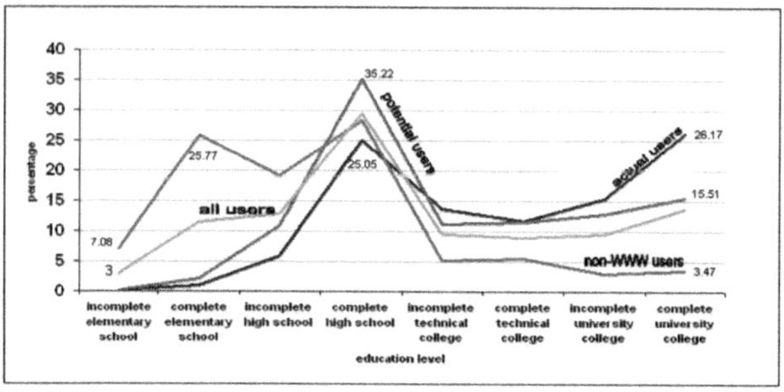


**Fig. 2.** Percentage of users per education level

Adoption also varies with education. Fig. 2 shows the distribution of education level for actual users, potential users, non-WWW users, and all users.

We observe that college education and adoption are dependent (the probability of those variable being independent is near zero: p= 1.55E-05 for Pearson's $\chi^2$ test). We infer that the website's design is implicitly favouring highly educated people.

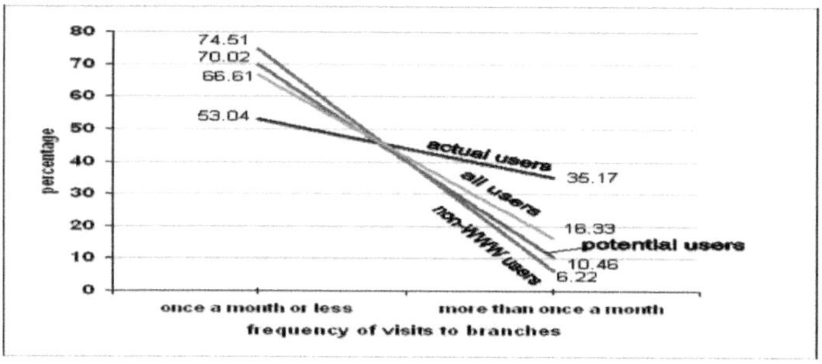


**Fig. 3.** Percentage of users that go to the agency's branches at each frequency

We found particularly interesting the differences in the frequency that respondents go to a brick-and-mortar branch of the agency. Fig. 3 shows the distribution of visits for actual users, potential users, non-WWW users and all users. 35.17% of actual users go to a branch more than once a month, which accounts for a professional pattern of behaviour. On the other hand, only 10.46% of potential users go as frequently. This statistics gave us the suggestion that the website was being adopted specially by intermediaries. In consequence, we studied further this phenomena and established hypotheses 2 to 5.0.

## 5.2 Comparison of Intermediary vs. Direct Users of the Website

For this comparison we considered as "intermediary users" those respondents that answered "yes" for at least one of the following questions: (1) do you go to a physical branch of the agency, visit the agency's website, or call to the agency, daily or weekly?; and (2) do you usually do the same kind of operation for several taxpayers, properties or automobiles at the same time? Those that answered "no" to both questions were considered as "direct users". For these statistics we used the whole sample, without regarding if they are users of the website.

According to these conditions, we found 26.26% of intermediary users in the sample, 70% of those use the website. Therefore, H2, since intermediaries have a significantly higher level of adoption compared with direct users (38%) (p=2.08E-23 for Pearson's $\chi^2$ test).

In order to test H3, we asked respondents for their subjective satisfaction with four typical tasks: mail address change, renegotiation of debt, bill print out and debt determination. For each task they answered one of this options: "never needed it", or "needed it but ...": "...could not perform the task", " ...could perform the task with difficulty", " ...could perform the task, with no opinion on difficulty"; and " ...could perform the task with satisfaction". Using Pearson's test, "Bill print out" task yielded a 6.08% probability of user role and satisfaction being independent. Hence, we can consider it dependent in most cases. The other three tasks did not show dependency. Therefore, H3 was accepted only for one task. However, as this task is frequently done, users may have learned by repetition: 69% of intermediaries said they do it at least every two months, while 39% of direct users said they do it so often.

Intermediary users are more experienced on computers and the WWW than direct users, as Fig 4 shows. The test for three questions showed p 0: use computers: p= 5.40E-25; use computers every day: p=0.00045; use the WWW: p= 5.11E-25. There is slight probability (p=0.04673) of independence between role of user and time since first use of computers. Therefore, H4 was accepted.

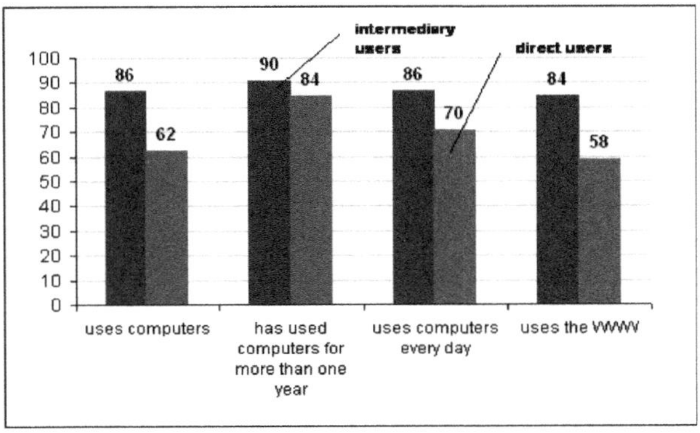


**Fig. 4.** Use of computers and the WWW by intermediary and direct users

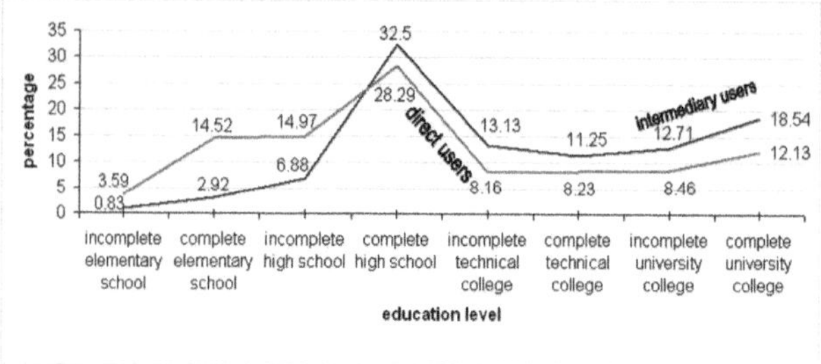


**Fig. 5.** Percentage of intermediary and direct users per education level

Intermediaries have a higher level of education compared with direct users. Fig. 5 shows how the percentage of intermediary users and direct users varies with the education level.

The difference is more evident at the level of complete college studies. The Pearson's test shows education level and role of users are dependent (p= 1.018E-23). Therefore, H5 was accepted.

# 6 Discussion

## 6.1 Effects of Usability: When a Difficult and Necessary Website Creates an Elite of Users.

Comparing actual and potential users we found the website is a useful tool, since it has been adopted by a fair percentage of users. However, it requires from the user skills that are above average. It may be necessary to have college studies or technical education to use the website. This may be derived from its technical language. It seems it also requires a high level of computational skills, which may be caused by a complex interaction design that results difficult for novice users.

It has been observed that business users and plain citizens have different behaviour when using e-government systems [12]. We may consider intermediaries as expert users. Most of them are adults or youngsters with technical or college education. They frequently use this website, as well as other ones to perform online transactions. They use to perform the same transaction for several properties or automobiles. Most of them are generally satisfied with the site, although some operations present difficulties. Despite all the objective difficulties for using our website, a high percentage of intermediaries have adopted it. We think that the members of this group are more motivated to cope with a long learning curve. Their motivations may be: (1) to maximize their efficiency to perform operations that would take more time and money if they are done in a physical branch; and (2) to catch clients that are obliged to fulfil their tax duties only through the website, but they do cannot to use the website (or they do not want to learn how to use it).

On the other hand, direct users may be considered to be novice and infrequent users. On average, they are older and less educated than intermediaries. As they are less satisfied with the website, we infer that, indeed, the website's usability may be playing a role in the process of contracting intermediaries for tax duties.

From these findings, we conclude that, in order to encourage a broad adoption, the new version should be easy to use and easy to learn. In order to achieve these goals, the new user interface should be self-explicative and use plain language. Experts use to learn the website's jargon and tricks, but those are too demanding for novices. The new version should be absolutely consistent and provide simple interaction techniques. Operations that are inherently complex and require accountancy skills are bound to be performed by an accountant that will intermediate for the taxpayer. We are not proposing that a usable interface design can replace intermediaries in these cases, but only in those where the design is artificially setting a barrier for a large group of users. We have found in the survey's results that, this website is being underused in general, but highly used by intermediaries. In further studies we will study if, a more usable design has any effect in the level of intermediation.

The benefits of usability on businesses are well studied [15] in terms on costs for the company. However, it is needed more research on the, social, economical, and political costs. Negative social effects may be associated with the poor usability of a mandatory and universal system, since it may be creating the need of contracting intermediaries. An unusable e-government website, far from benefiting all citizens, could be nurturing an elite class whose only advantage over the rest is that they know how to use a system. Obviously, contracting intermediaries is costing money, becoming a negative externality for taxpayers. This cost could be avoided designing a universally usable system.

Although we could not measure political costs, dissatisfaction with this website is certainly creating political costs to the government. Frustration with the government's inefficiency is likely to have an impact on elections.

### 6.2 Lessons Learned for a Methodology of User-Centred Design of e-Government

This real case set an opportunity for putting into practice the user-centred design methodology in the setting of an e-government project. We took advantage of an existent website to measure users' satisfaction and expectations on a real basis. The evaluation of the actual site was used as the first step of the development cycle.

The novelty of the user-centred design on an governmental setting is the challenge of designing for all, that is, the need of universal usability. In this case, the user interface should be designed to address the needs of the less skilled, and, in the process, making it easy for all. This decision may imply that the design is not as efficient as the expert users may need. After all, balancing different needs and options is what design is all about.

Users' participation during the design process increases their feeling of being taken into account, and stimulates the adoption of the new system [16].

## 7 Conclusion

E-government promises to offer useful and efficient services to all citizens. This may be challenged by an availability digital divide. However, poor usability may introduce an artificial digital divide, and actually plays a role in the behaviour of citizens. The difficulty of use of a necessary e-government system may encourage citizens to hire intermediaries, instead of adopting the system. We studied the phenomenon with respect to a concrete e-government Website, designed for universal use. We have found that there exists a huge gap on computer expertise and education level between actual users and potential users of the Website, the gap strongly corresponding to the gap observed between intermediaries and direct users. As a conclusion, we guessed that the majority of trained users are intermediaries. Furthermore, a relation of correspondence has been also established between expertise and satisfaction. The immediate implication is that the design serves the purpose of intermediaries, and does not serve accurately an universal audience. Further research is needed to explore the relationship between design and intermediation, and decide if the problem is exclusively related with usability, or there exist other hidden factors.

A possible solution for this situation is to implement a citizen-centred approach, that involves representative users from the beginning of the design process. However, this task seems not to be simple, because the definition of suitable user profiles [19], or system intermediaries [18] appears to be difficult when dealing with intermediation. Some new paradigms in profiling are necessary.

## References

1. Andersson, A. , Grönlund A.. e-Society Accessibility: Identifying Research Gaps. In: Proceedings of EGOV 2003, LNCS 2739. Springer, Prague, Czech Republic (2003).
2. Barnard, E., Cloete, L.,.Patel H.. Language and Technology Literacy Barriers to Accessing Government Services. In: Proceedings of EGOV 2003, LNCS 2739. Springer, Prague, Czech Republic (2003).
3. Bicharra Garcia, A. C., Maciel, C., Bicharra Pinto, F.: A Quality Inspection Method to Evaluate E-Government Sites. In: Proceedings of EGOV 2005, LNCS 3591, Springer, Copenhagen, Denmark (2005).
4. Davenport, E., Horton, K.: A Social Shaping Perspective on an e-Governmental System(ic) Failure. In: Proceedings of EGOV 2004. LNCS 3183. Springer, Zaragoza, Spain (2004).
5. De, R.. E-Government Systems in Developing Countries: Stakeholders and Conflict. In: Proceedings of EGOV 2005, LNCS 3591,. Springer, Copenhagen, Denmark (2005).
6. Finquelievich, S., Lago Martnez, S., Jara, A., Baumann, P., Prez Casas, A., Zamalvide, M., Fressoli, M., Turrubiates, R.: Los Impactos Sociales de la Incorporacin de TIC en los Gobiernos Locales y en los Servicios a los Ciudadanos. Los Casos de Buenos Aires y Montevideo. In: Cliche, G., Bonilla, M. (eds.): Internet y sociedad en América Latina y el Caribe. IDRC-FLACSO Ecuador, Quito (2001).

7. Flak, L. S., Moe, C. E., Sæbø, Ø.: On the Evolution of e-Government: The User Imperative. In: Proceedings of EGOV 2003. LNCS 2739, Springer, Prague, Czech Republic (2003).
8. Hewett, Baecker, Card, Carey, Gasen, Mantei, Perlman, Strong, Verplank: ACM SIGCHI Curricula for Human-Computer Interaction. www.sigchi.org/cdg/cdg2.html (March 14th, 2006).
9. Instituto Nacional de Estadsticas y Censos, Argentina (INDEC): Censo Nacional de Población, Hogares y Viviendas del ao 2001. www.indec.gov.ar/webcenso/index.asp (March 14th, 2006).
10. Kim, T. H.,Im, K. H.,Park, S. C. Intelligent Measuring and Improving Model for Customer Satisfaction Level in e-Government . In: Proceedings of EGOV 2005. LNCS 3591, Springer, Copenhagen, Denmark (2005).
11. Kuniavksy, M.: Observing the User Experience: A Practioner's Guide to User Research. Morgan Kaufmann, San Francisco (2003).
12. Lassnig, M., Markus, M.: Usage of e-Government Services in European Regions. In: Proceedings of EGOV 2003. LNCS 2739, Springer, Prague, Czech Republic (2003).
13. Lohr, S. L.: Sampling: Design and Analysis. Duxbury Press (1999). From: Palmas Velasco, O. A. (tr.): Muestreo: Diseño y Análisis. International Thomson Editores (2000).
14. Mayhew, D. J.: The Usability Engineering Lifecycle: a Practitioner's Handbook for User Interface Design. Morgan Kaufmann, San Francisco (1999)
15. Mayhew, D. J., Bias, R. G.: Cost-Justifying Usability. Morgan Kaufmann, San Francisco (1994).
16. Nielsen, J.: Usability Engineering. Morgan Kaufmann, San Francisco (1993).
17. Nuñez Miñana, H.: Finanzas Públicas. Macchi, Buenos Aires (1994).
18. Pasic, A., Sassen, A. M., Garcia, A. e-Government Intermediation. : Proceedings of EGOV 2004. LNCS 3183, Springer, Zaragoza, Spain (2004).
19. Pieterson ,W., Ebbers, W., Van Dijk, J. The Opportunities and Barriers of User Profiling in the Public Sector In: Proceedings of EGOV 2005. LNCS 3591,Springer, Copenhagen, Denmark (2005).
20. Posch, R. What Is Needed to Allow e-Citizenship? In: Proceedings of EGOV 2002.. LNCS 2456, Springer, Aixen-Provence, France (2002).
21. Shneiderman, B.: Welcome to the conference. In: Proceedings of the Conference in Universal Usability. ACM, New York (2000).
22. Wang, L., Bretschneider, S. , Gant, J. Evaluating Web-Based E-Government Services with a Citizen-Centric Approach. In: Proceedings of HICSS '05, the 38th Annual Hawaii International Conference on System Sciences, IEEE, Hawaii (2005).
23. Ware, C.: Information Visualization: Perception for Design. Morgan Kaufmann, San Francisco (2000) 107.
24. Yu, C-C.,Wang, H. : Measuring the Performance of Digital Divide Strategies: The Balanced Scorecard Approach. EGOV 2005: LNCS 3591,Springer, Copenhagen, Denmark (2005).
25. Yu, C-C.,Wang, H.: An Integrated Framework for Analyzing Domestic and International Digital Divides. EGOV 2004. LNCS 3183, Springer, Zaragoza, Spain (2004).

# Designing Government Portal Navigation Around Citizens' Needs

Rob Klaassen, Joyce Karreman, and Thea van der Geest

University of Twente, Dpt. of Communication Science,
P.O. Box 217, 7500AE Enschede, The Netherlands
http://www.gw.utwente.nl/cw/en/
{r.f.klaassen, j.karreman, t.m.vandergeest}@utwente.nl

**Abstract.** Improving the usability of government portal sites requires a focus shift from system to user in both research and design. Empirical studies into user behavior are needed to support decisions on navigation, labeling and search systems. This paper presents such a study. Through scenario based interviews data were collected on citizens' information seeking needs and search strategies. Additionally, server logs files were analyzed. The results demonstrated the complexity of the search task from a user perspective, and provided suggestions for user friendly portal design. On the basis of the results it was recommended that portal sites' navigation systems should be context-rich, and labeling systems should be adapted to citizens' colloquial speech.

## 1 Introduction

Providing government information, services, products and transactions electronically has the potential benefit of accessibility for a wider audience, political and administrative transparency and improved service delivery [1] [2] [3]. Many governments and public bodies have created general portal websites to give users (such as citizens and businesses) access to their information base. Such portals are aimed at making the information available to all citizens through one access point[1].

Research on providing access to large bodies of government information thus far has been predominantly sender-oriented. It has focused on methods for structuring the infobase and making individual items retrievable on the basis of precise specifications, or on the basis of taxonomies [4]. Although this work is important and fruitful, it puts the system at the center of the design process rather than the user (see also [5] [6] [7] [8]). This paper describes an effort to incorporate actual user behavior into the (re-)design of a government portal site.

The project was an initiative of ICTU, a Dutch ministerial agency that coordinates the portal site Overheid.nl ("Government.nl"). *Overheid.nl* is a portal that provides access to all online available government information, provided by a wide range of national, regional and local institutions and agencies. The website

[1] General portals are to be distinguished from personal portals, that contain information that is specifically targeted at the user. (see [9])

M.A. Wimmer et al. (Eds.): EGOV 2006, LNCS 4084, pp. 162–173, 2006.

was subject to a major reconstruction, and the research results were to be used as input in that process.

## 2 User Support Systems in Portal Web Sites

The main function of a portal is to give access to a wide collection of sources. The information contained in these sources is organized through some kind of structuring principle. However, the internal organization of the information base is not very relevant to end-users, as it can differ greatly from the way it is presented on screen. On screen, users are presented with different aids and means that should give them a grip on both the contents and structure of the information base. We call these user support systems. Three different systems can be distinguished [10]: navigation systems, search systems and labeling systems.

**Navigation System.** The navigation system is the complex of aids and means that enable users to find their way within the website. Some systems closely follow the information organization, resulting in for instance hierarchical lists of clickable topics. Other systems are more user-oriented, e.g. organized around frequently asked questions[2], or scenarios derived from actual contexts of use. A navigating user is well supported when he or she:

- is able to construct a global representation of the websites contents;
- is aware of his/her location within the portal site;
- knows where he/she is coming from;
- knows where he/she can go from here.

To enable the users to orient themselves, the navigation system should provide appropriate feedback. This feedback can be presented in the interface in many different ways, for example as breadcrumbs (which display the followed link path on screen), or as a sitemap which offers an overview of the information available.

**Search System.** The search system is the complex of means and aids that enable users to search directly for relevant information within the portal. A search engine within the site (ideally) offers direct routes to the desired information, relieving the users from the chore of browsing through multiple pages. Search engines work on the basis of user input, often (combinations of) keywords. It therefore is critical that users' keywords match the terms used in the information or by the search system (cf. [4]).

**Labeling System.** The labeling system is the complex of labels (terms, names) that is used to identify parts of the site's contents and references. Names are used for buttons, menus, site maps and links. They must provide a good view of the content behind the label. Most importantly, they must be comprehensible, logical and clear for the user.

[2] In principle, FAQ's are user-oriented because they are based on actual information needs of real users. In practice however, this principle is often neglected, and many FAQ's primarily represent the messages the site owner wants to send out.

Each of the three types of user support system leaves the designer with many options and choices. Decisions about how to realize the support system in the interface cannot be made without a thorough knowledge of users' information seeking needs and skills. Our empirical study was aimed at collecting data to support those design decisions about user-oriented navigation, search and labeling systems for the Overheid.nl portal.

## 3 Research Questions and Data Collection

The following three research questions guided our study:

1. Which search strategies do citizens use? (navigation system and search system)
2. How do citizens phrase their search questions? (labeling system and search system)
3. Which navigation system is best suited to citizens' needs? (navigation system)

We collected our data using three methods: 1) a comparative analysis of portal websites, 2) scenario-based interviews with citizens, and 3) an analysis of server log files. Due to time pressure in the portal design process, we decided to use the three methods in parallel.

*Comparative Analysis of Websites*: Thirty portal websites were analyzed and compared for their application of navigation systems.

*Interviews*: Thirty Dutch citizens who had recently used an online government information resource were selected randomly and interviewed. In the interviews respondents were asked to describe their most recent online government information search action in detail. Then twelve realistic scenarios were presented to them. Each scenario ended with a question. The respondents were invited to imagine how they would go about finding the necessary information to answer the question. The topics for the twelve scenarios were selected on the basis of the most frequently used search terms from the log files.

*Log File Analysis*: Two large server logs files were analyzed. One log contained the search terms that people had entered in the Overheid.nl portal's search engine. The second file contained the search terms that were used by people who had reached the portal site via a general search engine (like Google). Both log files contained the queries conducted from January until October 2005. The first log file contained 54.654 search terms and phrases. The second one the 100 terms and phrases most frequently used by the users who found Overheid.nl through a general search engine. For the study, both lists were combined into one comprehensive list. The accumulated list covered 787.144 actual queries of users. Table 1 contains an overview of the research questions and the contribution of the methods to the various questions.

**Table 1.** Overview of research questions and methods

| Research Question | Method |
|---|---|
| Which search strategies do citizens use? | *Interviews*: to determine citizens' search strategies by analyzing accounts of their latest search action and accounts of scenario-based projected) search actions. |
| How do people phrase their search questions? | *Interviews*: to determine citizens' phrasing by analyzing the questions and search terms they produced for their latest search action and for the scenario-based (projected) search actions.<br><br>*Server logs*: to determine patterns in the search terms used, by clustering the contents of the log file.<br><br>*Server logs + interviews*: to assess search action success by entering citizens' search terms in Overheid.nl and Google, and analyzing the results. |
| Which navigation system is best suited to citizens' needs? | *Site comparison*: to gain an overview of frequently applied classifications in information organization.<br><br>*Server logs*: to determine the match between logged search terms at one hand and frequently applied classifications at the other hand. |

# 4 Results

## 4.1 Navigation Systems and Their Match with Citizens' Needs

Thirty portal sites (twenty-one commercial ones and nine portals of governments) were analyzed for the classifications applied. Information can be organized in many different ways. For example: government information about unemployment could be organized in themes like Work and Income, but also around life events (Losing your job), or around specific groups in the larger population (information for the unemployed). Table 2 shows the six most frequently applied classifications.

To determine which classification system would fit the information needs of Overheid.nl visitors best, we used the server log data. The 350 most frequently used search terms from the server log file were analyzed and matched with four of the six most used classifications from Table 2: Thematical/hierarchical, Current issues/news, Organizations/Government agencies and Life events. The search terms were not classified by target groups, because they could not be attributed to target groups with sufficient reliability. The search terms were not classified by FAQ either, as the Overheid.nl website does not contain such a list. The last column in Table 2 shows the degree of coverage of the four classifications that were analyzed. Coverage was defined as the percentage of the first 350 terms that could be matched with each of the classification systems.

The classification on the basis of Current issues/news covered the smallest percentage of all search actions. Obviously, citizens did not go out to find information on topics just because they were current. The thematic/hierarchical appeared to be the most effective organizing principle for a navigation system on a portal site.

**Table 2.** Classifications found in 30 portal sites

| Classification | Applied in # of websites *(n=30)* | Coverage (%) |
|---|---|---|
| Thematical/hierarchical | 28 | 85 |
| Current issues/news | 23 | 9 |
| Groups within population | 17 | *) |
| Organizations / gvt. agencies | 8 | 52 |
| FAQ | 3 | *) |
| Life events | 2 | 22 |

### 4.2 Citizens' Search Strategies

In order to document citizens' search strategies, we analyzed the accounts the respondents gave of their most recent search for government information. The results show that the citizens mostly have open and complex questions, which are framed within a very individual and personal context. Only a few respondents had searched for government information with a clearly defined, non-complex question like: "I needed a mutation form for the rent subsidy". Most respondents had less well-defined questions like: "I was looking for information from the CWI, UWV , the city of [E] and the Internal Revenue Service, because I wanted to apply for social security."

Most respondents (17 out of 30) used only online resources to find an answer to their question. All of them reported that their search had been successful. The other 13 respondents also used web sites, but in combination with other channels, like telephone, or visits to agencies.

In the second part of the interviews, respondents were asked to describe their projected search strategy for twelve scenarios. Table 3 shows the channels respondents chose as a starting point for their search. We distinguished between online and offline channels, and between government and non-government sources.

Table 3 shows that respondents considered to use online and offline channels, government and non-government sources to an almost equal extent. However, preferred channels varied greatly between scenarios. People appeared to select the channel they used on the basis of the type of question they were confronted with. For some scenarios most respondents knew immediately which government agency to contact. This was the case for questions concerning Passport renewal, Unemployment benefit, Tax return (young workers), Driving license renewal, Road taxation, and to a somewhat lesser extent also forTax return (mortgage deduction) and Rental subsidies.

In these cases, where citizens seemed to know their way, the preference for offline channels appeared to be stronger than in the less obvious cases.

The other scenarios posed more problems for the respondents. In these cases, respondents started their projected search mostly with non-government sources. For instance, the scenario about Child day-care subsidy inspired respondents to

**Table 3.** Preferred channels and sources for 12 scenarios

| Scenario | Online gvt[1)] | Offline gvt | *Total gvt* | Online other[2)] | Offline other | *Total other* |
|---|---|---|---|---|---|---|
| Driving licence | 5 | 25 | *30* | 0 | 0 | *0* |
| Passport renewal | 9 | 18 | *27* | 1 | 2 | *3* |
| Tax return (young workers) | 16 | 10 | *26* | 1 | 3 | *4* |
| Unemployment benefit | 10 | 13 | *23* | 2 | 5 | *7* |
| Road taxation | 16 | 6 | *22* | 3 | 5 | *8* |
| Tax return (mortgage deduction) | 10 | 10 | *20* | 2 | 8 | *10* |
| Rental support | 11 | 6 | *17* | 6 | 7 | *13* |
| School holidays | 7 | 4 | *11* | 8 | 11 | *19* |
| Minimum wages | 6 | 3 | *9* | 17 | 4 | *21* |
| Child day-care subsidy | 4 | 4 | *8* | 7 | 15 | *22* |
| Lifecycle saving plan | 5 | 1 | *6* | 15 | 9 | *24* |
| Physiotherapy | 1 | 1 | *2* | 10 | 18 | *28* |
| *Mean (n=30)* | *8* | *8* | *17* | *6* | *7* | *13* |

1) gvt = government
2) other = non governmental organization, or individual person.

contact a day care center, or their employers. It seemed, that in these scenarios our respondents were less certain that their strategy would lead to success.

We also looked at the strategies respondents followed when they thought to use online channels. Table 4 shows the preferred strategies for the twelve scenarios.

**Table 4.** Projected online search strategies

| Scenario | Most popular search strategy [1)] | |
|---|---|---|
| School holidays | Google | |
| Minimum wages | Google | |
| Child day care subsidy | Google | |
| Lifecycle savingplan | Google | |
| Rental support | Google | URL, site's SE |
| Physiotherapie | Google | URL, site's SE |
| Driving license renewal | URL, site's SE[2)] | |
| Tax return (young workers) | URL, site's SE | |
| Unemployment benefit | URL, site's SE | |
| Road taxation | URL, site's SE | |
| Tax return (mortgage deduction) | URL, site's SE | URL, browse site |
| Passport renewal | URL, browse site | Google |

1) When two strategies were equally popular, both are mentioned. 2) SE = Search Engine

Table 4 shows that for the less clear scenarios, people reverted to a general search engine (always *Google*). For the other scenarios, people came up with an URL they would try. Those respondents reported they would continue their search action by using the site's search engine. Only a few respondents expressed a preference for browsing the target site. This finding contrasts with earlier user studies for Overheid.nl; it might well be a test artifact. Our respondents did not actually carry out the searches; they only had to imagine what they would do once they got to the website. It might be hard to imagine that you would browse a site when you are not actually visiting it.

Many of our respondents' comments suggest that they relied heavily on the website's contents and interface to guide them further. For example: "I expect there will be some information", "I'm sure that new regulations are on the site. I also expect a heading 'allowances overview' there".

In conclusion, citizens appear to focus their search process on finding the right source: the institution or agency that they expect to be able to answer their question. Citizens show a slight preference for direct ways of communicating with these sources (i.e. by visiting or telephone). The more certain citizens are about their choice for a source to consult, the more apparent this preference becomes. When, however, citizens are uncertain about which institution they should turn to, they prefer to use general search engines like Google to find relevant web sites. Once citizens find a (possibly) relevant website, they expect the website to guide them. Further, they have high hopes of the effectiveness of -their search engine use.

### 4.3 Citizens' Phrasing of Search Questions

We have analyzed the way in which citizens translate their information needs into concrete search questions in two ways. First, we analyzed the log files for patterns in the registered search terms. Secondly we analyzed the search terms that respondents chose in the scenario based interviews. Thirdly, the most frequently mentioned terms were entered in two search engines: Google and the search engine of Overheid.nl. The results for each term in both search engines were evaluated.

**Log File Analysis.** The combined server log files contained 54.754 search terms. However, this accumulated list contains many synonyms and near-duplicates We clustered related terms on the basis of four criteria:

1. Literal or near literal copies of the search term
2. Literal or near literal copies of the search term, combined with other terms
3. Synonyms
4. Semantically related terms

This produced a much clearer picture of the information the users were trying to find. Single keywords do not reveal much about the sort of questions that users have when they enter them. Seeing these keywords in a context of related search terms made interpretation easier. Table 5 shows the first 11 clustered items, the number of search actions performed with the original term, the number of related terms and the number of search actions with the clustered terms.

Each popular term in the log files had a high number of related terms that appeared further down in the list. For instance, "cao" (collective labour agreement) was related to 1095 other entries. "Diefstal" (theft) had the lowest number of related terms: 56. The average number of related terms was 409.

**Table 5.** Overview of formed clusters of related terms

| Original term | # search actions with the original term | # clustered (related) terms | # search actions with the clustered terms |
|---|---|---|---|
| Government | 24.758 | 876 | 58.781 |
| Theft | 9.746 | 56 | 10.091 |
| Constitution | 8.901 | 151 | 11.639 |
| Cao[1)] | 8.277 | 1.095 | 21.174 |
| Ministries | 6.837 | 754 | 22.905 |
| Saving | 4.149 | 133 | 6.136 |
| Vacancies | 3.155 | 271 | 15.666 |
| Passport | 2.752 | 182 | 5.040 |
| Rental support | 2.276 | 706 | 12.641 |
| Bpr[2)] | 2.198 | 58 | 2.678 |
| Civil lawbook | 2.180 | 215 | 4.960 |
| Total | 75.229 | 4.497 | 171.711 |

1) CAO stands for Collective Labour Agreement
2) BPR stands for National Registry of Personal Information and Travel Documents

Clustering was found to be an effective and efficient method for determining the actual information needs of the portal's users. The most popular terms were single terms. They revealed little about the types of questions users had. Clustering brought context to these terms in the form of related multiple term queries. This is best illustrated by an example. The search term "passport", for instance was entered 2752 times. The cluster "passport" contained 183 related search terms, that were entered 5040 times in total. A closer examination of the passport cluster shows that the term passport actually may have stood for many different questions. Some users searched for information on the number of years a passport remains valid, others wanted to know how to renew their passport, yet others wanted to register their children on their passport; some wanted to know what to do when a passport gets damaged, or how to renew a passport from abroad etcetera. This type of information is very useful for web site designers. It can help them decide on the topics for (for instance) a portal site.

**Interviews.** From our interviews it became clear that respondents found it very hard to phrase usable search questions and search terms. Presented with the twelve scenarios hey seemed to regard the scenarios as the search questions, and they tended to copy search terms from the scenario text. Of course, in normal life citizens will not often search for information on the basis of a given scenario. However, it seems probable that they will still use terms and phrases that are closely connected to their own interpretation of the problem situation.

**Table 6.** Search results for 18 frequently mentioned search terms

| Ranking of first usable answer | Score (n=18) in Google | Score (n=18) in Overheid.nl |
|---|---|---|
| nr. 1 | 5 | 5 |
| nr. 2 to 5 | 4 | 2 |
| nr. 6 to 10 | 0 | 1 |
| nr. 10 to 50 | 2 | not analyzed |
| No usable answer within first 50 (Google) or first 10 hits | 7 | 10 |

Also, day-to-day language usage will dictate the search terms people will come up with. People will try any term they assume to be connected with their question. A good example was given by one of the respondents, when he reports one of his experiences: "I got a heavy tax assessment, and didn't understand how this could have happened. Had something to do with overhevelingstoeslag[3]". The respondent visited the Internal Revenue Service website, and tried entering the term in the site's search engine. The respondent: "It didn't help. I searched for about 5 to 10 minutes, and I didn't make any progress."

Our results show clearly that respondents lack the notion that in order to search successfully they have to translate their personal problem situation into phrases and terms that match those used by the chosen sources and channels (for instance a government portal website).

The respondents did not seem to have an adequate mental model of their search situation. They had no overview over the sources and channels they used, the information available within these sources, and the structure of these sources. Put simply: respondents only have their own context to bring to the search process. This context does not always correspond very well to the official jargon. For instance, one of the scenarios ended with the question: "How would you try to find out whether your daughter's low salary is legal?". While any civil servant would immediately connect this question to the term "minimum wage", less than half of our respondents made the same connection.

**Effectiveness of Citizens' Search Terms in Two Search Engines.** In our scenario based interviews we asked the respondents to name suitable search terms for each specific problem: terms that could be entered into a search engine. We tested all 18 search terms that were mentioned by more than 3 respondents, by entering them in Google and the current government portal website (overheid.nl). We were able to establish the quality of the search results ('the search engines' 'hits'), by determining if any of the 'hits' provided in the search results contained the information needed for solving the problem described in the scenarios. We analyzed the first 50 hits in Google. Since Overheid.nl is a government website it seemed fair to apply a stricter criterium. Therefore we decided to analyze only the first 10 hits in Overheid.nl.

[3] 'Overhevelingstoeslag' is a technical term in Dutch Tax Law.

Many of the 18 search terms that were frequently mentioned by the respondents delivered no results. However, several topics were well covered. "passport renewal", "driving license renewal", "holidays", "rental support", and "lifecycle saving plan" lead directly to the right information. These topics are either standard government themes, or themes that have been in the news a lot in recent times. With the other, less clear cut scenarios people are bound to be much less successful.

## 5 Conclusions

This paper demonstrates that user oriented research in the field of government portal design is valuable in two ways. First, observing actual users carrying out search tasks is a powerful method for obtaining insight into users' search strategies, information needs and search skills. Second, these insights provide designers with concrete suggestions for developing user friendly government web portals.

**Citizens' Search Strategies.** Citizens' search questions often are complex rather than simple. They can be characterized as follows:

- The question is open ended.
- There is more than one 'good' answer or adequate solution.
- The search question originates from a certain (personal) context. The search results have to be evaluated permanently for their applicability in this context.
- The search question is one step in an already complicated process. Often separate steps have to be taken towards separate government agencies or institutions.
- Different information sources have to be combined to produce an adequate answer.

The respondents' search strategies in this study resembled what Choo, Detlor & Tornbull (2000) have described as 'situated action'. Situated action means that search questions are not static througout the search process. Each newly found snippet of information can lead to the question being altered, refined and developed, or even to completely new questions.

The complex nature of search questions and the fact that information needs develop over the course of the search process have important consequences for portal website design. They have to enable users to constantly evaluate the relevance and applicability of the information they find on their personal situations. And they must enable users to decide whether to continue the search or not, and if so in what direction. Our results match findings from earlier studies [11] [12].

Our results also support claims that users benefit when answers are presented together with extra information about the context (see [13][14]). Users may not only be interested in the exact answer, but also in related information. Merely presenting users with seemingly 'exact' answers may not be sufficient to meet users' needs. Presenting them with related information may trigger a new search question, that the user could not have conceived by him or herself.

**Phrasing of Search Questions.** Citizens approach online government services, expecting to be understood when they use colloquial speech. Most citizens find it hard to translate their personal situation, or question into terms that match government vocabulary. They tend to use single general terms. Only a minority uses multiple term search phrases.

A closer analysis of log files shows that many different questions can be hidden behind one general term. Clustering terms provides some insight into this.

Not only is it difficult for citizens to phrase their questions 'correctly', even if they know the right terms, it still may lead them nowhere. The search engines, the most popular navigation system with our respondents, too often deliver disappointing results.

**Navigation Systems and Citizens' Needs.** Our study confirms that citizens need a lot of support when they search for information online. Many systems and tools can be used to provide this support. However, we believe that the following criteria should always guide government portal design.

1. Navigation systems should be contextually rich. Instead of merely presenting ordered lists of links and documents, the user should have the opportunity to evaluate the relevance of each link or document before opening it. Providing necessary context can be done by adding short descriptions to each link provided.
2. Labeling systems should be adapted to citizens' colloquial speech. The system should not only recognize government jargon. The issue of complexity of formal government language is relevant to more contexts than just portal sites. However, in an online environment citizens have to find the right terms themselves, and the dominance of formal language becomes even more problematic.
3. For a limited number of important and frequently searched for themes the portal site should provide information pages written in colloquial language, on which all information related to that theme is gathered, ordered and provided with context information. This will give users a necessary overview of all possibly relevant information. Moreover, they will not have to browse through endless lists of search results, without any guarantee for success.

The information pages should be made accessible both from the portal homepage and the site's search engine. The search engine should direct anyone who enters a related search term to these information pages. The clustered terms could be used in the design process as an indicator of possible content.

## References


1. European Union (2005, november) Ministerial Declaration on E-government: Transforming public services. Retrieved February 14, 2006, from http://www.egov2005conference.gov.uk/proceedings/.
2. Beyond e-Government. Report for the UK Cabinet Office. Maclean (VA): Booz Allen Hamilton.

3. West, D.M. (2004). E-Government and the Transformation of Service Delivery and Citizen Attitudes. Public Administration Review 64, (1). 15-27
4. Sacco, G.M. (2005). Guided Interactive Information Access for E-Citizens. In: M.A. Wimmer, R. Traunmller, Å. Grönlund, K.V. Andersen (Eds.). Electronic Government: 4th International Conference, EGOV 2005, Copenhagen, Denmark, August 22-26, 2005. Proceedings. Lecture Notes on Computer Science 3591. 261- 268.
5. Thomas, J.C., & Streib, G. (2003). The New Face of Government: Citizen-Initiated Contacts in the Era of E-Government. Journal of public administration: research and theory 13, (1). 83-102.
6. Klaassen, R.F. (2004). Voorlichtingskundig Ontwerpen: De Totstandkoming van Postbus 51-Campagnes [Public Information Design: The Development of Postbus 51 Public Information Campaigns]. Assen, The Netherlands: Van Gorcum Publishers.
7. Van der Geest, Th. (2004). Tax to the max: Designing Web Services for Ordinary People. Document Design 12, (2). 213-218
8. Deursen, A. van, Dijk, J. van, & Ebbers, W. Why e-Government Usage Lags Behind: Explaining the Gap Between Potential and Actual Usage of Electronic Public Services in The Netherlands (in press).
9. Tatnall, A. (2005). Web portals : the new gateways to Internet information and services. Hershey (PA). Idea Group.
10. Rosenfeld, L, & Morville, P. (2002). Information architecture for the World Wide Web. Beijing: O'Reilly.
11. Albers, M.J. (2004). Communication of Complex Information; User goals and Information Needs for Dynamic Web Information. Mahwah (NJ): Lawrence Erlbaum Associates, Publishers.
12. Choo, C.W., Detlor, B. & Tornbull, D. (2000) Web work : information seeking and knowledge work on the World Wide Web. Information science and knowledge management; vol. 1. Dordrecht, The Netherlands: Kluwer Academic Publishers.
13. Burger, J., Cardie, C., Chaudhri, V., Gaizauskas, R., Harabagiu, S., Israel, D., Jacquemin, C., Lin, C.-Y., Maiorano, S., Miller, G., Moldovan, D., Ogden, B., Prager, J., Riloff, E., Singhal, A., Shrihari, R., Strzalkowski, T.,Voorhees, E. and Weishedel, R. (2000), Issues, tasks, and program structures to roadmap research in question & answering (q&a), NIST DUC Vision and Roadmap Documents.
14. Lin, J., Quan, D., Sinha, V., Bakshi, K., Huynh, D., Katz, B., and Karger, D. R. (2003), What makes a good answer? the role of context in question answering, Proceedings of the Ninth IFIP TC13 International Conference on Human- Computer Interaction, Zurich, Switzerland.

# Municipalities on the Web: User-Friendliness of Government Information on the Internet

Menno de Jong[1] and Leo Lentz[2]

[1] University of Twente, Faculty of Behavioral Sciences,
Institute for Behavioral Research,
P.O. Box 217, 7500 AE Enschede, The Netherlands
m.d.t.dejong@utwente.nl
[2] Utrecht University, Utrecht Institute for Linguistics (UIL-OTS),
Trans 10, 3512 JK Utrecht, The Netherlands
l.lentz@let.uu.nl

**Abstract.** Municipal websites are highly visible manifestations of e-government developments. Though the content and functionality of these websites are rapidly expanding, the usability of municipal websites is as yet underexposed. This paper reports on the results of a scenario-based evaluation of 15 Dutch municipal websites. Despite the often positive scores of the websites in national checklist-based rankings, an overwhelming number of usability problems was found with each scenario. A qualitative description is given of two important categories of user problems: navigation and perspective-taking. Both problem categories suggest that a strict HCI perspective on website evaluation may not suffice: it is the interplay between context, content and interface that will be crucial for the optimization of municipal websites.

## 1 Introduction

The internet offers considerable advantages for the communication between municipalities and citizens. Some of these advantages relate to the possibilities of sharing municipal information. Thanks to the internet, it has become feasible to offer large amounts of information at relatively low costs, and to do so 24 hours a day and seven days a week. Visitors can easily and effectively be referred to relevant information provided by other organizations. And, finally, municipalities have the opportunity to add, update and modify information very quickly and relatively easily. Another cluster of advantages stems from the various aspects of interactivity: website visitors are enabled to react to, select in and interact with the information offered. As a result, web designers have numerous possibilities to support visitors' navigation through the information offered-starting with navigation aids such as links and menus but evolving to the principles of user profiling [1]-and to relieve them of potentially difficult subtasks such as calculating, searching or combining information. A third cluster of advantages relates to the principle of connectivity: the internet provides many possibilities to maintain a two-sided relationship between a municipality and its citizens. It is, in principle, possible for web visitors to react to the information provided, e-mail

M.A. Wimmer et al. (Eds.): EGOV 2006, LNCS 4084, pp. 174–185, 2006.

the municipality with specific questions, submit an application, fill out a form, or discuss topics with other visitors, to name a few of the possibilities. Other typical aspects, such as multi-modality (the possibility to combine text, pictures, video and sounds in a natural and meaningful way), are as yet underexposed on municipal websites but may grow out to be important features.

Many of the municipal services currently offered in the local town hall or in decentralized municipal offices will in the near future be offered via the internet. National governments have stimulated local authorities for some years to invest in internet communication, and have been successful doing so in many respects. In the Netherlands, for instance, all municipalities have their own website, and there is a tendency to provide more and more service and transaction possibilities on municipal websites. These positive developments may obscure the problems municipal web designers have to face in designing user-friendly websites. Particularly the complexity of the municipal organization – with its many departments, each with potentially different claims for their presence on the website – and the enormous amount of administrative information available place high demands on the designers' expertise in user-centered design.

In spite of the overall complexity of the municipal web design task, the managers of municipal websites are often confronted with a lack of administrative power and limited resources. Compared to commercial organizations, municipalities have been less flexible in making organizational adjustments in order to meet the new demands placed by the central role of the internet. Furthermore, only relatively small budgets were made available to realize this type of innovation.

Given these tensions, it will not be surprising that for years municipalities have mainly focused on accomplishing a presence on the internet and on expanding the content of their websites, without bothering too much about usability research. Formative evaluation studies, particularly those that focus on an in-depth analysis of user problems in actual use-situations, are still rare in the context of municipal websites. If municipal web designers are at all confronted with indications of the quality of their websites, this feedback is often based on checklist-based assessments [2,3] or questionnaires, which focus more on overall impressions than on specific usability problems in actual use situations.

In our view, it is crucial for the future success of e-government initiatives that the usability of municipal websites will be placed higher on the agenda, both by web designers and by academic researchers. An ongoing disregard of usability issues may seriously limit the practical usefulness of municipal websites, despite all new technologies, content and functionality that may have been developed. Academic research in this area could focus on two aspects: (a) the development and validation of usability evaluation methods for this type of websites [4,5], and (b) the lessons about effective website design that may be learned from the results of usability research [6]. The research described in this paper is an example of the latter.

In the following sections, we will discuss two important types of usability issues in municipal websites. We have conducted a scenario-based evaluation study of

15 municipal websites in the Netherlands, and compiled the results regarding two design issues: navigation and perspective-taking. Based on the results, we will describe some of the main problems municipal web designers have to face. Before discussing these problems, we will first briefly describe the scenario method we used.

## 2 Scenario Evaluation

There are many methods available to evaluate the usability of municipal websites. Some of these methods stem from the HCI usability tradition [7,8], others originate from the discipline of document design [9,10]. One of the most common approaches of usability testing is by using think-aloud protocols: participants are asked to perform a set of tasks using a website and are asked to verbalize their thoughts. The results give an indication of the overall degree of success of the participants, and, more importantly, of the exact problems they experienced during task performance. In this study, we used a related, but different technique: scenario evaluation.

A scenario evaluation is an expert-focused evaluation approach [9,11], which means that the website is not evaluated by a sample of the intended users, but by professional experts. The experts are given realistic usage scenarios and the assignment to walk through the website using these scenarios and to record all potential usability problems they encounter. The experts are thus placed in a surrogate user role, which appears to be beneficial for their sensitivity for user problems [12,13].

In brief, the method we developed consisted of five realistic usage scenarios, which covered a wide variety of possible use situations on a municipal website [cf. 12 for an exhaustive overview of the method and its backgrounds]. In each

*Johan is a young carpenter who started working a few years ago. He has earned some money and bought a small house in the city. Recently, he planned to build a dormer window at the back side of his house, as large as possible. He needs information about formal permits that may be required.*

Questions:
1. Does Johan have the obligation to apply for a permit for this renovation, or is it possible for him to start renovating without any formal actions?
2. Which procedures does Johan have to follow?
3. Who can Johan turn to in the case of any questions about the formal settlement of his renovation plans?

User characteristics:
1. Johan does not like to read long texts.
2. Johan is not a very skilled reader.
3. Johan is rather impatient. When he has found something which looks like an answer to his question, he will not look for more information elsewhere.

**Fig. 1.** Example of a scenario for municipal websites

scenario, three related questions had to be answered using the website. Besides, additional information was given about characteristics of specific audience segments. In Figure 1, one of the five scenarios used is presented.

The scenario information was accompanied by a heuristic with types of problems to focus on. The problem types were limited to: (a) navigation (clarity and effectiveness of the route between home page and destination page), (b) content quality (comprehensibility, correctness and exhaustiveness of the information offered), (c) transaction and interaction possibilities (possibilities to contact the municipalities or settle things on the website), and (d) the search support offered by the site map and the search engine.

The use of the scenario evaluation method resulted in the detection of many potentially serious usability problems. For each scenario, serious doubts were raised about the extent to which the websites actually help citizens in finding the information that is relevant for them. Below we will discuss two clusters of design issues. First we will present user problems with the navigation in municipal sites, and after that we will concentrate on problems with perspective-taking in the textual content.

## 3 Navigation and Structure

Navigation has always been one of the key issues in discussions about the quality of informational websites. There are many reasons why visitors like Johan – as introduced in the scenario presented in Box 1 – may get lost on a municipal website. Visitors are often confronted with confusing homepages that offer little orientation to the information offered deeper in the site, with link labels that are hard to interpret, search engines that offer unreliable results, and design choices in secondary pages that reinforce their feelings of disorientation. In this section we will discuss and illustrate some of the recurring categories of problems we found.

Figure 2 presents the homepage of the city of Dordrecht. For several years, the site has won the award for the best municipal website in the national competition for governmental websites. The ranking for this award was based on heuristics for user-friendliness, transparency, interactivity, services, and accessibility. Still, the use of the scenario method reveals many user problems on the website.

On the top bar of the page, seven primary links are shown. The link labels are:

- Current affairs
- E-counter
- Administration and organization
- Visit Dordrecht
- Economy and large projects
- Living and districts
- Education, work and welfare

This is how the city of Dordrecht organizes a huge amount of information into seven categories. Visitors of the site have to translate their specific question into one of these categories. In what category would someone like Johan search for information about building dormers? There are two options: it has something to do with the *administration* as well as with *living*. Experienced web surfers might know that municipalities organize many of their services in something like a *digital counter*. In their perspective, a building permit is a *product* delivered by the municipality. Having little experience with municipal sites, however, it is unlikely that Johan will relate his question to this *E-counter*. This is one of the main problems in municipal home pages: visitors have difficulties in making their first choice.

**Fig. 2.** Homepage of the city of Dordrecht (www.dordrecht.nl)

This problem is strongly related to the labels of primary links. What is the meaning of the word *living* in the link *Living and districts*? An ordinary dictionary presents twenty definitions for the main entry *living*. Does the combination with *districts* limit the range of possible meanings? The final link about *Education, work* and *welfare* might be another indication of a restricted meaning of *living*: probably the meaning of *living* is not working, education and welfare. One way to find out the meaning of *living* is to click on the link and see what happens. In the left frame of the new page another menu is opened with eleven new links. The first one is *Districts* and the last one is *Living*; in between, there are links like *Parking, Spatial zoning plans, Environment, Market, Safety,* and *Public space*. This is puzzling; the fact that these links are offered should mean that they are all aspects of *districts and living*. On the other hand, the first and the last link indicate that they do not belong to these aspects. What is the meaning of this second link Living? Has its meaning changed, just because it is no longer a primary link but a secondary link? Clicking on the secondary link *Living* results in a new menu with six links: *Looking for a house, Building new houses, Renovation, Figures and trends, Policy, Research into foundations.* Indeed, the meaning of the word *living* now seems to be restricted to things that have to do with housing: citizens are looking for houses, they want to change things, they worry about the foundation of their houses because of the groundwater level, and the administration does some monitoring and develops a policy in this domain. This is the section that Johan needs to read about the permit.

A positive interpretation of this procedure may be that a visitor like Johan probably will end up finding the information he needs. But more fundamentally, it shows that in order to navigate efficiently, visitors have to interpret complex link labels, wrapped up in combinations of apparently everyday words. In this website, the word *living* has two different meanings: as a primary link it indicates all things related to the environment people live in, and as a secondary link the domain is restricted to the houses people live in. These interpretations are by no means conventional for municipal websites. Every visitor has to find out what the specific meaning is in the context of the site he or she has entered.

Apart from these at first sight rather easy labels, web visitors are also confronted with many labels that immediately seem difficult to interpret, like *general information, on line, service, public information, themes*, etcetera. These labels are hard to grasp, because they are very general. A visitor with a specific question about building dormers will not be able to guess whether these links will disclose that information. Finally, we found unfamiliar link labels, which seem to have been specifically created in the context of municipal sites, such as *digital counter, e-counter, product catalogue, and digital city.* These labels may create problems as they will be new for inexperienced visitors of municipal websites; such visitors will not be able to make a correct interpretation of their meaning.

One way to avoid these difficulties, of course, would be by using the search engine. The site of Dordrecht presents the search engine on a rather unusual location: at the bottom of the screen on the left side. In most municipal sites, the search engine is exactly at the opposite side of the screen: the upper right corner, where Dordrecht shows a button with a question mark (indicating an index and a FAQ). One of the problems we encountered in the scenario evaluation was that municipal sites sometimes offer more than one search engine. In our view, visitors do not want to worry about which search engine works best for them, in particular because it is practically impossible to fully grasp the differences between, for example, *searching the website* and *searching the administrative information.* Other problems with search engines concern the search results. Some search engines appeared to produce highly unreliable results: they did not report any hits on a certain keyword, even though the menu-based navigation had yielded clearly relevant findings. Other search engines produced unorganized output without any indication of relevance (for instance, mixing up the municipality's decisions on earlier applications and the general public information about applying for a permit).

A way to escape all difficulties is by contacting the civil servant responsible for building permits. Many sites offer a contact link (in Figure 1 this link is indicated by an envelope on the *utilities bar*). After clicking on this link, a form opens that enables a visitor to react. Very often, it is entirely unclear to whom this reaction will be directed. In most cases the button is not related to the context of the web page: the contact link always opens the same general form, even though, in Johan's scenario, the visitor would in fact want to specifically contact the civil servant who is responsible for building permits. In many sites, the exact function of *react* or *contact* links is unclear.

Finally, visitors of municipal websites can also be expected to experience navigation problems due to a lack of cohesion and structure in the site. This also happens to Johan in our example, who may have found a link to the information about building permits, following *Living and districts > Living > Building or renovation > Building permit*. During the first steps of this sequence, the aforementioned original menu with primary links remains visible at the top of the screen; on the left side, an altering menu is shown containing links within the domain, whereas the body text is presented in a white font against a black background. After the final link, however, everything changes: no more menus, no more blue, red and black, no more utilities, but an orange background with a large grey table with many cells containing questions and answers on building permits. This information is presented in a new window, which completely covers the original window: visitors may be expected to become disoriented by these sudden changes, and may not understand why the browser menu with the popular back button does not work anymore.

To summarize, the scenario evaluation we conducted on 15 municipal websites resulted in a set of navigation problems that probably will not be easily detected using a set of heuristics as the national monitor for government websites does. These heuristics are formulated in terms of the presence or absence of specific features, like *contact* links and search engines, but they do not invite the evaluator to enter deeper levels of the site and to interpret the navigation process from the perspective of a user with specific information goals.

## 4 Content and Perspective-Taking

As important as the navigation support for municipal website users may be, presumably even more important is the quality of the textual and visual information offered on the website. After all, that is what the users are navigating and searching for. The problem of tailoring functional documents to the needs, preferences and expectations of readers has been a focal point of interest within the discipline of document design for years [14]. In thirty years of research, the responsibility for successful communication has increasingly been placed with the writer of documents (instead of the reader), and the criteria for document quality have evolved from correctness to readability, and from readability to a multi-faceted concept of effectiveness. High-quality documents are optimally geared to the users and their use situation in all respects.

Document design researchers have shifted their attention to the context of internet communication, discovering that presentation formats may have changed, that more research may be needed on document use in online environments, but that the basic principles of document design are still valid [15]. In this section, we will discuss the main problems we encountered in the municipal websites with the textual content.

There are many eye-catching problems with the content of municipal websites, which raise serious doubts about the care with which the web content is produced. First of all, we found many instances of text dumping on municipal websites: textual information that was made available without any processing to make it suitable for external target audiences, for instance in pdf-format. On the internet, in general, the distinction is disappearing between public information aimed at general audiences and administrative information addressing specific stakeholder groups. Citizens who are looking for public information about building permits must find their information among overviews of permits granted in the past. Citizens who want to submit a request for a sandpit or a skate ramp in their neighborhood must find their information among reports about the long-term spatial planning and the municipal identity.

We also found several cases of database-supported information, with a problematic fit between the database and the specific information. In the website of Dordrecht, for instance, the following overall structure is used for tables with information about, among other things, building permits (like in Johan's scenario), making an appointment with a civil servant, opening hours of the city hall, or local taxes.

- What does the product mean?
- What are the conditions?
- How to apply for the product
- How is your application handled?
- Tips and cautions
- Costs
- Time frame
- Delivery
- Bring along/send
- Result
- Legislation
- Authority
- More info available at ...
- Webforms (etc.)

Not all headings are used for all topics, but on every page, there are examples of headings that do not fit at all with the topic. For instance, few citizens will see a building permit as a *product*, and even fewer will think of an appointment with a civil servant or an overview of the opening hours of the city hall in those terms. If headings do not apply, they are perfunctorily answered in the overview. For instance, in the information about opening hours, it reads: *Delivery: Not applicable; Result: Otherwise; Authority: Not applicable.* This, of course, is a way of presenting information that may be convenient for the municipality, but is not compatible at all with the users' perspective.

In many cases, information is presented that does not correspond well with the heading. For instance, on the page about moving and emigration, the heading *What does the product mean?* is answered by an elaborate description of the various situations users may experience (moving from Dordrecht to another city in the Netherlands, moving within Dordrecht, or coming from abroad). In other cases, a lot of detailed information must be presented under a particular heading, which makes the table a rather awkward presentation format. For instance, in the table about local taxes, five different types of taxes are described in one of the table's cells (which amounts to almost 60 lines of text). The table structure leads to rather unstructured descriptions about the various taxes. A longstanding research tradition into instructive communication has resulted in the undisputed insight that effective instructions are chunked into small, task-related segments. Despite a full score of 100 % on usability in the national monitor, the site of Dordrecht does not comply with this guideline.

A more fundamental issue is that of perspective-taking. In government information, roughly, two perspectives may be competing with each other: (a) the policy and/or administrative perspective, and (b) the users' perspective. Information presented from the policy or administrative perspective is organized according to the municipal organization, the municipal policy or legislation; information presented from the users' perspective starts with possible needs of target audience segments. One of the basic guidelines in document design is that information should be presented from the users' perspective. Many examples of a violation of this principle may be found in municipal websites. In fact, the majority of the information is not presented from the users' perspective.

An example of such a violation is found when the building permit scenario is used on the website of Dordrecht. Johan wants to know whether he will need a building permit for his dormer window. Navigating through the website's menu he will come across the page *Building and renovation, regular building permit*, which essentially gives a description of the "product" building permit. In the product description, he will read that "a regular building permit is only needed for the larger building or renovation projects; for a number of smaller projects, only a light building permit or no permit at all is required." No information is given about the criteria for no vs. light. vs. regular building permits. Johan is referred to the website of the Ministry of Housing, Spatial Planning and the Environment, where he is linked to the homepage, without any clue as to where the desired information may be found. This is the e-variation of being sent from pillar to post.

On the website of Dordrecht itself, two other pages may shed some light on the criteria for building permits. At the bottom of the page, links may be found to the "products" *Building and renovation, light building permit, and Building and renovation, when do you need a building permit*? Both pages, however, do not contain any clue to decide whether a citizen will need a (regular or light) building permit or not. Despite the overall impression of offering many "products" on the municipal website, no useful information whatsoever is given for citizens who want to build or renovate a house. From the municipality's perspective, three products are offered; from the users' perspective only the scent of information is given.

These, of course, are only a few examples to illustrate our overall observation that the quality of information on municipal websites is often problematic. The scenario-based evaluation brought to light many problems with the applicability and the comprehensibility of the information offered. Scenarios facilitate the detection of such problems, because they force an evaluator to actually try and use the information offered. The information is actually put to the test.

## 5 Discussion

Researchers who want to evaluate the quality and user-friendliness of e-government initiatives, such as municipal websites, have many ways of collecting data to their disposal. One of the choices they will have to consider is whether to conduct a user-focused or an expert-focused evaluation [9]. A user-focused evaluation is conducted with a sample of users from the target audience, who may be given the assignment to use the website to answer specific questions or to judge the website. Many specific methods are available for this type of evaluation research. An expert-focused evaluation is conducted by professionals with specific expertise, for instance on internet communication.

Both types of evaluation have their merits and restrictions. One could argue that the real proof of user-friendliness is only given when a website is used or evaluated by potential users. They are the ones who can best tell us what works and what does not work for them on a particular website. On the other hand, in the daily practice of municipalities, an expert-focused evaluation approach is often more feasible than user-focused approaches. And the results presented in this article show that there are many serious problems with the user-friendliness of municipal websites that can be easily detected by experts. It is, in our view, disputable whether the quality of municipal websites in the present state warrants the use of user-focused evaluation approaches.

Another choice that must be made involves the goal of the evaluation. De Jong and Schellens distinguish three possible functions of formative evaluation research: (a) verifying the overall quality of an artifact, (b) troubleshooting in order to improve, and (c) facilitating a choice between alternative designs [10]. Their distinction is based on the assumption that one particular document or website is evaluated and optimized. In the context of municipal websites other, more generic, evaluation goals appear to be important as well. Evaluation research may be used to shed light on the ranking of websites (which corresponds to the verifying function), or to diagnose crucial problems users are confronted with when using municipal websites in general (which corresponds to the troubleshooting function).

The aforementioned Dutch national award competition for government websites is an example of the first approach. Based on a relatively simple set of heuristics, it aims at ranking the municipal (and other government) websites according to their quality. Another example of the same approach is the worldwide inventory of municipal websites by Holzer and Kim [16]. Such rankings probably stimulate local authorities to invest in their websites, in the hope of getting a higher ranking in the future. The goal of our study was not to rank sites, but to detect potentially serious usability problems in municipal websites. We have conducted a thorough evaluation of fifteen Dutch websites, and described the most conspicuous problems, not in quantitative terms but in terms of typical examples.

While arguments can be given for both types of research (ranking and diagnostic evaluation), we think that the condition of many municipal websites calls for more emphasis on the diagnostic research. In the early years of web design, the main concerns were getting a presence on the internet, solving technological problems, benefiting from technological possibilities, and expanding the content and the transaction possibilities on the website. In this situation, it is possible to monitor the progress of municipal websites using straightforward and relatively simple evaluation criteria. But the websites have evolved to a new phase: the quality of the website content is becoming increasingly important for the success of e-government products.

Both in the organizational practice of municipalities and in the academic research on e-government, the quality of textual and visual information on websites has been underexposed. Within municipalities, the problem of making available enormous amounts of information has dominated the web design activities. The monitoring instruments just check whether information is offered on a range of topics without attention for the user-friendliness of the navigation process and the presentation of the information. An evaluation based on user-focused scenarios, performed by experts in website usability, results in clear sets of problems that give a realistic indication of problems that citizens will experience while using these sites.

In addition to our plea for more qualitative and diagnostic analyses of the user-friendliness of municipal website, we would also like to stress that a refinement of the website ranking methods would be an important improvement as well. The heuristics used for assessing municipal website quality often focus on rather superficial characteristics of the website. That is, they strongly focus on general interface characteristics, and neglect the context(s) in which the website will be used in, and the content offered on the website. The resulting scores may easily obscure the view on the user-friendliness of particular websites. Many of the user problems on municipal websites, whether they affect the navigation or the perspective-taking, deal with the interplay between context, content and interface. Scenarios, in principle, offer the possibility to develop a more context- and content-sensitive approach for the ranking of municipal websites. Instead of qualitative problem descriptions, accompanying quality metrics may be developed that provide an indication of website effectiveness. It may, for instance, be possible to formulate metrics based on (a) the amount of uncertainty for each scenario regarding the first link to use on the homepage, (b) the number of links to follow from the homepage to the information that is needed, (c) the quality of the information offered, (d) the exhaustiveness and selectivity of the search engine results, etcetera. The development of a scenario evaluation method that may also be used for ranking purposes is, in our view, one of the challenges for future research.

## Acknowledgment

This article is based on a research project that was financed by the Netherlands Organization for Scientific Research (NWO). It forms part of the research program. "Society and the Electronic Highway".

## References


1. Pieterson, W., Ebbers, W., Van Dijk, J.: The opportunities and barriers of user profiling in the public sector. Lecture Notes in Computer Science, 3591 (2005), 269-280
2. Garcia, A.C., Maciel, C., Pinto, F.B.: A quality inspection method to evaluate e-government sites. Lecture Notes in Computer Science, 3591 (2005), 198-209
3. Maciel, C., Noguiera, J.L.T., Garcia, A.C.B.: An x-ray of Brazilian e-gov web sites. Lecture Notes in Computer Science, 3585 (2005), 1138-1141
4. Gray, W.D., Salzman, M.C.: Damaged merchandise? A review of experiments that compare usability evaluation methods. Human-Computer Interaction, 13 (1998), 203-261
5. De Jong, M., Schellens, P.J.: Toward a document evaluation methodology: What does research tell us about the validity and reliability of evaluation methods? IEEE Transactions on Professional Communication, 43 (2000), 242-260
6. Spool, J.M., Scanlon, T., Schroeder, W., Snyder, C., DeAngelo, T.: Web site usability: A designer's guide. San Francisco, CA: Morgan Kaufman. (1999)
7. Nielsen, J.: Usability engineering. San Diego: Morgan Kaufman (1993)
8. Dumas, J.S., Redish, J.C.: A practical guide to usability testing. Revised edition. Exeter: Intellect (1999)
9. Schriver, K.A.: Evaluating text quality: The continuum from text-focused to reader-focused methods. IEEE Transactions on Professional Communication, 32 (1989), 238-255
10. De Jong, M., Schellens, P.J.: Reader-focused text evaluation: An overview of goals and methods. Journal of Business and Technical Communication, (1997), 402-432
11. Sweeney, M., Maguire, M., Shackel, B.: Evaluating user-computer interaction: A framework. International Journal of Man-Machine Studies, 38 (1993), 689-711
12. De Jong, M., Lentz, L.: Scenario evaluation of municipal Web sites: Development and use of an expert-focused evaluation tool. Government Information Quarterly, 23 (2006), in press
13. Hinds, P.J.: The curse of expertise: The effects of expertise and debiasing methods on predictions of novice performance. Journal of Experimental Psychology: Applied, 5 (1999), 205-221
14. Schriver, K.A.: Dynamics in document design. Creating texts for readers. John Wiley, New York (1997)
15. Spyridakis, J.H., Wei, C., Barrick, J., Cuddihy, E., Maust, B.: Internet-based research: Providing a foundation for web-design guidelines. IEEE Transactions on Professional Communication, 48 (2005), 242-260
16. Holzer, M., Kim, S.T.: Digital governance in municipalities worldwide. An assessment of municipal web sites throughout the world. The E-Governance Institute/ National Center for Public Productivity, Rutgers State University of New Jersey, Newark, NJ (2003) http://www.andromeda.rutgers.edu/egovinst/Website/Report%20-%20Egov.pdf

# “Open Choice”: Improving Public Sector Performance with Process Reorganization Methodology

Martin Brüggemeier[1], Angela Dovifat[2], and Klaus Lenk[3]

[1] FHTW University of Applied Sciences, Dept. of Public Management, Treskowallee 8, D-10318 Berlin
bruegge@fhtw-berlin.de
[2] Graduate School of Modern Governance, Faculty of Social Sciences and Economics of Potsdam University, Am Park Babelsberg 14, D-14482 Potsdam
dovifat@fhtw-berlin.de
[3] University of Oldenburg, Ret. Chair of Public Administration
D-26111 Oldenburg
lenk@aon.at

**Abstract.** E-Government is not yet harnessed to New Public Management so as to act as a driver for the modernization of public services. To change this situation, a comprehensive framework for modernization processes based on Business Process Reorganization is proposed. It combines a modularization of operative processes in public administration with a fresh look at the institutional framework in which such processes are executed. This framework supports the creation of new networked forms of service production and delivery.

## 1 Introduction

Public sector modernization in Germany has not made much progress during the last two decades. The general impression is one of slimming down the public sector in a haphazard and fairly unintelligent way. A closer look reveals some interesting improvements, especially at the local level. International comparisons are often unaware of these developments since public administration in Germany is almost entirely located not at the federal level, but at the Länder and local levels. Yet it can safely be said that so far neither “New Public Management” (NPM) nor E-Government drove public sector reform in a significant way.

The German version of NPM, the so-called “New Steering Model” concentrated on introducing modern management instruments, on financial management, and on cutback management [1]. Also, in the wake of NPM introduction, a diffusion process of some improvements in government / citizens relationship occurred. Increased responsiveness and better service quality were achieved, mainly through local government one-stop shops [2]. Based on the traditional correctness of German public administration, these improvements contribute significantly to

M.A. Wimmer et al. (Eds.): EGOV 2006, LNCS 4084, pp. 186–194, 2006.

an overall image of a good and reliable public administration where reform needs were not felt as acutely as in other countries. IT was instrumental in bringing about these benefits at a very early stage already [3], but these were unrelated to NPM. Interestingly enough, the new wave of using IT which "E-Government" as a movement brought about, hardly took notice of these achievements, concentrating as it did on the introduction of online transactional services which so far are hardly accepted by the public.

We feel that broadening the concept of E-Government to include the IT use in the back office, which in Germany has a tradition of several decades, would help to harness the more recent wave of E-Government to what remains of NPM, thereby opening avenues for a big step of change in the public sector [4].

Such a work programme of activating the potential which E-Government offers for "producing more with less" can take advantage of recent conceptual efforts from "(New) Public Governance" and from "Virtual Organization", which pave the way for new types of production of public services [5]. These include a radical version of the purchaser / provider split which NPM introduced. Governments should no longer strive to produce all public services themselves. As much as possible, they should limit their role to guaranteeing that a certain service is produced and delivered, in the spirit of "steering, not rowing". The concept of "Gewährleistungsstaat" (the "ensuring" state) points into this direction [6]. Here, the role of the state changes from a service provider to a service ensuring function.

This perspective suggests new institutional arrangements for the delivery of public services. These have been discussed already for a while [7], but the enabling role of IT for designing new types of production arrangements hardly played a role in these discussions.

## 2 E-Government – Key for Optimizing Public Performance?

With regard to this situation, the present spate of E-Government projects appears as a mixed blessing. There is much talk about improving public administration by making use of technology, but action seems to be mainly technology-centred, not yet bridging the gap between technological prowess and practical reform requirements. In order to advance toward meaningful reforms, the current path of E-Government development has to be left. In a recent research project, we analysed six advanced E-Government projects [8]. This research indicated very clearly that actors in the public sector did not yet recognize the full potential of IT for the reorganization of public services. E-Government solutions still focus on the relationship between single organizations and clients in order to automate processes and to offer online access for citizens and enterprises.

To change this situation, we propose a methodology for improving public performance based on E-Government. Its main characteristics are an interorganizational perspective, and a holistic, business-driven approach to process reorganization.

In the German context, the interorganizational view is of particular relevance. Public services are often delivered in a fragmented way. Up to four levels of administration may take part in producing a public service: The federation (Bund), the state level (Bundesländer), and two tiers of local authorities (Landkreise, Gemeinden). On each level, service production and delivery may be further distributed among several agencies and departments. Every organization has its own duties, responsibilities and competences. Therefore it is not very useful to re-engineer processes in every single unit leaving out other actors.

The focus on business process reorganization allows for a more fine-grained approach to matters of institutional choice and of policy instruments than the one taken so far. In our approach, the basic unit about which make-or-buy decisions are made, is no longer an entire "product" or service, i.e. a "task" together with the entire business process required to fulfil that task. The focus is put not on an entire business process, but on its modules. Such modules are obtained by analysing a process in detail.

## 3 "Open Choice": The Reorganization Methodology

The methodology developed in our "Open Choice" framework consists of four steps [9] (see fig. 1).

**Step One:** The first step is an evaluation of whether or not a business process for producing a service should be maintained or not. The main questions here are: What is the rationale of a given business process? Which task or political programme is it meant to fulfil? Is it effective, in the sense of producing the politically desired impact? Also, the consequences of abolishing this process altogether or of stripping it of its character as "public service" are assessed. This step should prevent from optimizing processes, which are no longer useful because of changed circumstances or expectations.

**Step Two:** In a second step, the "as-is" processes to produce a service are analysed and new (ideal) processes are designed. Such a design may be a very rough one, not specifying a process step by step, with every single activity needed to carry it out. The design may also be refined in iterations. The comprehensive form of process analysis and design, which is the hallmark of "Open Choice" takes place on the level of business logic, and it is fully IT-independent. Starting from the end of the process, i.e. the desired outcome (impact) of the process, process stages are identified and the process is broken down into modules. The methods used partly stem from software development, but are chiefly based on a business view and on socio-technical process design. They are sketched in the next section.

**Step Three:** In step 3, the results of step 2 – the "to-be" process broken down into several modules – will be used to make decisions about who could deliver such modules. Institutional choice in this sense therefore is about potential "module suppliers", and not about allocating or outsourcing entire tasks (business processes). Each module may require specific competences, know-how or target

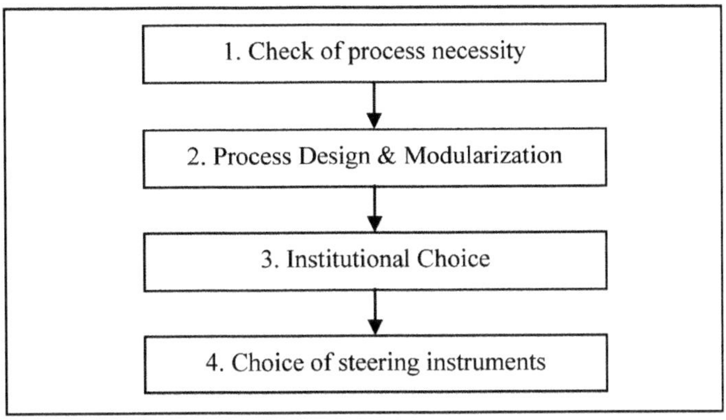


**Fig. 1.** The "Open Choice" Framework

group knowledge, and this should guide its allocation to a competent actor. Modules which are strategically relevant may remain under public responsibility, whilst less important modules may be handed over to other private or public organizations which harbour specific skills. In accordance with transaction cost theory, the criteria for the decision to outsource a module or to reallocate it to a different body within the public sector are "strategic relevance" or "specificity" (a.o. due to specific resources needed that can only be used to carry out the activity under consideration) [7]. So far these criteria had been suggested as a guide to decisions about the outsourcing of whole tasks. We use them instead at the level of process modules.

In addition to using transaction cost theory, the choice of the right institution for delivering a service could also start from the interests of citizens, customers, or political considerations. Typically, several private or public organizations are involved in public business processes. Many public services relate to privately produced services or products. To build a house, a building permit is needed, driving a car requires that car to be registered first, etc. Such public services could conceivably be delivered by suppliers of these goods, e. g., architects or car sellers. They could become part of the public production chain, in new forms of "electronic mixed economies".

An important feature of step 3 is the introduction of an inter-organizational perspective. Increasingly, public services are produced and delivered in "networks of interaction" which constitute public service grids. To support the formation of such grids, process reorganization needs to cross the boundaries of single organizations.

**Step Four:** The fourth and last step of the model is the choice of adequate management tools for steering and controlling the new process, which may span several organizations. The potential of IT to minimize information asymmetry by forwarding information or data immediately should also be used to create interorganizational steering systems. Furthermore, new contractual relationships have often to be invented, and self-steering by involved actors has to be harnessed to the overall aim of the process at stake.

## 4 Step Two of "Open Choice" in Detail: The Basics of Business Process Design in the Public Sector

In the following section, we concentrate on step 2 of the model, i.e. the design and modularization of business processes. Most important here is a holistic understanding of such processes. To reach such an understanding, many commonly used methodologies are only partly useful, since they are aimed at the elicitation of requirements for software engineering or customization. Due to the restricted languages which they employ, important elements of human action and of the context in which processes are executed, are not mapped. This observation does not only apply to software engineering but also to methodologies which, like ARIS[10], explicitly address a technology-independent business logic. Their ultimate aim is building software, with an underlying view toward automating business action as far as possible. This may yield good software for many types of processes, especially many auxiliary (housekeeping) processes, where the human element is less important. But in the case of more complex business processes, both at an operative and a managerial level, these methodologies do not support a holistic optimization of the entire work situation which results from the complex socio-technical interplay of human and computer activities. Hence our search for something more fundamental which combines the four most important paradigms of E-Government, as enumerated in [11]: Citizen service, Process Reorganization, CSCW, and Knowledge Management.

The following elements are characteristic for process analysis and design within the "Open Choice" methodology [9; 12]:

- The large *variety of business process types* in the public sector is acknowledged. Typically, operative processes (and partly also managerial and auxiliary processes) range from being predominantly executed by human actors to fully automated. The present situation is such that only highly automated processes (addressed here as "production processes") are adequately supported by IT, whilst decision-making processes and also many services processes, which both rely on situated human action, are supported only in a very rudimentary way.
- *Process modelling* takes place in several "*swimming lanes*", according to the number of key actors (or organizations) involved. An example is given in fig. 2, which shows several stages of a typical process for granting a license. Taking the standpoint of key actors involved is particularly important in the public sector, since very often the goal of IT support is not a narrow optimization of the work of one agency, but of a multi-polar network involving other agencies, citizens, private business etc. In order to avoid sub-optimization and to find a satisfactory way of producing public goods, the perspectives of individuals (costumers), the society (represented by politicians and public administration departments) and service providers (commercial or non profit) have to be taken into account.

- Rough *reference models* are built for typical public sector processes like licensing, registration, person-related services, welfare transfers, etc. The characteristics of every stage of these models are analysed.
- Based on the process stages identified in these reference models, a *modularization* of these processes takes place, which yields "building blocks" of different size (granularity). The building blocks obtained through modularization may either be fully automated (like e.g. an online payment system or any other web service not involving human agency) or based on a tandem-like human-machine interaction of different intensity. The latter is particularly relevant for decision-making activities at the operative level of the public sector, which are of the most various kinds. Finding the right criteria for this modularization is a particularly difficult task. Professional criteria (e.g. legal training of a role incumbent) or considerations of job enrichment may be important here. Other criteria are the suitability of a module for full automation, as well as the ease of plugging together ("articulating" or "orchestrating") various modules in a "Legoland" fashion so that the required business process will be constituted.
- The automated modules thereby obtained (building blocks), as well as the supporting IT part of human-machine tandem modules, are subject to *multiple use* in a large number of business processes. This should considerably promote IT support for the very large number of public business processes required by law, which seldom occur, as well as for more or less complex ad-hoc processes.
- Modules can be recombined so as to constitute *human-machine service grids* of different size and shape. This will allow to automate parts of those types of business processes which so far were entirely carried out by human actors. Advances in the field of service economy point into this direction [13]. This could considerably promote a mass customization in the service sector. Health care is one field where this type of thinking is already fairly advanced.
- Eventually, this approach paves the way towards a *Government Application Integration* on a wider scale. Such an integration will not only take place at the technological level, but includes an organizational integration (which is dealt with in detail at step 3 of "Open Choice").

## 5 An Example: The Car Registration Process

The connection between process reorganization and institutional choice, which is the most salient feature of "Open Choice" shall be illustrated by an example: The German car registration process. Up to now, car registration in Germany is done by car registration departments, which are part of the local district (county) authorities (Landkreise) or of the bigger, district-independent cities. This makes for a total of more than 400 units. Every district or district-independent city administrates its own car numbers. A citizen moving from one district to another is obliged to change her car registration number into one from the new district. This practice requires the actualization of the car registers in every district,

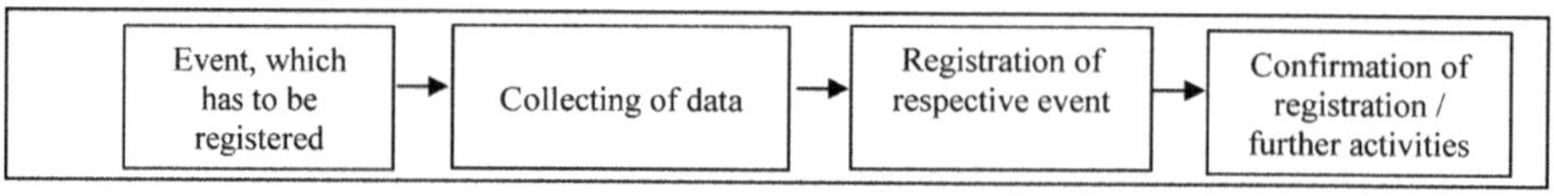


**Fig. 2.** Reference phases of a registration process

as well as communicating the new car number to insurance companies, to tax authorities and to the federal central car register. Proposals already abound for streamlining this rather complicated process, but so far they have failed due to a complicated federal-state legal situation. Almost all of these proposals took a view which was centred on one or more focal organizations, so that the question of centralization (one national car register) became the main discussion point.

The "Open Choice" approach starts with a rough reference model of a registration process (see Fig. 3). It then proceeds to map the contributions of various actors in "swimming lanes". Actors in the car registration process are: the buyer of a new car (or the person moving from one district to another), the seller of the car (private person or trader), the insurance company, the tax authority, the federal traffic authority, and the local car registration department. Fig. 4 shows the relevant "swimming lanes".

The process shows that several organizations collect the same data. Such data could easily be shared, and the burden of data reporting for various actors (including the citizen) minimized. One way of achieving this would be the creation of a pooled register which can be accessed by all organizations involved.

| | Event, which has to be registered → | Collecting of data → | Registration → | Confirmation of registration / further activities |
|---|---|---|---|---|
| **Car buyer** | • Buys a car<br>• Transfer of personel data to the vendor<br>• Choice of insurance | • Transfer of personal data about the purchase and insurance to tax authority, local car registration department, and traffic authority<br>• Completes data if requested | | • Collects confirmations of insurance company, tax authority and traffic authority<br>• Pays requested tax<br>• Pays insurance fee |
| **Car vendor** | • Sells a car<br>• Collects personel data about the buyer to draft contract | | | |
| **Insurance company** | • Offers general insurance information<br>• Needs car registration information to offer adequate insurances in general<br>• Collects data about buyer and car to draw up insurance offer | | | • Collects insurance fee |
| **Local car registration department** | • Offers general registration information | • Collects personel data about buyer, insurance and car<br>• Check of completeness of data according to the reqirements of registration | • Registers new car | • Hand out of car number and registration documents<br>• Answers inquiries of insurance companies, police, etc. |
| **Tax authority** | • Offers general tax information | • Collects personel data about buyer and car<br>• Check of completeness of data to calculate motor-vehicle tax | • Calculates individual tax fee | • Collects tax fee |
| **Traffic authority** | • Needs information about number and type of cars in use | • Collects data about buyer and car<br>• Check of completeness of data according to the reqirements of plannings | • Completes own planning data | • Confirms driving allowance to buyer |

**Fig. 3.** Reference phases of car registration process

Creating centralised registers is a demand often heard. The true advantages of "Open Choice" lie in the multi-polar view upon the entire process. Taking this view prompts new ways of redistributing tasks among the actors involved. Only those parts of the process which require a public authority to be in charge will be kept with the registrating authority (which may be either a central or a decentral one). Other actors could concur both in the production of different steps like forwarding information and in service delivery. New forms of an "electronic mixed economy" may result from this.

## 6 Conclusion

The suggested approach places public business processes into a wider context. Analysing public business processes at the level of modules prompts interesting solutions for delivering public services. It supports developing an interorganizational view taking into account the expectations of customers and other stakeholders. Solutions obtained in this way will exhibit a higher degree of customer orientation and of efficiency than the usual E-Government projects.

In our view, modularization is the missing link for bringing the philosophy of "steering, not rowing", which is underlying NPM, to bear on government reality. Especially important in this respect is the fact that strategically important process modules could remain under public responsibility whilst for other modules of the same (type of) process, the advantages of private production know-how could be exploited. In cases where a summary evaluation would lead to the conclusion that a certain task can no longer be financed, our analytical approach would conclude that outsourcing certain modules of that process would be sufficient to ensure its economic viability, so that the spiral of downgrading and privatising public services could be stopped, without removing responsibility from public actors.

Also, specialization among several actors, e.g. local governments, in the form of "shared services" can be encouraged; economies of scale can be realised at the level of single process modules without there being a need for the organization in charge to divest itself of the entire process.

"Open Choice" bridges the gap between public administration theory and practice, on one side, and the potential of IT and E-Government, on the other. Contrary to more superficial approaches and to much lip service being paid to harnessing NPM and E-Government for the modernization of the public sector, it focuses on operative business processes and thus on the daily practice of public administration, without giving in to restricted representations of that practice.

## References

1. Reichard, Christoph: Local Public Management Reforms in Germany. In: Public Administration 2003, pp.345-363.
2. Jann, Werner; Bogumil, Jörg; Bouckaert, Gert; Budäus, Dietrich; Holtkamp, Lars; Kißler, Leo; Kuhlmann, Sabine; Mezger, Erika; Reichard, Christop; Wollmann, Hellmut (Hrsg.): Status-Report Verwaltungsreform. Eine Zwischenbilanz nach zehn Jahren, Berlin 2004.

3. Lenk, Klaus: Electronic Service Delivery – A Driver of Public Sector Modernization. In: Information Polity 7 (2002), pp.87-96.
4. Lenk, Klaus: Der Staat am Draht, Electronic Government und die Zukunft der öffentlichen Verwaltung – eine Einführung. Berlin 2004.
5. Schuppan, Tino: Strukturwandel der Verwaltung mit E-Government. Eine Untersuchung am Beispiel von Kreis und Gemeinde. Berlin 2006.
6. Reichard, Christoph: From Public Management to Public Governance: A Changing Perspective in the German Public Sector. In: Mussari, Ricardo (Ed.): Dal Management Pubblico alla Governance Pubblica, pp. 31-46, Siena 2004/2005.
7. Naschold, Frieder; Budäus, Dietrich; Jann, Werner; Mezger, Erika; Oppen, Maria; Picot, Arnold; Reichard, Christoph; Schanze, Erich; Simon, Nikolaus: Leistungstiefe im öffentlichen Sektor, Berlin 1996.
8. Brüggemeier, Martin; Dovifat, Angela; Kubisch, Doreen; Lenk, Klaus; Reichard, Christoph; Siegfried, Christine: Organisatorische Gestaltungspotenziale durch E-Government, Berlin 2006.
9. Brüggemeier, Martin; Dovifat, Angela: "Open Choice" – Reengineering der öffentlichen Leistungserstellung auf Basis von E-Government. In: Klischewski, Ralf; Wimmer, Maria (Ed.): Wissensbasiertes Prozessmanagement im E-Government, Münster 2005, pp. 28-42.
10. Scheer, A.-W.: ARIS – Vom Geschäftsprozess zum Anwendungssystem, 3rd Ed., Berlin 1998.
11. Lenk, Klaus; Traunmüller, Roland: Broadening the Concept of Electronic Government. In: Prins, J. E. J (ed.), Designing E-Government, Amsterdam 2001, pp. 63-74.
12. Lenk, Klaus: Prozessmodelle für E-Government, In: Kubicek, Herbert et Al. (Eds.): Innovation@Infrastruktur, Heidelberg 2002, pp. 199-205.
13. Meier, Roland; Piller, Frank T.: Systematisierung von Strategien zur Individualisierung von Dienstleistungen, Arbeitsbericht Nr. 24 des Lehrstuhls für Allgemeine und industrielle Betriebswirtschaftslehre, TU München 2001.

# Organising Municipal e-Government Systems: A Multi-facet Taxonomy of e-Services for Citizens and Businesses

Yannis Charalabidis, Dimitris Askounis, George Gionis, Fenareti Lampathaki, and Kostas Metaxiotis

Decision Support Systems Laboratory, National Technical University of Athens, 9 Iroon Polytechniou Str., 15773 Zografou, Greece
{yannisx, askous, gionis, flamp, kmetax}@epu.ntua.gr

**Abstract.** As various e-Government initiatives are being realised throughout the world, policy makers and technology providers start to understand the importance of local administration e-Government systems. Municipalities are often the closest Point of Service for the European citizens and enterprises, having access to all the necessary information and usually providing the final service – a fact that makes their e-Services Portals a very important link in the e-Government chain. After attempting a positioning of municipality systems in the taxonomy of e-government systems, the present paper analyses the set of services that a Municipality Portal should be able to offer, focusing on eEurope – related capabilities. Based on this service directory, a multi-faceted classification mechanism is proposed, leading to an extendible taxonomy of e-Services to be offered by Municipality e-Government systems. A set of facets is analysed for each service, allowing for classification of services based on their main purpose, nature, orientation, means of provision, and various functional characteristics. Through populating, viewing and querying this multi-faceted classification, the design, development, deployment and impact assessment of e-Government systems for Municipalities can be systematically addressed.

## 1 Introduction

As the information society services advance, more and more e-government systems start their operation, promising to revolutionize government and its interaction with citizens, businesses and other authorities. The use of digital government enables people to have immediate access and response, reducing the number of personal interactions with government employees, realising the concept of "putting citizens online instead of in line" and aiming for up to 45% of productivity savings in the public sector [1]. Moreover, e-Government information systems are available in a 24 X 7 basis to all citizens, non – discriminating on age, colour or gender.

As indicated in the latest European Commission Report on Electronic Public Services [2], the availability and sophistication of e-Government systems in

M.A. Wimmer et al. (Eds.): EGOV 2006, LNCS 4084, pp. 195–206, 2006.

the European Member States concerning the 20 Basic Public Services presents a high standard deviation, of more than 20%, from the average of 42%, indicating that there are still many steps towards full availability of online services This fact is a lot more important when regional and municipality systems are taken into consideration, where the availability is significantly lower and almost 20% of the administrations do not even have a basic internet site, as the same Report points out. As indicated in Figure 1, the Registration Cluster, which contains 5 electronic services that are usually performed through a regional / local administration site, has a quite low sophistication level, ranging from 15% to 80%.

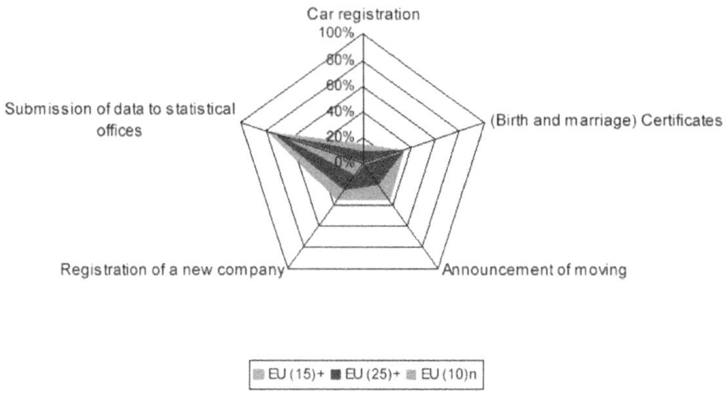


**Fig. 1.** e-Government full online availability of basic public services – Registration Cluster [2]

This lag of Municipality e-Government systems has many causes, stemming both from the non-determined policy drivers behind such systems as well as from the technological gap between the current status and the envisaged future capabilities. On the other hand, most of the current research attention is paid to Central e-Government Systems (such as Income, Corporate Taxation or VAT systems), not targeting the relevant Regional and Local Administration systems.

In order to effectively pursue the creation and successful operation of Municipal e-Government systems, further analysis of the offered services has to be made – leading to the definition of target infrastructure, new means of service provision, establishment of the technical challenges and in-depth analysis of the expected impact for the public administration and the collaborating citizens / enterprises. In the following chapter, an analysis of the electronic services to be offered by the municipalities is being performed, based on the non-digital services already provided by European and North American Municipalities as well as on the relative research being performed at European and International level.

After the initial analysis, a complete taxonomy is proposed in Chapter 3, introducing the various taxonomical dimensions for Municipal e-Services in the form of a Service Description Record stating the various facets of a service. Based on this taxonomy, various decisions can now be made concerning the various targeted configurations, the possible deployment steps, the needed interconnections with existing systems, as well as security, personalisation and authentication issues.

Conclusions and further research directions are presented in Chapter 4, giving way to discussion on the various patterns identified at the problem and solution space as well as on the most important issues to be overcome for the Municipalities in their quest for electronic service provision.

## 2 Discovering the Electronic Services of Municipalities

In order to provide a taxonomy of services that should be offered by European cities, the list of the "20 Basic Public Services" as defined by the eEurope+ initiative [3] was first taken into consideration. Analysing this list of electronic services, information on the nature of services, the orientation and the providing administration (central or local/municipal) have been identified, as depicted in Table 1.

Each of the above Basic Public Services has a prescription of the Target Sophistication Level, based on the e-Government Stage Description as proposed by Layne and Lee [4] and adopted by the European Commission, which applies

**Table 1.** Categorisation of the 20 Basic Public Services, based on the definitions of eEurope [3]

| Service | Service Orientation | Providing Administration | Cluster | Target Level |
|---|---|---|---|---|
| 1. Income Tax | Citizens | Central | Income Generating | 4 |
| 2. Social Contribution for Employees | Businesses | Central | Income Generating | 4 |
| 3. Job Search | Citizens | Central / Local | Returns | 4 |
| 4. Corporate Tax | Businesses | Central | Income Generating | 4 |
| 5. Social Security Benefits | Citizens | Central | Returns | 4 |
| 6. Value Added Tax (VAT) | Businesses | Central | Income Generating | 4 |
| 7. Personal Documents | Citizens | Central | Permits & Licenses | 3 |
| 8. Registration of a New Company | Businesses | Central / Local | Registration | 4 |
| 9. Car Registration | Citizens | Central | Registration | 4 |
| 10. Data Submission to Statistical Office | Businesses | Central | Registration | 3 |
| 11. Application for Building Permission | Citizens | Local | Permits & Licenses | 4 |
| 12. Custom Declaration | Businesses | Central | Income Generating | 4 |
| 13. Declaration to the Police | Citizens | Central / Local | Returns | 3 |
| 14. Environment-related Permits | Businesses | Local | Permits & Licenses | 4 |
| 15. Public Libraries | Citizens | Central / Local | Returns | 4 |

**Table 1.** (*Continued*)

| Service | Service Orientation | Providing Administration | Cluster | Target Level |
|---|---|---|---|---|
| 16. Public Procurement | Businesses | Central | Returns | 4 |
| 17. Birth and Marriage Certificates | Citizens | Local | Registration | 3 |
| 18. Enrolment in Higher Education | Citizens | Central | Permits & Licenses | 4 |
| 19. Announcement of Moving | Citizens | Local | Registration | 3 |
| 20. Health-related Services | Citizens | Central | Returns | 4 |

for Central, Regional and Municipal Administration and refers to the following levels:

- *Level 1 – Information only / static content.* In this level, formal but limited web presence of the municipality is established through a website which provides users with static information regarding the municipality, events and press releases, in addition to contact information with public officials regarding offered services.
- *Level 2 – One-way Interaction / dynamic content.* Municipality's web presence begins to expand. Content consists of dynamic information that is frequently updated and links to other pages are provided. Information regarding the procedure for completing a service and the required supporting documents are also available online in downloadable format.
- *Level 3 – Two-way Interaction.* Services ranked in level 3 offer citizens and businesses the potential to submit a request form, which they can download or fill-in through the portal and then receive the service deliverable in person. In services of this level, security and personalisation issues must be regarded. This is the maximum target level for services that are sensitive to personal presence and identification.
- *Level 4 – Full Case Handling.* This level refers to services that are fully handled. Submission of requests and supporting documents, status interrogation and retrieval of service deliverables is accomplished online from beginning to end. Security, authentication and personalisation issues are critical. This is the target sophistication level for most services.

Leaving behind the 20 Basic Public Services monitored by the eEurope initiative, the contemporary European municipality is currently offering a variety of services towards citizens, businesses, visitors and other agencies. These services are described in National laws and directives, usually under the Ministry of Interior or Internal Affairs of each member state. Although current studies indicate that there does not exist a unified framework setting the scope of municipal services worldwide [5], a common denominator can be found by studying both certain country frameworks and reports [6, 7, 8] as well as existing research projects and country initiatives within the European research space of e-Government [9, 10, 11, 12]. Such an analysis yields the following 7 main Municipality e-Service Categories:

- *News and Announcements*, usually oriented towards all citizens, visitors, enterprises or collaborating agencies. The non-electronic form of such services is fulfilled through ordinary bulletin boards, local newspapers or even radio / TV broadcasting stations. Also, the municipalities usually re-emit news originating from other sources.
- *Municipality Organisation Information*, relating to the internal structure of the City administration / Mayor Office, Municipal Agencies and Organisations including their history and evolution. These services may be provided through telephone, printed informative leaflets, static or dynamic web sites.
- *Municipal Information for the Public*, covering a vast range of subjects like: transportation means and destinations, places of interest for tourists and citizens, cultural events, recreational and athletic sites. These generic information services are usually offered towards citizens, visitors, businesses or other collaborating agencies.
- *Services to Citizens*, where the majority of interaction with the public is taking place. Major sub-categories for these services include Citizen Registry Services (various registrations and certificates, voting rights and centres, births, marriages, deaths), Land Registry Services (registrations, permits, urban planning, road construction, land usage zones), City Property & Income Services (local taxes and fees, water supply, drainage, cemeteries), Security, Cleaning and Waste Management, Employment, etc.
- *Services to Businesses*, providing enterprises of the city / region with various Registrations, Permits and Certificates, ways to pay Local Taxes and Fees, ways to participate in Public Procurement and Tenders [13].
- *Participative Services* for citizens, through offering the ability for meeting Public Officials, discussing with them on various subjects of common interest, even taking part in open Forums or informal voting campaigns.
- *Information and Knowledge Discovery Services*, where citizens, enterprises or visitors are assisted in finding necessary information within the various forms of municipal knowledge bases – be them in digital, paper or tacit/oral form.

In their effort to provide the above services, even in the standard non-electronic way, the Municipalities have deployed various internal back-office systems ranging from plain document creation, registration and management to complex Finance and Accounting, Geographical Information and other Management Information Systems, that now will need to become interoperable with Municipal Portals for Electronic Service Provision. The impact of this complete, one-stop, interoperable infrastructure is then projected as very important for citizens and businesses [14].

## 3 The Municipality e-Services Taxonomy

In order to classify the various electronic services towards citizens, businesses, visitors or other agencies, a Service Classification Record has been constructed that contains all the Taxonomy – related information of a Service, not aiming at the description of its internal structure. There are 11 identified "facets" for a service, taking values from restricted lists of values, as shown in Table 2.

**Table 2.** The Service Classification Record

| Service | Service Title / Description |
|---|---|
| Facets: | |
| Service Category | Classification Hierarchy (is-A classification tree), as defined in Chapter 2 |
| Service Nature | Informative / Income Generating / Registration & Certificates / Permits & Licenses / Returns / Participative / Information Discovery |
| Service Orientation | Citizen / Business / Agency / Visitor |
| Providing Organisation | Central / Regional / Municipal administration |
| Target Level of Sophistication | Information / One-Way Interaction / Two-Way Interaction / Full Handling |
| Means of Service Provision | Internet Browser / Web Service / Mobile / Telephone / ITV |
| Interoperability Need | Municipality / Regional / Government Systems / Other |
| Authentication Need | None / Basic / Advanced |
| Security Need | None / Basic / Advanced |
| Legal & Statutory Framework coverage | Whether the service is covered by legal framework (Yes / No) |
| Self-inclusiveness | Whether the Service is self-inclusive – OneStop (Yes / No) |

The purpose of each facet is to describe specific external characteristics – that is not related to internal structure, organisation or functionality – of an e-Service in a methodological and coherent way that will facilitate the organisation of the services into a taxonomy. The objective of this taxonomy is to provide the means – based on its structure – for the systematic analysis of the contained services in order to deduct conclusions regarding, for example, the impact of the provided services, the required sophistication level and others. To this end each facet that has been identified describes in a straightforward way – through a set of predefined values – certain defining features of the service, specifically:

- The Service Category facet describes the categorization of the service based on the seven distinct categories of municipality e-Services that have been identified in chapter 2 (e.g. News and Announcements, Municipality Organisation Information, Services to Citizens, etc). The value of the facet is in the form of a full path of an is-A classification tree. That is, each value comprises the entire path from the root of the tree (which is always the name of the category) to the level of the tree before the leaf (which is the service name). For example the value of the facet for an e-Service delivering the Announcements of the Mayor would be: "News and Announcements/News" (for the specific classification tree from which the previous value arises may refer to figure 3 of this paper).

- The Service Nature facet represents the category of needs, both at the level of municipal, regional and central administration that the service covers. For example, information (informative), creating income of the administration (Income Generating), etc. "The Service Orientation facet identifies the group of potential users for the service and defines the extent to which a user friendly approach oriented to "life events" or "business episodes" needs to be adopted. Naturally, every electronic service can have several types of users but the specific facet aims at identifying the group of users that the service is mainly targeted based on the functionality that the service provides or the needs it facilitates.
- The Providing Organisations facet identifies the level of administration that provides the service – Central, Regional and Local (Municipal).
- The Target Level of Sophistication facet states the level of service provision according to the four stages that have been adopted by the European Commission – Level 1 Information only, Level 2 One Way Interaction, Level 3 Two Way Interaction, Level 4 Full Case Handling.
- The Means of Service Provision facet identifies the technological infrastructures that are needed in order to access the service – Internet Browser, Mobile, Telephone, ITV.
- The Interoperability Need facet describes the requirements for systems interoperability between the different levels of administration that must be achieved in order for the service to be realized effectively. The values of the specific facet may vary significantly according to the service – from the interconnection of a frond-end website to a relatively simple back office information system at municipality level to advanced Application to Application interconnection among ERP systems at Central, Regional and Municipal level.
- The Authentication Need facet identifies requirements for user authentication about the provided service and matches them to existing methodologies – e.g. basic authentication needs which are covered through User ID/Password infrastructures.
- The Security Need facet, similarly to the Authentication Need facet, matches security needs to the underlying technologies that are used – e.g. advanced security level through HTTPS/SSL.
- The Legal and Statutory Framework facet yields whether the legal and statutory framework is in place to provide the necessary legal coverage to the electronic service. Furthermore, the present facet also identifies specific guidelines that stem from legal issues and affect technological aspects for the electronic provision of the service.
- The Self Inclusiveness facet refers to whether an e-Service can constitute a One Stop Shop or not. That is, it yields whether the service can conclude its purpose by its own mean or it has to call upon other services to do so.

Each of the above defined facets serves a specific purpose towards the realisation of a Municipal e-Government Service Point (e.g. a City Internet Based Portal). Three main purposes are served by the various facets, as depicted in Figure 2:

- The definition of the User Interface of a municipal portal or service, by means defining the basic structure of offered services and their positioning in the navigation tree. The main Service Category, the Service Nature, the Service Orientation and the Means of Service Provision are views of a service that assist the definition of the needed usability for the internet user.
- The definition of the needed Functionality and Integration, server by the facets of Target Level if Sophistication, Interoperability Need, Providing Organisation and Self-Inclusiveness of the provided service.
- The definition of the needs for data protection, ensuring the authenticity of the transmitted information by end-users and the need for following specific

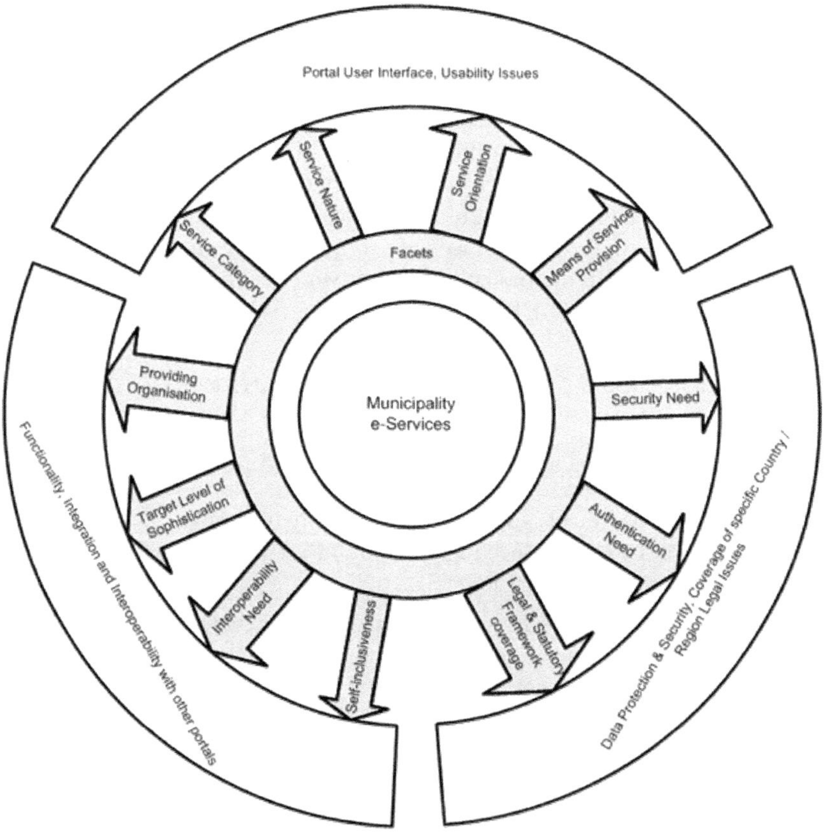


**Fig. 2.** How the various view-points of a Service contribute to the e-Government Services Definition

regulations imposed by the National Legal and Statutory Framework for the services in question. The facets of Security Need, Authentication Need and Legal & Statutory Framework coverage are contributing towards this direction.

## 4 Populating the Multi-facet e-Services Taxonomy

Following on the work of discovering and analyzing Municipality-related services, more than 100 electronic Municipal Services have been inserted in the above multi-facet classification scheme, yielding a taxonomy that can now be viewed and queried, providing interesting input for the construction of Municipal e-Government Systems and related electronic service centres. As depicted in Table 3, where an example of service classification is provided for two usually requested services from Citizens and Businesses, the descriptive means of the classification scheme is adequate for quickly categorising the analysed service.

**Table 3.** Example Classification for Birth Certificate and Local Enterprise Tax Payment

| Service | Birth Certificate | Local Tax Payment |
|---|---|---|
| Facets: | | |
| Service Category | Service to Citizens / Citizen Registry / Registry Certificates | Services to Businesses / Payments |
| Service Nature | Registration & Certificates | Income Generating |
| Orientation | Citizen | Business |
| Providing Organisation | Municipal administration | Municipal administration |
| Target Level of Sophistication | 4 : Full Handling - Certificate Issuing | 4: Full Handling – On-line Payment |
| Means of Service Provision | Internet Browser | Internet Browser |
| Interoperability Need | Municipality Back Office Systems / Registry | Municipality Systems / Accounting. Banking Systems. |
| Authentication Need | Basic (ID / Password) | Advanced (Digital ID) |
| Security Need | Basic (HTTPS) | Advanced (HTTPS/SSL) |
| Legal & Statutory Framework coverage | Yes (Certificate Form, Required Information to be submitted) | No |

The resulting overall populated taxonomy is maintained in a relational DBMS, providing the basic mechanisms for creating, updating, modifying and deleting service nodes as well as for querying the whole multi-facet tree. An extract of the graphical representation of the overall scheme, along the Service Category and Service Nature facets is provided in Figure 3.

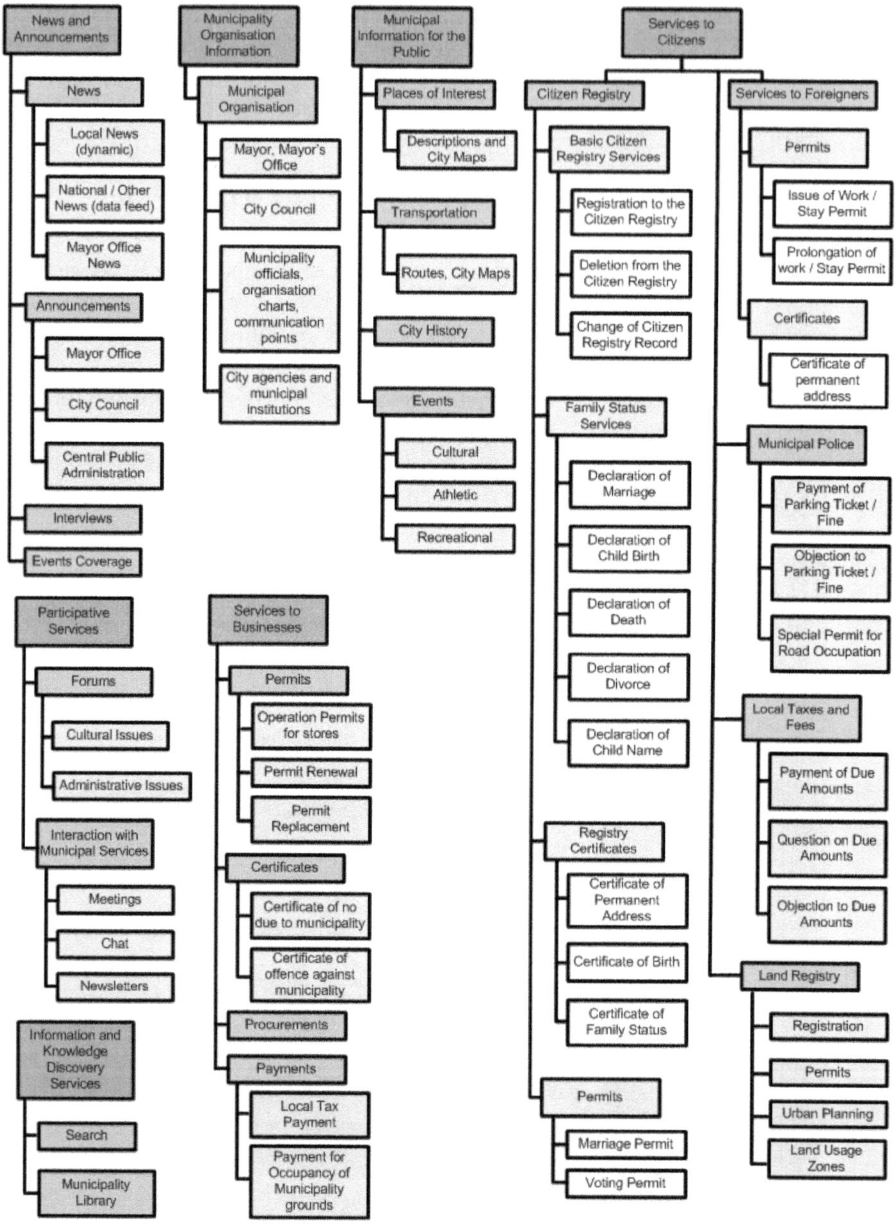


**Fig. 3.** Extract of the taxonomy, along the Service Category and Service nature facets

## 5 Conclusions

The Multi-Faceted classification of electronic services for municipalities proposed in this paper aims to facilitate the design, development, deployment, impact assessment and redesign of e-Government systems for Municipalities. Using the classification of e-Services for Municipalities, a spherical view of the services to be deployed for citizens or businesses on a municipal level can be obtained, including the level of sophistication that can be achieved, the requirements for security, personalisation and authentication and the means of service provision. The approach can be used for issuing guidelines for the presentation layer of municipality systems, the integration / interoperability needs or the level of security and conformance with existing legal and statutory regulations at national and regional level.

By populating and using the proposed multi-faceted taxonomy, comprehensive answers can be provided to questions such as:

- Which services we need to deploy for citizens or businesses on a municipal level?
- What level of sophistication should be achieved for each service?
- What are the requirements for security, personalisation and authentication for the various services?
- What are the means for provision that we need to deploy?
- Which can be the basis for the redesign of deployed services in a municipality?

Future work along the proposed approach includes classifying architectures and proposed solutions, based on best practices, for the implementation of the various services at each sophistication level, thus providing a taxonomy of the solution space in municipality e-government systems.

Furthermore, the analysis of the foreseen impact of each service, for the municipality organisation and the users of the service – be them citizens or enterprises – will allow for a cost/benefit analysis supporting the decision on what services to deploy.

Finally, providing the entire taxonomy and query output in XML schema will allow for easier exchange of data in a universal format, further assisting the population and the extraction of results from such a taxonomy.

## References


1. McKinsey Quarterly, "Putting citizens online, not in line", April 2001.
2. eEurope, "Online Availability of Public Services: How is Europe progressing? Web based survey on electronic Public services", Prepared by Capgemini, European Commission – Directorate General for Information Society and Media, 3 March 2005.
3. European Commission / eEurope Initiative: "List of Basic Public Services", http://www.eu.int/information_society/eeurope/2002/action_plan/pdf/basicpublicservices.pdf.
4. K. Layne, J. Lee, Developing fully functional e-government: A four-stage model. Government Information Quarterly, 18, pp. 122-136, 2001.

5. M. Holzer, S. T. Kim, "Digital Governance in municipalities worldwide. An assessment of municipal Web sites throughout the world. The E-Governance Institute/National Center for Public Productivity, State University of New Jersey, Newark, NJ. Retrieved February 03, 2006, from http://www.andromeda.rutgers.edu/egovinst/Website.
6. "Public Administration Services", North American Industry Classification (NAIC), Canadian Statistical Agency, Retrieved February 16, 2006 from http://stds.statcan.ca/english/naics/2002/naics02-title-search.asp?criteria=91.
7. Charles Kaylor, Randy Deshazo, David Van Eck, "Gauging e-government: A report on implementing services among American cities", Government Information Quarterly 18 (2001) pp. 293-307.
8. "Local e-government Services List- LGSL", Local e-Government Standards Body, Office of the Deputy Prime Minister, ODPM, UK, Retrieved February 15, 2006 from http://www.localegov-standards.gov.uk/.
9. "E-governance Practices, Strategies And Policies Of European Cities", Intelcities FP6/IST Project, European Commission, 30 July 2004, Retrieved from http://www.intelcitiesproject.com.
10. "Municipal Services – Analysis, Requirements and Usage scenarios", eMayor FP6/IST Project, European Commission, 20 December 2004, http://www.deloitte.com/dtt/section_node/0,1042,sid%253D28578,00.html.
11. "e-Government Interoperability Framework Version 6.1", Cabinet Office, UK e-Government Unit, Retrieved February 15, 2006 from http://www.govtalk.gov.uk/documents/eGIFv6_1(1).pdf.
12. "Definition of Municipal eGovernement Portals", Greek Digital Strategy 2006-2013, Retrieved December 2, 2005, from http://www.infosoc.gr.
13. Y. Charalabidis, V. Karakoidas, S. Theotokis, D. Spinelis: "Enabling B2B Transactions over the Internet through Application Interconnection", in P.Cunningham, M. Cunningham (eds.), "eAdoption and the Knowledge Economy: Issues, Applications, Case Studies", IOS Press 2004.
14. Y. Charalabidis, D. Askounis, G. Gionis: "A Model for Assessing the Impact of Enterprise Application Interoperability in the typical European Enterprise", Interoperability for Enterprise Software and Applications Conference, I-ESA'06, March 22nd – 24th, 2006, Bordeaux France.

# Time Model for Managing the Dynamic of Normative System

Monica Palmirani and Raffaella Brighi

C.I.R.S.F.I.D, University of Bologna,
via Galliera 3,40100 Bologna, Italy
{palmiran, brighi}@cirfid.unibo.it

**Abstract.** An important need is arising in the eGovernment era: to produce updated law corpora in order to improve democracy and justice in the European new enlarged system. This article intends to propose a formal model for managing the dynamic of the norms in the time with twofold objectives: provide a set of rule for designing a legal information system able to produce in automatic way the law in force; guarantee the main principles of the theory of law such as coherence of the normative system, certness of the legislative order, knowness of the law in force.

## 1 Introduction

Several problems are affecting the Italian legislative system, and also some European legislative system, due to the impossibility to manage in the proper way the legislative system in the dynamic and efficacy way:

- *normative overproduction*: the Italian law corpora is composed of about 50.000 law acts since 1861 to now. Especially in the last 60 years, during the republican period, the proliferation of production reaches a pathologic situation;
- *fragmentation and overlapping of the modifications*: there are a lots of little modifying laws that impact in different way on the same normative set and in not coherent way;
- *emerging new soft law sources*: the crisis of the main historical institution under the political trust deontological codes, authority acts, new institutional bodies, etc.) that have a no well-defined behaviour on the hierarchy of the law system (how they act in the law system is not fixed by a robust law of theory);
- *unclean law-making and legal drafting processes*: the inclusion of norms not pertinent with the main topic of the main law is a common politics practice, as well as to adopt implicit abrogation, modifications, or conditioned abrogation depending to future events. These worst practices produce disorienting information;
- *misleading about the range of competences assigned to national and regional bodies*. The recent modification to the Italian Constitution Act, Title V inverts the relationship between central and regional powers. In this situation it is not clear who is in charge to do what and sometime the competencies of the two authorities are overlapped.

M.A. Wimmer et al. (Eds.): EGOV 2006, LNCS 4084, pp. 207–218, 2006.

These considerations are confirmed by some statistical data. The Italian laws, or acts with the same power, approved in the last XIII and XIV legislations (period from 1996 to 19/5/2005) are about 2400 (data from the Parliament Office "Rapporto 2004-2005 sullo stato della legislazione", Deputy Camber, Legislation Observatory, "Servizio Studi su dati forniti dal Servizio Commissioni",11 July 2005, pag. 293). In France in the period 1990-2004 were approved about 1340 laws and in Spain in the same period about 700 and in Germany about 1900. The Swiss corpora is composed by the 23 heterogeneous legislative systems (26 cantons with different rules of production and 27 information systems). The problem is in different way affecting several countries in Europe and consequently the eGovernment innovation process.

Certainly, these problems produce on the eGovernance and eGovernment applications some relevant side effects:

- the unknown law domain makes not possible to identify in a cert way the historical set of law and consequently of the law knowledge;
- this affects the able to access to the norms not only in Internet. Internet makes more evident this gap because the end-users are used to do that for the other kind of information;
- the uncertain law applicable, that means that is not known the law corpora currently in force, affects the able to determine the status of the normative system applicable to a concrete case;
- the eGovernment applications based on the legal knowledge (e.g., one-shop-stop) are severely affected by this undefined situation (several eGovernment software applications produce a decision support system on the base of the knowledge extracted by the current legal framework).

This considerations are not only expressed in the Italian eGovernment Action Plan 2000 and 2002, but are included as key points also in the European Action Plans eEurope2002, eEurope2004 and in particular inside of the Com (2003) 71 titled "Updating and simplifying the Community acquis" and implemented with the Action Plan in the COM(2004) 432 "The Implementation of the framework action 'Updating and Simplifying the community acquis"'. This recommendations from the EU Commission expresses clearly six main actions for facing the above listed obstacles: simplify the law systems; consolidate the acts; promote codification approach; cancel the obsolete laws; adopt transparency measures; maintain all the law systems in line with these principle in the time. All the mentioned issues produces a high social and economic costs for the citizens, for the economic actors, for the administration bodies that is more and more evident if it is compared with e-commerce trend.

These problems constitute a relevant obstacle to the eGovernance strategy that aims to improve not only e-services by Internet, but moreover to increase democracy, direct participation of the citizens and groups, consciousness of the rights and obligations, justice in the unique European space.

This article intends to propose a formal model for managing the dynamic of the normative system in the time with twofold objectives:

- (a) for managing and querying a normative information system where the law in force is build in semi-automatic way; (b) for guaranteeing the main principles of the theory of law.

## 2 Norms and Time: Definitions

The normative system is defined by the Bulygin [2] and Guastini [10] as a sequence in the time of legislative system and the legislative system is the set of the valid norms in a due time. Therefore a legislative system is a static photo including all the valid norms in a due instant t. For valid norms in the time t we define a set of norm that respects the rules of law production imposed by the constitutional level effectiveness in the time t. Therefore starting to these concepts the normative system is a diachronic system flexible and mobile in the time [2]. The modifications of the normative system in the time is due in principle at three macro categories of events:

1. exit of a norm to the legislation system;
2. introduction of a new norm;
3. modification of the norm in general sense.[10]

In theory of law and in philosophy of law the concepts before mentioned (validity, applicability, enter in force, normative system, legal system, etc.) are strongly discussed under several point of view due to different doctrines [Kelsen, Ross, Hart, Bobbio]. Therefore if the objective is to describe a theory of the diachronic normative system in the time useful for designing a legislative information system, a new model should be formalised. In a previous work [14] we defined the main element of this model that we resume hereafter.

By *legislative unit* we mean an abstract concept of the legislative normative document (e.g. Italian Act 59 at 1997).

By *legislative text* or *document* is meant a virtual text of law showing all the modifications made to it, textual modifications and modifications affecting the text's validity and applicability. A text so described is an updated text: it results from a function whereby all the modifications Mj-1 are made to a document Dj-1 yielding an updated document Dj. An updated legislative text yields a virtual version of the legislative text as is (prior to the modifications to be built into it): this prior legislative text, D0, is called an historical text (e.g. the third version of the Italian Act 675 at 1999 is the D3($\alpha$) where is the legislative unit). The Mj-1 is a vector with all the modifications. It is possible to associate for each type of modification a weight w in order to produce a formula for calculating the impact of the modification on the D (1).

$$\begin{aligned} &\text{f(Dj-1}(\alpha)\text{, Mj-1)} = \text{Dj}(\alpha) \\ &\text{Mj-1(m1*w1,m2*w2,m3*w3,m4*w4,...,mx*wx)} \end{aligned} \tag{1}$$

A legislative text's *versioning chain* is the set of all the text's virtual versions. This versioning chain is a set of versioned text linked with the abstractness concept of the legislative document D (e.g, Italian Act n. 675 of 1996 is the legislative document D).

$$\textit{versioning chain } \mathrm{vc}(\alpha) = \sum \mathrm{Dn},\ \mathrm{n} = [0, \infty[ \tag{2}$$

A legislative text's *normative chain* is the set of all the versioning chains affecting the way the versioning chain itself is created.

$$\textit{normative chain } \mathrm{nc}(\alpha) = \mathrm{vc}(\alpha) + \sum(\mathrm{vc}(\mathrm{Mj})) \tag{3}$$

A *legal system* is defined as follows:

$$\begin{array}{l} \mathrm{LS(t)} = \{\text{a system of norms N that satisfy at least one} \\ \text{membership criterion at a given time t}\} \\ \text{Legislative system is the synchronic view of the norms} \\ \mathrm{LS(t)} = \mathrm{Dt}(\alpha)\ ,\ \mathrm{Dt}(\beta),\ \mathrm{Dt}(\gamma),\ \ldots \mathrm{Dt}(\omega) \\ \text{where:} \\ \alpha,\ \beta,\ \gamma,\ \ldots,\ \omega = \text{legislative unit} \\ \text{t is a fixed time in a discrete representation} \end{array} \tag{4}$$

A *normative system* is defined as a sequence of legislative systems over time [10]

$$\mathrm{NS} = \{\mathrm{LS(t1)}\ ,\ \mathrm{LS(t2)},\ \mathrm{LS(t3)},\ \ldots \mathrm{LS(tj)}\}\ \mathrm{j} \in \mathrm{N} \tag{5}$$

A normative information system is an information system that includes:

- all the original legislative texts; and
- all the modifications made to them and the corresponding versioning chains.

The two foregoing inclusions give us the entire normative chain of all the texts involved; that is, they yield the normative information system itself.

Following this model it is possible to assign a weight for each kind of modification and calculate the index of complexity a due normative system in relation with the number and the quality of modifications acting on the normative system itself.

$$\begin{array}{c} \mathrm{NIS} = \sum \mathrm{nc}(\gamma) \\ \text{for each legislative unit} \end{array} \tag{6}$$

A *norm* is a rule issued by an authority authorised and competent to do so. Within a norm, or normative text, a *provision* is any part expressing a complete legal meaning. Several provisions can combine into and express a norm, which can accordingly be broken up into provisions. For the sake of expository simplicity, we will only consider here single-provision norms.

A *modifying provision* (ActiveNorm) is a provision that modifies one or more target provisions (PassiveNorm).

## 3 Provision vs. Disposition

Since now we have defined a model for modelling the norms in the time where for norms we intend the behaviour prescriptive or regulative. Now we are moving to the disposition or the sequence of word that express the norms or better the textual expression of the norms. The norms are also defined as the interpretation of the dispositions [12] [3].

In order to avoid the interpretation factor we pass now to formalise the disposition:

- (a) disposition express a norm or a set of norms;
- (b) several disposition could express the same norm.

## 4 Static Time Elements of the Legislative Unit

Now we are able to analyse the time elements that impact on the legislative unit, on the legislative text Dj and on the dispositions.

A legislative document as abstract representation of all the version chain of D has static time elements, meaning dates that do not change over time but for major events such as renewals of an expired document.

Every legislative unit has three main static dates:

- enactment date when the document is delivered by the authorised legislator and signed by the competent person (president, Queen, prime minister, etc.);
- publication date when the legislative unit is published by the official journal;
- entry into force for the enter act when the legislative unit

Other dates, such as a text's coming into existence and its promulgation (for laws), bear little on the purposes of this work and often coincide with the time elements just mentioned.

## 5 Dynamic Time Elements for the Legislative Text

Each version of a legislative unit (version unit) has driven by the *date of application* of the modifications. Mj-1 is a vector of modifications applied to a legislative unit $\alpha$ in the time j-1. The same document M can produce a new vector of modification in the time j+n or j-n with n>1. Sometime a modifying document produce changes in the destination document (PassiveNorm) in different times. So the same modifying document can produce more of one versioning of $\alpha$.

## 6 Dynamic Time Elements for the Dispositions

For this project, we have modelled the dynamics of norms over time with respect to three temporal axes:

- the *norm's force*, the time when the norm enters in the normative system;
- its *effectiveness* as the time when the norm is operative;
- its *application* when the norm produce some effect.

This enables us to express each provision as a logical proposition (7).

$$\begin{array}{l}(\text{a}:t_x \Longrightarrow \text{c}:t_y)t_z \\ \text{where:} \\ t_x \text{ is the time marking the beginning of the norm's effectiveness} \\ t_z \text{ is the time marking the beginning to enter in force of the normative text} \\ t_y \text{ is the time marking the beginning of its de facto application}\end{array} \quad (7)$$

# 7 Modificatory Provisions

Modificatory provisions require special attention because they affect the entire normative system. As Rescigno [15] puts it, a modificatory provision is a meta-rule, or a rule about a rule.

$$\begin{array}{l}\text{Disp:Mod(Disp:Repeal(Norm)}:t_x \Longrightarrow \text{Disp:Realed(Norm)}:t_y):t_z \\ \text{where:} \\ t_z \text{ is the time of enter in force of a norm expressing a modification} \\ t_x \text{ is the modification's time of effectiveness} \\ t_y \text{ is the time when the modification is applied to the target text}\end{array} \quad (8)$$

Times tx, ty, and tz usually coincide with the modificatory norm's enter in force, but there are cases in which they all differ from one another.

**Table 1.** Examples of cases in which times tx, ty, and tz differ from one other

| |
|---|
| *Example 1.* Substitution, announced in 2005 but deferred to 1 January 2006<br>Tz = 1 January 2005, Tx = 1 January 2006, Ty = 1 January 2006 |
| *Example 2.* Substitution to be made in 2007, announced in 2005 but deferred to 1 January 2006<br>Tz = 1 January 2005, Tx = 1 January 2006, Ty = 1 January 2007. |
| *Example 3.* Retroactive substitution going back to 2003, announced in 2005 but deferred to 1 January 2006<br>Tz = 1 January 2005, Tx = 1 January 2006, Ty = 1 January 2003. |
| *Example 4.* Retroactive substitution going back to 2004, announced in 2005 and applicable in 2005<br>Tz = 1 January 2005, Tx = 1 January 2005, Ty = 1 January 2003 |
| *Example 5.* Substitution conditional upon a possible future event, announced in 2005 and applicable in 2005<br>Tz = 1 January 2005, Tx = 1 January 2005, Ty = NULL. |

A *modifying provision* can be modelled thus:

- ActiveNorm(position);
- PassiveNorm (position, internal/external);
- Behavior(type, duration, date_application, implicit/explicit);
- Times (inforce(i,f), efficacy(i,f));
- Topic, used to comment a modification, as by specifying any postponements, extensions, or authorized interpretations;

- Space, used to specify a geographical area to which the modification applies (thus, a regional law might be marked "only for Emilia-Romagna Region");
- Conditions (event, space, domain), a condition is an effect dependent on an event, a geographic space, or a class (or domain) of application.

Disp:Mod(Disp:Repeal(ActiveNorm):tx $\Longrightarrow$ Disp:Repealed(PassiveNorm):ty):tz
Disp:Mod(Disp:Repeal(ActiveNorm):tx, s1 $\Longrightarrow$
Disp:Repealed(PassiveNorm):ty, s2):tz, s1
where s1 and s2 may differ. (9)
*Example 1.* A regional law (s1) enacted by the government of Sicily repeals from a national law an article (s2) having an effect only on the territory of Sicily (s1).
*Example 2.* A ruling of a constitutional court (s1) annuls a regional law (s2).

The national and government *NormeInRete* project [1] includes in the DTD definition a part dedicated to the modifications that permits to implement in XML this model coming from this research.

## 8 A Model for Expressing Conditions

*Conditions* are expressed as complex strings of conjoined or disjoined elements that identify space, event, and domain attributes and that may need predicates to this end. Events are either sure to happen or not (certain or uncertain) and they may result in consequence of certain actions or simply in consequence of the passing of time.

**Table 2.** Examples of expression for conditions

| |
|---|
| *Example 1. A modification conditional upon an uncertain event.*<br>Law no. 328 of 8 Nov. 2000 (validity/applicability: 28 Nov. 2000)<br>Art. 30 – Abrogations<br>(2) On the date when the legislative decree referred to in the foregoing article 10 is set to come into force, all IPAB regulations passed with law no. 6972 of 17 July 1890 shall be abrogated. |
| *Example 2. A modification conditional upon a class or domain.*<br>Law no. 393 of 2 Aug. 1975 (published in Gazzetta Ufficiale no. 224 of 23 Aug. 1975), titled "Norms regulating the siting of nuclear power plants and the production and use of electric energy"<br>Article 15<br>The present article shall not be applicable before 31 Dec. 2003 for all thermo-electric and turbo-gas power plants that run on conventional sources of energy and whose total thermal power exceeds 300 MW (art. 1, legislative decree no. 7 of 7 Feb. 2002, passed into law with amendments with law no. 55 of 9 April 2002). |

## 9 Ontology of Modifications

### 9.1 Taxonomy of Modification

The taxonomy of the modifications (Fig. 1) is a fundamental step for the logic model framework.

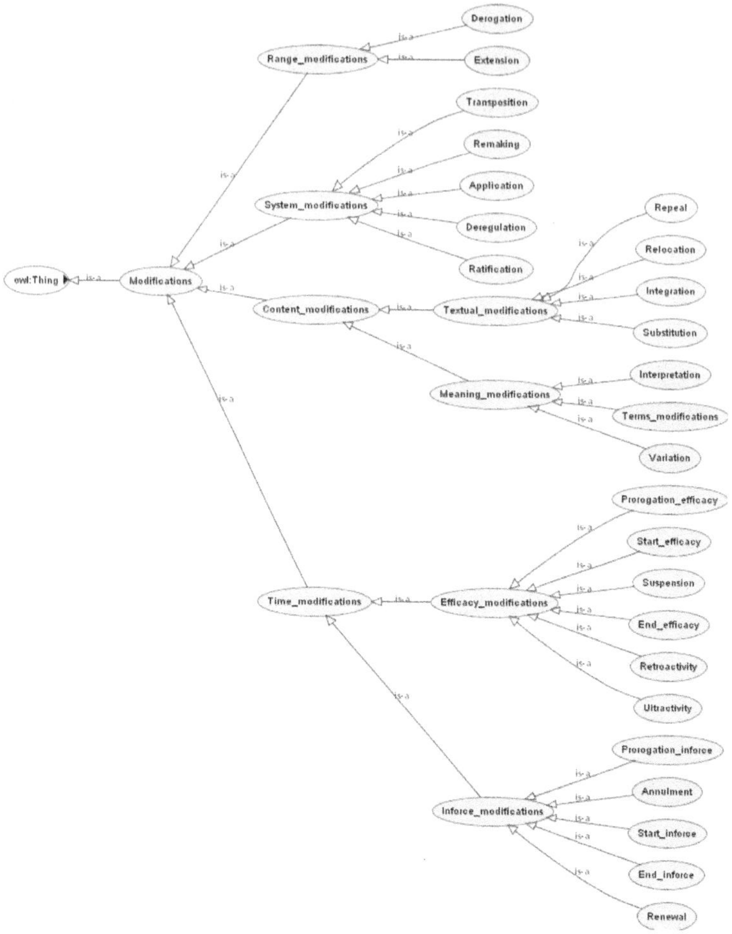


**Fig. 1.** Taxonomy of modification

The disposition of modifications, respect this research, are divided in two main category: (1) modification of the norms; (2) modification of the normative system.

The first category models the modifications that have impact directly on the norms included in the documents and consequently on the relationship betweens two or more documents.

The second category models the modifications that occur to the normative system in general and not to a specific document. It is the case of approval of an International Act inside of the national normative system. No modification of the International Act occurred, simply this legislative document enter in the national normative system.

The modification of the norm are divided in other three sub-categories:

- modification of the content;
- modification of the range;
- modification of the time.

The modification of the content is sub-divided in: (a) modification of the text; (b) modification of the meaning.

The *modification of text* essentially change a part of wording. The *modification of meaning* can change the sense of the norm without modify the text (e.g. interpretation). The *modification of range* extend or restrict the spectrum of application of the norm (e.g. extension or derogation). The *modification of the time* modify the time of enter in force or the time of effectiveness (e.g. retroactive actions).

This classifications, showed in the Fig. 1, permits to build relationship and to make assertion among the disposition of modification: so we are able to define an ontology of modifications [4].

### 9.2 Ontology of Modifications

The modifications can be applied instantaneously, in the past or in the future.

The modifications in the past, generally speaking, are not allowed in the Italian normative system (by Constitution). Nevertheless several norms take action retroactively. In these cases the versioning chain can not be cancelled

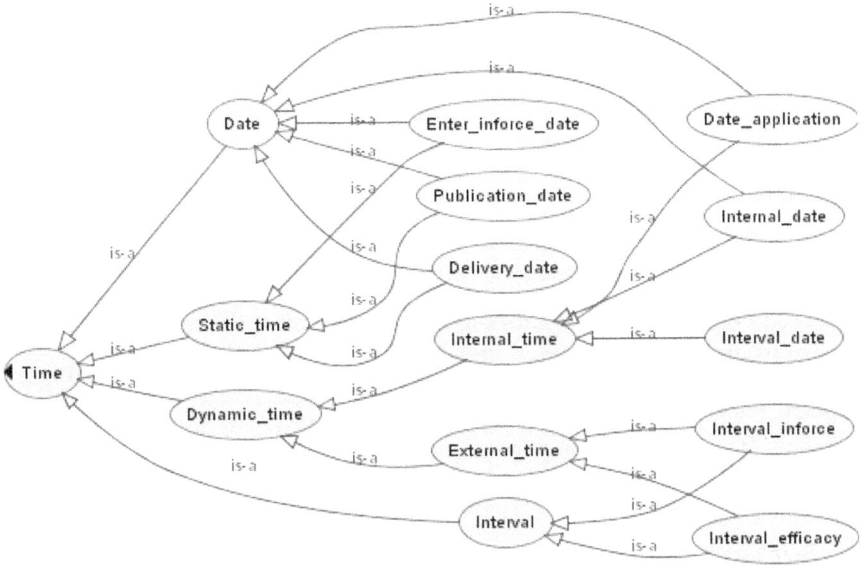


**Fig. 2.** Ontology of times

because for a cert period the norms act some effects, on the other hand since the time of the new declaration we shell consider the norm destination of the retroactive modification in a new way.

Therefore a versioning model occur for managing the normal case and the retroactive cases. Fig. 2 shows the main typology of times used in our model.

## 10 A Versioning Model

In this model of modification is possible to define a model for managing the dynamicity of the normative system by the technique of versioning.

The versioning model is designed to create a new document only when this document goes through changes over time: a new document is thereby created that carries the changes it underwent through the agency of another document.

Versioning is run on the time axis Ty, in other words the date of application of modifications drive the versioning chain. Because of each document in our normative system is referred by a URN defined by the standard *NormaInRete* ([1], [5], [6]), it is possible to build an easy model of versioning adding to the URN the time of application of the modification. Therefore for each set of modifications with the same date of application and the same destination, a new version of the document is created an a URN is created thus: namedoc@Ty. Each document URN@Ty will satisfy a period of validity as either $[Ty, \infty[$

Thus, to select all the documents that are in force at time k, we will filter all URN@Ty documents using y<=k.

**Table 3.** Example of versioning chain for the code on privacy, legislative decree 196/2003

| |
|---|
| 1. urn:nir:decreto.legislativo:30-06-2003;196 → original document |
| 2. urn:nir:decreto.legislativo:30-06-2003;196@29-12-2003 → version as modified by a legislative decree |
| 3. urn:nir:decreto.legislativo:30-06-2003;196@27-02-2004 → version as modified by the law through which the modified legislative decree was passed into law |

If I need legislative decree 196/2003 in its valid state as time 1/1/2004=k, I will have to present version no. 2, meaning URN@Ty with maximum y<=k.

If instead I need legislative decree 196/2003 in its applicable state at time 1/1/2004, I will have to get into the XML document or access the database that stores every document's period of applicability (and in the future of every article's period of applicability).

## 11 Forking of Versioning Chains

Certain modifications can change out of recognition the effect that flows from a norm. There are four such modifications:

- legislative decrees that have lapsed out of force;
- retroactive modifications;
- annulments;
- authentic interpretations.

Each of these types of modifications can fork the versioning chain into two chains, of which one shows all past modifications and the other all the new ones.

Thus, if we look at a retroactive modification (example 3, section 7), we will have the following:

- URN - original document
- URN@1-1-2002 ' by effect of a substitution made in 2002
- URN@1-1-2004 ' by effect of a substitution made in 2004
- URN@1-1-2005 ' by effect of a substitution made in 2005

and URN@1-1-2003 ' after the *retroactive substitution* introduced on *1 July 2005* At this point the chain starts up again from URN@1-1-2003; the rest of the chain, meaning versions (c) and (d) need to be dismissed and placed out of service (or *frozen*). This parallel chain can only be consulted by running a query having two parameters: *time of force* and *time of observation*.

A chain in common (living chain)
a) URN → original document
b) URN@1-1-2002 → by effect of a substitution made in 2002
Forke of single chain into two chains:
first chain (a dead chain)
c.1) URN@1-1-2004;1-7-2005 → by effect of a substitution made in 2004
d.1)URN@1-1-2005;1-7-2005 → by effect of a substitution made in 2005
second chain (a living chain), marking the point from which to resume
c) URN@1-1-2003→ by effect of a substitution made in 2005
d) URN@1-1-2004→ by effect of a substitution made in 2004
e) URN@1-1-2005→ by effect of a substitution made in 2005.

Document URN@1-1-2003 marks the point from which all previously applied modifications start up again, in that the text has changed and we may have a stratification on the modifications themselves (thus, for example, all the modifications above, (a) through (d), carry an effect on article 3). We will then have the situation described above.

## 12 Conclusion

The model presented is able to manage the dynamic over time of the normative system under the legal point of view and to produce valid legislative versioning respect the main principles of the legal theory. Several legislative information systems are arising for improving the eGovernment, nevertheless only few of them can be pointed out as valid normative system. The pure automatic process applied to the text are not enough to guarantee and preserve the legal results. This model would like to join the automatic process with the legal validity of the results, and moreover it wants to provide to citizen and to judge different view perspective. This model is now implemented in several legislative information system of Italian public administration (e.g. Court of Cassation) trough the Norma-System software architecture ([13], [14]).

## References


1. AA. VV., Studio di fattibilità per la realizzazione del progetto "Accesso alle norme in rete". Informatica e Diritto No. 1, 2000.
2. Alchourrón C., Bulygin E., Normative Systems, Pringer-Verlag, Wien, 1971.
3. Bobbio, N., Teoria generale del diritto, Giappichelli, Torino, 1993
4. Brighi, R., Norme e conoscenza: dal testo al metadato, Giuffrè, 2004, Milano.
5. Circolare 22 aprile 2002 n. AIPA/CR/40, "Formato per la rappresentazione elettronica dei provvedimenti normativi tramite il linguaggio di marcatura XML", Gazzetta Ufficiale n. 102, 3 May 2002.
6. Circolare 6 novembre 2001 n. AIPA/CR/35, "Assegnazione dei nomi uniformi ai documenti giuridici", Gazzetta Ufficiale Serie generale n. 262, 10 November 2001.
7. Commission of the European Communities, White Paper of the Commission on the European Governance COM(2001) 428, 25.7.2001, Brussels.
8. Communication from the Commission, European Governance:Better lawmaking, COM (2002) 275, 5.6.2002, Brussels.
9. Communication from the Commission, The Role of eGovernment for Europe's Future, COM(2003) 567, 26.9.2003, Brussels.
10. Guastini, R., Teoria e Dogmatica delle fonti. Giuffrè, Milano, 1998.
11. Hernndez, R. M., Sartor G., Time and Norms: A Formalisation in the Event-calculus. In Proceedings of the Seventh International Conference on Artificial Intelligence and Law, ACM, New York, 1999, pages 90-100.
12. Kelsen, H., Reine Rechtslehre, Deuticke, Wien, 1960, it. translation Torino, Einaudi, 1966.
13. Palmirani, M., Norma-System. In the series "Filosofia, Informatica, Diritto", Bologna, Clueb, 2000.
14. Palmirani, M.,Time Model in Normative Information Systems, in the proceeding of workshop "The Role of the Legal Knowledge in the eGovernment", ICAIL2005.
15. Rescigno, G.U., L'atto normativo, Zanichelli, Bologna, 1998.

# Semantic Portal for Legislative Information

Matti Järvenpää, Maiju Virtanen, and Airi Salminen

University of Jyväskylä, PL 35 (Agora), 40014 Jyväskylä, Finland
first.lastname@jyu.fi

**Abstract.** Semantic portals enabled by Semantic Web technologies have been suggested to provide a point of access to an integrated body of information about some domain. In the area of e-Government there are multiple possible domains for semantic portals, one of them being legislative work. In this paper we propose a semantic portal based on a rich metadata repository to support the retrieval of legislative information. The portal provides process oriented semantic browsing capabilities. A prototype of the portal has been implemented for the retrieval of Finnish legislative information.

## 1 Introduction

Public sector in many countries has been active in building new kinds of *e-Government* services, enabled by the Internet and Web technologies. For example, various e-Government services provide legislative information for the needs of people working in legislative organizations or needing the information outside the organizations. *Legislative information* includes information about the ongoing and past legislative processes in a country, documents and other content created in the processes, as well as information about human and organizational actors participating in the processes. The information is important to legal experts, politicians, media, various interest groups, and laypersons. Some ongoing legislative processes may create wide interest both among professionals and public. The legislative information is, however, typically scattered in a number of services structured, organized and classified in many different ways. Following legislative processes and finding information about them requires both knowledge about these processes and about various information sources and services.

The World Wide Web Consortium (W3C) has initiated the development of Semantic Web to improve utilization of information resources. The *Semantic Web* is intended to be "an extension of the current Web in which information is given well-defined meaning, better enabling computers and people to work in cooperation" [2]. The well-defined meaning is added to the Web by means of metadata. The *metadata* is information about resources either accessible or identifiable on the Web. The meta-data is given in a formal, standardized format, readable and interpretable by software. The Extensible Markup Language (XML) and the Resource Description Framework (RDF) create the basis for the standard formats [4] [11]. Formal presentation of the metadata can be used to facilitate automated reasoning about the meaning and trust-worthiness trustworthiness of resources.

M.A. Wimmer et al. (Eds.): EGOV 2006, LNCS 4084, pp. 219–230, 2006.

Ontologies are used to express semantic metadata. An *ontology* defines formally the concepts and their relationships in an application domain [7] [8]. In semantic information portals ontologies facilitate semantic search.

*Semantic portals* enabled by Semantic Web technologies have been suggested for improving information sharing for a community of users [19]. They are intended to provide a point of access to an integrated and structured body of information about some domain [16]. In this paper we introduce new ideas for a semantic portal to support *transparency* of legislation by providing an extensive body of contextual information along with legislative documents. The prototype of the portal, called the RASKE semantic portal, has been built for the Finnish legislative information. The portal is intended to facilitate semantic browsing, to connect the legislative documentation to the different activities of the legislative process, and to provide different views to the documentation according to the activities. The approach puts explicit representation of the legislative process at the central position in the portal. The rest of the paper is organized as follows. Section 2 discusses the characteristics of information management in legislative environments. Section 3 describes the design principles and basic characteristics of the RASKE semantic portal. Section 4 provides evaluation of the prototype in respect to the semantic portal solutions presented in earlier research. Section 5 concludes the paper.

## 2 The Legislative Information in Context

Legislative information is created in the activities of legislative processes which give the context for legislative documents. As a means to increase the transparency of legislation we propose improving, not only the accessibility of documents, but also accessibility of the contextual information.

A *legislative process* consists of a set of successive activities where the goal is to update rules of the society by yielding new legislation. Following the content management framework used by [17], the resources in legislative processes can be roughly divided into three types: actors, systems, and content items. *Actors* are organizations and persons performing activities in the process. In the future also software agents may have an important role as actors. *Content items* consist of legislative documents and other stored data produced and used in the activities. *Systems* consist of the hardware and software used to support the performance of activities. In the remaining section, the characteristics of information management in legislative environments are discussed from the perspective of the four entities: activities, actors, content items, and systems. The Finnish legislative environment will be used as a reference point.

*Activities.* The procedure of a legislative process originates from laws, regulations and traditions in the particular country or region. In Finland, legislative process of ordinary laws can be divided to four chronological phases: preparation of the legislative proposal in a ministry, handling of the legislative proposal in the Government, handling of the Government Bill in the Parliament, and ratification and publication of the law. The actual instances of the legislative processes, in the following also referred to as *legislative projects*, can vary greatly in terms of time and complexity. For example, in the Finnish legislative process, simple projects are finished in months and involve only a small number of actors while in complex cases the project may involve hundreds of people and take several years to complete. Legislative processes are dynamic and knowledge-intensive political processes, where alternative courses, iterations, and cancellation are possible, and many events take place outside the official documentation. However, emergent aspects of all legislative projects are constrained by the formal procedure that sets structure for the handling process and limits the amount of different paths that it may take. For the public, understanding the dynamics and the role of politics might be an important aspect in the transparency.

*Actors.* New legislation is typically created in an interorganizational process participated by many public organizations. In the Finnish legislative process, for example, the central organizational actors are the Government, the ministry on the domain of the law, the Parliament of Finland, Special Committees of the Parliament, and the President of the Republic. Hundreds of people in these organizations participate in the work and include officials, politicians, and administrative personnel. As a public process with far-reaching implications, the legislative process also attracts the interest of many actors outside these organizations. Actors such as interest groups, citizen groups, citizens, experts of different domains, companies, and other government organizations participate in the process indirectly by commenting legislative proposals, taking part in the hearings, and otherwise communicating with officials and politicians. Currently the role played particularly by external actors may be extremely difficult to determine and understand even to legal experts.

*Systems.* The systems involved in legislative work consist of a number of different types of software applications. The backbone of the system resources is formed by the applications supporting creation, storage, and dissemination of documents. This category includes office applications, document management systems, and legal databases. Additionally, applications such as voting systems, decision support systems, and information visualization tools may have more or less direct role in legislative processes. The third category of information systems contains applications that allow citizens and other external actors take part in the legislative process by means of information, consultation, and direct participation [10]. Currently, at least in principle, the systems are connected by networks, either by intranets, extranets, or the internet. In many countries legislative information is made widely available to the public through various web sites. However, at least in Finland, lack of interoperability between information systems of different organizations scatters the online legislative information under multiple differently structured services. Resultantly, tracking of legislative processes and finding information about them requires both knowledge about these processes and about various information sources and services. We argue that transparency of legislation should be achieved without requiring knowledge about many different systems.

*Content items.* A great deal of the information produced in the legislative activities is recorded in documents. Documents such as memos, legislative proposals, bills, minutes, communications, and law documents are created, circulated, discussed, and decided throughout the legislative process. Another essential category of content items is the metadata related to documents. Ongoing transformation toward digital and structured forms of information and networked environments increases the importance of metadata constantly [6]. The problem with the metadata in the Finnish legislative process is that although large portion of the metadata is created systematically in every project, its use is hampered by the lack of integration. Metadata is dispersed over multiple documents and information systems. There are also differences in work practices of different organizations affecting the production of metadata.

We see rich metadata describing content, context, and structure of legislative documents as an important means to improve the transparency of legislation. The metadata should be in a standard form facilitating the use of the data by different systems and thus enabling building integrated services for the retrieval of legislative information. RDF provides the standard format for the purpose. Figure 1 shows the RDF metadata schema creating the basis for the portal introduced in the following section.

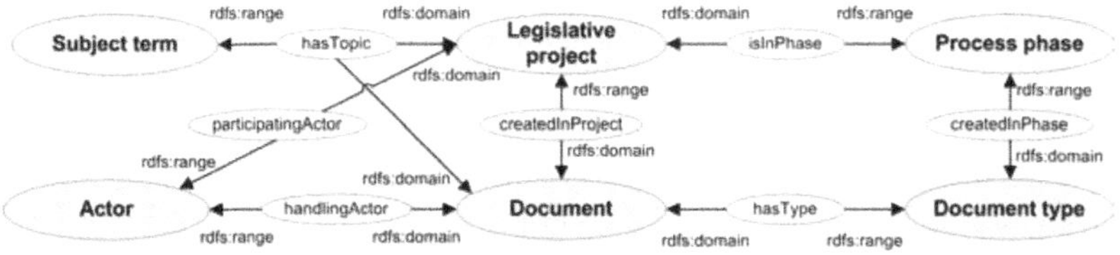


**Fig. 1.** Metadata schema for legislative information

## 3 The RASKE Semantic Portal

The RASKE semantic portal is a prototype of an e-Government portal designed to gather information, within one user interface, about the whole Finnish legislative process. Although the portal is presented in the context of the Finnish legislative process, many of its central ideas are applicable to other legislative processes as well.

The architecture of the prototype is based on the idea of having an *integrated metadata repository* on the background of the portal. Various RDF ontologies describe the organizations, process phases, documents types, and associated metadata. RDF has also proven to be adequate modeling language for the ontology used in current version of the prototype. However, it is possible that more complex modeling language such as OWL will be used in the future to identify more detailed relationships between the concepts.

The prototype uses XHTML [15] combined with Cascading Style Sheets for the user interface and server-side scripting language PHP for the generation of the user interface. Additionally, RDF API for PHP (RAP) [14] is used as application interface for querying RDF modeled ontologies and metadata. RAP was chosen because of its support for SPARQL query language which is W3C candidate recommendation. In the current version of the prototype intended for research and demonstration purposes, metadata repository is only a small collection of manually created RDF and RDF Schema documents.

The current user interface of the portal follows top-down approach where the user is first provided with a general overview of the information that he or she can use to focus on more constrained aspects of legislative projects. Accordingly, the interface consists of two main parts. First, there is a semantic *project search interface* for finding legislative projects. Second, the *project-specific interface* facilitates information retrieval inside a single legislative project. Description of these two interfaces will be provided in the following subsections.

## 3.1 Project Search Interface

The project search interface supports both traditional search and semantic browsing. Figure 2 shows a screen dump from the interface where the text is written in Finnish. The main window is divided into four principal components. The panes on the sides are intended for semantic search, those in the middle for traditional search (the upper pane), and for the list of the found projects. *Traditional search* enables the user to search projects by their identifiers or names, or by words in their textual description. The semantic search capabilities

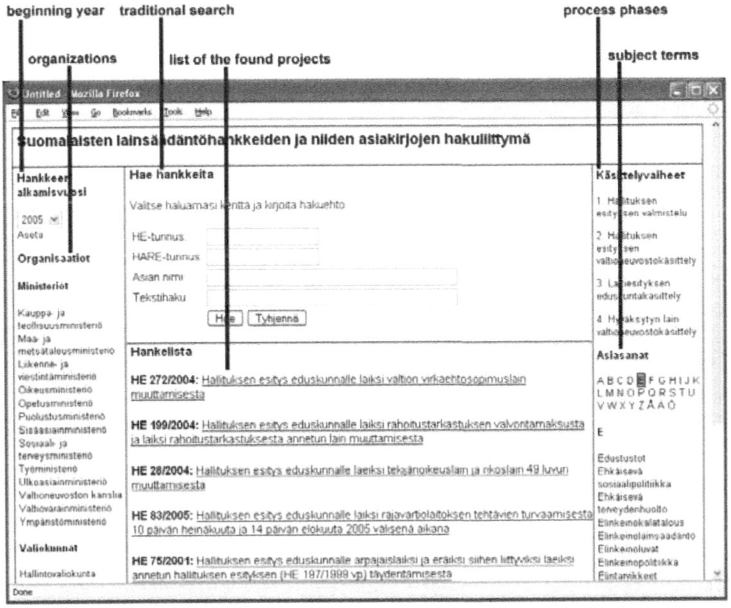


**Fig. 2.** Project search interface

are intended for situations, where the user is not sure what he or she is looking for. The search result is shown in the *list of the found projects*, which can be filtered by successive searches.

The semantic search panes show categories that are used to constrain the search result. From the left pane the user is able to choose the *beginning year* of the project or *organizations* participating in legislative work. The right pane shows the *process phases* classified to four main phases, and subject terms, which are used to describe the content of the resources with the concepts of the domain. With the help of the categories, the user is able to filter the search result little by little. For example, the user might choose (if the terminology of the portal were expressed in English) the category *Ministry of Social Affairs and Health*, the phase *preparation* and a subject term childcare to retrieve all legislative projects which are prepared by the Ministry of Social Affairs and Health, currently in the preparation phase, and concern the subject 'childcare'.

The benefit of the semantic search mechanism is that the user has no need to know any exact information about the project, for example, about its identifier or a particular word in the description of a project. Instead, the user can reasonably freely browse the knowledge base. It can also be seen, at a glance, which concepts are used in the knowledge base.

### 3.2 Project-Specific Interface

The project-specific interface consists of two different views. The summary view provides basic information about the examined project while the *detailed information view* provides access to documentation of the project and allows the user to track its progress through different activities of the legislative process. The summary view helps the user in deciding whether the presented project is worth closer examination. Detailed information view is illustrated in the figure 3.

The summary view is displayed after the user has chosen the name of the project in the list of found projects. Provided basic information includes the description of the project, a list of subject terms, actors responsible for the preparation, and references to other legislative projects and international treaties related to the project under examination. Additionally, both the summary view and detailed information view share two functionalities marked in figure 3.

First, the area marked *name history* informs the user about the current and past names of the legislative project. It is common for a legislative project to change its name at least once when the Government Bill is created. This is also the case in the figure. The upper name is the name of the legislative project during the preparation and the lower the name of the Bill.

Secondly, *semantic recommendations* of other legislative projects related to the current project are presented on the left and right panes. On the left-hand side there are links to the projects that are related to the current project by their content, while projects listed on the right are currently being prepared by the same ministry.

In the detailed information view (see Figure 3), the instance level process description is represented by the *activity row*. The *sub-activity row* provides

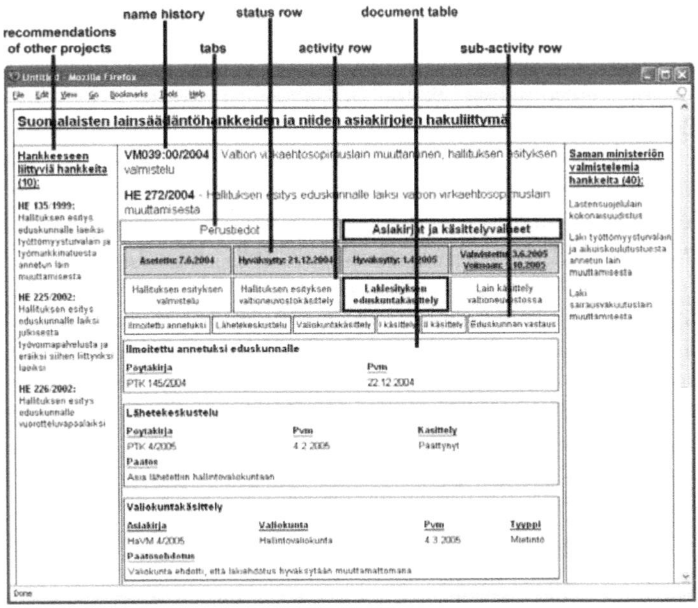


**Fig. 3.** Project specific interface. Detailed information view.

access to the documents and decisions of the legislative process and shows the status and schedule of the project.

The cells in the activity row of Figure 3 correspond to the four high-level activities of the legislative process mentioned in Section 2. The status row shows the status of the high-level activities. Each cell of the *status row* is related to the high-level activity of the same column. A cell of the status row can be in three different states. First, if the corresponding activity has not yet ended, the status cell is white. Secondly, if the activity has ended successfully, the cell is green. In case of Figure 3, the project has passed all activities of the legislative process and as a result all cells of the status row are green. Thirdly, it is possible that activity has ended exceptionally. For example, the project may have been cancelled in the course of particular high-level activity or the President might have left the law without ratification. In this case, related cell of the status row is shown in orange.

The activity row is a functional part of the interface and allows the user to navigate between different activities by clicking the cells of the row. In the figure, the currently chosen activity is *Lakiesityksen eduskuntakäsittely* (Handling of the Bill in the Parliament). Consequently, the sub-activity row and the *document tables* shown to the user are related to this activity. If the user chooses another activity from the activity row, the sub-activity row and the document tables change to match the chosen activity. Only the activities that have resulted in documents and decisions can be chosen by the user. Other activities are shown in the activity row but marked as unavailable with shading and gray color.

Most legislative projects follow the similar high-level structure but exceptions in details are possible. For example, the President may leave the law unratified and return it to the Parliament for new handling. The interface is able to reflect these kinds of exceptions by utilizing the flexibility of the XHTML tables.

Both finished and ongoing or expected future sub-activities related to the chosen high-level activity are shown in the sub-activity row. In a case of handling of the Bill in the Parliament, the sub-activities shown in the subactivity row represent the default handling process described in Section 2. However, if a completed sub-activity results in deviation from the default process, future sub-activities are changed to match the situation. For example, if the Bill is amended in the first reading it must be handled by the Grand Committee, leading to changes in the remaining handling process. In this case, sub-activities following the first reading are changed automatically to match the altered handling procedure, as the decision of the first reading is made available for the system. In order to do this, deviations need to be modeled in advance to RDF process ontology. In practice, this can be done without extensive modeling effort as the number of possible deviations during the Handling of the Bill in the Parliament is limited on the chosen level of abstraction and they are well documented in laws and regulations affecting the process.

Each document table provides document metadata, links to actual documents, and decision-making information related to single sub-activity. For example, in the figure the second document table from the top corresponds to the preliminary debate. This document table contains link to the minutes where the preliminary debate is recorded, the date of the debate, status of the debate, and decision to which it has resulted. Depending on the reflected activities, document tables may also contain information about participating actors, voting results, and document types.

## 4 Evaluation

The prototype portal has been tested only with a limited number of legislative projects and its usability has not been tested systematically. However, representatives of the case environment have given positive feedback about the prototype and implementation of more extensive prototype has started. In this section related e-Government research is first compared to our research and then the properties of legislative processes identified in the section 2 are discussed in respect to the portal.

During the last years a number of semantic portals enabled by Semantic Web technologies have been introduced. The idea of the semantic web portal implemented in the OntoWeb project is to support knowledge sharing in a community [19]. The portal creates its knowledge base automatically by harvesting information published and annotated according to a shared ontology by members of the community. In our approach, the metadata is stored upon creation to a centralized repository. Ontologies developed in OntoWeb project concern similar topics than ours including actors and documents but unlike our work they do not describe activities. KAON infrastructure of the same project [22] provides several practical tools for ontology creation, storage, retrieval and maintenance. These tools, especially tools for ontology storage, may prove useful in the later implementation phase of our portal.

In the area of e-Government, a number of studies seek to enhance web services with "semantics by applying ontologies" [20], [13]. Purpose of these ontologies is to describe to transactional government services and support web service composition, orchestration, and management while the purpose of our ontologies is to improve legislative information retrieval with contextual metadata.

Other studies related to e-Government portals focus on strategic decisions and semantic interoperability [9] and on designing "one stop" e-Government portals [21] and intelligent e-forms environments [5]. While most of the e-Government research focuses on providing integrated access to government services for citizens, our goal is to support information retrieval related to legislative information performed both by expert actors and citizens.

In the area of legal informatics, the focus has been on ontologies describing legal information [1] while our work has concentrated on legislative information. Even if these areas overlap, in the latter area much more specific information is needed about the context in which the information is produced. In E-POWER project [3] automated processing of annotated legal sources is used to generate legislative ontologies. In our approach, ontologies are designed during the metadata analysis and design. Additionally, our research does not focus on content and structure of legal documents but on semantics and information related to their originating context. For this reason, we cannot utilize vocabularies used to describe contents of legal documents such as Norme in Rete [12] or Metalex produced in E-POWER project. However, structural metadata concerning legislative documents such as minutes could be used in the future to automate population of the metadata repository.

Even if the prototype was designed in the context of Finnish legislative process, many of its features are based on properties of the legislative processes in general. In the following, the content management framework presented in section 2 is used to identify issues and design principles applicable to other legislative processes.

*Actors.* Legislative work involves many types of actors both as producers and users of information. In the production side, legislative information is often dispersed under multiple services because of interorganizational nature of legislative processes. The portal addresses the problem by providing a single point of access to information created in the process. In the user side, actors face information created by large number of different actors. For this reason, organizational actors are used as one of the constraining categories in the project search interface. Actor information is also central in many other parts of the interface, for example, in document tables. Finally, the architecture of the portal based on metadata repository and dynamic generation of user interface makes it technically straightforward to create customized interfaces for different user groups.

*Content items.* As legislative work is very document centered activity, documents and related metadata have central role also in the portal. The interface of the portal can be described as information retrieval interface where legislative documents are presented in the rich set of contextual and semantic metadata. We see that bringing the metadata to the foreground does not only support the tasks of finding the relevant information and making sense to legislative documents but it is also important for transparency of the legislative process. Metadata allows users to gain lot of information without reading documents.

*Activities.* Activities are represented in the interface of the portal by the instance-level process description of the legislative process consisting of activity row, sub-activity row, and status row. We see that instance-level visualization of legislative process could help users of the related information retrieval interface to gain an overview of the decided issue and put information in its proper context. Our preliminary experience suggests that an application generating such descriptions on basis of RDF process metadata can be implemented without complex architecture as level of abstraction of the resulting descriptions can be quite high. The task of creating such applications is aided by the controlled nature of exceptions especially during the formal parts of legislative processes.

*Systems.* Underlying information systems are hidden from the users of the portal. Nevertheless, they remain a considerable technical challenge for further implementations of the prototype. Metadata repository must be populated with the information residing in heterogeneous information systems used to support the legislative process. In short term, our goal is to transfer limited amount of information to the metadata repository in order to perform further testing and evaluation of the portal. However, if the portal is to be taken in production use, the underlying metadata repository must be embedded as stable part of the work process. This is very likely to require a full-scale integration project with all technical and organizational challenges that such projects typically entail in the domain of government [18].

## 5 Conclusion

The RASKE prototype portal has been developed in parallel with the specification of the metadata repository, and its functionality is still relatively limited. One of the purposes of the prototype has been to motivate further development and the demanding task of metadata standardization in the target organizations by showing benefits of such work. The prototype provides semantic browsing and recommendation services based on RDF metadata. Compared with earlier work, our approach has a strong process orientation and thus the semantics of our ontologies concern particularly the process environment with different activities, document types and actors.

The development of the prototype continues further. There are interesting open questions left concerning, for example, the level of details in process models described with RDF Schema. How accurately the models concerning the default process and process deviations are possible and reasonable to describe? Several interesting questions concern the utilization of automation in the ontology and metadata generation. The research has not included so far problems concerning the development of the subject term ontology. Currently people in the Finnish Parliament and ministries have varying practices in attaching subject terms to projects and documents, and the work for identifying a joint subject term vocabulary has not started yet. Extending the vocabulary from a set of terms to include relationships between terms as well would give interesting possibilities for semantic recommendation in the user interface.

After the ontologies have been designed, the next step will be to populate the RDF database and to initiate the process of metadata creation according to the ontologies. The goal is to automate the metadata creation as much as possible. Investigation for the utilization of automation has started on the following sub areas: generating metadata by a system at the time of content production, extracting metadata from the elements of structured documents, and extracting metadata from the user profiles.

## References

1. Benjamins, V., Casanovas P, Breuker, J. & Gangemi, A. (2005). Law and the Semantic Web, an Introduction. In Law and the Semantic Web: Legal Ontologies, Methodologies, Legal Information Retrieval, and Applications. Lecture Notes in Computer Science, Vol. 3369, Springer Verlag.
2. Berners-Lee T., Hendler J. & Lassila O. (2001). The Semantic Web. Scientific American, 284(5), 34-43.
3. Boer A., Engers T. & Winkels R. (2003). Using ontologies for comparing and harmonizing legislation. In Proceedings of the 9th international conference on Artificial intelligence and law, Scotland, United Kingdom, 60-69.
4. Bray T., Paoli J., Sperberg-McQueen C., Maler E. & Yergeau F. (2004). Extensible Markup Language (XML) 1.0 (Third Edition). W3C Recommendation.
5. Georgiadis, P., Lepouras, G., Vassilakis, C., Boukis, G., Tambouris, E., Gorilas, S., Daven-port, E,. Macintosh, A., Fraser, J. Lockhead, D. (2002). SmartGov: A Knowledge-Based Platform for Transactional Electronic Services. In Proceedings of EGOV 2002, Aix-en-Provence, France, 362-369.
6. Gilliland-Swetland, A. (2000). Introduction to metadata: Setting the stage. Retrieved from http://www.getty.edu/research/institute/standard/intrometadata/
7. Gruninger M. & Lee J. (2002). Ontology applications and design. Communications of the ACM 45(2), 39-41.
8. Klein M. (2002). Interpreting documents via an RDF Schema ontology. In Proceedings of the 13th International Workshop on Database and Expert Systems Applications, Aix-en-Provece, France, 1-5.
9. Klischewski R. (2003). Semantic Web for E-Government. In Proceedings of EGOV 2003, Prague, Czech Republic, 288-295.
10. Macintosh, A. (2004). Characterizing E-participation in Policy-Making. In Proceedings of the 37th Annual Hawaii International Conference on System Sciences. Big Island, Hawaii, USA.
11. Manola F. & Miller E. (Eds.) (2004). RDF Primer. W3C Recommendation.

12. Marchetti, A.,Megale F., Seta E. & Vitali F. 2002. Using XML as a means to access legislative documents: Italian and foreign experiences. ACM SIGAPP Applied Computing Re-view 10 (1), 54-62.
13. Medjahed B., Bouguettaya A. & Ouzzani M. 2003. Semantic Web Enabled E-Government Services. In the Proceedings of 3rd NSF Conference for Digital Government Research, Boston, USA, 237-240.
14. Oldakowski, R., Bizer, C., Westphal, D. (2005). RAP: RDF API for PHP. In Proceedings of the Workshop on Scripting for the Semantic Web, Heraklion, Greece. Retrieved from http://www.semanticscripting.org/SFSW2005/papers/Oldakowski-RAP.pdf
15. Pemberton, S. et al. (2000). XHTML 1.0: The Extensible HyperText Markup Language. W3C Recommendation.
16. Reynolds D., Shabajee P. & Cayzer S. (2004). Semantic information portals. In Proceedings of the WWW2004-conference, New York, New York, USA, 290-291.
17. Salminen, A. (2005). Building Digital Government by XML. In Proceedings of the 38th Annual Hawaii International Conference on System Sciences. Big Island, Hawaii, USA.
18. Scholl, H. (2005). Interoperability in e-Government: More than just smart middleware. In Proceedings of the 38th Annual Hawaii International Conference on System Sciences. Big Island, Hawaii, USA.
19. Spyns P., Oberle D., Volz R., Zheng J., Jarrar M., Sure Y., Studer R. & Meersman R. (2002). OntoWeb – a Semantic Web Community Portal. In Proceedings of Fourth International Conference on Practical Aspects of Knowledge Management (PAKM), Vienna, Austria, 189-200.
20. Tambouris E., Gorilas S., Kavadias G., Apostolou D., Abecker A., Stojanovic L. & Mentzas G. (2004). Ontology-enabled e-Gov Service Configuration: An Overview of the OntoGov project. In Proceeding of 5th IFIP International Working Conference on Knowledge Management in Electronic Government (KMGov 2004), Krems, Austria, 122-127.
21. Traunmüller, R. & Wimmer, M. 2001. Web semantics in e-government: a tour d'horizon on essential features. In Proceedings of the WISE 2001 Conference and Workshops, Kyoto, 132-140.
22. Volz R., Oberle D., Staab S. & Motik B. 2003. KAON SERVER – A Semantic Web Management System. In Alternate Track Proceedings of the Twelfth International World Wide Web Conference, WWW2003, Budapest, Hungary, 20-24.

# The x-Leges System: Peer-to-Peer for Legislative Document Exchange

Luca De Santis[1], Caterina Lupo[1], Carlo Marchetti[2,3], and Massimo Mecella[2]

[1] Centro Nazionale per l'Informatica nella Pubblica Amministrazione (CNIPA)
Via Isonzo 21/b, 00198 Roma, Italy
{luca.desantis, lupo}@cnipa.it

[2] Università di Roma "La Sapienza", Dipartimento di Informatica e Sistemistica
Via Salaria 113, 00198 Roma, Italy
{carlo.marchetti, mecella}@dis.uniroma1.it

[3] Senato della Repubblica, Servizio dell'Informatica
Palazzo Madama, 00186 Roma, Italy
carlo.marchetti@senato.it

**Abstract.** Among the recent initiatives in the context of the Italian *e*-Leges program, which concerns the exploitation of IT technologies for the life-cycle management of laws and related documents, there is the design and implementation of a cooperative system supporting the processes underlying the drafting and the publication of laws. In this paper we describe the architecture of such a system, referred to as *x*-Leges, highlighting its peer-to-peer architecture. The *x*-Leges system guarantees *(i)* autonomy of all involved organizations, *(ii)* the reuse of information stored in legacy systems and *(iii)* efficient process support and analysis.

## 1 Introduction

In the context of the renovation process of the Italian Public Administration (PA), in 2000 Financial Law has launched a program concerning the use of IT technologies for the management of laws and related documents. In order to give effectiveness to such a program, the *Centro Nazionale per l'Informatica nella Pubblica Amministrazione* (CNIPA - National Center for IT in the PA) has launched an overall project, referred to as *e-Leges*, consisting of various action lines. Among them, the *x-Leges* one has been recently started, involving different PAs, namely the Senate, the Chamber of Deputies, the Office of the Prime Minister, the Ministry of Justice with its National Printing Office, with the aim of supporting the cooperative processes underlying laws approval, drafting and publication on the Official Journal.

The *x*-Leges system will support legislative production processes through the *(i)* the exchange of documents (e.g., draft of the laws to be discussed, accompanying documents, etc.), *(ii)* the management and the exchange of added-value information related to the overall process and its phases and *(iii)* the possibility to receive notifications when relevant events happen. A strict design requirement is that users need to maintain the full control over their activities, i.e., the

M.A. Wimmer et al. (Eds.): EGOV 2006, LNCS 4084, pp. 231–242, 2006.

system should not be proactive towards operators. The cooperative process is traced-back "a posteriori".

The aim of this paper is to present the overall $x$-Leges architecture, that offers some interesting and innovative features, such as its pure peer-to-peer design, the use of Web Service technologies, as well as the pervasive adoption of XML as exchange information format and as a mean to represent metadata. The contribution is thus twofold: from one side, some specific design choices and technical solutions are interesting and worthy of considerations in similar $e$-Government projects; on the other side, it's one of the first "real" $e$-Government projects in which the peer-to-peer paradigm and Web Service technologies are adopted.

The paper is organized as follows: in Section 2 we briefly illustrate some related works and systems; Section 3 describes the context of the project, namely the basic principles of the $e$-Leges initiative, whereas in Section 4 the principles underlying the system design are introduced. Section 5 and Section 6 describe the technical details of the system, focusing on the XML structure of the exchanged documents and the peer-to-peer architecture. With Section 7 the paper ends remarking the implementation and validation schedule for the project and discussing future work.

## 2 Related Work

In the last few years, information technologies are changing the way legal documents are managed and accessed. A growing number of initiatives are today in progress, some of them reaching significative results.

Many standards and systems, enabling and simplifying juridical documents management processes, have been proposed [10,6,3]. All these standards are based on XML, thus simplifying interoperability among different systems.

In Italy, the *NormeinRete* (NIR) project[1] [8] started in 1999. It was proposed by CNIPA jointly with the Italian Ministry of Justice with the aim of building a distributed cooperative system to have access to juridical documentation, achieved through the standardization of the information format. As far as the standardization, the main results are a national standard for XML representation of laws [2], and a national standard for persistent identification of laws [1]. The $x$-Leges project is considerably based on the results of NormeinRete, specifically it adopts the two cited standards.

Also the Irish Parliament has recently been involved in an XML publishing project. The project aims *(i)* at developing a "common IT platform" to be used in the publication of parliamentary documents, and *(ii)* at pushing the use of XML as a solution to publishing requirements. Moreover, this platform will be used to develop Web-enabled, XML-based authoring, editing and publishing systems. More information can be found in [5].

An initiative similar to $x$-Leges is the Pan African Parliamentary Interoperability (PAPI, [12])framework. It aims to enable Parliaments across Africa to

[1] http://www.nir.it

easily share data. The PAPI framework aims *(i)* at defining common building blocks in a single model that can be applied to each (or at least most of) Parliamentary documents, and at *(ii)* providing tools for managing drafting and the publication process on the Web.

The peer-to-peer computing paradigm and the Web Service technologies are currently proposed in many research contexts, including *e*-Government, as a viable solution to solve interoperability issues between heterogeneous systems [4]. Even if the research community basically agrees on the usefulness and advantages of such paradigms and technologies, "real world" examples are still missing, due to the inherent difficulties in developing this kind of systems, to the novelty of technologies and the lack of skills in Public Administrations and software vendors/developers. Therefore, mission critical applications are not yet designed and implemented by adopting peer-to-peer and Web Services. The $x$-Leges system presents therefore a great interest as one of the first real, mission critical systems in the *e*-Government area that has been conceived, since its inception, as based on such technologies and paradigms.

## 3 The Context: The Italian e-Leges Project

During the last few years, the Italian Parliament promoted many national projects in order *(i)* to provide free access to juridical documents, in particular to the *in-force* version of the law (i.e., the law containing all the changes introduced by following related laws), and *(ii)* to increase the spread of IT technologies in the whole life-cycle of laws.

The main issues that have been identified in order to fulfil these objectives are the following: *(i)* making available over the Internet the in-force version of the primary Italian legislative corpus, by means of specialized document management systems freely available; *(ii)* supporting the evolution of Italian national standards for the representation of laws as electronic documents; *(iii)* studying legislative drafting and classification problems and testing software products to simplify these tasks; *(iv)* designing and implementing a cooperative system to support exchanges of electronic documents among the institutions involved in the law production process, from the early stages till the official publication.

In this context, CNIPA started a general initiative, referred to as *e-Leges*, that covers all the previous aspects, from standardization up to the software infrastructure for accessing laws. The initiative consists of several different projects, including the $x$-Leges one, which deals with the exchange of electronic documents among the institutions that take part in the law production processes.

Italy has a *perfect bicameral parliamentary system*: to become a law, the same (possibly amended) proposal has to be approved without modifications by both the Chambers. Laws approved by one chamber with modifications are submitted to the other chamber for a new discussion, limited to the parts affected by amendments. This "back & forth" occurs through physical (motorized) exchange of signed paper documents, making the process expensive and inefficient. CNIPA has proposed the design and implementation of a distributed system, based on Web Service technologies, in which documents are exchanged in XML format compliant with the NormeinRete standard. CNIPA has carried out a feasibility study and a design of the system, in which the processes for law production have been deeply investigated and the wanted solution has been designed. In the following sections, the results of this study are presented.

## 4 x-Leges Requirements

The process that allows the production of a law consists of intra-organization activities together with inter-organization ones, such as transmission of (drafts of) documents, coordination among the different involved subjects and their integration. $x$-Leges is designed to make more effective the latter kind of activities, characterizing cooperation between organizations. All the internal aspects of the processes inside organizations are out of the scope of the system.

From a technical point of view, the $x$-Leges system seems to be more a document management system with groupware features than a proper workflow management system [7]. It indeed aims at tracing the state of the normative production process, not at defining "a priori" and then enacting the process itself. Other requirements of the $x$-Leges system architecture are the following: *(i)* to be implemented using a distributed architecture, in order to preserve administrations' autonomy and technological/organizational independence; *(ii)* the use of standard cross-platform technologies; *(iii)* the possibility to perform document exchanges on top of the *certified e-mail* infrastructure that is currently under development in most of the Italian PAs[2].

The overall architecture of the $x$-Leges systems is based on such requirements, with the support and continuous collaboration of IT representatives of all involved organizations.

## 5 Conceptual and XML Structure of the Exchanged Documents

The first task of the $x$-Leges project has been to clearly identify the documents and information to be transmitted among cooperating organizations during the laws approval and promulgation process. In order to represent the data flow, let us consider the following metaphor, shown in Figure 1:

[2] The certified e-mail infrastructure is a system in which electronic metadata, with legal value, concerning the effective sending and receiving of the message, are provided to the end-points (like in the ordinary postal service). In order to build such a system, a set of technical standards have been defined (e.g., for interoperability among different thrusted e-mail providers, how to certify a mail provider, etc.). See also: `http://www.cnipa.gov.it/site/it-IT/In_primo_piano/Posta_Elettronica_Certificata__(PEC)/`.

- the cooperative process that produces a new law creates a "container" (a kind of directory) of documents [3];
- each process step, performed by a different organization, enriches the container with a folder;
- in a given folder (i.e., the object exchanged at the end of a given step) there are the current versions of the law, reports, notes, further information, i.e., files, that are referred to as "documental objects" in the following of this work.

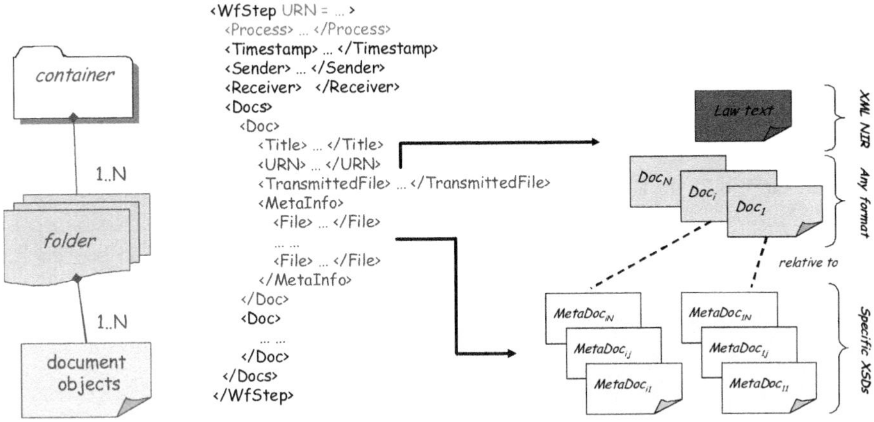


(a) The container intuition

(b) XML format

**Fig. 1.** The $x$-Leges exchange format

As shown in Figure 1(a), a container consists of 1..N folders and a folder consists of 1..N documental objects. At each cooperative process step, only the documental objects produced in the last stage are put in an apposite folder, which is then transmitted through $x$-Leges to the appropriate institution. If an organization wants to collect the documents belonging to a container (and the related process history), all involved organizations are considered using query/access functions.

Figure 1(b) shows the exchange format, i.e., the structure of objects transmitted at each step, consisting of:

- a set of "strict" documental objects, that are the official documents currently transmitted on paper; in particular the law text is transmitted as an XML document compliant with the NormeinRete (NIR, [2]) format, while other document objects can be in any electronic format (PDF, MS Word, scanned images, etc.);

[3] In Italian we have a nice term to indicate it, namely *faldone*, which is physically the big box in which you were used to put all folders (each one containing different sheets) in old paper-based archives.

- meta-information, considered as "extended" documental objects; their transmission is one of the added-values of the system. They heavily depends on the specific process step, on the typology of normative act, etc. Such document objects are XML documents compliant with XML Schemas (XSDs) that have to be defined "ad hoc";
- workflow information to identify documents and folders belonging to the same container, i.e., process instance. The system uses identifiers compliant with the IETF URN specification [9], the format of such identifiers being defined as an Italian national standard [1,11]. Specifically they are: *(a)* a unique flow/container identifier (an URN); *(b)* a unique step/folder identifier (an URN); *(c)* a timestamp; *(d)* a sender ID; *(e)* a receiver ID; *(f)* a title and an identifier (an URN) for each strict documental object being transmitted; *(g)* references to the XML documents with meta-information related to this step, and the references to the transmitted extended documental objects. Note that 0..N extended document objects can be associated at each strict document object; therefore the workflow keeps track of the relationship between these two kinds of document objects, and this should be stored and transmitted.

Workflow information are therefore exchanged as an XML document according to the previous format, shown in Figure 1(b).

## 6 The x-Leges Peer-2-Peer Architecture

The $x$-Leges system is a distributed, cooperative system based on a peer-to-peer architecture[4]:

- each involved organization deploys an identical copy of a subsystem, referred to as x-*Leges peer* in the following;
- the whole system consists of the combination of the $x$-Leges peers deployed by all the organizations constituting the system;
- the overall behaviour is obtained through peer interactions; these interactions can change according to different scenarios: sometimes an organization subsystem can start the system execution (thus acting as a "client" towards the other subsystems), and other times it waits for an invocation (acting as a server).

The system aims at transmitting documents and (some) meta-information produced during the cooperative process of the law production; other piece of information is not sent along with the documents, but is rather stored by the organizations of origin, yet being accessible on demand by other subsystems.

[4] In this paper we consider a distributed system as peer-to-peer if each sub-system belonging to it acts both as a client and as a server with respect to the set of functionalities the whole system offers. In the $x$-Leges system, there is not any centralized component, thus making it a "pure", i.e., "non-ibrid" peer-to-peer system.

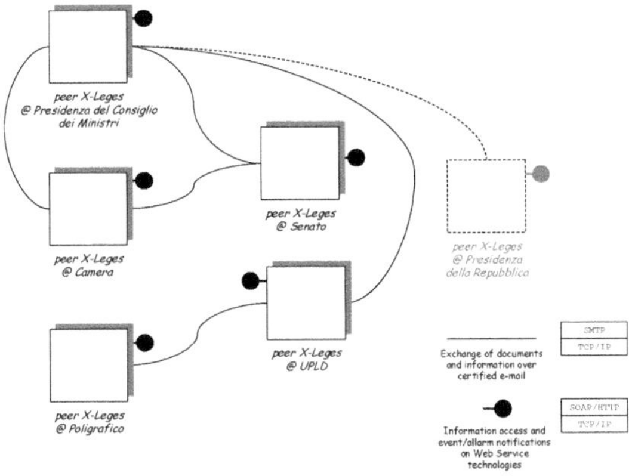


**Fig. 2.** The P2P x-Leges distributed architecture

In such a way the system is able to manage documents and meta-information, and trace-back cooperative workflow sequences by using distributed queries to all involved subsystems. Moreover the system delivers *(i)* notifications related to transmissions/receptions of documents and their related meta-information, to organizations subscribing suitable categories of events, and *(ii)* delivers alarms when given deadlines are exceeded.

The system does not show one of the features of a workflow management system, i.e., the ability of acting proactively towards users, to respect the correct activity timings; this happens also because processes managed by the system are not repetitive, as the production of each law is a different case (technically an instance), with respect to both process steps and timings. For this reason the system is not required to manage the process schemas, to which all instances must be compliant. Conversely, the system supports document exchange and, ex post, the cooperative workflow history construction; however process advances for exclusive initiative of those users/organizations that use the system: it can be considered more as a groupware system than a genuine workflow management system.

Documents and information exchanges are achieved through certified e-mail. Conversely, *(i)* access to information belonging to organizations, and distributed query functionalities, as well as *(ii)* functionalities of subscription to events and alarms, and related acknowledgements, are deployed through Web Service technologies. Figure 3 shows the architecture of a single $x$-Leges peer, consisting of:

**Database $x$-Leges.** This component manages the persistence of documents transmitted during the cooperative workflow, and of meta-information related to them. The database implementation is based on relational DBMS technology, with suitable extensions to manage XML documents.

**Subscriptions, Transmission Events and Alarms Database.** This component manages the persistence of subscriptions to transmission events and to alarms, moreover it manages all the information needed to handle the

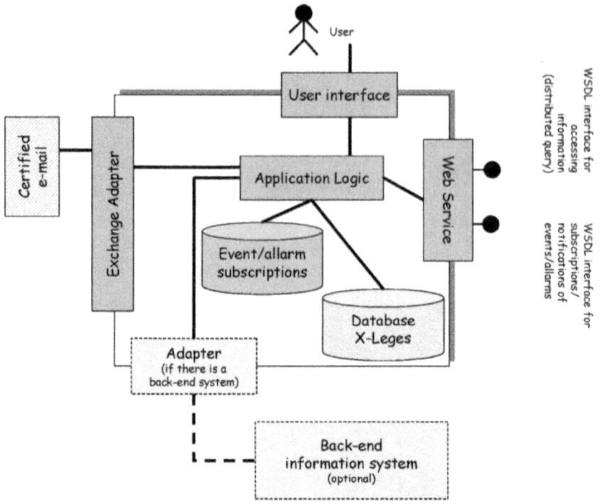


**Fig. 3.** The x-Leges peer architecture

related acknowledgements. Different $x$-Leges peers host identical copies of such a database, with a Web Service interface managing their synchronization. Its implementation can be based on a DBMS or on a Publish & Subscribe engine.

**Application Logic.** It is the system engine, as it controls interactions among all components. Indeed the components forming a peer can not interact directly, so in order to maintain consistency between them, application communications between components are always controlled by the application logic layer acting as a "master" towards the other components ("slaves"). In particular, application logic acts as a façade towards the other system components and as a mediator; its application-oriented interface exposes both request/response methods and events notification functionalities. It is published in order to allow the different organizations to autonomously develop their adapters towards pre-existing systems. Its implementation must be based on a component-oriented technology, hosted on a suitable application server.

**User Interface.** It allows interaction with users, i.e., organization operators working with the $x$-Leges system. Its implementation must be based on the thin web client paradigm, for this reason this interface will be deployed on a web server, able to manage and host both static HTML pages and dynamic modules (as servlet, JSP, ASP, CGI, etc.), suitably interfaced with the application logic. When the user interface is used during the document and information transmission and reception phases, it must provide automatic information completion capabilities, by collecting data from the back-end systems, thus simplifying users work and making intra-organization systems more and more integrated with the $x$-Leges system. Moreover through this UI it is possible to configure alarms, to make subscriptions both to alarms and to transmission events.

**Web Service.** Access to information kept by each peer is possible using suitable remote interfaces built on Web Service technology. For example, when an operator wants to know a cooperative process evolution, he/she makes a request to the peer of the organization he/she works (by using the user interface), then the application logic layer manages a distributed query to all the other peers, done through Web Services offered by them. Using a Web Service is also possible to synchronize different copies of subscription events and alarms database, and to manage their notifications. This component implementation must be based, as much as possible, on the application server platform hosting application logic.

**Transmission Adapter.** When a document, and the meta-information related to it, must be sent from one organization to another during the cooperative process, the application logic manages the transmission, using this component interfaced to communication systems, i.e., certified email, and, if in place, a digital protocol system.

**Adapter.** If the organization hosting a peer is equipped with its own information system, and *(i)* such a system manages information of interest to $x$-Leges, or *(ii)* it wants to allow such a system to access part of the $x$-Leges information, then an appropriate adapter deals with interfacing between the two subsystems. In particular, the adapter interfaces $x$-Leges with the organization information system in some specific moments:

- when a folder is sent, in order to access information already stored in the back-end system, and to notify the event to the back-end system;
- when a folder arrives, in order to notify the back-end system the event and let the back-end system access the new information;
- each time the back-end system needs to access information in $x$-Leges (and vice-versa).

The two components are loosely coupled ("read-only"): the update of the database $x$-Leges is never triggered by the back-end, but the $x$-Leges always acts as a client (it updates itself on its own initiative); the back end system is never updated by $x$-Leges: it is notified and then, the back-end, according to its own business logic, accesses information and possibly updates itself.

In summary, a peer is a subsystem needing to interface with 4 different elements: *(i)* operators, *(ii)* other peers, *(iii)* possible pre-existent elements in the hosting organization, and *(iv)* electronic transmission systems. User interface, Web Service, adapter and transmission adapter are the components that allow the $x$-Leges application logic to interface with the external elements.

## 6.1 Deployment Architecture and Security Concerns

From a theoretical point of view, all the information exchanged through the $x$-Leges system is public, as it represents documents that according to the Italian law are accessible, in any moment, by any citizen. Therefore strict confidentiality

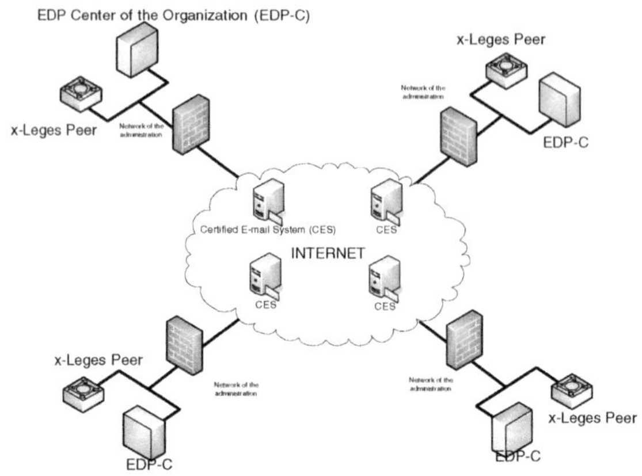


(a) The overall deployment architecture

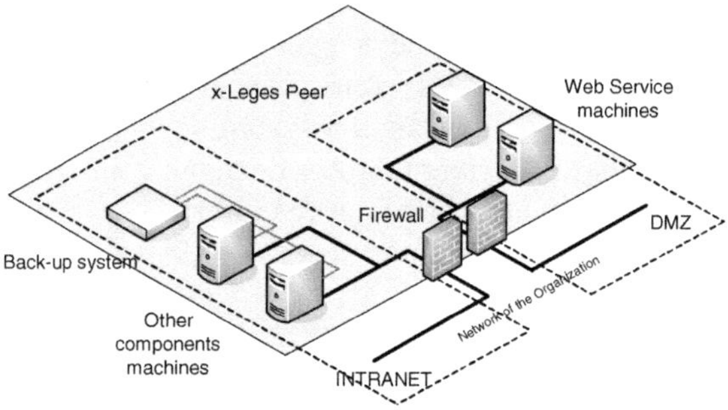


(b) Detail of the single peer

**Fig. 4.** The $x$-Leges deployment architecture

requirements should be not needed for the system. However, from a more pragmatic point of view, the loss of image due to a possible attack to $x$-Leges, with high visibility, is likely to result very high (e.g., the reader should imagine the effect and visibility gained by an hacker/cyber terrorist who can claim to have successfully attacked the system for producing the Italian laws). Therefore, specific security (in particular integrity) and availability requirements for $x$-Leges have been considered and are briefly presented in the following paragraph.

As a first measure, all exchanged information (both sent in certified e-mail messages and exchanged through Web Service technologies) is ciphered.

From a deployment point of view, each $x$-Leges peer consists of the different previously considered software components, which need to be deployed on logically independent hardware systems. In particular, only the Web Service is accessible/reachable from outside the organization hosting the $x$-Leges peer: as shown in Figure 4(b), it is deployed on appropriate machines in the DMZ of the organization, whereas all other components are internal to the organization, and therefore deployed on different machines on its own intranet. This implies that the Web interface is accessible only inside the organization, guaranteeing, through appropriate organizational measures, that only users of the organization may use the system (in general, only specific personnel is in charge of drafting and transmitting the documents concerning laws).

Both the machines deploying the Web Service and those ones deploying the other software components are arranged in redundant clusters, in order to guarantee high availability of the whole peer [13], and therefore of the whole $x$-Leges system.

With such arrangements, shown in Figure 4(a), a single node has only two physical contacts with the general Internet: the Web Service, in the DMZ, and the Certified E-mail system; the provider of the latter, according to the Italian standard, need to guarantee high security, and therefore, with the previous design, only the Web Service needs to be accurately made secure.

Besides requiring the Web Service of each organization to implement the WS-Security standard, a specific attention has been paid to authentication and access control. More in details, during the interactions between organizations, each one presents itself to the other by providing appropriate credentials granting access to the offered operations (e.g., for querying the container, or subscribing to an event); internally the organization adopts a Role Based Access Control (RBAC) method for authenticating and authorizing its own operators to use the operations offered by the $x$-Leges system (in such a way a user $\mathcal{U}$ with role $\mathcal{R}$ in organization $\mathcal{A}$, is granted by $\mathcal{A}$ to execute an operation); then, when the $\mathcal{A}$'s Web Service needs to interact with another organization $\mathcal{B}$, the latter grants access on the basis of the credentials presented by $\mathcal{A}$, i.e., the ones presented by the Web Service, in an independent and transparent way with respect to the specific user. With such a 2-layer security architecture, the complex management of users is restricted to single organizations, guaranteeing autonomy and different policies that may exist.

## 7 Conclusions and Future Work

In this paper the $x$-Leges system has been illustrated. This system will enable digital exchange of documents among the institutions involved in the legislative production process. The architecture is fully decentralized: each node is independent and holds a subset of the information of the whole system. Exchange is based upon XML documents, containing both the law proposal and the metadata needed to rebuild the law workflow instance. The use of Web Services as interfaces and a strong security implementation complete the system.

The Call for Projects by possible software vendors/developers has been launched at the end of May 2006, and the winner (the effective subject realizing the system) should be defined within the autumn 2006. The start of the development activities is foreseen for 2007, then, after the completion, the Senate, the Chamber of Deputies, the Prime Minister Office, and the Ministry of Justice should start to use the system, even though the traditional exchange system will continue to be used in parallel during this experimental phase.

## References

1. AIPA. Definizione delle Regole per l'Assegnazione dei Nomi Uniformi ai Documenti Giuridici. Circolare n. AIPA/CR/35 (in Italian), http://www.cnipa.gov.it/site/_contentfiles/00127800/127896_CR_35_ 2001.zip, November 2001.
2. AIPA. Formato per la Rappresentazione Elettronica dei Provvedimenti Normativi tramite il Linguaggio di Marcatura XML. Circolare n. AIPA/CR/40 (in Italian), http://www.cnipa.gov.it/site/_contentfiles/00127500/127544_CR_40_2002.pdf, April 2002.
3. A. Boer, R. Hoekstra, R. Winkels, T. van Engers, and F. Willaert. Proposal for a Dutch Legal XML Standard. In *EGOV 2002 Conference*, 2002.
4. M. Contenti, M. Mecella, A. Termini, and R. Baldoni. A Distributed Architecture for Supporting e-Government Cooperative Processes. In *TED Conference on eGovernment (TCGOV 2005)*, 2005.
5. P. Doran. Legislative XML in the Irish Parliament: Our reasons for, and Experience of, Migration to XML. In *3rd Workshop on Legislative XML*, 2005.
6. F. Grandi, F. Mandreoli, P. Tiberio, and M. Bergonzini. A Temporal Data Model and Management System for Normative Texts in XML Format. In *5th ACM International Workshop on Web Information and Data Management*, 2003.
7. F. Leymann and D. Roller. *Production Workflow - Concepts and Techniques.* PTR Prentice Hall, 2000.
8. C. Lupo and C. Batini. A Federative Approach to Laws Access by Citizens: The "Normeinrete" System. In *EGOV 2003 Conference*, 2003.
9. L. Masinter and K. Sollins. Functional Requirements for Uniform Resource Names (RFC 1737). http://www.faqs.org/rfcs/rfc1737.html, 1994.
10. M. Palmirani and R. Brighi. Norma-System: A Legal Document System for Managing Consolidated Acts. In *13th DEXA Conference*, 2002.
11. P. Spinosa. Identification of Legal Documents Through URNs (Uniform Resource Names). In *EUROWEB 2001 Conference "The Web in Public Administration"*, 2001.
12. UNDESA. Pan african parliamentary interoperability. http://www.parliaments.info/PAPI/index.htm, 2005.
13. P. Verissimo and L. Rodrigues. *Distributed Systems for System Architects.* Springer, 2001.

# Flexibility of Information Architecture in e-Government Chains

Victor Bekkers

Department of Public Administration/Center for Public Innovation Erasmus University, P.O. Box 1738, NL-3000 DR Rotterdam
Bekkers@fsw.eur.nl

**Abstract.** How can the flexibility of an information architecture in e-government chains – defined as a set of multi-rational agreements – be achieved, if one acknowledges the fact that the use of ICT may automate the status quo between organizations which work together in a policy chain? Research shows that flexibility cannot only be achieved by looking at technological requirements and agreements. Also other agreements should be considered which express other (political, legal and economic) design rationalities and values. Moreover, flexibility is also influenced by the structure and dynamics of the power and trustworthiness of the relationships between the organizations involved.

## 1 Introduction

E-government refers to production and delivery of government information, interaction and transaction services through the use of ICT, which are closely related tot the execution of rules and regulations [24]. In this process different (semi-) public and private organizations as well as their back and front offices fulfill specific but interrelated tasks for which they have to exchange information. The concept of a policy chain and a policy network may help us to understand the dependencies between these tasks, which is very important in relation to the development of e-government. In this study e-government chains and networks will be defined as semi-permanent collaboration arrangements between organizations, in order to produce – in a routinized way – specific services and provisions [30]. In a chain the dependencies between crossorganizational working processes have a sequential character, while in a network the dependencies have a reciprocal nature [33]. Chain or network computerization can be understood as the use of information and communication technology (ICT) to support and/or redesign the working and coordination processes and the sharing of information between (inter)dependent organizations in order to enhance the efficiency and efficacy of implementation and service delivery processes. However, there is a shady side. The effective use of ICT presupposes the formalization and standardization of working processes and information exchange relations. Stability and predictability are important conditions for the effective use of ICT. ICT may automate the status quo, freezing organizations into patterns of behavior and operations that are difficult to change, once they have been computerized, and thus contributing to a process of bureaucratization [1]. Hence, an important issue in chain

M.A. Wimmer et al. (Eds.): EGOV 2006, LNCS 4084, pp. 243–255, 2006.

and network computerization is flexibility, for instance if the law one which the service delivery process has been based, is changed. Will organizations that collaborate in a policy chain be able to adapt to changing circumstances, once they have computerized cross-organizational working and information exchange processes?

This article investigates how flexibility has been achieved in the development of an information architecture – defined as a set of multi-rational agreements – that facilitates the exchange of information and the use of ICT within three Dutch egovernment chains. What factors account for the flexibility of an information architecture within a e-government chain? In order to answer this question, we have to explore the nature of (the shaping of a) information architectures (section one) as well as how flexibility as a requirement can be achieved (section two). Based on these theoretical explorations, we will develop in section three a theoretical framework and research strategy in order to empirically investigate the research question. In section five we will describe three how flexibility of the information architecture has been achieved in three Dutch e-government chains. In section six we draw some conclusions.

## 2 Designing Information Architectures

From an information management perspective, an information architecture can be defined as a conceptual framework for the future organizational ICT-infrastructure. An architecture is a plan for the structure and integration of the information resources in or between organizations in order to support the information needs of organizations which are related to the specific processes within the organizations and the tasks and goals of an organization [1][34]. However, how neutral is an architecture? An architecture can also be perceived as a social and political constructed 'artefact', which embodies different interests and values as well presenting a set of playing rules which influence the exchange of information and the use of ICT [5]. Some reasons, stemming from different bodies of knowlegde, can be given.

The development of an interorganizational information architecture challenges the existing interests, working practices and domains of organizations, because information and ICT are powerful resources that organizations use to protect their position in a service delivery chain or network [3] [7] [ 15]. However, essential is how organizational stakeholders perceive the nature and degree of the uncertainties and dependencies that result from a more intensive and coordinated exchange of information [29] [36]. They are willing to set up an architecture, if they are able to minimize their dependency on other organizations or maximize the dependence of other organizations on them [4]. Therefore, chain and network computerization can be understood in terms of 'information politicking', resulting in conflict, competition, exchange, negotiation and co-operation [12] [13].

From a public management perspective the development of an information architecture development can also be defined as a governance challenge [2] [3].

Governance refers to the process of horizontal coordination, in which different actors try to create a shared understanding and definition of the relevant problems and solutions [14]. Chain and network computerization can be defined as the co-production of a common information domain through interaction, communication, negotiation and exchange [30]. It is important to define a dynamic balance between (qualitative and quantitative) costs and benefits (in the short run but also in the long run), so that a 'win-win' situation emerges based on the recognition of interdependency [35]. However, this implies that core values and vital interests will be respected [2] [14] [27] [28]. Moreover, trust, reputation and social capital within a policy sector seem to be important to achieve productive information exchange relationships [6] [35] Furthermore, positive collaboration experiences, stemming from the past, influence the degree of trust which is important to define win-win situations. Experiences with opportunistic behavior or even 'power play' can enhance distrust [37]. Trust can also be a quality that facilitates the preparedness of an organization to re-consider existing information exchange agreements, and thus contributing to flexibility. Moreover, the specification of the agreements, which are laid down in an architecture, can be understood as the expression of trust or even distrust too [37].

From a political science perspective, it is important to look at the specific values, based on different but competing design rationalities, that play a role in the design of an information architecture. Four rationalities, with their own internal logic and legitimacy and stressing specific core values, should be taken into account [31]. The political rationality deals with the question 'who gets what, when and how', if we look at the political challenges with which a political community is confronted [21] [32]. Information and ICT are important policy instruments that governments use to realize specific political values like efficiency, security, liberty, equity or accountability. Moreover, they use ICT to deliberately influence the information position of actors and their relationships [11] [22]. The legal rationality stresses the importance of the rule of the law, which e.g. implies offering legal security, consistency and legality. The economic rationality focuses on cost-efficiency, due to the scarce amount of resources which is available in order to achieve specific goals (in terms of benefits). The technological rationality emphasizes the question, how to design effective, efficient and trustworthy tools and interventions strategies which are based on specific professional knowledge, in this case information management and computer technology knowledge.

Hence, we conclude that in the development of information architecture competing design rationalities and values play an important role, which also touches upon existing interests, practices and positions of organizations.

## 3 Flexible Information Architectures

From an information engineering perspective, the flexibility of an information architecture can be addressed in two ways. Allen and Boynton distinguish a 'low' and 'high' road [1]. Following the low road, flexibility can be achieved through a highly decentralized approach. Data, computers and networks, applications, programming and all the supporting resources are pushed as far down in the organization as possible. Variety is seen as pre-condition for flexibility. Efficiency advantages can be accomplished through a) the definition of a common, but minimal set of standards and definitions for the exchange of information and building networks that link dispersed work stations, data bases etc; b) ensuring that there is full access of information in stead of restricted access, primarily based on trust; c) ensuring the integrity of the data definitions and network standards. Hence, the emphasis is on specification of minimal, but critical standards and interfaces that makes it possible to exchange information between rather autonomous organizational units in order to create a minimum of uniformity in the framework of organizational heterogeneity [1]. Therefore, an information architecture should only regulate a number of minimal but vital issues, which prevent the break-down of the organization as whole [25] [10].

The 'high road' focuses on creating flexibility and efficiency through uniformity, based on centralization: corporate wide networks, central data collections, common application systems, standardized hardware, operating systems and databases. Core applications are designed to be organizationally independent, which are immune to the restructuring of an organization. The development of a central imposed, homogeneous information architecture and infrastructure is seen as the road to meet the changing conditions, without fundamentally changing the systems themselves [1].

However, the changing nature of the technology itself does also changes the way in which flexibility can be achieved. ICT has become more flexible itself, because it has increasingly been based on open, thus flexible, and international accepted standards, like XML. Moreover, the rapid development of the internet and the World Wide Web has provided a basic and publicly available infrastructure that can be used to achieve connectivity and communality in order to facilitate new collaborative arrangements [26].

## 4 Theoretical Framework and Research Strategy

An information architecture consists of a number of agreements which facilitate the smooth exchange of information and the use of ICT between organizations in a policy chain. These agreements reflect different design rationalities. Therefore, we will first focus our attention on the *object and nature of the agreements* which organizations have developed to exchange information within a policy chain The following agreements are relevant:

- political and administrative agreements, referring to the interests and the information domains that are at stake as well as to the political goals to be achieved. For instance how to deal with the autonomy of the participating organizations?
- technological agreements, which refer to a) the definition of the (standardized and formalized) information to be exchanged, b) the use of ICT to support this exchange and c) the management and control of the use of ICT;

- economic agreements, which refer to the specification and allocation of costs and benefits, related to the exchange of information and the use of ICT;
- legal arrangements, which refer to specific rights and obligations which are laid down in rules and regulations and to more fundamental rights, like privacy.

Furthermore, it is important to look at the way in which these agreements are specified [37]. The nature of the agreements refer to questions like: Are the agreements specified in detail or are they vague? Do they focus on minimum requirements or are they rather elaborated and detailed?

The second step is to understand how the nature and object of these agreements have contributed to the flexibility of the architecture.

Thirdly, it is important to explain why these arrangements have been made. In this research project we have look for explanations which refer to the *structure of the chain*; in particular, we have looked at the relevant interests, positions of the organizations involved and the dependency relations between them as well as the resources they can mobilize to protect these interests. An architecture may reflect the power relations and positions within the policy chain or network. However, these relationships are not static, but dynamic due to the interactions between the organizations involved.

This implies, fourthly, that also the *quality of the collaboration process* between the involved organizations should be considered. Especially the trustfulness of past and present interactions and the way in which a common challenge has been defined, may have influenced the object and nature of the agreements made and the way in which flexibility is being perceived as an important characteristic of the architecture [37].

Another issue in our research strategy has been the selection of three chains in which flexibility was an issue; chains that also resemble the high and low road of architecture design and that will be studied from a case study perspective. The low road has been followed in the design of the vehicle license chain, in which the Vehicle License Agency focuses on the standardization of linkage between different local and autonomous systems. The second case is the Suwinet architecture in Dutch social security which resembles the high road, in which a complete nation-wide standardized exchange infrastructure has been developed. The third case is a combination of the low and high road. This case is the urban zoning plan chain, in which central and nation wide data exchange and professional data definition standards have been developed.

## 5 The Practice of Developing Flexible Information Architectures

In this section we present the results of our comparative case study research. First, a short description of the backgrounds of the three chains will be given. Secondly, we will focus on the object and nature of the agreements made as well try to understand how they contributed to the flexibility of the architecture.

Thirdly, we explain why these arrangements have been made in relation to the structure and dynamics of the policy sectors in which the chains are located.

## 5.1 Preliminary Description of the Policy Chains

The first case is the Vehicle License Chain, which resulted from Vehicle License Registration Act (1995). This chain consists of different sub chains that share the New Vehicle License Registry (NKR). The Registry is owned by the Vehicle License Agency on behalf of the Traffic Ministry. This registry was established to improve traffic safety – in terms of liability of vehicle ownership (mostly used cars) – through a better exchange of information. The registry is a central, common pool database in which information about the status of a vehicle and its owner is stored and can be used by other organizations, such as the Tax and Customs Administration (in order to assess road taxes), garages (when they periodically execute safety checks on cars, older than two years), insurance companies (to assess the legal status of a car in order to handle insurance requests) and post offices (when functioning as the front office of the Vehicle License Agency for citizens to provide information about the status of a car when they sell or buy a used car). On the one hand, the Vehicle License Agency is dependent on private garages, insurance companies and post offices in order to execute a number of tasks on their behalf. On the other hand, the Agency – based on the use of her legal competences as owner of the registry – attempts to control the discretion of the organizations through the introduction well specified information processing and exchange procedures and norms.

The second case is the Work & Income Chain which started in 2002. In order to implement this chain a technological network (called Suwinet) has been installed. It connects 131 local job employment organizations – that fulfill tasks in the assessment and delivery of social benefits to unemployed people as well help these people to find new jobs – and some nationwide social security agencies. This network supports the execution of Law on Work & Income, which generates a chainlike sequence of operational procedures and actions between different organizations and as well as corresponding information processing activities. There is a joint responsibility of the Ministry of Social Affairs, the association of local job employment centers and some national agencies to create an effective and efficient exchange network. Based on this joint responsibility, a central co-ordination committee which facilitates and monitor the exchange of information within the chain, has been erected.

The third case is the exchange of digital planning zone information, which is used to approve plans and to render local spatial planning permits. The approval is done by local, regional and central planning authorities, which generates a rather intensive exchange of information. This exchange is based on the sequence of a number of legal procedures (based on the Spatial Planning Act) that have to be obeyed. In this project – started in 2003 and based on voluntary co-operation – the emphasis was on the development and implementation of data exchange and professional data definition standards. The Ministry of Spatial Planning which is formally responsible, has been the initiator, focusing on boosting the project.

### 5.2 Architectural Agreements and Flexibility

Based on our case study approach, we are able to reconstruct the object and nature of the agreements which are laid down in the three chain information architectures. We will the discuss the most essential agreements and link them to the nature of the agreements that have been made and the motives which lay behind them. We have also asked key-figures, which agreements have contributed substantially to flexibility of the information architecture?

The most important agreement in the Vehicle License Chain to achieve flexibility is to respect the administrative and informational autonomy of the participating public and private organization. This also facilitates the inclusion of new partners. ICT should not immediately intervene with internal working procedures and routines. Therefore no complex negotiations take place in order to integrate external and internal information processing processes and to formulate all kinds of exceptional technological working conditions. As a consequence, the Vehicle License Agency does not develop their own networks, but the agency uses the already available networks of the involved partners, like the network of the garage association and the post offices. This political agreement also influences the technological agreements that have been made. They focus on the standardization and certification of the interfaces between the local information systems and the third party network as well as between the third party network and the agencys information systems in order to establish effective, efficient and reliable links and interfaces. By following the 'low road' of architecture development the Vehicle License Agency aims to achieve a flexible architecture. The costs for the regular exchange of information are based on an annual price/tariff per message. This also enhances flexibility, because complex budget negotiations about the allocation of a fixed budget can be avoided. Moreover, it respects the factual intensity of the exchange. Furthermore separate financial agreements are made, if legal changes lead to additional investments, for which an additional budget will be given. These political, economic and technological agreements are laid down in 'service level agreements'.

Not only the contents of the specific agreements have contributed to the flexibility of the chain, but also the fact that only very firm agreements have been made; agreements which only specify the minimal and critical requirements that are needed to have reliable interfaces.

In the Suwinet information architecture the most important agreement refers to the establishment of a data exchange network, based on international accepted and open (XML) message standards, compulsory sharing of specific databases, and the definition of specific data. This is compulsory for the participating organizations. In order to achieve compliance a rather detailed set of service level agreements have been formulated, which address the technological standards which should be taken into consideration as well as the speediness and the reliability of the information to be exchanged. These agreements focus on the chain as a whole as well as on the rights and obligations of a specific group of functional identical links in the chain, like the group of local employment agencies. The most important political agreement is that the chain itself is a self-organizing chain in which the steering of the chain is a joint responsibility of the partners involved. Therefore a chain coordination committee has been erected. The ministry of Social Affairs is only responsible for the functioning for the chain as a whole as well as for the financing of the chain information infrastructure as a whole. The most important legal agreement is the specification of the data which should be obligatory exchanged, which are further elaborated in exchange guidelines and the earlier mentioned service level agreements.

What does this imply for the flexibility of the work & income chain? On the one hand the use of a nation wide technological infrastructure, based on solid and rather minimal, open and international accepted technological standards such as XML do contribute to the flexibility of the chain, because it diminishes all kind of 'legacy' frictions and it tries to achieve flexibility for the long term. Moreover, the willingness of the Ministry of Social Affairs to finance the development and exploitation of the network, thereby facilitating the inclusion of new organizations, has contributed to the flexibility of the chain. On the other hand, the flexibility of the chain is frustrated, because the conditions under which specific data sets should be exchanged, have been worked out in very detailed mandatory regulations, operational information policy guidelines and service level agreements, which strongly intervenes with internal working processes. Furthermore, these guidelines change frequently, which generates all kinds of additional implementation costs as well as resistance.

In the urban planning zone chain flexibility has been achieved to use proven, internationally accepted information exchange standards (like GML) and international professional accepted geographical information models, which define the contents of specific professional object-oriented geographical information. Therefore the emphasis primarily lies on the development on a number of technological agreements, which has also let to an elaborated system of ICT management and data model management arrangements. Also the voluntary nature of the chain has contributed to its flexibility. Local and regional governments are free to participate. Voluntary participation generates more support to make the necessary changes, because participants are easier to be convinced of the need to change and to make additional costs. The agreement is that each organization should pay its own expenses, because the idea is that the benefits will be larger than the possible costs.

### 5.3 Flexibility as a Social and Political Quality

In this section we investigate how the structure and dynamics of the relationships between the organizations that constitute a chain, have influenced the agreements which have been made, which in the end also influences the perception of the flexibility of an information architecture.

In the Vehicle License Chain the nature and object of the agreements can only be understood in relation to the powerful position of the Vehicle License Agency as well as the ability of the agency to (re)produce trustful relationships with those organizations that fulfill tasks on behalf of the agency. After all, the agency controls the Vehicle License Registry, which contains authentic and highly reliable information about the legal status of a vehicle which is used for different, but related administrative operations. The agency uses her legal competences and ICT (knowledge) resources to position herself as the spider in a web of interrelated policy implementation chains, thereby weaving new ties with new organizations and new activities in vehicle safety related sectors under the political condition to respect the internal informational autonomy of the participating organizations. These legal and ICT resources enable the Agency to impose specific agreements which can be altered rather easy, if conditions change as well as to determine which organizations is included or excluded in Agencys chains. On the other hand the agency acknowledges that it is dependent on the co-operation of these other organizations to fulfill a number of tasks on behalf of the agency, like the safety inspection of cars by certified garages. Sheer power politics would create resistance and would frustrate the ability to change the architectural agreements. Hence, the agency has explicitly invested in the creation and reproduction of trust. Trustfulness has been defined as a necessary condition for flexibility, because garages, post offices and insurance companies can be easier seduced to make the necessary changes in their ICT systems, if they are convinced of the good intentions of the agency. This has been elaborated in three ways. First, the agency recognizes the importance of making firm and clear agreements, addressing only the most critical requirements which are necessary to exchange information. The ability to formulate minimal but firm agreements is seen as the expression of trust. Rather detailed agreements in which eventualities have been described, are perceived by the agency as well as the other involved organizations as the expression of distrust. Secondly, if changes are necessary, the agency and its partners together, analyze and assess the impact of the changes for all the parties involved. These joint impact assessments are being perceived by all the stakeholders involved as important instruments to generate trust. They create an open agenda for negotiation, based on a systematic assessment of possible positive and negative effects. For instance, the allocation of costs and benefits of the ICT-measures to be implemented is a recurrent theme on this agenda. Thirdly, the agency has developed an elaborated system of customer relation management, using account managers as the eyes and ears of the agency in order to detect problems in an early stage.

The key respondents who represent different organizations in the Work & Income Chain also define the flexibility of an information architecture as the outcome of the relationships between them, because the history of the chain is one of the suspiciousness. Collaboration was imposed through a blue-print, based on the Work & Income Law. To the participating organizations the law offered less opportunity to shape the functioning of the architecture according their own wishes. Tailor-made solutions were not possible. Respondents perceive these detailed rules, prescribing which organization should receive or send information and under what conditions, as the expression of distrust. Recurrent changes in legislation led to ongoing and difficult negations about the nature of the implementation rules and how to translate these rules in specific information policies, which themselves had to be translated in an already detailed information architecture and all kind of service level agreements. Suspiciousness was also increased by the fact that the chain lacks as an organization which was actually capable to steer the operational functioning of the chain, although formally the Ministry of Social Affairs was responsible. The chain coordination committee which was foreseen in the law, had limited competences and only grew slowly in significance, once its added value had been proven. Originally, this led to an elaborate system of consultation and negotiation arenas, which frustrated the ability to change. Compromises which have been reached in one arena, were cancelled in another one; or divergent solutions were worked in different arenas. The fact that the new law has also imposed changes in the tasks and competences of the organizations involved, has also contributed to distrust. Issues that addressed the design and redesign of the information architecture, were consequently defined as competence questions. Information politicking was the result. Moreover, the re-allocation of competences among the organizations involved did also influence the internal working and information processing processes within the participating organizations. Existing working and information processing practices were challenged, which led to resistance; resistance which persisted when new legal changes had to be translated in the information architecture.

However, recently the relationships within the chain have improved, which enhanced the flexibility of the information architecture. First, the already foreseen coordination committee has acquired more credit and is regarded as a useful mechanism to diminish the intensive consultation rounds. Second, parties have switched their primarily internal focus towards a common external goal: putting clients first. Through this common frame of reference it is easier to legitimize changes in the information architecture.

The last chain is the planning zone chain. According to our respondents there is a relationship between the flexibility of the information architecture and the political principle that participation of local and regional government in the chain is voluntary. This generates support which makes it more easy to propose and implement changes. They all share the same goals, because they are all convinced of the benefits of the digital exchange and drafting of the spatial plans, although they have to bear all the costs. The voluntary character of the project has also led to specific arrangements for consultation and negotiation. In contrast to the previous chain, these arrangements are perceived as contributing to the flexibility of the architecture, because specific wishes and interest can easier be heard and are not suppressed by the most powerful organization. Tailor-made solutions are possible. Furthermore, this bottom-up process facilitates an evolutionary process, in which the project can develop itself according in its own pace; in this process of 'trial and error' an open attitude towards changes did prevail. Moreover, the fact that digitalization of the urban spatial plan did no challenged the existing distribution of tasks and competences was also being defined as a contribution to trustworthy relationships.

## 6 Conclusions

The aim of this article is to investigate what factors contribute tot the flexibility of an information architecture defined as a set of agreements – that facilitate the exchange of information and the use of ICT in e-government service delivery chains. However, these agreements do not only reflect technological requirements. They also refer to the political, legal and economic rationality and corresponding values which are important if policy programs or rules – on which e-government services are based – are computerized and information architectures are being developed. Moreover , it is important to take into account the structure and dynamics of the relationships of the policy sector in which a chain is located, because information and ICT are important resources which organizations use to protect their domains and interests.

From an information planning or information engineering point of view two roads of achieving flexibility have been distinguished, which have been translated into our case study selection. Following the 'low' road flexibility can be achieved through the specification of minimal, but critical standards and interfaces that makes it possible to exchange information between rather autonomous organizational units. The 'high road' focuses on creating flexibility and efficiency through uniformity, based on centralization. Core applications are designed to be organizationally independent , i.e. are immune to the restructuring of an organization. Our cases show that the choice for one of these roads or the combination of both contributes to the flexibility of an architecture. Arguing from a technological point of view, all the respondents were satisfied about the way technology did contribute to the flexibility of the chain. However, they stress that flexibility is being achieved through the combination of different kinds of agreements that are laid down in an architecture, in which more issues are specified that only technological requirements.

In the Vehicle License Chain flexibility is achieved through the combination of a technological agreements, specifying the linkages between a variety of systems and networks, and political and administrative agreements that try to respect the autonomy of the participating organizations and their internal processes. In the Work & Income Chain flexibility was frustrated by the detailed legal requirements that have to be translated in detailed information policies and regulations, which, ultimately, influenced the internal working and information processing procedures and routines in the participating organizations. In the Planning Zone Chain flexibility was achieved through the combination of choosing unambiguous, international accepted and proven standards and the political agreement that participation should be based on a voluntary basis.

Economic agreements are also important. Flexibility can be achieved if a tariff structure per message is being used (Vehicle License Chain) or one party takes all the operational costs (Work & Income Chain) and/or the strategic investments (Vehicle License Chain and Work & Income Chain). Complicated budget allocation discussions can be avoided, focusing on who gets what funds in relation to expected amount of messages. In the Planning Zone Chain we see that the established economic agreements begins to frustrate flexibility because costs and benefits are no longer in balance.

The flexibility of an architecture is also influenced by the nature of the agreements made. In the Vehicle License Chain and the Planning Zone Chain one has chosen for unambiguous, firm agreements, specifying only these vital conditions under which the chain could work. In the Work & Income Chain flexibility was diminished through the use of very detailed agreements, which try to foresee in all kinds of eventualities.

The research also showed the importance to relate the flexibility of an information architecture to the power relationships between the participating organizations and the quality of their collaboration process. These two factors also influence the object and the nature of the agreements which are made as well as the readiness to reconsider existing architectural agreements. The powerful resources of the undisputed Vehicle License Agency contribute substantially to the flexibility of the information architecture, but at the same this has not led to the misuse of power, because the agency want to establish trustworthy relationships. In the Work & Income Chain there is no powerful, undisputed organization which could impose the necessary changes. The idea of self-regulation by the chain itself lead to distrust and a continuous battle about competences in different arenas, which is expressed in continuously changing and detailed agreements. A dominant chain director is also absent in the Planning Zone Chain, but the fact that all the participating organizations share the same vision how to improve the exchange of zoning plans contribute to a shared understanding of how to proceed and how to make changes. This was absent in the Work & Income Chain.

These results have important implications for architecture development in policy chains. Successful development, in terms of creating flexible architectures, implies that it is important to recognize the multi-rational kind of agreements which have to be made in order to exchange information, while at the same time it is important to take into account the structure of power relationships between the chain partners as well as the quality of the relationships between them.

## References


1. Allen, B.R., Boynton, A: Information architecture: in search of efficient flexibility. In: MIS Quarterly, 15 (4), (1991) 435-445.
2. Bekkers, V.: The governance of back office integration: some Dutch experiences, In: Wimmer, M. et al. (ed.), Electronic Government, Springer, Heidelberg (2005) 12-25.
3. Bellamy, C., Taylor, J.: Governing in the Information Age. Buckingham: Open University Press (1998).
4. Beynon-Davies, P.: Information Management in the British National Health Service: The Pragmatics of Strategic Data Planning. In: International Journal of Information Management, 14 (2), (1994) 84-94.
5. Bijker, W., Hughes, T, Pinch, T (ed.): The social construction of technological systems, MIT Press, Cambridge (1987).

6. Butler, J., Cantrell, S.: Communication factors and trust: an explanatory study. In: Psychological Reports, 74, (1994) 33-34.
7. Davenport, T., Eccles, R. Prusak, L.: Information Politics. In: Sloan Management Review, 34 (1), (1992) 53-65.
8. Dawes, S.: Interagency information sharing: expected benefits, manageable risks. In: Journal of Policy Analysis and Management, 15 (3), (1996) 121-147.
9. Hasting, C.: The new organization, McGraw Hill, Maidenhead, (1996).
10. Hood, Ch.: The tools of government, McMillan, London (1993).
11. Homburg, V.: The Political Economy of Information Management, SOM, Groningen, (1999).
12. Knights, D. & F. Murray: Politics and Pain in Managing Information Technology: A Case Study in Insurance. In: Organization Studies, 1992, 13 (2), (1992) 211-228.
13. Koppenjan, J., Klijn E-H.: (2004), Managing uncertainties in networks, London: Routlegde.
14. 15. Kumar, K., van Dissel, H.: Sustainable collaboration: managing conflict and collaboration in interorganizational information systems. In: MIS Quarterly, 1996, 20 (3), (1996) 279-300.
15. Laswell, H. : Politics: Who gets what when and how? World Publ., Cleveland (1958).
16. Margetts, H.: Computerising the tools of government. In: Snellen, I., van de Donk, W. (eds.), Public administration in the information age, Amsterdam (1998) 441-460.
17. 23. Martin, J. Leben, J.: Strategic information planning methodologies, Prentice Hall, Englewood Cliffs (1998).
18. Moon, M.: The Evolution of E-Government Among Municipalities: Rhetoric or Reality? In: Public Administration Review, 62(4), (2002) 424-433.
19. Morgan, G.: Riding the waves of change, Jossey-Bas, San Francisco (1990).
20. Monge, P. Fulk,J.: Communication technology for global network organizations. In: De- Sanctis, G., Fulk, J. (eds.), Shaping organizational form, Sage, Thousand Oaks (1999) 71-100.
21. Orlikowski, W.: The duality of technology: rethinking the concept of technology in organizations. In: Organization Science, 3 (3), (1991) 398-427.
22. Orlikowski, W.: Using technology and constituting structures. In: Organizational Science, vol. 11(4), (2000) 404-428.
23. Pfeffer, J., Salancik, G.R.: The external control of organizations. Harper & Row, New York, 1978.
24. Rhodes, R.: Understanding governance, Open University Press., Maidenhead (1997).
25. Snellen, I.:Boeiend en geboeid, Samson, Alphen (1987).
26. Stone, D.: The policy paradox, Norton, New York/London (2000).
27. Thompson, J: Organizations in Action, McGraw Hill, New York (1967).
28. Turban, E, McLean, E. ,Wetherbe, J.: Information technology for Management, Wiley, New York, (2002).
29. Uzzi, B., Social structure and competition in interfirm networks: the paradox of embedddedness. In: Administrative Science Quarterly, 42(4), (1997) 35-68.
30. Van de Ven, A., On the nature, formation and maintenance of relations among organizations. In: Academy of Management Review, (1976) 24-36.
31. Williamson, O.E , The economic institutions of capitalism, Free Press, New York (1985).

# Local Networking for e-Services: A UK Case Study

Rony Medaglia

Department of Innovation and Society
University of Rome 'La Sapienza' Via Salaria 113 – 00198 Rome, Italy
r.medaglia@polity.it

**Abstract.** This paper deals with the networking at local level for e-government policies. Focusing on the case of the e-government local partnership in the County of Surrey in the United Kingdom, I analyse the characteristics and the development through time of the networking activity, using the theoretical framework provided by the literature on policy networks. By analysing data collected from primary sources, including focused interviews, I show the changes occurred in the partnership networking for local e-government policy, and point out some independent variables for explaining them. I conclude suggesting new directions of research on the topic.

## 1 Introduction

As e-government strategies progress across different countries, some paths of development can be recognized in the way e-government services policy is being shaped. One of the directions the e-government agenda is taking is in emphasizing the role of the local level of administration and of the networking activity within it. An increasing empowerment of the role of the local tier of government in the delivery of e-services to citizens is being carried out by providing for the creation of local networks for the implementation of e-government policies.

Being this dimension a new focus in e-government policy-making, it is of big interest to analyse which are the processes occurring within local networks for e-government: what is the structure and what are the features of the networks in time, if and how they change and what stimulates the change. An analysis of the characteristics of the networking among local actors for developing and implementing e-government policies can in fact provide a deeper insight on what is behind the actual e-government policy outcomes, and what is the trend of change in the fundamental dimension of back office activity – a side that has been too often neglected in e-government research [1], [2], [3]. In order to achieve this, in this paper the development of a partnership between Local Authorities in the UK is taken as a case study. By analysing the features of a network of Local Authorities joined up in a Strategic Partnership for e-government, the paper aims at showing the changes occurred through time in the networking process, relate it to a theoretical framework and point out some underlying factors beneath them.

M.A. Wimmer et al. (Eds.): EGOV 2006, LNCS 4084, pp. 256–268, 2006.

The paper is structured as follows: first I set my focus on the networking for local e-government policies, drawing on a gap stressed within a brief review of the literature on e-government (2). Then, after describing the features of the Surrey Partnership as the case selected for the study and the methods I have used for collecting the empirical data (3), I carry out an analysis of the features and changes occurred in the networking activity distinguishing between three dimensions: the institutional setting (4), the actors' composition (5) and the network structure (6). Eventually, I assess the results of the analysis of the data against the theoretical framework of policy networks as provided for by Marsh and Rhodes (7) and try to individuate some underlying factors for explaining the changes analysed. In the conclusion (9), I suggest new research questions opened by the study for further inquiry.

## 2 The Research Object: Partnership Networking for Local e-Government

Research on e-government almost unanimously points out that e-government policies express much of their potential at local level [4], [5], [6], [7], [8], [9], [10], [11], [12]. Motives underlying such an importance recognised in the local level of e-government can be summarised in three main features:

1. The local tier is the ideal level for the delivery of services, following the principle of *subsidiarity* [13], [14];
2. The local actors are the main empowered ones within the processes of *administrative devolution* [15], [16];
3. Local government represents the main 'access gate' for citizens to the public administrative system [17].

Within this rationale, local e-government is included among the main issues of local government decentralisation, coordination and networking. Being the local policy actors charged with increasing responsibility in the delivery of e-government services, the creation of networks between them is being seen as a response to this.

More in particular, the main drives for stimulating partnership work at local level in e-government policies can be summarized as follows:

- A technical need for shared infrastructures and compatible standards, that is the need for *systems interoperability*;
- An efficiency need for creating *economies of scale*, and avoiding uneconomic duplications;
- An administrative need for inter-institutional coordination between different agencies for creating integrated single access points to the citizen/customer, in a *one-stop shop* way [8].

In such a context it is of big interest to analyse how the networking activity between policy actors involved in the delivery of e-government service works and develops through time. Nevertheless, scientific publications on e-government have frequently focused on the customer's use of electronic services – the so-called *demand side* of e-government policies [18], [19], relatively neglecting the *supply side* of e-government policies – the one dealing with the dynamics in the process of e-government policies and with the behaviour of the organisations that deliver them. Only more recently there has been a growing awareness among the scientific community that e-government is more about organisational change and policy-making development than just about technological improvement. As Curthoys and Crabtree put it, as far as e-government policies are concerned, 'organisational change is as much a priority as technological implementation' [5, p. 58], so that the focus must be concentrated on 'organisational change, not electronic change. The purpose is to reform, not just rewire' [5, p. 61].

## 3 The Case Study and Methods

As far as the UK context is concerned, recently particular attention has been put on joint e-government implementation between Local Authorities and other public sector agencies [20], [21], [22], [23].

The formal framework within which networks for a joined approach to local e-government policy making are formed is the one of Local Strategic Partnerships, as provided by national guidelines [24]. Since June 2002 a special fund for e-government projects submitted by local authorities joined in LSP has been established, and 69 Local Strategic Partnerships and 7 Regional Partnerships have been formed across the country.

The County of Surrey has been one of the areas where a joint approach to e-government policy has been kicked off very early. Since 2001, the first year of the national strategy, Local Authorities across Surrey County started networking for delivering the first e-government projects. This makes the case of Surrey County an ideal one for following the development of the network approach from the very beginning of the national policy process.

For collecting the data three different sources have been used:

- Analysis of official documents. I have analysed documents from institutional sources both at central and local level. These include central government's White Papers, Office of the Deputy Prime Minister (ODPM) Action Plans and guidelines, Local Government Association publications, Best Value Performance Indicators scoring, Local Authorities' annual IEG (Implementing Electronic Government) statements.
- Online web survey. I have surveyed the content of central government and Local Authorities' websites, Surrey Partnership web portals and online documents from several other sources (Improvement and Development Agency, National Projects[1], Directgov[2], Localegov[3]).

[1] www.localegovnp.org
[2] www.direct.gov.uk
[3] www.localegov.gov.uk

– Background interviews. I have conducted semi-structured interviews with two officials at Surrey e-Partnership: Programme Manager for Business Development and Product Manager in July 2005.

In the following paragraphs I will present an analysis of the features and the development in time of Surrey County Local Strategic Partnership for e-government in the three areas of institutional setting, actors' composition and network structure and relations.

## 4 The Institutional Setting: Towards a More Formalized Framework

A first framework for networking to develop a joined e-government strategy in the Surrey County has been established in 2003, with the constitution of the Surrey e-Partnership. Today, the Surrey e-Partnership is made of 47 organisations coming from four sectors: Local Authorities; Health Services; Higher Education; Crime and Disorder. However, the structure of the partnership that brings together these actors has not always been the same. As a chronological analysis can show, the pattern of the institutional setting linking the actors involved in the partnership has changed through time.

The evolution of partnership working in Surrey county can be divided in two main phases: the first one, before the formal constitution of the Surrey e-Partnership, and the second one after it. Initially, the proposals for e-government projects across Local Authorities in the county of Surrey in response to the national funding bids tended to be formulated at the individual authorities' level. Even at this early stage, however, with time the need for coordination and for joint work between institutional actors emerged as a priority. As a consequence, forms of partnership started to develop between different Local Authorities within the County to better formulate and implement at local level the e-government agenda, kicked off by the central government through guidelines, external support and funding bids [24], [25], [26], [27].

By the year 2000, the first year of the national e-government strategy [28], a joint project within the framework of the National Pathfinder Programme has been activated. This is the case of SurreyAlert[4], the first project that a partnership across Surrey County came to deliver.

In 2003 the formal partnership as it is now was established, under the name of *Surrey e-Partnership*, with 13 Local Authorities signing in. The partnership provided for each Local Authority to make an annual financial contribution in exchange of a final say on the products to deliver. A Programme Board has been

[4] The SurreyAlert project provided for both an Extranet infrastructure between Local Authorities for inter-institutional information exchange and data sharing, and for a service to the citizenship through a website providing a single access point to real-time information in emergency cases, such as fires, floods, etc. (www.surreyalert.info).

established as the main body for the strategic decisions by the e-Partnership, made of representative members of each Local Authority.

Each project on the agenda is directed by a Project Board, a technical body that puts together a team of experts working on the individual projects, while Project Teams are made of IT professionals, project executives, commercial suppliers and other specialized practitioners, depending on the nature of the project.

Summarizing, the initial informal approach to networking has been shifting through time towards a higher degree of formalization, with the constitution of official institutional bodies for the network management.

## 5 The Actors: Shifting Away from the Hegemony of IT Professionals

Similarly to the institutional structure, also the nature and the role of the actors involved have changed through time.

For the first projects (SurreyAlert and SurreyJobs) the type of personnel involved was mainly project-dependent. Thus, while for instance SurreyAlert brought together mainly practitioners of emergency, the second project, SurreyJobs[5], has been carried out mainly by Human Resources managers and other actors with similar professional backgrounds. Furthermore, all the project boards by which the first projects have been led saw also the predominant presence of Information Technology professionals.

As the partnership became more formalized, there was a shift away from the *ad hoc* project actors' composition in terms of backgrounds. The role of IT professionals tended to loose its central and determining position. Both the trend of moving away from homogeneity in actors' backgrounds and skills, and of downsizing of the role of IT professionals has been contemporary to the introduction of the strategic Programme Board.

The diminished role of IT professionals can thus be put in a wider picture: the downsizing of the role of IT professionals in formulating and implementing the projects is to be interpreted within a trend of moving from a previous *technology-centred* approach to partnership making for e-government, to a *governance-centred* approach, in which a non-technical body as the Programme Board is given increasing power to steer the policy.

## 6 The Network Structure and Relations. Leadership and Degree of Openness

The last key issues concern the nature and the development of relations within the network. This includes both the question of the leadership role and the degree of openness of the network.

[5] A website providing information and access to databases of job vacancies across the county, allowing personalized queries through an integrated search engine (www.surreyjobs.info).

### 6.1 Leadership: From Weight-Based to Consensus-Based

As regards the leadership of the partnership, the development through time and the constitution of the formal e-Partnership framework introduced a shift from a type of leadership naturally stemming from the main Local Authority administrative weight, to one that increasingly has to ground on consensus from the members, and is faced with potential conflict.

In the initial phase Surrey County Council assumed almost naturally the leadership, as a consequence of its intrinsic role and importance among the County's Local Authorities, due to its administrative size[6].

The Surrey County Council leadership has never been seriously questioned. Nevertheless, the complexity of the leadership issue goes beyond a nominal framework as, for instance, in day-to-day matters like the meeting logistics. This latter example is a good one for showing internal underlying tensions concerning the leadership consensus which, even though did not explicitly break out so far, are yet present and active.

Meetings of the Programme Board are usually scheduled in the Mid Surrey Office in Leatherhead, situated in the Mole Valley district, approximately in the geographical centre of the county, where the offices of Surrey e-Partnership are based. Nevertheless, this happens not to be only a neutral logistic issue since, as one of the interviewees points out, there is also a sensible leadership issue at stake in the choice of the meeting place:

> We try not to meet in Surrey County Council building and this is absolutely essential not to give the wrong impression. We spent a lot of time and effort in the last 2/3 years trying to make sure that the partnership team activity that happens around the core team [the Programme Board] or that the core team administers is very much seen as not being County-driven, but is actually moving away from that.

In other words, the former natural Surrey County Council's strong unquestioned leadership has been giving space to a more delicate situation, where each member's involvement has to be given voice, even at a precautionary stage and in apparently secondary questions as the one of the choice of meeting places.

### 6.2 Degree of Openness: From Compact Communities to Strategic 'Open Door' Approach

The partnership network has seen changes also as far as its degree of openness is concerned. The recent development of the partnership saw a shift from a more closed and rigid network structure, towards one that tends to be more flexible and to work in a different way in terms of openness and internal cohesion.

In the first phase of the networking process, different project teams worked structured as relatively small, internally homogeneous groups, with little effective

[6] Surrey County Council employs 25,000 people, managing an annual budget close to 900,000,000£, while a typical Local Authority usually has 300/400 employees and works with an annual budget of around 10-15,000,000£.

boundaries from the outside, and a fair level of internal autonomy and cohesion. With the step of the creation of the formal e-Partnership, a new framework provided for both an extended and more organic coordination through the new strategic Programme Board, and for 'opening up' the relatively autonomous and closed groups of actors. The e-Partnership membership now is formally renewed by each member every three years, and members willing to opt out can do it by giving a six-month prior notice.

In addition, some parts of the network (specific Local Authorities) showed to have reached different levels of electronic services implementation, making the network less even in its internal structure and therefore needing a more flexible organization than the one that worked at the initial stage:

> At the beginning we were trying to involve all the partners because of the nature of the funding [that had wide Local Strategic Partnership forming as a conditionality]. But from a practical perspective this is very difficult to achieve. So we shifted to a different approach in the last twelve months: you cannot work in an 'all or nothing' approach, so now we look for those who want to be involved in the project and then just work with those, and then we go back to the main group in terms of progress on that, but also *leaving the door open* for those who want to join [*my stress*].

Summarizing, the network in the early phase was structured as a closed community of actors with common backgrounds, fair autonomy from the outside, and tight relations between actors working together. With the creation of the formal e-Partnership and with the progress of the policy implementation, the network began to loosen its internal cohesion, and to assume a more open and more flexible structure.

## 7 From Policy Community Towards Issue Network: Membership, Integration, Resources, Power

The overall changes occurred in the partnership, including all the dimensions of institutional setting, actors' composition, leadership and network structure can thus be summarized as follows:

**Table 1.** Overall changes occurred in the partnership

| *Area involved* | *Change occurred* |
|---|---|
| Institutional setting | From informal to formal |
| Actors composition | From technology-centred to governance-centred |
| Leadership | From weight-based to consensus-based |
| Network structure | From closed community to open network |

In this paragraph I will relate this set of changes to the theoretical framework of policy network analysis, mainly drawing on the contribution of David Marsh and Rod Rhodes [29], [30]. I will argue that the changes emerged in the data analysis are part of a general shift from a network of the type of *policy communities*, towards one of the type of *issue networks*.

It is now worth recalling the characteristics of policy communities and issue networks as described in [29], summarized in the following table:

**Table 2.** Types of policy networks: characteristics of policy communities and issue networks

| *Dimension* | *Policy community* | *Issue network* |
|---|---|---|
| *Membership*: | | |
| No. of participants (*a*) | Very limited, some group consciously excluded | Large |
| Type of interest (*b*) | Economic and/or professional interest dominate | Encompasses range of affected interests |
| *Integration*: | | |
| Frequency of interaction (*c*) | Frequent, high-quality, interaction of all groups on all matters related to policy issue | Contacts fluctuate in frequency and intensity |
| Continuity (*d*) | Membership, values and outcomes persistent over time | Access fluctuates significantly |
| Consensus (*e*) | All participants share basic values and accept the legitimacy of the outcome | A measure of agreement exists, but conflict is ever present |
| *Resources*: | | |
| Distribution of resources within network (*f*) | All participants have resources; basic relationship is an exchange relationship | Some participants may have resources, but they are limited, and basic relationship is consultative |
| Distribution of resources within participating organizations (*g*) | Hierarchical; leaders can deliver members | Varied and variable distribution and capacity to regulate members |
| *Power*: (*h*) | There is a balance of power among members. Although one group may dominate, it must be a positive-sum game if community is to persist | Unequal powers, reflecting unequal resources and unequal access. It is a zero-sum game |

(Source: [29, p. 16])

We can try to assess the features of the Surrey partnership case against the single items as indicated in the framework.

The number of participants (a) in the e-government partnership in Surrey has not changed dramatically through time. The only case of one of the 13 Local Authorities opting out does not really account for relevant changes in the partnership size. What can be said, instead, is that the number of actors has become *potentially* large with time, while in the early stages it was indeed 'very limited', with some groups implicitly excluded – i.e. the hegemony of IT professional and specialized practitioners.

Directly linked to this issue there is the one of the type of interest (b) connecting the network actors. The dominance of 'professional interest' clearly matches the early stage of the partnership, when either the IT professionals leading the project groups or *ad hoc* teams of specialized practitioners (HR managers, practitioners of emergency, etc.) gathered around the first projects. The later stage instead tends to comprise a wider range of affected interests, i.e. the more governance-driven ones of the politically appointed members of the Programme Board.

On the frequency of interaction (c), instead, the collected data can actually say something significant only in an indirect way. More extensive research (requiring means not available in this context) would be needed in order to fully explore the issue of the 'interaction of all groups on all matters related to policy issue', as mentioned in Marsh and Rhodes' framework. However, it can be pointed out that reasonably the more closed, tighter relations between network actors of the early stage also featured to some extent 'frequent and high-quality' interactions. Supposedly, with the 'loosening' of the network structure (more diverse composition, easier optouts, weaker cohesion in implementation) also contacts between actors relatively diminished in frequency and intensity.

A similar point can be made regarding the issue of continuity (d). The later stage can be described as featuring access that – if not 'significantly' – anyway does fluctuate: both *in reality* (as in the case of an actual Local Authority opting out) and *potentially* (with the setting out of a formal framework). This situation, typical of a network of the type of the issue network, has changed in comparison with the beginnings, when membership and values tended to be persistent over time in a context of a more closed policy community. On the other hand, little in this case can be said about 'persistent *outcomes* over time', a topic which would be the object of different research than the one carried out here – that is an analysis of the services delivered: the *front office* electronic products.

The consensus item (e) basically follows a similar trend. The IT community that used to lead the policy implementation process did it by sharing 'basic values and the legitimacy of the outcome', as the common background and the consequent shared vision they featured suggest[7]. The shift towards the issue network ideal-type occurs when (at least potential) conflict between actors rises over visions, as the example of the delicate issue of meeting logistics (6.1) can show.

As far as the distribution of resources is concerned (within the network and within participating organizations) (f; g), the resulting picture is less clear. In the

---

[7] This is a similar phenomenon to the one pointed out in the pioneering case study on local e-government carried out by Lawrence Pratchett [31, p. 741], when dealing with 'the shared values and appreciative system of the ICT community'. Pratchett points out the influent presence of two core beliefs on the role of technologies that 'glue' the network: belief in the need for continued technological advancement; emphasis on quantifiable returns on investments (ROIs) and visible improvement in effectiveness.

case of Surrey partnership a shift from everyone to only some participants having resources does not emerge: since the beginning resources have been distributed evenly for most of the projects by the central authority of the ODPM, with the exception of one project (SurreyJobs). However, if we consider resources as including also knowledge and expertise, it is true that the progress in the e-government implementation process increased unevenness among the individual Local Authorities, some of which can thus be considered as now featuring 'limited resources', compared to others.

Regarding the distribution of power (h), the comparison with Marsh and Rhodes' framework is a rather problematic one. It cannot be said that at the initial stage of Surrey partnership for e-government there has been a clear-cut situation of 'balance of powers among members': the question of the spontaneous leadership of Surrey County Council accounted for a scenario with a particular actor de facto leading the process, due to the unchallenged power and resources available.

Trying to summarize, we can say that in the Surrey partnership case there is *a trend of shift* from a policy community type of network towards an issue network, better than an accomplished one. The Surrey partnership network is not clearly classifiable as an issue network at the present moment. Of the 8 items typical of issue networks described by Marsh and Rhodes, for three of them (*a, f, g*) the data display a controversial scenario, while to put further light on item c we would need a different type of survey than the one carried out in this study. However, better than the single items analyzed, it is the comprehensive picture of the difference between closed and rigid policy communities and open, flexible issue networks that suggests the presence of this trend in the Surrey partnership case.

In the next paragraph I will analyze the factors pushing for this shift.

## 8 Finding Independent Variables

I indicate two factors as pushing the Surrey case of partnership from a policy community towards an issue network: the constitution of a formal framework (the Surrey e-Partnership) and the progress of the e-government policy process.

The formalisation occurred with the constitution of the Surrey e-Partnership represents a major factor in the 'opening' and 'loosening' of the network structure, towards the pattern of an issue network. The ways through which the formalisation process has kicked off the shift are:

- The introduction of an explicit set of rules for: buying in and opting out; choosing the leadership;
- The creation of the Programme Board, that took away power from the closed IT community.

The second factor influencing the shift occurred is the progress of the e-government policy process. This latter has particularly affected the network structure and its degree of openness. As the partnership members progressed in the e-government policy implementation, the previous even situation has been replaced by an uneven scenario, in which different members work at different paces, show different degrees of progression and feature different visions on the policy itself. Such a transformation has been crucial in making the need of a different network structure clearly emerge: flexibility besides a new agency for strategic coordination was needed. This has pushed for the creation of the Programme Board, set within the constitution of the formal framework of the e-Partnership.

The following model can illustrate the role of the two push factors in the shift from policy community towards issue network:

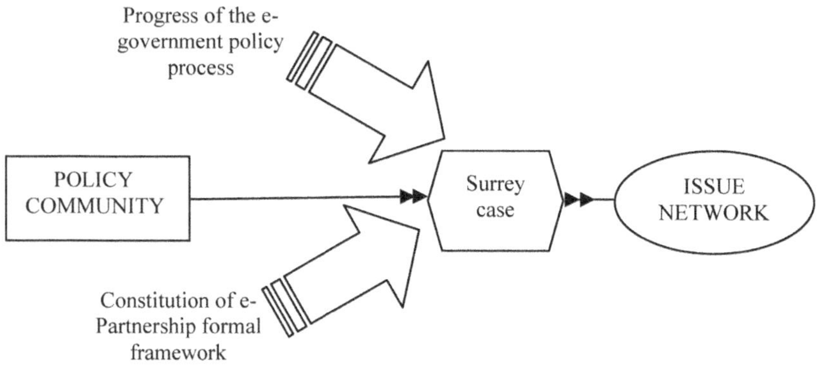


**Fig. 1.** The push factors of the Surrey case shift

## 9 Conclusion

As regards further development of the research on the topic area, at this stage comparative studies would be useful, in order to allow some degree of generalisation in the findings. Does the same trend of changes occur in other similar initiatives of networking for e-government policies at local level? And do they occur as a result of the same (or similar) push factors?

The findings of this study itself raise further research questions as well. An interesting issue to be investigated would be the link between the partnership networking for e-government (a typical supply side *back office* issue), with the integrated features of the delivered services (a supply side *front office* issue). The question to be addressed would be, in other words: how does the capacity to network for delivering electronic services affect the final delivered product in terms of its integration?

In more general terms, a perspective for further investigation is the observed phenomenon of shift from what can be called a *technology-centred* approach, to a *governance-centred* one. Is it possible to generalise this trend to other cases of networking for e-government policies? And what are the broader implications of this shift in terms of the meaning to be given to e-government?

A potential hypothesis could be that, as the e-government policy progresses by leaving the pioneering stage of foundation towards a more mature stage, the technology-centred approach is replaced by one that looks at e-government policy making as a whole new form of *governance*, and not as just a technical means to some ends (efficiency, savings, value for money, etc.) anymore.

## References


1. Gronlund, A.: State of the Art in E-gov Research – A Survey. In: Tranmuller, R. (ed.), Electronic Government: Third International Conference, EGOV 2004, August 30 – September 3 (2004)
2. Gronlund, A.: What's in a Field – Exploring the eGovernment Domain. Proceedings of the 38th Hawaii International Conference (2005)
3. Lofstedt, U.: E-government – Assessment of Current Research and Some Proposals for Future Directions. International Journal of Public Information Systems, No. 1 (2005) 39-52
4. Bhatnagar, S.: E-Government. From Vision to Implementation. Sage, New Delhi (2001)
5. Curthoys, N., Crabtree, J.: SmartGov: Renewing Electronic Government for Improved Service Delivery. The Work Foundation, London (2003)
6. Gronlund, A.: Managing Electronic Services. A Public Sector Perspective, Springer, London (2000)
7. Heichlinger, A.: eGovernment in Europe's Regions: Approaches and Progress in IST Strategy, Organisation and Services, and the Role of Regional Actors. EIPA (2004)
8. Jaeger, P. T., Thompson, K. M.: E-government Around the World: Lessons, Challenges, and Future Directions. Government Information Quarterly, Vol. 20, No. 4 (2003) 389-394
9. OECD: OECD E-Government Flagship Report. 27th Session of the Public Management Committee, Chateau de la Muette, Paris (2003)
10. OECD: e-Government for Better Government. OECD Publishing, Paris (2005)
11. Ho, A. T.-K.: Reinventing Local Governments and the E-Government Initiative, Public Administration Review, Vol. 62, No. 4 (2002) 434-444
12. Torres, L., Pina, V., Acerete, B.: E-government Developments on Delivering Public Services Among EU Cities. Government Information Quarterly, Vol. 22 (2005) 217-238
13. European Commission: E-Europe 2005 Action Plan. European Commission, Brussels (2002)
14. OECD: The E-government Imperative: Main Findings. OECD Observer, http://www.oecd.org/publications/Pol_brief (2003)
15. Denters, B., Rose, L. E. (eds.): Comparing Local Governance: Trends and Developments. Palgrave Macmillan, Basingstoke (2005)
16. Fedele, P., Ongaro, E.: A Common Trend, Different Houses: A Comparative Analysis of Devolution in Italy, Spain and the United Kingdom. Paper presented at the EGPA conference, Bern (2005)

17. Capocchi, A.: Il processo di e-government nel quadro UE e in particolare la situazione in Gran Bretagna. In: Capocchi, A.: Il processo di E-government nel sistema delle amministrazioni pubbliche. Giuffré, Milano (2003)
18. Kuk, G.: The Digital Divide and the Quality of Electronic Service Delivery in Local Government in the United Kingdom. Government Information Quarterly, Vol. 20, No. 4 (2003) 353-363
19. Mellor, W., Parr, V.: Government Online: an International Perspective, Taylor Nelson Sofres, unpan1.un.org/intradoc/groups/public/documents/APCITY/ UNPAN007044.pdf (2002)
20. Eifert, M.: National E-Government. Routledge, London (2004)
21. Ferguson, M.: Local E-government in the United Kingdom. In: Druke, H. (ed.): Local Electronic Government: A Comparative Study. Routledge, London (2005)
22. ODPM: One Year On. Office of the Deputy Prime Minister, www.localegov.gov.uk (2004)
23. ODPM: Two Years On: Realising the Benefits from our Investment in E-government, Office of the Deputy Prime Minister, www.localegov.gov.uk (2005)
24. Department of Environment, Transport and Regions (DETR): Promoting E-government – Best Practice in Local Authorities. www.odpm.gov.uk (2001)
25. Department of Environment, Transport and Regions (DETR): Delivering Local Government Online: Milestones and Resources for the 2005 target. www.lga.gov.uk/lga/infoage/deliver2001.pdf (2001)
26. Department of Environment, Transport and Regions (DETR): Modern councils, modern services – access for all, www.odpm.gov.uk/stellent/groups/odpm_ localgov/documents/page/odpm_locgov _605195.hcsp (2001)
27. Department of Environment, Transport and Regions (DETR): Detailed National E-Local Government Strategy. www.odpm.gov.uk (2001)
28. Cabinet Office: E-Government: A Strategic Framework for Public Services in the Information Age. Stationery Office, London (2000)
29. Marsh, D. (ed.): Comparing Policy Networks. Open University Press, Buckingham (1998)
30. Marsh, D., Rhodes, R.A.W. (eds.): Policy Networks in British Government. Clarendon, Oxford (1992)
31. Pratchett, L..: New Technologies and the Modernization of Local Government: An Analysis of Biases and Constraints. Public Administration, Vol. 77, No. 4 (1999) 731-750

# Why E-government Usage Lags Behind: Explaining the Gap Between Potential and Actual Usage of Electronic Public Services in the Netherlands

Alexander van Deursen, Jan van Dijk, and Wolfgang Ebbers

University of Twente, research program Governments and ICT,
Department of communication studies
P.O. Box 217, 7500 AE Enschede, The Netherlands
a.j.a.m.vandeursen@utwente.nl

**Abstract.** Most of the EU-15 countries illustrate a gap between potential usage and actual usage of electronic public services. Using a model of four successive kinds of access to digital technologies a number of explanations are sought. They are tested in the case of current Dutch electronic governmental service usage. Motivational access indicates that there is a part of the Dutch population that doesn't have sufficient motivation for using computers and the Internet. It also appears that even in the Netherlands, a top country regarding Internet and broadband connections, physical access cannot be taken for granted. Insufficient digital skills produce serious problems as well. But the most striking facts are found in the context of usage access. Here we have observed a lack of user orientation in Dutch e-government services. It appears that the Dutch government doesn't know what citizens want, how they use ICT en what the consequences for citizens are.

## 1 Introduction

As a result of increasing development and use of the Internet over recent years, almost all public authorities of the European countries have waged efforts to offer electronic services. These efforts have reached different degrees of sophistication in European countries [1]. While some countries have already developed services of full online transaction, communication and service handling, others are only offering basic information. Increasingly, entire procedures are planned or designed in such a way that they can be settled fully electronic [2]. Both public authorities and citizens are able to benefit from online services. For governments potential advantages are increased competition, increased efficiency by reduced redundancy and system integration, a stimulation of democratic principles by more transparency of governmental processes and the improvement of service provision for citizens and companies [3].

Potential advantages for citizens of electronic government are summarized by Michael Cross (Guardian Online 16.07.98): Round the clock government,

M.A. Wimmer et al. (Eds.): EGOV 2006, LNCS 4084, pp. 269–280, 2006.

one-stop shops (tell the government only once instead of form filling for different departments), electronic benefits (no more queuing and information-sharing across departments reducing fraud) and open and cheaper government (better public access to information encouraging efficiency and democracy). A necessary condition for citizens to make use of these advantages is physical access to the Internet. In Table 1 the percentages of individuals in the EU-15[1] who accessed the Internet in the three months prior to a Eurostat survey are summarized.

**Table 1.** Percentage of individuals who used the Internet in the three months prior to the survey

| Country | DK | DE | EL | ES | FI | IE | LU | NL | AT | PT | SE | UK |
|---|---|---|---|---|---|---|---|---|---|---|---|---|
| 2003 | 71 | 54 | 16 | 37 | 66 | 31 | 53 | 64 | 41 | 26 | 77 | 61 |
| 2004 | 76 | 61 | 20 | 40 | 70 | 34 | 65 | 69 | 52 | 29 | 82 | 63 |

Source: Eurostat

Table 1 shows the potential number of individuals that could make use of the electronic government services offered. In Table 2 the actual use of the internet for obtaining information from public authorities' websites is summarized.

**Table 2.** Percentage of individuals who used the Internet in the three months prior to the survey for obtaining information from public authorities' websites

| Country | DK | DE | EL | ES | FI | IE | LU | NL | AT | PT | SE | UK |
|---|---|---|---|---|---|---|---|---|---|---|---|---|
| 2003 | 39 | 23 | 6 | 20 | 39 | 10 | 25 | 15 | 14 | 10 | 41 | 19 |
| 2004 | 43 | 31 | 7 | 22 | 43 | 11 | 36 | 17 | 18 | 10 | 36 | 20 |

Source: Eurostat

Interesting findings are exposed while comparing Table 1 with Table 2. The tables show that none of the EU-15 countries have a 100% match between potential and actual usage of online governmental information. There are several possibilities to explain this discrepancy. In some countries geographical distances may encourage citizens to use e-government services, other countries may have a successful multichannel approach that divert citizens from the web to call centers and service desks. And last but not least, variables such as quality and user friendliness of e-government services may influence the take up of e-government usage. However, these factors mainly address the supply side of electronic governmental services. We would primarily search the reasons for the gap between potential and actual use of these services more close by, that is at the demand side and with the actual access by users to the technology required.

In this article we will demonstrate that a model of successive kinds of access to digital technologies [4,5] is able to serve as a framework for a number of explanations of the actual choice and usage of electronic government channels

[1] Belgium, France and Italy are excluded in Table 1 and 2 because of unavailable data for these countries.

in the case of the Netherlands. This model presupposes a broad conception of access as a full appropriation of technology by users, from the motivation to use the technology to its actual usage. The choice of the Netherlands is particularly interesting because according to CBS Statline (2005), only 24% of the Dutch citizens used the Internet for visiting public authorities' websites in 2004. The low level of usage in the Netherlands is remarkable considering the fact that this country is the second country of the world in broadband diffusion, after South Korea [6]. The Internet diffusion in this country is comparable to, for example, Denmark, but in Denmark the use of public authority electronic services is more than two times as high!

The next section introduces the model of successive kinds of access to digital technologies, followed by a large section that elaborates the Netherlands as a case study. Finally, section four contains the concluding remarks.

## 2 A Model of Successive Kinds of Access to Digital Technologies

To explain the discrepancy described in the previous section we will focus on the different kinds of access that are required for using electronic services. A model of successive kinds of access to digital technologies is introduced the figure below.

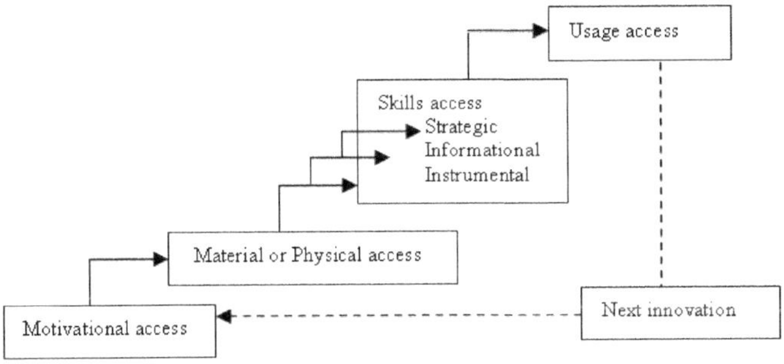


**Fig. 1.** A cumulative and recursive model of successive kinds of access to digital technologies [4,5]

In figure 1 van Dijk [4,5] distinguishes four kinds of access that are necessary to obtain full access to a specific digital technology. The model is called accumulative and recursive because the types of access follow on top of each other (e.g. motivation is a condition for the purchase of physical access) and because the whole process recurs with every distinct new innovation in digital technology. The first condition, motivational access, is an adequate level of motivation of potential users to adopt the technology. This mental barrier varies from little interest in or need of the technology, to real computer anxiety. The second condition is material or physical access. People need enough material resources to acquire the necessary hardware, software and services. Evidently, public opinion and public policy are strongly pre-occupied with this kind of access. After motivational and physical access users need to have an adequate level of digital skills to handle the services offered. The final type of access is usage access. This primarily means the number, type and diversity of applications used. When someone has a computer and Internet access, and is able to work with them, it is not at all granted that this person will actually use them. This will only happen when a particular application is needed. In this context, usage access will not explain the exact statistical figures of the gap between potential and actual usage, but it can help to shed light on the restraints that the usage statistics suggests, the most important restraint being actual need or a supply of applications that meets demand. This will be demonstrated in section 3.4. The kinds of access are not just simply present or absent. The measure of presence, for example the level of digital skills attained and the diversity of applications used also is important.

According to this model the gap between potential and actual usage might be explained by aspects of the following types of access that will specify the paragraphs in the following section: Motivational access, Material access, Digital skills, Usage access;

## 3 The Dutch E-government Usage Case

The development of electronic public services in the Netherlands is rather ambitious. In 1996 the Ministry of Internal Affairs introduced the OL2000-project, that was developed to realize provision of services controlled by the demands of citizens and companies and not by the supply-side view and organization of traditional government departments. Many other programs were introduced to promote and advance the development of electronic services. For example the 'Actieprogramma Elektronische Overheid' (Action Program Electronic Government), issued in 1998, proposed and realized a 25% online availability of all public services in 2002. In 2003 this program proposed to extend this result setting the next objective at an electronic settling of 65% of all public services in 2007. Driven by the opportunities of the technology, the goals of government such as a realization of New Public Management objectives, attention in the media and the supposed needs of citizens, a lot of governmental information was presented online and several services were offered electronically. But, as the gap to be explained clearly demonstrates, the policy to offer as much as possible online does not match actual demand.

To (partly) explain the gap between the big and fast growing supply of electronic public services and the demand that is lagging behind the four types of access discussed will serve as a framework for the presentation of relevant usage data. Our analysis is based on a number of national studies published earlier and on data we received from several national and municipal governmental departments. It needs to be emphasized that many of the government organisations addressed did not appear to collect user data and were not able to deliver useful information.

## 4 Motivational Access

The first access condition is motivation. Research in the Netherlands that explores motives whether or not to use the Internet is scarce. Citizens that lack motivation to use computers and the Internet have several reasons as shown in Table 3. This lack of motivation might be induced by shortcomings in confidence, a lack of interest or need, or it might be due to computer anxiety [4,5].

**Table 3.** Reasons not to use Internet at home 2002-2004 (amongst non-possessors)

| | 2003 | 2004 |
|---|---|---|
| Not interested, not useful | 33 | 34 |
| No suitable PC | 30 | 29 |
| Too expensive | 17 | 16 |
| Thinks he or she is too old | 10 | 11 |
| Lack of knowledge, skills | 9 | 9 |
| Has Internet access elsewhere | 8 | 10 |
| Other | *21* | *21* |

Source: CBS Statline

Most of the respondents indicate that they simply are not interested in using the Internet. Another group indicates that they don't have a suitable PC. Other barriers for using the Internet at home are that it is too expensive or that they lack the knowledge or skills required. If we specify Internet access further to the use of governmental sites, there is no relevant research considering motivational access. Some municipalities did surveys amongst their inhabitants but this has produced only superficial reasons, such as the citizens of Dordrecht that never used the municipal website because they did not need it (56%) or because they did not have access to the Internet (32%).

It won't be easy to close the motivational gap in using governmental sites on the Internet. People that consider access too expensive can be motivated by providing physical access in public places or, in some cases, subsidize the purchase of computers and connections [4,5]. However, just granting physical access will not be sufficient. Without in-depth knowledge about the citizens motives to (still) prefer traditional channels instead of electronic channels, the government will not be able to take the necessary steps to meet the preferences of citizens.

Although little research has been done for the motivation to use electronic government services in the Netherlands one can safely say that motivational access is a problem because it is a general reason for not having access to the Internet. So, it also might be a first potential explanation for the discrepancy described. However, we don't think it is the main problem when we consider electronic *government* services. According to Table 2 usage of governmental websites in Finland and Denmark is high, while there is no obvious reason to assume that the people in these countries differ from the Dutch in motivations for using the Internet. According to the international comparison of cultures by Hofstede [7]

Dutch and Scandinavian culture are rather similar. The same goes for the nature of the welfare state and the political system of the countries concerned. So, although a part of the Dutch inhabitants lacks motivation, the causes of the discrepancy considering electronic public services probably has to be sought elsewhere.

### 4.1 Physical Access

According to Table 1 the amount of Internet users in Netherlands is among the highest. In international perspective the Netherlands has a very high penetration of broadband Internet access, just under leader South Korea. In Table 4 the Internet possession of households and individuals is summarized.

**Table 4.** PC-ownership with Internet access of the Dutch population over 12 years of age (2000-2004)

| | PC-ownership with Internet access | | | | |
|---|---|---|---|---|---|
| | 2000 | 2001 | 2002 | 2003 | 2004 |
| % per household | 38 | 48 | 55 | 59 | 64 |
| % per person | 45 | 56 | 64 | 68 | 73 |

Source: CBS Statline

Although the percentages of possession are quite promising, statistics about the actual usage of computers and the Internet differ considerably. In Table 5 ICT usage is illustrated for Dutch citizens that have access to computers and the Internet.

**Table 5.** ICT usage in the Netherlands of persons over 12 year of age (%)

| | 2003 | 2004 |
|---|---|---|
| Used a PC | 72 | 74 |
| Used a PC (% of PC owners) | 83 | 84 |
| Frequency PC usage at home (% van PC-bezitters) | | |
| daily | 40 | 45 |
| once a week | 35 | 33 |
| once a month | 8 | 7 |
| not at all | 17 | 16 |
| Uses Internet at home (% of Internet owners) | 79 | 81 |
| Frequency Internet usage at home (% of Internet owners) | | |
| daily | 32 | 37 |
| once a week | 38 | 37 |
| once a month | 9 | 6 |
| not at all | 21 | 19 |

Source: CBS Statline

According to Table 5, only 81% of the people that have Internet access at home actually use this medium. This is divided in 37% daily, 37% once a week and 6%

once a month, indicating that only 74% of Internet owners can be considered as regular users. Nineteen percent of the people that have Internet access at home (73% in 2004) do not use this medium at all. Thus, only 59% of the Dutch population in 2004 used the Internet more or less, and 41% not at all.

This lack of usage exists not only among the usual groups lagging behind, seniors and people with low education. Young people also are different in physical access and actual usage. Particularly considering the extent and variety of usage low educated youngsters and youngsters living in low income households spent less time on the Internet. The assumption of some governments that the Internet is a commonly available channel, or will be in some years, is not valid and it is dangerous. There still are deep divides in the possession of computers and Internet connections in Europe [8]. The main demographics explaining these differences are age, education, income and ethnicity [5] [8].

Even though the Netherlands is one of the top countries in the number of Internet connections, a more thorough examination proves that this does not mean that all those connected actually use the Internet. So, physical access is an important aspect one should not take for granted. However, this also goes for a series of other countries in Table 3 that reveal a much higher use of electronic government websites than the Netherlands.

## 4.2 Skills Access

The next potential cause is a lack of digital skills. According to the model in figure 1 van Dijk [4,5] divides digital skills in operational skills (the ability to operate a computer, network connection and websites or web applications), informational skills (the ability to find, select and process electronic information) and strategic skills (the ability to use electronic information and services to realize a specific goal and to improve ones social position).

**Table 6.** Digital skills of the Dutch population divided by social-economic position, people aged 18-65, 2001 (means) on a *nine*point-scale

| | Employed | η/R [1] | Unemployed | η/R [1] | Unemployable | η/R [1] | Housewife/ man | η/R [1] | Total | η/R [1] |
|---|---|---|---|---|---|---|---|---|---|---|
| Male | 6,13 | 0,20 | 5,02 | 0,16 | 3,31 | 0,28 | 2,20 | 0,03 | 5,80 | 0,28 |
| Female | 4,76 | | 3,82 | | 1,59 | | 1,87 | | 3,81 | |
| 18-29 | 6,52 | -0,23 | 5,47 | -0,35 | 5,82 | -0,22 | 4,02 | -0,37 | 6,55 | -0,39 |
| 30-39 | 5,94 | | 4,54 | | 2,14 | | 3,10 | | 5,46 | |
| 40-54 | 4,91 | | 3,06 | | 2,29 | | 1,75 | | 4,27 | |
| 55-64 | 4,14 | | 1,52 | | 1,96 | | 0,92 | | 2,35 | |

1. η (eta) is an association measure for nominal variables (sex), R is the linear effect of an ordinal variable (age). Source: CBS

Table 6 points out that specific groups of citizens, like seniors (55+) and housewives/men that have computer access, do not, or barely have the necessary skills to operate their computers according to self-reports in a survey. The skills measured in these self-reports were a combination of mainly operational skills and some information skills. If these groups score low on these general skills, it might be reasonable to expect that they will not be able to use specific electronic government services, when the design of these services is not appropriate for them. These services presuppose not only that citizens possess operational and informational digital skills but also particular knowledge about the workings of government and its uses of information technology and the strategic skills to use this knowledge for own purposes.

Research that tries to estimate the level of digital skills of Dutch citizens is very scarce and it is often based on self evaluation. Performance tests of actual skills possessed are better. In a Ph D project Eszter Hargittai [9] [10] practiced such performance tests of a number Internet tasks among experimental subjects. Giant differences of success or failure of these tasks and the time required to finish them were recorded among subjects with different age, educational background and sex. This is alarming since people will be inclined to finish the task they are charged with in an experimental environment. When they cannot find or accomplish something in the real life of Internet use people will stop searching and using the application much earlier.

Just like we did with motivation and physical access, we have to conclude here that the Internet is not (yet) a generally accessible information, communication and transaction channel for citizens. Van Dijk [5] claims that people with higher social class, higher education, males and youngsters are the first and best in developing digital skills. According to Claeys and Spee [11] experienced Internet users have developed a further set of complex skills for finding and processing information, in this way increasing the chance that the gap deepens between early and skilled users and the late majority and laggers that only posses basic skills.

The problem of being short of skills becomes urgent when governments suppose that citizens are able to do about everything on the Internet. There are recent examples in Dutch government communication that indicate this. For example the municipality of Nijmegen sent its citizens a letter about the real estate appraisal-value of their houses. This letter referred to the Internet for more specific information about the value of their houses and comparative real estate used for the appraisal. This led to huge problems, not only because the website wasn't ready on the date specified, but also because a lot of citizens didn't have the skills to access their real estate information on the municipality's website.

Again, there is not much reason to think that the digital skills of the Dutch population are so much inferior to those of the Scandinavian peoples, or other people from countries with more frequent public authority website use, that they would be able to explain the difference. So, we will have to look further.

### 4.3 Usage Access

The last kind of access is usage access. This section covers the types of electronic public services that people choose or do not choose to use. It doesn't provide a statistical proof, but it might help to discover the deeper causes of the gap between potential and actual use. To gain more insight in the type of services used and in the level and diversity of usage, we gathered information on both the national and municipal level. The availability of information often was limited to simple web statistics that do not carry much information about actual usage. We discovered that different organisations used different methods for keeping up with their data. Organisations that could provide the most useful and reliable information are included in this section. But as mentioned before, we found that many government organisations did not appear to collect user data at all.

Bongers et al. [12] conducted research to get a clear overview of the desires, expectations, conditions and experiences of citizens in relation to e-government. They concluded that Dutch citizens do not undertake as much activities on governmental websites as on other websites, for instance in e-commerce. Online facilities such as using interactivity (e.g. asking questions or giving opinions), sending forms or performing transactions are scarcely used. Most people only use online public services to gather information about products or services.

On the municipal level usage is extremely varied. There still are small municipalities that only have one webmaster who can spend 16 hours a week on site development, while other bigger municipalities are granted large amounts of money for the development of electronic services. In Eindhoven, one of the bigger municipalities that have put much effort in the development of electronic services, almost 45% of the visitors of their website were searching for addresses of municipal institutions [13]. The main reasons for visiting the website were searching for information, reading news (25%), searching for contact (7%) and visiting the digital service counter (2%). The few people that did use the electronic counter mainly used it for passing on removals and applying for forms [14].

In Amsterdam one of the main conclusions was that 41% of their website visitors were searching for general information. A large part (29%) was only looking for opening hours of the office. In the municipality of Dordrecht 18% of citizens used the digital service counter on the website in 2003. Users were asked for the purpose of their visit. Most people were searching for information (67%). Another part visited in order to make service desk appointments for their driving license or passport. The most important reasons for citizens of Sint Michielsgestel for using the website were searching for opening hours, reading current news and curiosity. Most services that the website offers are hardly ever used. From the people that use the Internet, only 44% is aware of the fact that their municipality offers a digital counter desk. Seventy percent of this group never used products and services available on the website.

Enschede is one of the municipalities that is financially supported for developing electronic services by national government. This resulted in a broad variety of online services. However, most of these services are barely used. Only a few products seem to be appropriate for online settlement. In Table 7 three of these services are shown. This table indicates that even in one of the most successful municipalities the most frequent services are still used occasionally, despite the fact that these are still simple services and that citizens were given a discount for retrieving birth register statements online.

**Table 7.** Comparison between electronic and traditional channels for three products in 2004

| | Electronic | Traditional |
|---|---|---|
| Births | 426 | 2.454 |
| Divorces | 34 | 276 |
| Birth register statement | 1130 | 18.991 |

Source: Municipality of Enschede.

In the municipality of Beverwijk 15% of the website visitors also visited the product catalogue of which only 6% eventually used a form. A direct comparison with traditional services is not available but the municipality indicates that the proportion of traditional services to electronic services is roughly 95 to 5 percent.

On the national level the Belastingdienst is one of the success stories regarding public electronic service delivery. The Belastingdienst is the Dutch Tax and Customs Administration. The number of electronic tax declarations is reasonably high, what is also caused by the fact that Dutch citizens are obliged to fill tax forms themselves. Unfortunately, very few data are available that show who performs the declarations, citizens or their financial advisers. Table 8 contains the percentage of electronic declarations from 2000 until 2004.

**Table 8.** Number of electronic declarations (%)

| | 2000 | 2001 | 2002 | 2003 | 2004 |
|---|---|---|---|---|---|
| Total % of electronic tax declarations | 31 | 35 | 76 | 81 | 81 |
| By disk | 26 | 44 | 59 | 50 | 40 |
| By modem | 74 | 56 | 41 | 50 | 60 |

Source: Belastingdienst

**Table 9.** Number of users of the different channels of the Informatiebeheergroep

| | 2001 | 2002 | 2003 | 2004 |
|---|---|---|---|---|
| E-mail | 204.000 | 227.000 | 237.000 | 260.000 |
| Internet visits | 1.500.000 | 2.100.000 | 3.000.000 | 4.300.000 |
| Modifications using the by Internet | 37.000 | 77.000 | 123.000 | 187.000 |
| Question and answer module | 232.000 | 538.000 | 859.000 | 1.480.000 |
| My IB-Groep new users | - | 17.600 | 72.000 | 100.000 |
| My IB-Groep consultations | - | 23.000 | 184.000 | 378.000 |

Source: Informatiebeheergoep

Another successful Dutch public institution regarding electronic services is the Informatiebeheergroep, which is responsible for the execution of several services such as student grants. The website counted 4.3 million visitors in 2004, a large number compared to earlier years. A third of the visitors used the FAQ (almost doubled compared to 2003). Table 9 illustrates the number of users of the different channels. The UWV is the Dutch body responsible for paying social benefits such as unemployment benefits. In 2004 the website added a FAQ module that seems to have satisfied an important need. The amount of questions rose from 7.000 in April to 54.000 in December 2004. At least 400.000 customer questions were answered using the FAQ in 2004.

The main conclusion in this section is that as far as statistics show the largest part of the Dutch citizens only use simple electronic government services, both on the national and the municipal level. On municipal websites citizens appear to mainly search for information like addresses and telephone numbers. On the national level FAQ modules are popular. So, the main function of online pubic service delivery in the Netherlands is providing information. Other, more advanced services, are hardly used. This means that the more advanced services that are supplied do not meet demand. One of the few exceptions are the popular transactions of the electronic tax declaration. Others might become popular as well, but the problem is that the Dutch government does not know what advanced services of communication and transaction the different sections of the Dutch citizenry want. Dutch e-government is strongly supply-side oriented. A recent EU survey showed that the Dutch are in the forefront of using e-commerce on the Internet (CBS Statline, 2005). Table 3 shows that they are in the middle or the back accessing e-government. This strange contradiction can only be explained by a unsatisfactory match of government supply and citizen demand, in our view. This is a matter of usage access as potential usage is not realized because of insufficient popular usage opportunities.

## 5 Conclusion and Further Research

In this article we have shown that insufficient access to digital technologies might explain the conspicuous gap of potential and actual usage of electronic government services in the Netherlands. A lack of motivation, physical access and digital skills is very important for the general lag of usage of these services. However, they cannot explain the large differences of the actual use of electronic government services between the Netherlands and, for example, Scandinavian countries and the surrounding countries of Germany and Luxemburg, comparable countries regarding physical Internet access. Dutch e-government gets stuck in problematic usage access, a mismatch of the supply and demand of services. Dutch government organisations pay a lot of attention to supply, offering as much electronic services as possible. This quantitative approach goes at the expense of a more qualitative approach that tries to identify the specific services different segments of the Dutch population are interested in and tries to focus supply on this demand. Such a quantitative approach would be unthinkable in e-commerce, but apparently e-government can get away with it .... for some time. Possibly, the gap between potential and actual usage of electronic government services in some other European countries, as revealed in the comparison between Table 1 and Table 2, also is to be explained by a mismatch of supply and demand. Generally speaking, a supply orientation dominates European e-government policy as exemplified by the benchmarks for e-government such as those offered by Accenture and the European Union. These benchmarks reveal a strong preference for the supply of the most advanced and extended electronic public services. The attention for the actual demand and usage of services by European citizens is only secondary, to put it mildly. Further research has to investigate whether a mismatch between supply and demand also exists in these countries. Or that the other types of access (motivation, physical access and digital skills) are comparatively more important. In a much larger international comparison of all important supply and demand factors of electronic government services in Europe it would be important to also pay attention to the supply side factors of the social, technological, political and public administration systems in these countries. All these factors taken together might give a full explanation of the conspicuous gap between the potential and actual use of electronic government services in Europe.

## References

1. Accenture: Leadership in Customer Service: New Expectations, New Experiences. Accenture (2005)
2. Eurostat: e-Government 2004: Internet based interaction with European businesses and citizens. Statistic in focus, n. 35 (2005).
3. ISC: eGovernment, More than an automation of government services http://www.isc.ie/downloads/egovernment.pdf. (2003).
4. van Dijk, J.A.G.M.: A Framework for Digital Divide Research. Journal of Communication/ Revue de Communication Electronique, Volume 12, Nrs 1 and 2 (2003).
5. van Dijk, J.A.G.M.: The Deepening Divide, Inequality in the Information Society. London: Thousand Oaks (2005).
6. Centraal Bureau voor Statistiek (2006). De digitale economie 2005. CBS Voorburg-Heerlen.
7. Hofstede, Geert H. (2001), Culture's Consequences: Comparing Values, Behaviors, Institutions, and Organizations across Nations, Thousand Oaks: Sage Publication Inc.
8. Eurostat: The digital divide in Europe. Statistic in focus, n. 38 (2005).
9. Hargittai, E.: Beyond Logs and Surveys: In-Depth Measures of People's Web Use Skills. Journal of the American Society for Information Science and Technology. 53(14):1239- 1244 (2002).
10. Hargittai, E.: Second-Level Digital Divide: Differences in People's Online Skills. First Monday. 7(4) http://firstmonday.org/issues/issue7_4/hargittai/ (2002).
11. Claeys, L. and Spee, S.: Een virtuele illusie of rele kansen? Gender in de netwerkmaatschappij. Antwerpen: Steunpunt Gelijkekansenbeleid (2005).
12. Bongers, F., Holland, C., Vermaas, K. en Vandeberg, R.: Burgers aan bod. Dialogic innovatie en interactie, Utrecht (2004).
13. Staps, K.: Het digitale loket. Een nieuwe revolutie op het gebied van dienstverlenen? Dienst Algemene en Publiekszaken gemeente Eindhoven (2005).
14. Besseling, E. en Boom, E.: Veelbelovend Eindhoven. Onderzoek naar www.eindhoven.nl. Uitgevoerd door NetPanel, in opdracht van de gemeente Eindhoven (2002).

# Limits of Public Procurement: Information Systems Acquisition

Carl Erik Moe[1], Anne Cathrine Risvand[2], and Maung K. Sein[1]

[1] Agder University College,
Box 422, 4604 Kristiansand, Norway
{Carl.E.Moe, Maung.K.Sein}@hia.no
[2] Agresso AS, Pb. 4244 Nydalen, 0401 Oslo, Norway
anne.risvand@agresso.no

**Abstract.** In this paper, we identify the tensions that exist inherently in the public procurement process as it applies to the acquisitions of larger information systems. The tensions are a result of government organizations trying to acquire the best information system possible while at the same time having to adhere to public procurement regulations. Based on case analysis of two information system acquisitions in a Norwegian municipality, we uncover three tensions inherent to the procurement process. Our findings reveal that municipalities employ a variety of strategies to deal with these tensions. However, in doing so, new tensions are created. The findings have implications for development of e-Government as these tensions needs to be taken into account when procuring new systems.

## Background

In the last few decades, the public sector has been facing the challenge of doing more with less. Hence it is becoming increasingly dependent on the effective application of information technology (IT). The Norwegian public sector is no exception. It has launched several initiatives with the final goal being electronic administration. Among a plethora of e-Government initiatives, is e-procurement. The public sector however, is required by law to follow certain rules and regulations when procuring goods and services, including IT-equipment and IT-systems. This sets the public sector procurement process apart from that of the private sector.

## 1 Introduction

e-Procurement systems have not been adopted as fast as was expected [1-5]. One reason for slow adaptation may be that e-Procurement and procurement regulations may not be suitable for acquisition of certain goods and services. In particular, acquiring information systems may not be optimally done through standard procurement policies. Yet, municipalities are required to follow the rules. The question then arises, how do municipalities meet the twin requirements

M.A. Wimmer et al. (Eds.): EGOV 2006, LNCS 4084, pp. 281–292, 2006.

of following the strict procurement regulations and at the same time meeting systems requirements that are often difficult to set up front? On one hand they would want to acquire the best system possible, this is of vital importance to development of e-Government. On the other hand, they have to adhere to strict procurement regulations. Certain tensions are likely to arise due to this.

The objective of this paper is to examine how Norwegian municipalities deal with the inherent difficulties of the public procurement process and what strategies they adopt in order to deal with these. To do so, we conducted case studies of systems acquisition at a Norwegian municipality. Before describing the method and the case studies, we examine the public procurement process and discuss systems acquisition briefly. We conclude by listing implications for practice and directions for further research.

## 2 Public Procurement

Várday [6] states that public procurement is the process of acquiring goods, works or services with public money for the society to promote the public good. This procedure is governed by rules and regulations and is essentially open and provides equal opportunities for participants. Following is a brief description of this procedure.

When the decision of what to acquire has been made it is necessary for the municipality to develop a basis for competition. This consists of vendor qualification criteria, a system specification and the contract award criteria. Vendor qualification criteria are technical qualifications, organizational, financial and economical statements as well as certificates of good conduct. The system specification may not place higher demands on performance than is necessary.

One of the main project problems is writing a technical specification that is "good enough". The vendor who ultimately wins the contract is only required by law to deliver exactly what the tender and ultimately the contract, specifies. If the technical specification is lacking in detail then the system might not be what the municipality envisioned and thus jeopardize the success of the project. Another main problems faced by public organizations is the lack of in-house competence and the resources needed to craft a sufficient specification. However, as they are often also insufficiently funded, hiring consultants is an expense they may not afford [7]. There exists however, strict regulations that govern the level of contact the public sector is allowed to have with vendors prior to a tendering. Prior contact could favour a vendor during the selection process. The government organization must be very careful not to let it influence the process.

For tendering the public authority must choose one of the three procedures: the open, the restricted, or the negotiated procedure [8]. The first thing to consider is whether there is a framework agreement. This can be defined as an agreement with one or more vendors which intent is to determine the conditions, especially price and amount, for a series of contracts to be awarded during a specific timeframe. A non-binding framework agreement does not have an impact on the procedure selection as the public entity is not committed to making purchases off such an agreement. If no binding framework agreement exists, the value of the acquisition decides the procurement procedure. The process is regulated by Norwegian legislation in addition to both EU-regulations and agreements reached through the World Trade Organization (WTO).

Certain procedures need to be followed when the value of the acquisition exceeds a threshold-value. The current threshold-values are 1.15 million NOK for central government and 1.8 million NOK for municipal government. Acquisitions above these values must be announced in both the national and the EU databases for procurement announcements. In addition the Norwegian government has made it mandatory to announce acquisitions between 500 000 NOK and the threshold values in the DOFFIN-database. Acquisitions of a value below 500 000 need not be announced but offers must be collected from two or more vendors [9].

The norm is to have an open or restricted open tender. In an open tender the purchase is first announced for tendering, interested vendors then receive the basis for competition documents from the public sector entity and finally submit their offer. Open or restricted tendering does not allow for any negotiations between the vendors and the public sector. The negotiated procedure is the most flexible but the least transparent. For acquisitions above the threshold value it can only be used if certain narrowly construed conditions are met [9]. Examples are when the risk of the system is so great that a price cannot be set in advance or when a sufficiently accurate system specification cannot be devised making it impossible to decide on a bid when following the rules of an open or limited tendering.

## 3 System Acquisition

The acquisition of a new information technology system is often very expensive and risky. Systems sometimes fail entirely to provide the expected benefits, or they may commit an organisation to a particular approach that can be very costly to change if it proves to be inappropriate. The importance of clear, stable system requirements has been stressed in system acquisition research [see e.g. 10]. In addition, system requirements are difficult to get right and techniques for specifying such requirements in terms of functionality, performance, etc. have yet to improve sufficiently [11].

System specification is an integral part of the public procurement process. A specification is found to be necessary even if the system to be purchased is a standard off-the-shelf system [12]. The difficulty of expressing all needs up front means that the specification that the contract is to be awarded on may not be complete. This indeterminacy also harms the supplier when he tries to estimate the scope of the project [13, 14].

Another factor that is important to the success of the acquisition is the choice of procedure. Most manufactured goods are mass produced, have standardized characteristics and are typically purchased at list price. Other goods, such as information systems are tailored to fit the buyer's need. In the public sector competitive bidding is perceived to select the lowest cost bidder, prevent corruption and favouritism, and offer a clear yardstick with which to compare offers. Bajari et al. [15] found that in the private sector most of the larger, complicated projects are more likely to be awarded by negotiation than by auction. Their work suggests that auctions perform poorly when projects are complex, contractual design is incomplete and there are few available bidders. With increased project complexity the importance for communication and coordination between the buyer and vendor also increases. Bajari et al. as cited (op.cit) conclude that auctions stifle communication, preventing the buyer from using the contractor's expertise when designing the project.

Competitive bidding for fixed price contracts performs especially poorly when the product designs are incomplete as substantial adjustments may be required, according to Bajari and Tadelis [16]. General system acquisition literature emphasizes the importance of the vendor's competence [10]. The environment of public sector purchasing has become more complex then ever before [17]. Today, purchasing agents confront rapidly emerging technologies, increasing product diversity and choice, environmental concerns, and the growing emphasis on quality and best value (not simply lowest price). The acquisition of a large IT-system is for most organizations an infrequent activity.

## 4 Method

To obtain an in-depth understanding of the context and the process, an interpretive case study method was the most appropriate choice. We employed a multiple case study approach where the level of analysis was the system and not the organization. Our data collection method was mainly interviews supplemented by document analysis. We conducted four semi-structured interviews, three face-to-face and one over the phone. The respondents were selected based on their strong involvement and prominent roles in the procurement process of two large information systems: an ERP system and a portal system. Two of the respondents were employed by the main vendors bidding for the contracts and were responsible for the bids and all communication with the municipality; the other two were employees at the municipality and responsible for running the procurement processes.

From the transcribed data, we extracted content, before we identified and categorized themes. Then we used the themes from interviews and from prior research to identify tensions inherent to the public procurement process and the strategies that were applied to deal with these tensions.

## 5 The Case Studies

The research site was the municipality of Kristiansand (henceforth KM), which is a fairly large municipality in Norway, it has a population of above 75 000 and employs around 6000 people. The IT budget for 2005 was 22 million NOK.

### 5.1 Case 1: The Portal Acquisition

Since 1995 the municipality has had a portal that was developed in-house. It had long been the intention to substitute this for a more standardized system. For various reasons a previous attempt was cancelled after a tendering process. KM regarded the acquisition of a standardized portal as part of their strategy for "an electronic municipality". A survey was conducted in the various sectors of the municipality in order to identify different stakeholders such as employees, customers and partners. The survey revealed which systems would potentially be integrated with the portal as well as the stakeholders' requirements for the portal solution. The results of this survey led to a high-level system specification.

According to the IT-manager the basis for competition was to give the vendors the necessary understanding of the extent of the portal project. The basis for competition documents stated that an open tendering competition would be conducted with the option of using negotiations. The contract design was that of a framework agreement which was to include assistance in development of a high-level system specification, assistance in planning the implementation and the implementation of the inter-, intra- and extranet solutions. Vendor 1 won the contract. We identified the following issues in the procurement process for the portal:

- *The nature of the acquisition influenced the system specification*: The informants all agreed that the system specification is both an important and a very difficult part of the procurement process. The quality of the system specification affects much of the rest of the procurement process and the outcome of the system implementation. The nature of this acquisition was that there would be several development projects within the whole of the project. The strategy was to let the vendor help create the specification.
- *The importance of vendor qualification:* Inherent in the procurement regulation is that the municipality must select the best offer and not the vendor. It is therefore important to ensure that the vendors in the competition are of a certain standard. The procurement regulations give the municipality the opportunity to pre-qualify the vendors as it was in this acquisition. The vendors were pleased with the formal procedure of pre-qualification of vendors. The procedure is seen as more professional and fair than those of the private sector.
- *Negotiated procedure is superior*: Among the informants there is consensus that the offer with negotiations procedure is superior to the open tendering procedure.
  "*Open tendering means that no changes can be made to the system requirements. This procedure is not very suitable [for larger IT-acquisitions] and is generally used too often.*" (Vendor 2)
  If the open tendering procedure is used the offer from the vendors can only be as good as the system specification. In this case this was not a problem as the vendor was to collaborate with the municipality on the creation of the system specification. Even so, the procedure for this acquisition was that of offer with negotiations.

- *Fixed price contracts may lead to cost overruns*: The vendors agree that offering a fixed price based on a specification of poor quality is very difficult and that market conditions often force them to offer a much lower price than what the contract is actually worth in order to win the contract. When the time comes to implement the system disputes often arise between the municipality and the vendor about what functionality the price actually includes.
- *Framework agreement reduces the need for change orders*: While the contract was awarded based on the offered fixed price per hour it is the belief of the winning vendor that the framework agreement will allow them to give accurate price estimates for projects that will be called off the framework agreement. The IT-manager emphasized that the municipality is not obligated to call-off a specific number of hours on the framework contract. They decide how many projects they want to call-off the contract.
  "*The vendor gambles on there being a lot of projects.*" (IT-manager)
- *Standard contracts favour municipalities*: Both vendors commented very specifically on the standard contracts developed by the Norwegian state agency; Statskonsult [18, 19] that are used by most municipalities. They both felt that the standard contract is very much in favour of the municipality and other public organizations that use them.
  "*If the specification is vague and problems arise, it is more or less implied that we should have understood what the client wanted. We take the risk. [The implication is that] the client should not necessarily have created a better specification, our specification of what we intend to deliver should have been more detailed.*" (Vendor 1)
  "*The standard contracts that are used are in favour of the client. All the risk is passed on to the vendor.*" (Vendor 2)
  The IT-department of KM has long experience in dealing with vendors and is said to have a lot of competence in this area. While this municipality does have a procurement department and a legal department and the IT-department claims to make frequent use of these professionals, the vendor commented:
  "*They would benefit from strengthening their administrative side. If there were procurement professionals working on this [portal] acquisition we've never met them.*" (Vendor 1)

In summary, the municipality felt that specifying all the different projects up front would be very time consuming. It would also be very difficult to get the specifications to a level of quality where the municipality would be comfortable on basing the tendering competition on it. A high-level specification was crafted. The contract was designed as a framework agreement so that the municipality would be able to develop the specifications for the individual projects with the selected vendor and not having to announce a new tendering competition for each project. The vendor was happy with the contract design and felt that the framework agreement was a good solution for this type of contract. The vendor was not happy with the quality of the contract the municipality wanted to.

### 5.2 Case 2: The Financial System Acquisition

KM had used their financial system since 1994. This system would be phased out by the vendor by 2004. A decision was therefore made to replace it with an ERP system. A pilot project was held prior to the announcement of the tender. The system specification was created as a result of this pilot and with the help of an independent consultancy firm that was subsequently excluded from the tendering competition because of this. The procedure for this acquisition was that of offer with negotiations. In the final the vendors were to give a demonstration of their respective systems. They were given a description of processes in the municipality and were asked to show how their system could improve these processes. They were also given a set of data to use while demonstrating the systems. It is believed that this is the first time such a demo case has been held for acquisition of an information system in a Norwegian municipality.

A panel of members of stakeholder departments in the municipality was present at the demonstration checking the information produced by the systems against the data that were entered. After the demonstration the municipality had a list of functionality that had to be implemented in order to meet the demands of the municipality. We identified the following issues in the procurement process.

- *The nature of the acquisition influenced the system specification*: A system specification lacking in quality would be a big problem in a project of this size and impact potential.
  "*We wrote a very specific specification [...]. The specification was detailed almost down to the specific key strokes [...].*" (Procurement professional)
  The very detailed specification was prepared to ensure that KM would get all the functionality needed to support their business processes. The high level of detail in the system specification was also meant to ensure that the vendor can give a more accurate and realistic price estimate and the need for change orders should be at a minimum.
- *Negotiated procedure foster quality*: The procedure for this acquisition was that of offer with negotiations. All the informants agree that using the negotiations procedure can have a positive influence on the acquisition process. It gives the municipality the opportunity to learn from the vendors' offers and act upon this new information. The informants also agree that this procedure should be the norm for IT-acquisitions of this value. The procurement professional worried that the procurement regulations might hinder the municipality in getting the best possible system:
  "*Our task is to make sure that the municipality gets the best systems or products available. It is a shame if the law prevents us from doing that. It would be nice if we were allowed to use tendering with negotiations more often.*"
  While the IT-manager tries to apply the negotiations procedure as often as possible the vendors stated that this is not what generally happens in Norwegian municipalities. They believe that the procedure is often not used even when it is allowed.

*"Often purchasing professionals do not wish to use offers with negotiations. They are worried about doing something that is not legal."* (Vendor 2)

- Potential problems are discovered before contract is awarded: The municipality chose to organize the demonstrations in the final phase a little differently than what is normal. According to the IT-manager vendors only show the positive aspects of their systems in demonstrations and not the less favourable ones. They wanted to make sure that they got the best system possible and adopted a strategy to solve this problem.
  *"Normally the vendors use a set of data that means nothing to us; in this case we knew the data that went into the system and knew what results to expect to come out of the system."* (IT-manager)
  During the presentation a panel of experts from different departments looked at the results coming out of the system. The IT-manager feels that several flaws in the systems were discovered this way. One of the vendors commented that setting up the system to use the data supplied by the municipality was very time consuming and that the job was not done well enough by the vendors. The whole procedure caught them a little off guard. He also believes that the municipality got extra functionality implemented because of the strategy.

## 6 Discussion of Findings

Based on the analysis, tensions inherent to the public procurement process are identified.

Tension 1: System specification as integral part of the procurement process versus creating a complete specification before the procurement process starts System specification is a critical document in the public procurement process. An inadequate system specification could potentially cause problems throughout the procurement process. Our findings show that KM was aware of this tension. The strategies applied were different in the two cases due to the different nature of the acquisitions. The strategy adopted in the portal acquisition was to design the contract as a framework agreement and thus bypassing the need for creating a detailed system specification prior to awarding the contract. In the case of the financial system the strategy was to create a very detailed system specification.

These strategies may have inadvertently caused new tensions. Firstly, framework contracts are subject to discussion. Both long lasting and comprehensive framework agreements can be deemed to be in conflict with the procurement regulations fundamental principle of competition. The number of potential vendors may be reduced as there will be a lower number of contracts to compete for. Also, development projects within a framework agreement may have been won by another vendor if the project had been announced for tender. The government entity may not get the best system available.

Secondly, creating a very detailed system specification may also create tensions. Heseltine (in Fisher et al, 2001) has identified three main problems with the manner in which conventional system specifications are written. Design oriented specifications are not capable of eliciting enough or accurate information from vendors. Rather than asking questions statements are made. If a comprehensive system specification is created using design requirements, it may include assumptions or expressing requirements using system terms instead of explaining the situation that the system must solve.

Tension 2: Restrictions on use of negotiations versus the nature of information system projects which are difficult to specify.

Bajari et al. [16] have found that in an open or restricted open tender the principle piece of information the buyer receives from the vendors is the bid. In negotiations, the buyer usually discusses the project in detail with the vendors before the contract is signed. Vendors may have important information previously not known to the buyer. With increased project complexity the importance for communication and coordination between the buyer and vendor also increases. When it is possible to enter into a negotiation with the vendors the public organization can take the knowledge gleaned from the vendors' offers and add this to the specification. This can clear up misunderstandings and give a clear understanding of what is included in the offers. In both cases, both the public employees and the vendor representatives agreed that the rules governing the use of this procedure are too strict and that it should be the norm in information system acquisitions at this level.

The use of the negotiated procedure as a strategy may cause an additional tension. The negotiated procedure is the most flexible but also the least transparent procedure [8]. In the public sector competitive bidding is perceived to select the lowest cost bidder, prevent corruption and favouritism that are opposed to efficiency, and it offers a clear yardstick with which to compare offers [16]. The data collected implies that Norwegian municipalities do not use the negotiations procedure even when they are allowed. This tension could explain the reluctance.

Tension 3: Fixed price contracts versus the nature of information system projects where expectations are not always clear up front.

Failure to deal with the previous two tensions is very often materialized when a contract is awarded on a fixed price. Bajari and Tadelis [15] found ample evidence that ex post facto changes are the rule rather than the exception. If the offer is based on a system specification of low quality very often a tension will arise. The public organization might have expectations that go beyond what the vendor is prepared to deliver at that set price. Government entities often have very strong market positions; especially the larger entities and vendors' offers are priced very low in order to win contracts. In a fixed price contract, the vendor will not be willing to perform duties beyond those to which he is contractually bound without additional compensation.

Our analysis has shown that the municipality applied strategies to deal with this tension. In the case of the financial system the vendors were asked to demonstrate the system using a set of data supplied by the municipality. They were then asked to calculate the cost of the improvements needed. This cost was then added to the fixed price offer that had already been made. This made the price offers more accurate. The strategy applied in the portal acquisition was to design the contract as a framework agreement. The contract was awarded on a fixed price per hour but as the vendor and the municipality would collaborate on the project specifications the overall price should become more accurate.

These strategies may also cause new tensions. In the case of the financial system, each system has its unique selling points; a philosophy of how to perform tasks. These philosophies may help the buyer in finding new and improved ways of performing their tasks. If what is to be demonstrated is dictated solely by the government entity, this philosophy may be lost. In the case of the portal acquisition the total scope of the project is unknown.

## 7 Conclusions

Interesting implications arise for the practice of public procurement from our findings:

Our results indicate how important it is to create a system specification so that the vendors have a greater chance of preparing an offer that corresponds to what the public organization needs. If the resources and competence is not found in-house it is important to hire competent advisors. Be aware of how the specification is constructed. A system specification using design requirements or assumptions stating how the system should function instead of which issues it should resolve may exclude vendors from the competition and lock the public organization to a certain solution.

The procurement regulations state that the public organizations must select a system, not a vendor. However, the procurement regulations make it possible for public organizations to ensure that the vendors that submit offers are of a certain quality and have the necessary experience to deliver what they offer.

The negotiated procedure allows the public organization to acquire knowledge from the vendors' offers and add this to the specification. It is also an important tool to clear up misunderstandings and get a clear understanding of what is included in the offers. The negotiated procedure when used to its full advantage can help improve the quality of the acquisition as shown in the case of the financial system.

If potential problems can be discovered before the contract has been awarded, a more accurate fixed price offer can be made by the vendors. It is also less likely that the implementation project will be disrupted by unexpected problems and that the need for change orders will be minimized.

Interesting implications also arise for research on public procurement of information system. Our findings revealed tensions inherent to the procurement as well as the strategies applied to deal with these tensions. These strategies may have created new tensions. Both the strategies and the tensions they create are interesting areas of further research. The vendor demonstration using data and scenarios supplied by the municipality is also an interesting avenue for further research. The claims that the standard contracts for software acquisitions and development create a great risk for the vendors should be investigated further. While it would be natural for the public sector to try to transfer the risk, it might mean that some vendors could be reluctant to enter into contracts with the public sector thus limiting the number of vendors that compete for government contracts.

## References

1. Davila, A., Gupta, M., Palmer, R.: Moving Procurement Systems to the Internet: The Adoption and Use of E-Procurement Technology Models. Eur. Man. J. vol. 21, no. 1 (2003) 11-23.
2. Ageshin, E.A.: E-Procurement at Work: A Case Study. Prod. and Inv. Man. 1st. quarter, vol. 42, no. 1 (2001) 48-53.
3. Henriksen, H.Z., Andersen, K.V.: E-Procurement Adoption: Theory and Practice. In Traunmuller, R. (ed) Electronic Government. Sec. Int. Conf. EGOV 2003, Lecture Notes Computer Science 2739 121-124.
4. Seong, S.K., Lee, J.Y.: Developing e-Procurement Systems: A Case study on the Government e-Procurement Systems in Korea. Pub. Fin. Man. vol. 4 no. 2 (2004) 138-157.
5. Moe, C.E., Henriksen, H.Z., Andersen, K.V.: eProcurement: Love of Life and Overnight Temptations. In K.V. Andersen, A. Gronlund, R. Trunmuller, M. Wimmer. (ed) Electronic Government. Fourth Int. Conf., EGOV 2005, Trauner Verlag Schriftenreihe Informatik, Vol 13, Band 15: 351-357.
6. Vrday, G.: Public Procurement: Lessons from Three Years' Experience clarification of key basic principles. http://www.cipe.org/publications/cee/hungary/ procurement.htm [26.10.2004] (1998).
7. Valen, H.: Ikke fortvil - Forvaltningsnettsamarbeidet hjelper deg og ytterligere hjelp er underveis. http://www.foyen.no/index.cfm?doc=107 [15.01.2004] (1998).
8. Lovells: Public procurement: the expos - the truth behind the headlines! http://www.lovells.com/control/PublicationControl/pubId/772 [17.05.2005] (2002).
9. Ministry of Trade and Industry. Veileder Forskrift om offentlige anskaffelser. http://odin.dep.no/filarkiv/158061/NOK_Veileder_rev_2002-forskrift_om_offentlige_anskaffelser.pdf [17.05.2005] (2002).
10. Jawad, A.O., Reeves, R.: Successful acquisition of IT systems. www.cranfield.ac.uk/sme/rdman/research/students/aj.htm [04.01.2004] (2002).
11. Cegrell, T.: Systems Specification and Requirements Engineering. http://www.enersearch.se/knowledgebase/publications/books/ises/ISES9.pdf [01.05.2005] (1998).
12. V. Lilley. Managing procurement. Inf. Man. Report, vol. 12, no. 9 (1996) 16-19.
13. Warsta, J.: Contracting in software business - Analysis of evolving contract processes and relationship. http://herkules.oulu.fi/isbn9514266005/isbn9514266005.pdf [01.05.2005] (2001).
14. Fisher, S., Delbridge, R., Lambert, S.: Harmonising the process of procuring library management systems: a feasibility study. http://www.cerlim.ac.uk/projects/harmonise/ harmonise.pdf [07.05.2005] (2001).
15. Bajari, P., Tadelis, S.: Incentive versus transaction costs: A theory of procurement contracts. RAND J. of Economics, vol. 32, no. 3 (2001) 387-407.
16. Bajari, P., McMillan, R., Tadelis, S.: Auctions versus Negotiations in Procurement: An Empirical Analysis. http://www-econ.stanford.edu/faculty/workp/swp02007.pdf [08.05.2005] (2002).

17. McCue, C.P., Gianakis, G.A.: Public purchasing: Who's minding the store? J. of Publ. Procurement, vol 1, no 1 (2001) 71-95.
18. Statskonsult: The Software Development Agreement - Agreement relating to the development of software. http://www.statskonsult.no/it/ssa/avtaler/ssa-u-en.pdf [22.05.2005] (2003).
19. Statskonsult: The Purchase Agreement – Agreement regarding purchase, licensing and other performances. http://www.statskonsult.no/it/ssa/avtaler/ssa-k-en.pdf [22.05.2005] (2003).

# Digital Capability Assessment for eGovernment: A Multi-dimensional Approach

Anthony M. Cresswell, Theresa A. Pardo, and Donna S. Canestraro

Center for Technology in Government, University at Albany, SUNY, USA
{tpardo}@ctg.albany.edu

**Abstract.** Capability assessment can play an important role in the digital government domain in at least two ways: one is to provide a basis for judging whether agencies are ready to initiate some digital government innovation, and the other is to judge the impact of a digital government initiative in terms of improved capabilities. The problems of how to assess and enhance organizational capability are therefore central to virtually all efforts to improve government performance, particularly in the area of information technology innovation. This paper describes the approach used in developing a set of toolkits for use in assessing capability, with examples from versions developed for use in justice information integration projects and state-level digital preservation planning in the US. The paper includes the theoretical rationale for the design of the toolkits, methods for their use, and implications for use in practice.

## 1 Introduction

Capability assessment can play an important role in the digital government domain in at least two ways: one is to provide a basis for judging whether agencies are ready to initiate some digital government innovation, and the other is to judge the impact of a digital government initiative in terms of improved capabilities. Data on capabilities targeted by digital government initiatives can provide both baseline measurements and evidence of subsequent improvements. The problems of how to assess and enhance organizational capability are therefore central to virtually all efforts to improve government performance, particularly in the area of information technology innovation. This importance is recognized in the strategic planning or planned change models in the literature, which typically include an assessment of capability as an initial step in planning or reform efforts [1-3].

The importance of capability assessment became apparent and efforts to develop new assessment methods were launched. Those efforts have produced assessment toolkits for use in three types of digital government initiatives. This paper describes the approach used in developing these toolkits generally, with examples from versions developed for use in justice information integration projects and state-level digital preservation planning in the US. The paper includes the theoretical rationale for the design of the toolkits, methods for their use, and implications for use in practice.

M.A. Wimmer et al. (Eds.): EGOV 2006, LNCS 4084, pp. 293–304, 2006.

The toolkits are based on a common conceptual foundation that treats capability as a multidimensional phenomenon, embedded in organizational practice. From this foundation, described in more detail below, each toolkit is tailored to a different government practice context and problem. The first toolkit focuses on self-assessment of capabilities and needs for developing systems for access to electronic government information. The second and third, described here, are designed for use in complex IT innovation projects in government: information sharing initiatives among government justice agencies and state government efforts to plan and implement digital preservation programs for born-digital government records [4, 5]. The latter toolkits are available as both a paper-based and in an online interactive version.

The dimensions of capability in each of the separate kits are based on a combination of existing research and theory, combined with development and validation by highly qualified advisory groups from the professional and academic communities engaged in the respective fields of practice. In each case, dimensions were identified and vetted through the review of the advisory groups. For the latter two toolkits, detailed indicators (treated as subdimensions) were identified to provide detailed examination of capabilities that make up each of the overall dimensions. In the justice integration toolkit, for example, there are 16 dimensions, each with from 8 to 15 indicators, totaling 180 indicators overall.

## 2 The Need for Capability Assessment

Assesing capability for successful government IT projects, is particularly important when collaboration and information sharing across practice domains and jusridictions are central to the project. This is especially true of information integration initiatives in the criminal justice domain and in state-wide planning for digital preservataion. These initiatives can involve several different levels of government, various combinations of agencies, and a wide range of information types and technologies. Pennsylvanias JNET Project, for example, is a statewide justice information sharing effort that has developed a secure network infrastructure and web-based portal for access to driver license photos, mug shots, rap sheets, advanced photo imaging for investigations, and capacity for email and pager notification of security events or arrests. The Harris County (Texas) Justice Information Management System (JIMS) over a decade in development, involves 281 public agencies in the county (including Houston), and covers most aspects of both criminal and civil justice functions.

Initiatives like these are typically, difficult, and prone to failure. They are more likely to succeed if they are based on a comprehensive assessment of organizational and technical capabilities. The toolkits described here generate comprehensive information about those capabilities, to focus attention on strengths, weaknesses, and the strategic selection of sharing partners. The assessment results also help identify risks and risk mitigation strategies.

# 3 Approaches to Assessing Capability

The approach to assessing capability used in these toolkits is derived from three theory domains: capability maturity modeling in the software development domain, capability in organization theory, and capability as an aspect of work practices in an organizational context. From these three perspectives we have constructed a common approach to thinking about capability that has informed the design of these toolkits, namely treating capability as a multidimensional characteristic of the organizational setting. The result is a framework for capability assessment that combines both a social and technical analysis of the concept of capability.

## 3.1 Organizational Basis of Capability

The capability assessment approach presented here was initially developed for use in a specific kind of IT innovation: developing systems for sharing and integrating information among criminal justice agencies. This kind of project, involving many technical and organizational issues, tends to be highly difficult and failure prone (see for example,[6, 7]. Therefore assessing the organizational and technical capabilities to successfully engage in such an effort is an important part of the planning and preparation. Because of the range of issues, it seems appropriate to approach the task from a combined social and technical perspective, based on the growing body of theory and research emphasizing the importance of both kinds of influences [8-12].

The conceptualization of capability that guides this assessment approach is based on the organizational context. In the organizational context, capability (or at times competence) is central to a long line of organizational and economic theory. Richardsons seminal description of an organizations capability introduced the concept in its current form, It rested on three basic components, the appropriate knowledge, experience, and skills [13], p. 888), and is based in part on Penroses earlier work [14]. Williamson review of capability theory [3] describes capability more broadly, as a composite concept, concerned with several aspects of organizational process (p. 1106). Capabilities are also linked to organizational learning and knowledge resources [15, 16]. Various dimensions of capability have also been described in research on innovations in organizations (for example, [17, 18]). More general approaches to the analysis of information systems design and development also typically employ a multidimensional approach [19]. Given this foundation of a process orientation and multiple or composite conceptualization, a multidimensional method for defining and assessing in the social aspects of capability seem the most appropriate for these toolkits.

## 3.2 Capability and Maturity Models

A multidimensional approach to capability in a technical sense is common as well. The well-known Capability Maturity Model (CMM) for software development is based on multiple dimensions arranged in five maturity levels [20]. A similar maturity model for IT investment decisions from the U.S. Government Accountability Office employs a similar design [2]. These are what Averill describes as a hybrid reference model, combining both description and prescription [21]. They are thus idealized representations of organizational processes against which to judge the actual process in use and provide a path for improvement. The reference model in both cases is based on the metaphor of maturity. That is, a process capability assessment results in scoring the process on one several the progressively higher maturity levels (five in the CMM). Placement on any level above the lowest requires achievement of all the lower level goals.

Though widely accepted in software development, the maturity model appears too restrictive for the broader range of innovation activities of interest here. The maturity structure represented in the CMM and ITIM has two features which do not appear adequate to deal with the complexities of these projects: a linear progression and a simplistic model of interaction among the many factors involved in process performance. The building-block sequence of development in the maturity model seems to fit only a part of the collaboration and interorganizational processes we have observed. Some capabilities grow and become a stable base for subsequent improvements, while others are much more dynamic and unpredictable. This dynamic is more consistent with the alternative models described below. In addition, the interaction inherent in such a building-block model are based on restricted set of assumptions about interdependency: the levels are distinct, and higher values for factors at one maturity level cannot compensate for lower (immature) levels elsewhere. This seems unnecessarily restrictive and limiting for the many diverse processes that make up multi-organizational IT innovations.

### 3.3 Capability and Work Practices

Capability in action is embedded in work practices. In this sense, practice consists of the activities and context through which the participating persons and organizations design and develop information resources. The various agency work practices involved in these projects have different missions and traditions, different scope and internal structures and cultures. The capabilities to work in mixed practice settings therefore includes the ability to share knowledge, resolve interest conflicts, and craft the new technical and social arrangements that will yield a successful shared innovation.

The concept of practice that we use here has three major sources. Lave and Wenger [22, 23] described communities of practice as informal groups engaged in shared learning and work processes, independent of formal organizational structures or management controls. The community is one in which in which social structure and meaning are continually negotiated through participation [24], p. 152). Integrating information across organizations involves many different communities of practice in this sense, and may require the creation of new ones. Practice capability would include alignment and compatibility of social relationships and knowledge across organizations and sub-units. The idea of technology in practice is another source of theory material, which we draw from Orlikowskis framing of a practice perspective [8], including concepts of structuration following Giddens [25], and related work by [9, 26]. A similar, but dynamic view of practice learning and feedback informs the concept of capability in the process of information system development [10]. The important elements of the practice perspective in this body of work are related to the reflexive relationship between technologies and social structures. That is, neither social structures nor technology structures are treated as determining causes of practice, but rather interacting in mutual influence and restructuring. This view of practice is similar to the reflexive nature of social and technical structures in Bourdieus theory on the nature of practice [27]. In this view, the practice context, or habitus, is structured by the dispositions of the social and physical elements of the setting, and are in turn modified by the practices carried out in the setting, etc. (p. 72). In this sense practice is neither social nor technical, but action that is both influenced by and influencing the social and technical dispositions in which it is embedded.

This practice perspectives incorporates the role of human intention and agency in capability assessment. Some previous work has examined this question of human agency and goal-directed behavior in the information system development context. The participants in the process (individuals or organizations) can be treated as seeking to advance their own interests and acting in a goal-directed manner. Capability will therefore be influenced by divergence in individual and group interests and goals, the conflicts among them, and by the pursuit of individual and organizational strategies. These propositions follow in particular from the work of [12, 28], and agency theory generally [29], as well as descriptions of information system development as planned behavior [11].

### 3.4 Strategy and Resource Based Capability

Considerable research and understanding of organizational capability is founded in a resource-based model. That is, what accounts for differences in the capabilities among organizations are differences in their critical resources [30, 31]. These resources consist of assets that the organization owns or controls (physical assets, knowledge & skills, social relationships, etc.), as well as resources that it can mobilize or influence externally. The resource based view of capability does not hold that any particular mix of level of resources produces a corresponding capability, as in the maturity model sense, but that variations across diverse mixes of resources produce capability differentials [32]. Capability in the resource based view is not stable, but can be strongly affects by both internal and external changes in the organizational context [33, 34].

There is also evidence that organizational capability depends not only on the possession of resources, but also on alignment among technical (i.e., physical) resources, social and organizational norms & cultures, and knowledge resources. By alignment we mean that the characteristics of these elements of information systems and organizations are sufficiently similar and compatible that they allow for productive interactions and interoperability. This includes the ability of the participants to overcome or resolve differences in conceptual and technical structures, and language [18, 35].

## 4 Capability Dimensions in the Toolkits

These varied theory perspectives provide ample support for treating capability as an overall mix of characteristics of persons, devices, and organizations that are needed to complete a complex body of work. Moving that work forward consists of meeting a mix of social and technical requirements for success. These requirements include:

- coordinating and sustaining the overall work process
- solving problems of misalignment of technical and organizational characteristics of the practice setting, which include
  - resolving conflicts arising out of divergent interests, power, and culture, and
  - resolving conflicts arising out of incompatibilities and misalignment of technical resources

Since these main groupings can involve different methods, knowledge bases, actors, and types of problems, they may represent different practice settings for the innovation processes. This perspective on the nature of interorganizational information sharing formed the basis for seeking professional judgment and additions to the description of dimensions.

That professional input was obtained in a series of three workshops involving over 30 professionals and experts on criminal justice information systems, and subsequent field tests of the assessment tool. The existing dimensions and their detailed descriptions were developed using the judgements and discussion obtained from the workshop participants. In the first workshop they were presented with the overall theory approach and proposed design of the assessment process and asked to identify relevant dimensions and their descriptions. These results were collected, discussed in detail, and used as the basis for the second workshop. In that setting the participants revised and refined the dimension descriptions and produced lists of questions or indicators that could be used to assess capability along those dimensions. Those results were used to draft the assessment tool, which was presented at the third workshop. There the participants reviewed and critiqued the draft and provided substantial improvements. The results are the 16 basic dimensions, each of which has between seven and 16 specific subdimensions, or indicators associated with it (an example is shown in the Appendix). Altogether the 16 dimensions and their 180 subdimensions constitute the basis for capability rating, following the assessment methods discussed below. The relationships among the basic dimensions and the theory perspectives outlined above are shown in Table 1 below.

Some dimensions (4,11,12, &14) have implications for more than one problem area, and as developed include indicators and that span two columns. An argument can also be made for overlap for others that are not so marked in Table 1. Since these are complex conceptual domains and not subject to specific discipline-based definitions, it does not seem appropriate to make too fine a distinction for these types of activity.

**Table 1.** Theory Bases of Final Dimensions

| | Coordinating Work Processes | Resolving Social Problems | Technical Alignment |
|---|---|---|---|
| 1. Business Model & Architecture | | | X |
| 2. Collaboration Readiness | | X | |
| 3. Data Assets & Requirements | | | X |
| 4. Governance | X | X | |
| 5. Information Policies | | | X |
| 6. Leaders & Champions | X | | |
| 7. Organizational Compatibility | | X | |
| 8. Performance Evaluation | X | | |
| 9. Project Management | X | | |
| 10. Resource Management | X | | |
| 11. Secure Environment | | X | X |
| 12. Stakeholder ID & Engagement | X | X | |
| 13. Strategic Planning | X | | |
| 14. Technology Acceptance | | X | X |
| 15. Technology Compatibility | | | X |
| 16. Technology Knowledge | | | X |

## 5 Collaborative Assessment Methods

To be useful in an actual information sharing initiative, the dimensions must be part of a workable assessment method. The dimensions and subdimensions (indicators), must be understandable to those involved in the assessment. The assessment activity must be organized and conducted to generate meaningful results that can be applied to planning and initiative development. And the method must be adaptable to the wide variety of settings in which justice information sharing initiatives can occur. This section describes the way the justice toolkit employs the dimensions and assessment activities to meet these requirements. Additional details on the assessment materials and activities are available in the appendix.

### 5.1 Assessment as a Collaborative, Knowledge Sharing Process

The toolkit assessment process is based on the assumption that a collaboration and knowledge sharing are the best ways to ensure that the results reflect the multiple understandings of capability that exists across the organizations involved in information sharing. The work of the assessment is designed to take place in a kind of knowledge and information sharing network among the various participants. That is, the directions for the assessment call for forming groups to gather and summarize assessment information based on their shared knowledge and judgments. Ultimately this information is shared within organizational structures and through interorganizational and intraorganizational network relationships.

This kind of information sharing across organizational boundaries does not require the organizations to form new institutional structures as much as form new relationships based on information needs and coordination of work processes and IT systems. These relationships are much more like network forms of organization than formal bureaucratic structures [36]. Networks have long been associated with research on the influence and decision making aspects of the public policy process (e.g. [37]), but the treatment of networks as instruments of public management is relatively recent and still developing as a research area [38, 39].

The participation in network relationships as part of the assessment also provides a mechanism for identifying and resolving issues arising from diverse interests, cultures, and work practices across the participating organizations. Broad participation in the assessment provides for attention to the interests and concerns of the stakeholders before and during the development of the new IT-based initiatives [40]. As Brown argues, "[w]ith e-government, different stakeholders become critical to the survival of the project during different phases of the initiative.

### 5.2 Dimension Descriptions

In order to work with the dimensions as the basis for assessment, the assessment participants must apply a reasonably consistent understanding of the dimensions and indicators. For that purpose, the implementation materials include detailed descriptions of the dimensions themselves, and of how to interpret the higher and lower ranges of capability along each dimension. The assessment instructions also call for training workshops for the participants to prepare them for the process and develop consistent interpretation of the dimensions and indicators.

### 5.3 Assessment Process

Information sharing initiatives can vary greatly deal, so the toolkit offers options for organizing and implementing an assessment. Organizers decide how to manage the assessment ratings, who to involve in discussions and decisions using the ratings, how to organize their efforts, and how to compile and present ratings for use in interorganizational discussions. Some of the options rely on group consensus, others defer to executive decision-making. Data can be weighted in different ways and presented in qualitative or quantitative form. The implementation guide describes these options. The process is almost never linear; instead, it progresses through multiple iterations as information and analysis from one set of activities feed back into and modify earlier conditions and understandings.

The most complete data come from a process that begins with the individual organizational units engaged in the initiative assessing themselves and producing unitspecific results. These are then combined into results for each agency and combined again for the entire initiative. A more detailed view of this process is shown in figure 1, which illustrates how this might work in a setting with three agencies, each of which have two subunits involved in the initiative. Through this process participants build knowledge about their ability to contribute to cross-boundary sharing efforts.

## 6 Testing Results

Following the review of the toolkit by the professional workshops, five field tests were conducted during the time period of July November 2003. The field tests identified the usability of the toolkit in a variety of practical settings at the state and local level in three states (California, Colorado, and Illinois) and by a national and a state-wide panel of justice executives. The tests provided evidence of the validity of the dimensions, indicators, and procedures among the intended user population.

Two of the field tests were usability review by executives justice agencies, one chosen from a national organization, the Justice Information Sharing Practitioners (JISP), and the executive boards of a very large state integrated justice initiative: the Pennsylvania Justice Network (JNET). JISP is a professional organization made up of practitioners from the 50 states that are involved in Justice Integration initiatives. JNET is an integrated network of municipal, county, and state justice agencies in Pennsylvania. The JISP members reviewed the practicality and the use of the toolkit in each of their individual jurisdictions. The Executive Board and Executive Director of JNET organized a task force who provided a summary review of the dimensions and the toolkit and how it could be used within their enterprise. These executive review results supported the clarity and relevance of the dimensions and subdimensions from the practitioner perspective. Each of the field testers were in agreement as to the appropriate scope, content, and depth of the dimension and subdimension descriptions. There were no suggested changes to the dimensions from the field test results.

As a result of the JISP review, 3 individual jurisdictions offered to participate in an onsite administration of the toolkit by their integrated justice project team. Of these three field test sites, two were at a county integration initiative level, and one was at a state integrated justice enterprise level. The field tests consisted of a pre-workshop planning session, an assessment workshop, and a post-workshop review. The research team conducted the pre-workshop planning session for those who would be administering the assessment and jointly develop their field test plan. The subdimension ratings were collected in assessment workshops, which took different forms in each field test sites. Research team and field site staff analyzed the data and provided a presentation of the results to the executive boards. The post-workshop review allowed the team to gather additional data from the core teams from an implementation and logistical standpoint as well as assist the local teams with crafting the tactical plans resulting from the assessments.

Overall, the field tests provided strong evidence that the conceptual material and methods of the toolkit were relevant, accessible, and adaptable to a wide range of justice integration initiatives. Participants in the field tests were able to readily understand and apply the dimension and subdimension ratings to their situation. Each group was able to apply the results to strategic and tactical planning as well, focusing on those areas that were assessed as being low capability. The participants were able to easily customize the toolkit methods to their particular situation.

## 7 Implications for Theory and Practice

A number of important issues remain unresolved by this work. One is uncertainty about the effectiveness of the method to improve the success of innovation initiatives. The ready acceptance of the toolkit by practitioners suggests that it can be used as designed. At present, however, there is no direct evidence of the impact that such use would have on the progress or ultimate success of the projects. When the experience with the toolkit has accumulated sufficiently, retrospective studies of possible impacts can be conducted. It seem unlikely that statistical studies for this purpose would be feasible. The types of settings in which the toolkit would be used would likely vary greatly, making sampling among equivalent units very problematic. Qualitative studies of innovation processes and outcomes may be more useful, providing for comparisons across cases and new insights into how the basic capability approach can be improved.

Neither is it clear that the cost of the assessment process represents a good investment. The assessment could involve hundreds of hours of staff time and result in substantial work disruption. The most extensive field test of the justice agency toolkit required hundreds of hours of participant time to complete and review. Costs can be contained by choosing the extent of participation and number of iterations of assessment carefully. But too severe restrictions on the resources used could compromise the validity of the results. Further field testing is needed to obtain more detailed cost data.

We have not settled the basic issue of the relative advantages of multidimensionbased assessment versus the maturity level approach in the ITIM [2] and the Capability Maturity Model [20]. Modifications contemplated for the ITIM approach may include dimensions as an extension of these other models. Plans for the further development of the dimension-based approach described here include examining the possibility of including threshold or maturity-like components in the design Since there is nothing logically inconsistent in a combination of the two approaches, these further developments may be helpful in advancing the usefulness of these tools.

## References

1. A. H. Segars and V. Grover, "Profiles of Strategic Information Systems Planning," Information Systems Research, vol. 10, pp. 199-232, 1999.
2. U.S.Government Accountability Office, Information Technology Investment Management: A Framework for Assessing and Improving Process Maturity. Washington, DC: GAO, 2004.
3. O. E. Williamson, "Strategy research: governance and competence perspectives," Strategic Management Journal, vol. 20, pp. 1087-1108, 1999.
4. A. M. Cresswell, T. A. Pardo, D. S. Canestraro, S. S. Dawes, and D. Juraga, "Sharing Justice Information: A Capability Assessment Toolkit," Center for Technology in Government, Albany, NY November 2005.

5. T. A. Pardo, A. M. Cresswell, S. S. Dawes, B. Burke, L. Dadayan, S. Embar, and H. Kwon, "Building State Government Digital Preservation Partnerships: A Capability Assessment and Planning Toolkit," Center for Technology in Government, Albany, NY August 2005.
6. K. Lyytinen and D. Robey, "Learning failure in information systems development," Information Systems Journal, vol. 9, pp. 85-102, 1999.
7. H. Goldstein, "Who Killed the Virtual Case File?," IEEE Spectrum, vol. 42, 2005.
8. W. J. Orlikowski, "Using Technology and Constituting Structure: A Practice Lens for Studying Technology in Organizations," Organization Science vol. 11, pp. 404-428, 2000.
9. K. Lyytinen, "Empirical Research in Information Systems: On the Relevance of Practice in Thinking of IS Research," MIS Quarterly, vol. 23, pp. 25-27, 1999.
10. L. F. Luna-Reyes, Jing Zhang, J. R. Gil-Garcia, and A. M. Cresswell, "Information systems development as emergent socio-technical change: A practice approach," European Journal of Information Systems, vol. 14, pp. 93-105, 2005.
11. R. Hirschheim, H. K. Klein, and K. Lyytinen, Information Systems Development and Data Modeling: Conceptual and Philosophical Approaches. New York: Cambridge University Press, 1995.
12. M. C. Boudreau and D. Robey, "Enacting Integrated Information Technology: A Human Agency Perspective," Organization Science, vol. 16, pp. 3-18, 2005.
13. G. B. Richardson, "The Organization of Industry," Economic Journal, vol. 82, pp. 883-896, 1972.
14. E. T. Penrose, The Theory of the Growth of the Firm. New York: Oxford University Press, 1959.
15. C. E. Helfat and R. S. Raubitschek, "Product sequencing: Co-evolution of knowledge capabilities and products," Strategic Management Journal, vol. 21, pp. 961-979, 2000.
16. B. Kogut and U. Zander, "What firms do? Coordination, identity, and learning," Organization Science, vol. 7, pp. 502-518, 1996.
17. A. H. VandeVen and M. S. Poole, "Methods for studying innovation development in the Minnesota innovation research program," Organization Science, vol. 1, pp. 313-385, 1990.
18. T. A. Pardo, A. M. Cresswell, S. S. Dawes, and G. B. Burke, "Modeling the Social & Technical Processes of Interorganizational Information Integration," presented at Hawaiian International Conference on System Sciences Hawaii, 2004.
19. H. Barki, S. Rivard, and J. Talbot, "An Integrative Contingency Model of Software Project Risk Management," Journal of Management Information Systems, vol. 17, pp. 37-69, 2001.
20. M. C. Paulk, C. V. Weber, B. Curtis, and M. B. Chrissis, The Capability Maturity Model: Guidelines for Improving the Software Process. Reading, MA: Addison Wesley, 1994.
21. E. Averill, "Reference Models and Standards," StandardView Archive, vol. 2, pp. 96-109, 1994.
22. J. Lave and E. Wenger, Situated learning: Legitimate Peripheral Participation. Cambridge: Cambridge University Press, 1991.
23. E. Wenger, Communities of Practice Learning, Meaning, and Identity. New York City: Cambridge University Press, 1999.
24. M. Thompson, "Structural and Epistemic Parameters in Communities of Practice," Organization Science, vol. 16, pp. 151-164, 2005.
25. A. Giddens, The Constitution of Society: Outline of the Theory of Structuration. Berkeley, CA: University of California Press, 1984.

26. N. Levina and E. Vaast, "Competence in Practice: Implications for Implementation and Use of Information Systems," MIS Quarterly, vol. 29, pp. 335-363, 2005.
27. P. Bourdieu, The Logic of Practice. Stanford, CA: Stanford University Press, 1980 (translated 1990).
28. J. Rose and M. Jones, "The Double Dance of Agency: A Socio-Theoretic Account of How Machines and Humans Interact," Systems, Signs & Actions, vol. 1, pp. 1937, 2005.
29. S. P. Shapiro, "Agency Theory," Annual Review of Sociology, vol. 31, pp. 26384, 2005.
30. K. M. Eisenhardt and J. A. Martin, "Dynamic capabilities: what are they?," Strategic Management Journal, vol. 21, pp. 1105-1121, 2000.
31. S. Dutta, O. Narasimhan, and S. Rajiv, "Conceptualizing and Measuring Capabilities: Methodology and Empirical Application," Strategic Management Journal, vol. 26, pp. 277-285, 2005.
32. I. M. Cockburn, R. M. Henderson, and S. Stern, "Untangling the origins of competitive advantage," Strategic Management Journal, vol. 21, pp. 1123- 1145, 2000.
33. D. M. G. Raff, "Superstores and the evolution of firm capabilities in American bookselling," Strategic Management Journal, vol. 21, pp. 1043- 1059, 2000.
34. R. S. Rosenbloom, "Leadership, Capabilities, and Technological Change: The Transformation of NCR in the Electronic Era," Strategic Management Journal, vol. 21, pp. 1083-1103, 2000.
35. M. E. Sosa, S. D. Eppinger, and C. M. Rowles, "The Misalignment of Product Architecture and Organizational Structure in Complex Product Development," Management Science, vol. 30, pp. 1674-1689, 2004.
36. K. G. Provan and B. H. Milward, "A preliminary theory of interorganizational network effectiveness: A comparative study of four community mental health systems," Administrative Science Quarterly, vol. 40, pp. 1-34, 1995.
37. H. Heclo, A Government of Strangers: Executive Politics in Washington. Washington, DC: Brookings Institution, 1977.
38. J. Zhang, & Dawes, S., "Expectations and perceptions of benefits and barriers in public sector knowledge networks," Public Performance & Management Review, forthcoming.
39. R. K. Rethemeyer, "Conceptualizing and Measuring Collaborative Networks," Public Administration Review, vol. 65, pp. 117-121, 2005.
40. A. Pouloudi and E. A. Whitley, "Stakeholder Identification in Inter- Organizational Systems: Gaining Insights for Drug Use Management Systems," European Journal of Information Systems., vol. 6, pp. 1-14, 2004.

# Assessing the Intangible Value of G2G Endeavours

Luiz Antonio Joia

Brazilian School of Public and Business Administration of Getulio Vargas Foundation and Rio de Janeiro State University Praia de Botafogo 190 room 526 - 22253-900 – Rio de Janeiro – Brazil
luizjoia@fgv.br

**Abstract.** This paper was elaborated in order to measure the variation of the intellectual capital in public organisations involved in Government-to-Government (G2G) endeavours. Consequently, this study aims to assess the intangible outcomes of G2G projects within Public Administration. A heuristic frame was then developed to evaluate the impact of G2G endeavours on the components of the intellectual capital of a public agency. Applying this heuristic frame to thirty G2G endeavours in Brazil, it was concluded that a successful G2G undertaking has a positive impact on the intellectual capital of a public agency associated with it. Lastly, in addition to the research limitations, some conclusions and recommendations are set forth for public managers, practitioners and academics, so as to allow them to grasp the potential of using the intellectual capital theory to assess e-government initiatives.

## 1 Introduction

Since the beginning of the 1980s, a movement was fomented by academics and executives to use Information and Communication Technology (ICT) not only as a tool for processing data more rapidly, but also as a powerful strategic weapon. The need to use ICT as an enabler to reformulate old processes, rather than simply automate existing practices was perceived by these academics and executives (see, for instance, [1] and [2]).

As Internet technology became more readily available, the reformulation of productive processes in the public arena became a reality, leading all levels of government to strive for greater efficiency, efficacy and accountability in their relationship with their stakeholders, in what is now known as e-government [3].

In fact, the understanding of knowledge as a strategic weapon for a corporation is nothing new. Back in 1945, Frederick Hayek presented research about the use of knowledge in society [4]. In 1993, Peter Drucker analysed the new Knowledge Economy and its consequences [5]. Therefore, the importance of the intangible assets of a corporation, and even those of both countries and any other organisations – including non-profit entities – has been increasingly highlighted by academics, researchers and practitioners (see, for instance, [6],[7],[8],[9], to name but a few).

M.A. Wimmer et al. (Eds.): EGOV 2006, LNCS 4084, pp. 305–316, 2006.

Moreover, several publications deserve mention on their own merit, such as Kaplan and Norton's "The Balance Scorecard" [10] and "The Valuation of Intangible Assets", prepared by Arthur Andersen with The Economist Intelligence Unit [11]. However, a watershed was reached in July 1994, when a meeting was held in Mill Valley in order to establish how the knowledge of an organisation could be measured. Knowledge may be intangible, but that does not mean that it cannot be measured. As we know, markets do it when they value the stock of some very knowledge-intensive companies way above their book value.

In 1995, Skandia – the largest insurance and financial services company in Scandinavia – released its Intellectual Capital Annual Report, based on its Navigator framework [8]. Some other companies, like Dow Chemical, the Canadian Imperial Bank of Commerce, Posco, etc., to name but a few, have also entered this new era.

Hence, this paper draws on the fusion of these two former mainstreams, namely e-government and the strategic role of intangible assets in public agencies. It was elaborated in order to establish a heuristic frame that is capable of measuring the variation of the intellectual capital in public organisations involved in Government-to-Government (G2G) endeavours. Consequently, this study aims to assess the intangible outcomes of G2G projects within Public Administration, which is still considered a knowledge frontier in the e-government arena [12].

## 2 Bibliographical Review and Research Hypotheses

### 2.1 The Impetus Behind the Intellectual Capital Theory

There is no single definition for intellectual capital (IC). Kaufmann & Schneider [13], for instance, analysed several definitions for this construct. Most of them are associated with the definition of intangible assets and knowledge resources, as stated by Rastogi [14]: "*IC may properly be viewed as the holistic or meta-level capability of an enterprise to coordinate, orchestrate, and deploy its knowledge resources towards creating value in pursuit of its future vision*". In line with this, Petty & Guthrie [15] define IC as "*the economic value of the intangible assets of a corporation*".

According to Edvinsson & Malone [8], Roos et al. [6], Sveiby [7] and Stewart [16], the impetus for the development of an intellectual capital theory draws upon the increasing value of the ratio between the market and the book (M/B) values of organisations. Indeed, some authors, such as Ordonez de Pablo [17] not only agree with that but also support the claim that a firm's intellectual capital equals the difference between its market and book values.

Some might say that different depreciation policies might influence the book value (B) calculation. It is a valid point, and is the reason why Tobin [18] suggests the use of replacement cost, defining q as (market value)/(replacement cost of the assets). The replacement cost concept was developed in order to circumvent the differing depreciation policies used by accountants world-wide. If q is greater than 1, the asset is worth more than the cost of replacing it, thus it is likely the company will seek to acquire more assets of this kind. However, recently this explanation has not been capable of explaining the increasing M/B values.

## 2.2 Intellectual Capital Taxonomy

Based on research carried out by Edvinsson & Malone [8], Roos et al. [6], Sveiby [7] and Stewart [16], it is proposed that certain corporate capital taxonomy be used in this article. The taxonomy adopted is based on the following equation:

$$\texttt{Market Value = Book Value + Intellectual Capital} \tag{1}$$

This equation shows that stock value has a tangible portion (book value) in addition to an intangible component. Hence, assuming that the intellectual capital is greater than zero (IC>0), the market value/book value is greater than 1 (M/B>1). The more knowledge-intensive the company is, the higher the M/B value is.

The book value (also called financial capital) is then calculated by the following formula:

$$\texttt{Book Value = Monetary Capital + Physical Capital} \tag{2}$$

and intellectual capital, formerly called goodwill by accountants, is calculated using the formula below:

$$\texttt{Intellectual Capital = Human Capital + Structural Capital} \tag{3}$$

Human capital does not belong to the firm, as it is a direct consequence of the sum of the expertise and skills of its employees. Structural capital belongs to the company, and can be traded (at least theoretically), as it is the actual environment built by the firm to manage and generate its knowledge adequately. It is compounded by the internal structure or the day-to-day operations of the company, encompassing for instance its processes, databases, codes, culture, management style and internal networks (such as intranets), called organisational capital; the relationship capital that is concerned with the value of a firm's links with its customers, suppliers, subcontractors and other major players; and innovation capital, a direct consequence of the firm's culture and its capacity for creating new knowledge from the existing supply. Thus, the following formula summarises what has been said above:

$$\begin{aligned}&\texttt{Structural Capital = Organisational Capital +}\\&\texttt{Relationship Capital + Innovation Capital}\end{aligned} \tag{4}$$

Finally, the intellectual capital formula can be presented in conjunction as:

$$\begin{aligned}&\texttt{Intellectual Capital = Human Capital + Organisational Capital +}\\&\texttt{Relationship Capital + Innovation Capital}\end{aligned} \tag{5}$$

It can be seen that the intellectual capital is compounded by four constructs HC, OC, RC and InC – i.e. human, organisational, relationship and innovation capitals, respectively – each one of which interacts with the others [19].

### 2.3 Intellectual Capital in Public Administration

Intellectual capital has been widely used in the private sector. However, public administration lags far behind the business realm. There are several reasons for this, as stated by Cinca et al. [20]. According to the authors, unlike the private sector in which performance can be evaluated by financial measures, public agencies have multiple objectives of a non-financial nature. Moreover, although using similar production inputs – human resources, knowledge, money, raw materials and plant – the public sector takes greater advantage of the first two, which are intangible assets. Furthermore, the main output of public agencies is service, rather than products, and service cannot be measured directly. Finally, the authors point to lower motivation for the adoption of new management practices and methods in the public administration realm and the fact that public managers have less room to manoeuvre as two more hurdles to the implementation of intellectual capital-based projects in public administration [20].

Notwithstanding these obstacles, some academics have already developed research addressing the use of the intellectual capital theory in public administration. We can cite, for instance, Sveiby [7], who applied the intellectual capital theory in the Home Care Department of a Local Government and a Government Agency in Adelaide, Australia. There is also Dragonetti & Roos [21], who analysed AusIndustry – a state agency associated with Australia's department of Industry, Science and Tourism, as well as Bontis [22], who developed a national intellectual capital index for the Arab Peninsula.

However, there is a major difference between intellectual capital in the business and public realm, namely in the way that the measurement model is validated [23]. Often, the business sector validates its intangible asset measurement models statistically, by correlating the results accrued from them with a firm's M/B (market value/book value) ratio [24]. As public agencies do not have a market value, another way to validate the measurement model must be found [20]. In the public administration arena, the solution for this problem is to be found in the body of knowledge gathered from performance measurement [25].

According to Ballantine & Cunningham [26], increasing recognition of the need to monitor multiple dimensions of performance has led to the development of a substantial body of performance measurement literature. Among the earlier contributors to such literature, Checkland et al. [27] conceptualised performance measurement by using the concept of a system and the measures necessary for it to remain stable over time. Their research led to the recognition of three levels of performance which, they argue, should be used to monitor a system's performance (see also [28]):

- *Effectiveness*: Is the right thing being done?
- *Efficacy*: Does the means work?
- *Efficiency*: Is resource usage minimal?

Moreover, in public projects, accountability must also be evaluated. To Campos [29], this concept may be understood as a question of democracy. The more advanced the democratic stage, the greater the interest in democracy. And government account-ability tends to follow the advance of democratic values such as equality, human dignity, participation, transparency and responsibility.

Hence, these four dimensions – effectiveness, efficacy, efficiency and accountability – consolidated into a single dimension could avoid misconceptions on the part of the respondents. It could also replace the M/B ratio in order to validate the results accrued from the use of the intellectual capital theory to measure the intangible asset variation in the public sector due to G2G projects.

### 2.4 Research Hypothesis

So, based on the claims already presented, two research hypotheses can be established for testing in this study, namely:

*Ha: Government-to-Government projects between public agencies increase their intellectual capital*

*Hb: The impact of Government-to-Government projects is greater on the relationship capital of the public agencies involved*

The rationale for the first research hypothesis lies in the fact that Government-to-Government is supported by inter-organisational systems that can enable collaboration and be the locus of knowledge creation within public agencies (see, for instance, [30],[31],[32], to name only a few).

On the other hand, G2G endeavours can be seen as horizontal networks among public agencies. According to Nooteboom [33] and Koivisto & Ahmaniemi [34], horizontal networks are defined as cooperative arrangements among firms in the same field of business, such as in the Public Administration realm. Hence, it is expected that a G2G project has a major impact on the relationship capital of an organisation, as its purpose is to link two or more public agencies digitally enabling them to work in a collaborative way, which is known as the "sharing component" of a firm's organisational intelligence, according to Haeckel & Nolan [35]. Moreover, in a G2G undertaking the customers are the civil servants of the public agencies involved. Therefore, it would seem that the strongest influence of a G2G endeavour is on the relationship capital of an organisation, as this capital addresses the relationship of a firm with its customers, whoever they are. The second hypothesis tests this idea.

## 3 Research Design

The methodology used in this article draws from existing models set forth by Edvinsson & Malone [8], Roos et al. [6], Sveiby [7], Klein [36] and Winter [37]. In the latter article, the heuristic frame concept developed by Winter in his article "Knowledge and Competence as Strategic Assets" is heavily used, being the model proposed later in this research and classified as a heuristic frame.

As Winter says: "*A heuristic frame corresponds to a degree of problem definition that occupies an intermediate position on the continuum between a long and indiscriminate list of things that might matter at one end and a fully formulated control-theoretic model of the problem at the other. Within a heuristic frame, there is room for a wide range of more specific formulations of the problem – but there is also enough structure provided by the frame itself to guide and focus discussion. On the other hand, a rich variety of different heuristic frames may represent plausible approaches to a given problem*" [37].

A series of thirty successful G2G projects undertaken in Brazil was selected by the author for further analysis. All of them involved just two public agencies linked via a web-based inter-organisational system to work in a collaborative way.

A questionnaire was created for assessing each G2G endeavour. This form used a five-point Likert scale ranging from - 2 to 2. Intellectual capital (IC) was split into its components: human capital (HC); organisational capital (OC); relationship capital (RC); and innovation capital (InC). Four questions were developed in order to evaluate the impact of the G2G project on the above capitals, as presented below:

Q1: After the implementation of the G2G project, how have the improvements in terms of skills and competence of the organisation's personnel accrued from this specific undertaking been perceived? (*to evaluate the human capital variation*)

Q2: After the implementation of the G2G project, how have the improvements in terms of processes in the organisation accrued from this specific undertaking been perceived? (*to evaluate the organisational capital variation*)

Q3: After the implementation of the G2G project, how have the improvements in terms of relationships between the organisation and its main stakeholders accrued from this specific undertaking been perceived? (*to evaluate the relationship capital variation*)

Q4: After the implementation of the G2G project, how has the innovation capability of the organisation accrued from this specific undertaking been perceived? (*to evaluate the innovation capital variation*)

The questionnaires with the above four questions were answered by the two chief executives of the organisations linked via the G2G project. They were asked to agree with a single value to be marked in the questionnaire. They could say that the G2G project had jeopardized the specific capital greatly (-2); jeopardized it (-1); was neutral in relation to it (0); improved the specific capital (1) or improved it greatly (2). So, in this research, the intellectual capital variation of the two firms involved in the G2G project was consolidated into a single score as agreed by the principals of the digitally-linked firms. This can be considered a limitation of the method applied, as it is possible that the impacts are widely different in each public agency involved.

Thereafter, for each G2G project, the intellectual capital variation was calculated as depicted below [8]:

$\triangle$ICi= ($\triangle$HCi + $\triangle$PCi + $\triangle$RCi + $\triangle$InCi )/4; where i = the number of the G2G project and $\triangle$means the capital variation.

Afterwards, the averages and standard deviations of the intellectual capital variations accrued from the G2G projects were calculated and a single-tail t-test was undertaken, in order to test whether the IC average variation could be supported to be higher than 0, i.e., to verify whether there was an increase in the intellectual capital of the data set due to the G2G projects (Hypothesis Ha).

Using an ANOVA test, it was also verified whether the impact of the G2G projects on the capitals composing the intellectual capital was equal or whether there was a stronger influence on the relationship capital (Hypothesis Hb).

As suggested by Kannan & Aulbur [38], perceptual measures were used in order to validate these results. A questionnaire was then circulated among five employees of each organisation that took part in the G2G project, in order to assess their value perceptions accrued from the impact of the G2G project on their public agency's efficiency, efficacy, effectiveness and accountability. Before the questionnaire was filled out by the civil servants, the researcher had a meeting with them, explaining the objectives of the study and the performance measures adopted. A single value was then set by each respondent. A 5-point Likert scale ranging from -2 to 2 was also used. As explained before, they could say that their perceptions about their firms' performance were now: much worse (-2); worse (-1); neutral (0); better (1); or much better (2) than before. The averages of all perceptions were then calculated and statistically correlated with the intellectual capital variations, in order to avoid any bias from the answers of the principals of the public agencies.

All the G2G undertakings chosen and analysed by the author have been in regular use for more than one year.

The heuristic frame applied is then consolidated in Figure 1 below.

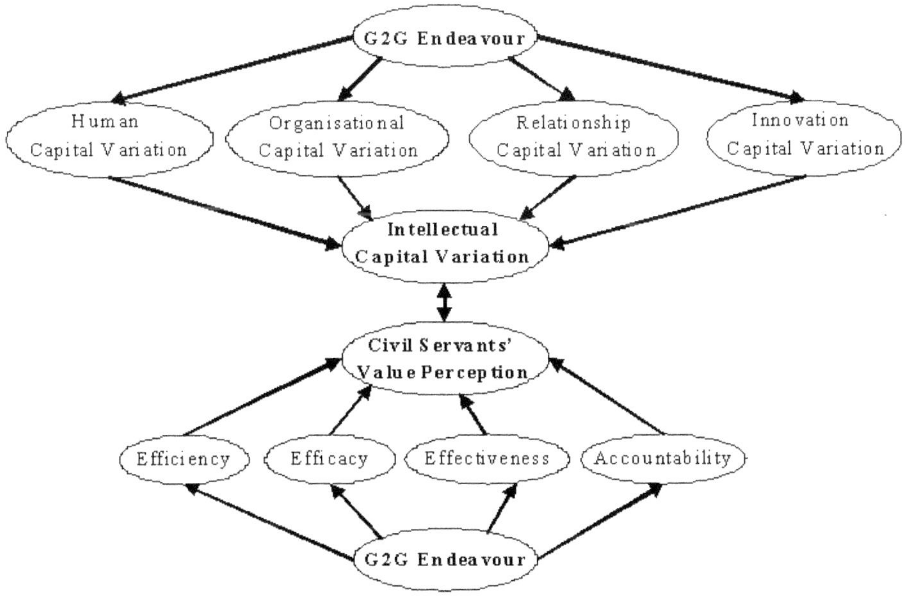


**Fig. 1.** An Heuristic Frame to Assess the Intellectual Capital Variation due to Government-to-Government Endeavours

# 4 Data Analysis

As stated earlier, thirty G2G undertakings were analysed. The principals of the public agencies involved in the Government-to-Government projects were contacted and they filled out the questionnaires relating to the influence of the e-government initiative on the public agency's intellectual capital.

First of all, the data were screened and no outliers were found. A chi-square test was used to verify the normality of the data set. The kurtosis and skewness of the sample were also calculated showing that the sample could be considered as having a normal distribution. The average and standard deviations of each intellectual capital component variation and of the intellectual capital variation of the firms involved in the thirty G2G projects were then calculated, as presented in Table 1 below.

**Table 1.** Average and Standard Deviations of the Capital Variations

| | Human Capital | Process Capital | Relationship Capital | Innovation Capital | Intellectual Capital |
|---|---|---|---|---|---|
| Average | 1.00 | 1.26 | 1.00 | 1.20 | 1.11 |
| St. Dev. | 0.78 | 0.78 | 0.64 | 0.79 | 0.46 |

Initially, the first hypothesis was tested as presented below:

*Ha: Government-to-Government projects between public agencies increase their intellectual capital*

- Hao (Null Hypothesis): Intellectual Capital = 0 (there was no improvement in the intellectual capital of the public agencies due to the G2G project)
- Ha1 (Alternative Hypothesis): Intellectual Capital ¿ 0 (there was improvement in the intellectual capital of the public agencies due to the G2G project)

Using a single-tail t-test, it was concluded that the Null Hypothesis cannot be supported at a 5% level of significance (p=5.43744E-14).

Therefore, the hypothesis that a G2G project has a positive impact on the intellectual capital of the firms involved in the G2G project cannot be rejected.

The second hypothesis was then tested as presented below.

*Hb: The impact of government-to-government projects is greater on the relationship capital of the public agencies involved*

- Hbo (Null Hypothesis): HC = OC = RC = InC

Using an ANOVA test, the following results were established, as presented in Table 2.

Since p-value = 0.4, the Hbo hypothesis cannot be rejected at a 5% level of significance ($0.98 < 2.68$), i.e. the G2G project influences the components of the intellectual capital equally. So, for this sample, the contention that the G2G undertakings have a major influence on the relationship capital of the public

**Table 2.** ANOVA test for the influence of the G2G project on the capitals

| SUMMARY | | | | |
|---|---|---|---|---|
| *Groups* | *Count* | *Sum* | *Average* | *Variance* |
| Human Capital | 30 | 30 | 1 | 0.62 |
| Organisational Capital | 30 | 30 | 1.26 | 0.62 |
| Relationship Capital | 30 | 30 | 1 | 0.41 |
| Innovation Capital | 30 | 30 | 1.20 | 0.65 |

| ANOVA | | | | | | |
|---|---|---|---|---|---|---|
| *Source of Variation* | *SS* | *df* | *MS* | *F* | *P-value* | *Fcrit* |
| Between Groups | 1.7 | 3 | 0.56 | 0.98 | 0.40 | 2.68 |
| Within Groups | 66.67 | 116 | 0.57 | | | |
| Total | 68.36 | 119 | | | | |

agencies cannot be supported. In fact, the G2G endeavours influence the human, organisational, relationship and innovation capitals of the organisations homogeneously.

Finally, as a way of validating the outcomes of the data analysis, the statistical cor-relation between the intellectual capital variations and the civil servants' value perception variation about their firm's efficiency, efficacy, effectiveness and accountability generated by the G2G endeavours were calculated. The rationale for using it is the same as that of applying the M/B ratio as an adequate proxy for the intangible assets of an organisation. The market value (M) is also a figure associated with the investors' perception about the business value.

The statistical correlation calculated was r=0.74 (p=2.9736E-06), which represents a strong correlation. Hence, according to the employees' perception of the firms involved in the G2G endeavour, this undertaking does influence the performance measures – i.e., the efficiency, efficacy, effectiveness and accountability – of their organisations positively. As this is a strong correlation, it can be said that in this case the results and the heuristic frame developed were validated.

## 5 Final Remarks and Research Limitations

As stated earlier, the assessment of e-government undertakings is still a challenge to public managers and academics [39]. This is due to the basic fact that most of the benefits accrued from an e-government project are intangible.

This paper developed and tested a heuristic frame based on the intellectual capital theory to evaluate G2G projects. Very interesting conclusions can be drawn from the findings of the test.

Firstly, the impact of successful G2G projects on the intellectual capital of a public agency is positive, which is in line with the ideas of Sveiby [7], Dragonetti & Roos [21] and Bontis [22].

Secondly, a successful G2G undertaking – despite linking different public agencies and aiming to allow these firms to work in a collaborative way – has a positive and homogeneous impact on all the components of the intellectual capital of a public organisation, i.e. its human, organisational, relationship and innovation capital. Interestingly, these results tally with the ideas of some researchers, who apply a systemic view to inter-organisational networks (see, for instance, [40],[41],[42],[43], to name but a few).

However, this research presents some methodological limitations that must be clearly addressed.

There are several different types of G2G endeavours as they have similarities with strategic alliances [44]. However, this research didn't take this fact into consideration and took it for granted that a G2G undertaking was developed successfully simply when an inter-organisational system between two public agencies was in use by their employees. Furthermore, this paper attempted to establish the value perceptions of the civil servants regarding the outcomes of the G2G endeavours. There are some limitations in this approach, as efficiency, efficacy, effectiveness and accountability are not such simple variables as to be clearly understood by the civil servants beyond all reasonable doubt, even after various meetings with the author. Indeed, a certain degree of subjectivity and bias from the respondents may have occurred [45]. This research also disregarded possible cross and reciprocal influences of the intangible capital variations resulting from G2G undertakings in a public agency, analysing each capital in a separate way, as well as not taking into account the externalities due to G2G endeavours in society as a whole. Moreover, only G2G projects involving two public agencies were analysed in this research. Lastly, the tangible outcomes accrued from G2G undertakings were not addressed in this paper.

E-government is still in its infancy, so a great deal of research is still needed in order to fully validate the frame developed, as well as to overcome this paper's afore-mentioned methodological limitations and to create new models to deal with the peculiarities of performance management and measurement in the public administration realm.

This paper tried to shed light on the evaluation of the intangible outcomes of G2G projects, taking into account that what gets measured gets managed and what needs to be managed needs to be measured.

## References

1. Davenport T.H. & Short J.E. : The New Industrial Engineering: Information Technology and Business Process Redesign, Sloan Management Review, Summer, (1990), 11-27
2. Venkatraman N. : IT-Enabled Business Transformation: From Automation to Business Scope Redefinition, Sloan Management Review, Cambridge, Vol. 35, No. 2, (1994), 73-87
3. Lenk K. & Traunmüller R. : Broadening the Concept of Electronic Government, In: De-signing E-Government, Prins J.E.J. (ed.), Kluwer Law International, (2001), 63-74.
4. Hayek F. : The Use of Knowledge in Society, The American Economic Review, 35:4, September, (1945).
5. Drucker, P. : From Capitalism to Knowledge Society, Post-Capitalism Society, Harper-Collins Publishers, Inc., (1993).

6. Roos, J.; Roos G.; Dragonetti N.; Edvinsson L. : Intellectual Capital, Macmillan Business, (1997).
7. Sveiby, K.E. :The New Organisational Wealth, Berret-Koehler Publishers, Inc., (1997). 8. Edvinsson L. & Malone M. : Intellectual Capital, HarperBusiness, (1997).
8. Davenport, T.H. & Prusak, L.: Working Knowledge, Harvard Business School Press, (1998).
9. Kaplan R. & Norton D. : The Balance Scorecard, Harvard Business School Press, Boston, MA., (1997).
10. Arthur Andersen & The Economist Intelligence Unit: The Valuation of Intangible Assets, Special Report No. P254, (1992).
11. Sharma S.K. : Assessing e-Government Implementations, Electronic Government: An International Journal, Vol. 1, No.2, (2004), 198-212
12. Kaufmann & Schneider: Intangibles: A Synthesis of Current Research, Journal of Intellectual Capital, Vol. 5, No. 3, (2004), 366-388.
13. Rastogi P.N.: The Nature and Role of IC – Rethinking the Process of Value Creation and Sustained Enterprise Growth, Journal of Intellectual Capital, Vol. 4, No. 2, (2003), 227-248.
14. Petty R.& Guthrie J. : Intellectual Capital Literature Review – Measurement, Reporting and Management, Journal of Intellectual Capital, Vol. 1, No. 2, (2002), 155-176.
15. Stewart T. A : Intellectual Capital, Doubleday/Currency, (1997).
16. Ordonez de Pablo P. : Intellectual Capital Reporting in Spain: A Comparative Review, Journal of Intellectual Capital, Vol. 4, No. 1, (2003), 61-81.
17. Tobin J. : A General Equilibrium Approach to Monetary Theory, Journal of Money, Credit and Banking, I, (1969), 15-29.
18. Hussi T. & Ahonen G.: Managing Intangible Assets – a question of integration and delicate balance, Journal of Intellectual Capital, 3 (3), (2002), 277-286.
19. Cinca C.S.; Molinero C.M.; Queiroz A. B. : The Measurement of Intangibles Assets in Public Sector Using Scaling Techniques, Journal of Intellectual Capital, Vol. 4, No. 2, (2003), 249-275.
20. Dragonetti, N. C. & Roos G. : La evaluacin de Ausindustry y el business network programe: una perspectiva desde el capital intelectual, Boletn de Estudios Econmicos, Vol. LIII August, No. 164, (1998).
21. Bontis N. : National Intellectual Capital Index: A United Nations Initiative for the Arab Region, Journal of Intellectual Capital, Vol. 5, No. 1, (2004), 13-39.
22. Joia L. A. : Using Intellectual Capital to Evaluate Educational Technology Projects, Journal of Intellectual Capital, 1 (4), (2000), 341-356.
23. Senz J. : Human Capital Indicators, Business Performance and Market-to-Book Ratio, Journal of Intellectual Capital, Vol. 6, No. 3, (2005), 374-384.
24. Joia L.A. & Zamot F.S. : Internet-Based Reverse Auctions by the Brazilian Government, The Electronic Journal of Information Systems in Developing Countries, http://www.ejisdc.org/ (9), (2002), 1-12.
25. Ballantine J.A. & Cunningham N. : Analysing Performance Information Needs, in: Heeks, R. (Ed.) Reinventing Government in the Information Age, Routledge: London, (1999), 331-349.
26. Checkland, P.B.; Forbes, P.; Martin, S. : Techniques in Soft Systems Practice. Part 3: Monitoring and Control in Conceptual Models and in Evaluation Studies; Journal of Applied Systems, 17, (1990), 29-37.
27. Checkland, P.B. : Systems Thinking, Systems Practice. Chichester: John Wiley, (1981).

28. Campos, A.M. : Accountability: Quando poderemos traduzila para o portugus?, Revista de Administrao Pblica, 24, 2, (1990), 30-50.
29. Powell W.W.; Koput K.W.; Smith-Doerr L. : Inter-organizational Collaboration and the Locus of Innovation: Networks of Learning in Biotechnology, Administrative Science Quarterly, vol. 41, no. 1, (1996), 116-145.
30. Zack M.H. & Serino M. : Knowledge Management and Collaboration Technologies, In: Knowledge, Groupware and the Internet, Smith D.E. (ed), Butterworth-Heinemann, (2000), 303-315. 32. Fountain J. E. : Building the Virtual State, Brookings Institution Press, Washington, D.C. (2001).
31. Nooteboom B. : Inter-Firm Alliance: Analysis and Design, Routledge, London, (1999). 34. Koivisto T. & Ahmaniemi R. Verkostoperustainen Yrityskäytäntöjen Kehittäminen, Edita, Helsinki, (2001).
32. Haeckel S. & Nolan R.: Managing by Wire, Harvard Business Review, September-October, (1993), 122-132.
33. Klein D. : The Strategic Management of Intellectual Capital: An Introduction, In: The Strategic Management of Intellectual Capital, Klein D. (ed.), Butterworth-Heinemann, (1998), 1-7.
34. Winter S. : Knowledge and Competence as Strategic Assets, In: The Strategic Management of Intellectual Capital, Klein D. (ed.), Butterworth-Heinemann, (1998), 165-187
35. Kannan G. & Aulbur W.G. : Intellectual Capital: Measurement Effectiveness, Journal of Intellectual Capital, Vol. 5, No. 3, (2004), 389-413.
36. Lau E. : Principaux Enjeux de l'Administration Electronique dans le Pays Membres de l'OCDE, Revue Franaise d'Administration Publique, Ecole Nationale d'Administration, no. 110, (2004), 225-244.
37. Luhman N. : Social Systems, Stanford University Press, Stanford, USA, (1995).
38. Stahle P.: Supporting a System's Capacity for Self-Renewal, Yliopistopaino, Helsinki, (1998).
39. Stahle P.; Stahle S.; Pöyhönen A. : Analyzing Dynamic Intellectual Capital: System-Based Theory and Application, Lappeenranta University of Technology, Lappeenranta, (2003).
40. Pöyhönen A. & Smedlund A. : Assessing Intellectual Capital Creation in Regional Clusters, Journal of Intellectual Capital, Vol. 5, No. 3, (2004), 351-365.
41. Dyer J.H. & Singh H. : The Relational View: Cooperative Strategy and Sources of Interor-ganizational Competitive Advantage, Academy of Management Review, Vol. 23, No. 4, (1998), 660-678.
42. Scandura T.A. & Williams E.A. : Research Methodology in Management: Current Practices, Trends, and Implications for Future Research, Academy of Management Journal, Vol. 43, No. 6, (2000), 1248-1264.

# Evaluation of E-Government Systems: Project Assessment vs Development Assessment

Rahul De'

Indian Institute of Management Bangalore, Bannerghatta Road,
Bangalore 560076. India
rahul@iimb.ernet.in

**Abstract.** Most reported literature on evaluation of e-government systems tend to focus on narrow aspects of project design and implementation. The larger context of development and related issues are not used for assessment. This paper presents a case for evaluation of e-government projects by using development theory as propounded by Amartya Sen. A single e-government system, the Bhoomi system of Karnataka, India, is used as a case, and it is evaluated using both a project assessment approach and a development assessment approach. The two approaches lead to different conclusions, providing insights as to the value of each.

## 1 Introduction and Motivation

E-government systems research is broadly covered under the topic of Information and Communication Technology (ICT) for Development. In the extant literature ICT for Development assumes a categorical significance and many publications, web sites and conferences use the same phrase as their title or subject category. As a theme this topic resonates across disciplines, be it information systems, development economics, development studies or administrative sciences. Papers have argued the role, function, use and relevance of ICT for development, as also the various meanings of development and its inclusion of ICT.

The contention of this paper is that e-government projects are also development projects and have to be assessed as such. At first glance this may appear to be a pointless exercise as by very definition this seems to be true and uncontroversial - e-government projects are a part of ICT for development. However, some points about the manner in which e-government systems have been written about in the literature show that the development aspects of e-government systems are not entirely clear and need to be highlighted.

First, most reported literature on e-government systems tends to focus on the narrow aspects of project design and implementation issues. The reports tend to evaluate the systems from the perspective of projects whose implementation goals have been tightly defined and that can be measured by parametric methods. Larger issues and impacts are considered, but in a peripheral manner, and are mainly used to show the achievement of project goals.

Second, in the developing country context, e-government projects are large public interventions that impact the lives of millions of people. Even though

M.A. Wimmer et al. (Eds.): EGOV 2006, LNCS 4084, pp. 317–328, 2006.

many projects have simple goals, such as reduce the time taken to acquire some document, or increase the transparency of some procedures, the projects affect the way thousands of people work and make a living. These systems introduce radical and disruptive changes in people's lives and their impact has to be understood in this larger context.

Third, by definition again, e-government projects are promoted and sponsored by government departments. Governments and government departments are accountable to the public and their role in initiating and building these projects has to be evaluated in the public space. Development theory brings to the fore the methods for understanding matters of public accountability (resulting from public policy). Thus, ICT projects are best understood when seen from the lens of development theory. This latter aspect is missing from the existing literature on e-government systems.

E-government projects are development projects, where the semantics of the word "development" is derived from the existing literature and the discipline of development studies. Prior literature has not explored the ramifications of this method of investigation of e-government systems. This paper makes such an attempt by examining a particular e-government system (in Karnataka, India) and this is its major contribution.

The rest of this paper begins with a discussion on the methodology used for this research, followed by a review of the understanding of development and a review of the current literature on e-government in developing countries. This is followed by an analysis of a particular e-government system using first a purely technical and project-oriented approach and then a development theory based approach. A contrast of the two approaches is presented and conclusions are drawn as to the implications for design and evaluation.

## 2 Methodology

This research relies on the case study method where a particular e-government project is studied extensively at its existing location. The advantage of the case study method is that it prescribes a rigorous and exhaustive way of analyzing a particular phenomenon and also enables bringing multiple tools and methods of analysis to bear on the subject of analysis[1,2]. More importantly, the case study methodology enables the researcher to include prior theories and analyses into the current analysis and draw from a larger canvas the data and issues for arriving at conclusions. The analytic generalizations [1, page 32-33] provided by the case study method help to validate the application of theory to the data.

For this study a single e-government project called Bhoomi from the state of Karnataka is used as the basis for conducting the case analysis. Secondary data was collected from published documents on Bhoomi, the Bhoomi web site, newspaper reports and published reports. Primary data was collected by structured and unstructured questionnaires, and interviews were conducted in many districts of Karnataka. The details of data collection are provided in the sections below.

## 3 Review of Development Theory and E-Government

It is important to understand the notion of 'development' from the perspective of the wider understanding and the implicit ideas in this word, as well as from the perspective of its theoretical treatment. The former is the discourse on development that informs public discussions, writing and policy related to development practice whereas the latter is the formal writing on development theory. The two discourses overlap and inform each other.

The wider understanding of development has to do with the economic policies and agendas for poverty reduction, economic growth, reform of trade policies, valuation of currency, spending on health and education, decentralization, monetary policy and environmental policy amongst others [3]. For many developing countries, such as India, it is widely believed that these agendas and policies are often driven by multi-lateral funding agencies such as the World Bank and the IMF that provide loans for structural adjustments. Although the actual process of policy formulation is a complex one and driven by competing interests of political parties, civil society organizations, the bureaucracy and the industrial groups, many amongst the elite in India argue that the multi-lateral agencies have the strongest role.

Academic theory on development draws from multiple disciplines, including economics, political science, sociology and anthropology. For the most part, researchers agree that development as an idea of modernity that brings about changes in 'under-developed' nations and societies, has basically failed [4,3]. Development interventions that seek to address issues of poverty, women's empowerment, sustainable growth etc, have failed to show results and have worsened if not improved situations.

Governance reform is a recent effort by multi-lateral agencies to address the failures of the past. The logic underlying these reforms is that economic programs and interventions fail because of poor governance in developing countries and hence the policy documents of agencies such as the UNDP, the World Bank, the DFID emphasize the importance and role of governance reform. Aid is tied to such reforms and the agencies provide support via funding and partnerships. The basic tenet of these reforms is a partnership of the state, the industry and the civil society in governance and targeting of specifics of governance such as efficiency, transparency, right to information, participation, legitimacy and freedom of association.

Prior research in ICT for development, and also in e-government, highlights the difficult problem of understanding such projects from the perspective of development theory. First, development theory is itself a contested terrain where neo-liberal and neo-Marxist theories 'talk past each other' and there isn't an overarching perspective that can be used consistently [5]. Second, the 'digital divide' tends to dominate the literature, where problems of development are translated into the problems of people's access to ICT resources. Third, the literature in ICT for development assumes either 'utopian' or 'dystopian' positions: where in the utopian view ICTs are, a priori, seen as highly beneficial; while in the dystopian view ICTs are seen to be imbued with values that hurt development rather than enhance it. The literature on e-governance defines it as a means to deliver governance more effectively and more efficiently [6,7]. Research in e-government systems in developing countries has mainly focused on issues related to technical design, cost-benefit analysis and on issues of managing change [6,8]. Other issues include legal and infrastructure issues for using e-governance [9], an understanding of best practices[10], and the broad developmental impact of e-government systems[11].

Despite the wide range of issues covered, the literature is biased towards technical and narrowly focused case studies [12]. Another gap in the literature is a clear theoretical and analytical understanding of the role of development theory in assessing and designing e-government systems. This paper attempts to fill this gap.

## 4 A Project Analysis of Bhoomi

### 4.1 A Brief Description of Bhoomi

The Bhoomi system of land records management was deployed in 2001 in Karnataka, via kiosks installed in 177 taluk (a sub-district) offices of the state. Each kiosk consists of a computer that holds the digitized land records of the taluk, and farmers can easily access their land records via the system for a nominal charge of Rs 15 (about $0.30 at the time of writing). The kiosks are in the office of the Tehsildar, a sub-district magistrate, and each record (also known as an Record of Rights, Tenancy and Crop Inspection Register (RTC certificate))is signed by a Village Accountant (VA) who also updates the data in the system. Farmers may also enter 'mutation' requests in the system, where these are requests to make changes to the land record upon change of ownership. Further details about the system are provided in [13].

### 4.2 Assessment of Bhoomi

**Objectives.** The stated objectives of the Bhoomi land records digitization project are as below (quoted from [14]):

1. Improving the quality of service to the citizens: (a) Allowing farmers / citizens easy access to their records; (b) Infuse transparency in providing the services to citizens
2. Ease of administration: (a) Facilitating easy maintenance; (b) Prompt updation of land records; (c) Making land records tamper proof
3. Generating meaningful MIS out of the system relating to land records
4. Ensuring self-sustainability of the project: (a) Robust revenue model; (b) Public-Private partnership, where possible.

**Achievement of Objectives.** Upon its launch in Karnataka, Bhoomi was immediately hailed as a highly successful system by the media. A survey of users conducted by an independent agency, the Public Affairs Council in Bangalore

(PAC), showed that the system was easy to use and an improvement over the manual system. The PAC survey was conducted in 4 districts of Karnataka and had 180 respondents. A summary of the survey results is as below [15]:

- Of the users who had used the earlier, manual system and also the Bhoomi system, 78% found Bhoomi to be simpler to use.
- In the manual system about 60% of the respondents had to meet 2-4 officials for their work, whereas with the Bhoomi system 79% could complete their work by interacting with kiosk staff itself.
- 74% of users of Bhoomi stated that their documents were error-free, whereas 63% said so for the manual system.
- 28% respondents had to make more than one trip to the kiosk.
- The average time spent in the queue is 27 minutes.
- 3% of users had to pay a bribe with the new system, as opposed to 66% in the manual system.

Bhoomi meets the first stated objective as the PAC report clearly shows that the system is easier to use and lesser number of officials have to be met to obtain an RTC certificate, takes less time to obtain the certificate and less bribes have to be paid. Transparency is provided by the mutation request procedure, where a queue discipline is forced by the system and citizens know the status of their requests from the queue details. With centralized facilities at the taluks, the records can be maintained better, and the bio-login procedures tamper-proof the records. MIS reports are not generated by the system, as the different taluks have not been connected up fully to obtain useful summaries. The revenues collected at the Bhoomi kiosks for RTC certificates and for mutation requests is sufficient to cover operating costs of the kiosks (with some surplus left over) so the project is self-sustaining.

In summary, it can be said that Bhoomi meets all of its stated objectives, except the one of generating MIS reports, and to this extent it is a successful system.

## 5 Bhoomi as a Development Intervention

When viewed as a project, Bhoomi is certainly a successful e-government system. It has won international recognition and within India the central government is planning to implement it across the country as a model of land records digitization. However, when viewed as a development intervention that has impacted the lives of almost 30 million people living in the state of Karnataka, its success or failure cannot be so easily framed.

### 5.1 Sen's Theory of Development

Nobel Laureate Amartya Sen's work on development is considered to be the most comprehensive and relevant for understanding issues of developing countries.

We use Sen's framework of capabilities and freedoms to understand a complex development intervention like Bhoomi.

Sen argues that development is not an end in itself but a means to an end [16]. The ends of development are achievement of freedom from hunger, poverty, illiteracy and deprivation. Most importantly the freedoms enable and are enabled by capabilities that citizens enjoy. Sen argues that the most important instrumental freedoms, required for development, are political freedoms, economic facilities, social opportunities, transparency guarantees and protective securities. Political freedoms allow citizens to choose their representatives and participate in setting the agenda for political discussions. Economic facilities are the freedoms citizens enjoy to transact in the market and to use available economic resources and entitlements. Social opportunities have to do with the facilities made available to citizens for health, education, and infrastructure that allow them to live healthily and participate in economic and political activities. Transparency guarantees have to do with the basic trust that citizens enjoy in their day-to-day transactions, with an assurance of disclosure and lucidity. Protective security is some measure of protection from basic deprivations such as poverty or unemployment or protection from natural disasters.

Focused questions about Bhoomi as a development project may now be thus posed:

- As a development intervention, in what way did Bhoomi facilitate citizens' access to economic resources such as credit and their ability to access markets?
- In what way did Bhoomi improve the transparency guarantees to citizens related to documents about their dealings with government officials and government services?
- Did Bhoomi increase the political participation of citizens about governance by allowing them to be involved in setting policies and agendas for governance?
- Did Bhoomi enable or enhance protective security to citizens, against droughts or other disasters?
- Did Bhoomi enable citizens to have improved access, directly or indirectly, to education, information, health care or judicial procedures?

## 5.2 Development Analysis

An analysis based on these questions is provided below. Data for this analysis was collected through structured and unstructured interviews of land-owning farmers, landless farmers, kiosk operators, bureaucrats and commentators in six districts and various government offices in Karnataka. The analysis is based on responses of about 120 individuals (some interviews had multiple respondents answering in a group and so the number is not exact). The interviews were conducted over a period of 3 years. The analysis also includes data from secondary sources such as government reports, newspaper articles and policy documents. For reasons of space all data are not presented, only the summary and analysis are included.

The analysis below includes several categories of stakeholders who belong to both the demand-side of the system, those who use the services of the system, and those who belong to the supply-side [17]. One group of demand-side stakeholders are landless farmers, those who farm land in Karnataka but have no papers to prove their ownership. There are one million landless farmers in Karnataka. They occupy and farm lands given to them through historical grants from landlords or sovereigns, or land that traditionally belonged to their tribes or communities. Another set of demand-side stakeholders are women who belong to farming households. It is estimated that about 56% of women who belong to landholding households in rural Karnataka participate in farming activities and 41% work as agricultural laborers.

## 5.3 Economic Resources

*Credit.* One of the main reasons that farmers purchased the RTC certificate is to obtain loans from banks. About 40% of the usage (as reported by the PAC study) for RTC documents is for obtaining loans. A statistical analysis based on secondary data showed that there is no significant increase in rural credit in Karnataka since the introduction of Bhoomi. Although land-owning farmers were better off with Bhoomi in terms of their access to the RTC document, this fact by itself did not improve their ability to access credit. Credit obtained through formal means requires a set of documents that have to be presented to the banks, of which the RTC is one, and invariably has a lead time of a few weeks to months. Informal credit through traditional moneylenders, who charge usurious rates, is more prevalent as it requires less paperwork and is available instantly.

Landless farmers who don't have RTC certificates and who cannot officially apply for formal credit are unaffected by Bhoomi. Their abilities to access credit remains unaltered as they participate only in the informal market.

*Markets.* Farmers who have RTC certificates can use these to sell their produce, in some cases, to government procurers at subsidized prices. RTC certificates are required to prove their status to the government department. This is an important application of RTC certificates but is not widely used, as it is only for special crops which the government procures via subsidies. Bhoomi has no direct links with the agricultural procurement departments to transfer the relevant information via an electronic link; farmers have to provide an RTC certificate as evidence of their agricultural production.

Bhoomi helps with the sale and transfer of agricultural land via the automated mutation system. Farmers can file a mutation request in the system and the queue maintained by the system ensures that their request is processed in the order in which it was received. Corrupt officials have tampered with the system to provide special access to certain customers who have paid bribes, but overall the system does enforce queue discipline. This has increased the transactions in land parcels in economically growing areas, such as in the periphery of Bangalore.

There is no market information provided to farmers about prices and commodity markets at the Bhoomi kiosks. This is a potential application Bhoomi designers are working on.

**Transparency Guarantees.** Bhoomi makes it easier for land-owning farmers to access RTC certificates and to ensure the queue discipline for their mutation requests. The system allows farmers to verify the status of their property. One respondent in Bidar district mentioned that the RTC certificate she had recently obtained showed a discrepancy in her land-holding. A part of her property had been removed. Upon verifying with a neighbor, she found that it had been annexed to his. They brought the matter up with the taluk authorities to correct the error. Another farmer in Kanakpura taluk mentioned that he checked his RTC regularly to see if any part of his large estate had been affected by land sharks operating in the area (Kanakpura is in the periphery of Bangalore). The transparency and easy access of RTC certificates is important for these farmers, something that was difficult in the manual system as the village accountant controlled all the records, as they can verify the status of their own lands and also check upon their neighbors' properties.

However, this easy access comes with a price. Respondents, in some districts, noted that with the new digital system the kiosk operators and taluk officials could introduce errors into the system, on the pretext of typographical mistakes, and then demand a bribe for the correction. With the manual system this was not possible as the underlying text would show the original text and the overwritten error. Although, the Bhoomi system is protected by a bio-login process, and changes to the data can be tracked, kiosk operators are able to pretend that deliberate data manipulation are unavoidable errors.

Landless farmers, some of whom have an unofficial sanction to the lands they farm, do not benefit from the enhanced transparency of the new system. These farmers own a document called a Saguvali chit, and this is an official record that states the right to farm on the land. This document is not part of the Bhoomi database and so the farmers cannot check their status on the system.

The transparency in the mutation process helps farmers see the status of their pending requests. This transparency has exposed, to a certain extent, the 'grease money' corruption in the system. As some respondents noted, if someone bribes the officials to move their documents faster, those ahead of the briber in the queue are also moved faster. Some respondents noted a negative consequence of the queue system, where officials would reject applications on trivial grounds to push out applicants from the queue and process the one that they had been paid to process faster.

The larger issues related to transparency in the land records adjustment and updation process though remain unaffected by the new Bhoomi system. Many respondents noted that their title deeds, which is their official record of ownership of land and is a unique document, had not been updated in many years, sometimes stretching back by decades. The cadastral maps, maintained by the VA, had also not been updated and few knew the status of the maps. Other documents related to land ownership and transfer, such as the Mutation Register, the

*Akarband* and *Tippani* registers, remained unaffected by the Bhoomi system and also remained unavailable to the citizens for scrutiny. Bhoomi has computerized only one document out of many that are used for land administration.

**Political Participation.** For the design of the Bhoomi system, none of the stakeholders on the demand-side were included in requirements determination. Many respondents had not even heard of the system until their manual certificates were declared illegal by the state and new Bhoomi RTCs were given to them. The farmers could not participate in the agenda-setting and design exercise for Bhoomi. The entire system was designed and implemented by the supply-side stakeholders such as the Project Champion and the private partners who implemented the system. VAs were included in the data digitization and error removal phase of the project.

Many bureaucrats interviewed for the research mentioned that initially Bhoomi was quite actively resisted by many in the taluks and required the Chief Minister's personal intervention to help implement the system. This resistance constitutes a different kind of political participation, albeit a negative one. Government officials resisted the system as it upset their existing ways of working as much as it was a new technology that they were not familiar with. Village accountants resisted the system as it reduced their authority by taking out of their control a document that had value to farmers.

Landless farmers rely on the VA for most of their needs related to documents about land. The VA is the principle sanctioning authority for their ability to farm land, and also the main person who is involved in confirming their rights to the land. Landless farmers were not directly affected by Bhoomi, but the reduced powers of the VA has affected them too. Several landless farmers mentioned that the VA is now harder to get as s/he is away at taluk headquarters and also the VAs services have become more 'expensive.' This latter aspect has affected land-owning farmers too.

For most farmers, the VA is a representative of the government they have easiest access to. Almost all matters of government documentation and recording is handled by the VA. Political leaders recognize this power and often try to include VAs in the campaigns during elections. VAs are thus able to impact agenda-setting for the parties to a certain extant. Some respondents argued with the new system in place the VAs role has changed somewhat, as some of the power has shifted to the taluk offices.

**Protective Security.** Bhoomi RTC certificates are required for crop insurance, but they are not primarily used for that purpose. Farmers have to purchase insurance when they apply for loans, as this is a requirement imposed by some banks. Thus insurance is purchased as an indirect requirement for loans. To this extent Bhoomi has ensured some protection against crop failure for land-owning farmers. Under conditions of drought, which some districts of Karnataka have suffered repeatedly over the last few years, loans are not granted easily by banks, and the crop-insurance that is needed under these conditions are also not purchased. Landless farmers do not have the facility of insurance available to them, and in cases of drought work as farm laborers to earn a living.

The data from Bhoomi is not used by the government to plan for and provide any sort of insurance or other protective package to farmers of Karnataka. This is a possibility that some supply-side officials have considered.

Some agents, who help with buying and selling of land (also known as document writers), in the Bangalore periphery region, said that Bhoomi data, since it was not protected and anyone could have access to it, was being used by land sharks to identify properties that were vulnerable (as the farmers owning them had suffered repeated droughts and many loans had been taken against them). Directed queries in the database were used to identify those farmers in the taluk who had not paid land taxes (usually a nominal sum) and such farmers were targeted. The sharks would then manipulate and bribe taluk officials to grab control of the land. Very little data could be collected as to the extent of this activity but several document writers corroborated this story. This data points to the reduced security of farmers that is helped by the Bhoomi system by the facility of database queries.

**Improved Access.** Bhoomi kiosks were not designed to offer a portfolio of applications similar to what is available in other states, where kiosks were designed to offer basic facilities in computer literacy, information about weather, prices of crops, markets, provide health care through tele-medicine arrangements and allow users to browse information on the Internet. So far Bhoomi has the largest reach of all the kiosk-based e-government systems implemented in India and a portfolio of applications would have greatly enhanced its appeal.

One significant second-order impact of Bhoomi, that we learned from interviewing people from diverse backgrounds, was the knowledge and awareness of computers and the value that they can have. Bhoomi kiosks and the technology of touch screen interaction, instant printing, bio-login procedures and computerized queue-lists, have informed citizens, who were not aware of such things, of the immense power of information technology. We found that citizens who are the most deprived in terms of the digital divide have learned about such technology and are beginning to examine the various possibilities of these devices.

Bhoomi certificates are used to apply for and obtain government grants for education. These certificates are also used obtain bail from courts and for adjudication by courts in cases of dispute.

Women from landholding families whose husbands have migrated to other places for work, or whose husbands are not available for some other reason, are affected by the Bhoomi system as now they have to leave their homes and travel to taluk headquarters to seek the RTC document.

## 6 Contrast of the Two Analyses and Conclusions

Prior research that has examined Bhoomi has reported mainly on the project aspects of economic feasibility, change management, process re-engineering, costs and benefits, and some user-based features for efficiency and transparency of transactions [6, pages 97-109] and [18]. Consider the issue of transaction efficiency for obtaining RTC certificates - making this particular aspect better was one of the primary objectives of Bhoomi. The PAC report clearly shows that with Bhoomi access is faster and with fewer number of officials to meet. With the development framework perspective, we find that this efficiency has helped land-owning, and not landless, farmers and has increased the transactions in land parcels too. Also, Bhoomi only eases access to RTC certificates, and leaves out a number of other documents that are needed and used by farmers for land management.

Another parameter that is important for project assessment is that of increased transparency in processes. This is an objective for almost all e-government projects in India. Bhoomi implements this in the queue discipline for mutation requests and the mechanism is successful. When seen in the development context, other aspects of transparency emerge: RTC certificates are enabling farmers to verify the status of their holdings and to protect and correct for errors; transparency is allowing land sharks to target vulnerable farmers (as Bhoomi makes it easier to view and select records).

One cannot conclude here that project assessment cannot raise and examine the issues raised by development analysis. That is certainly possible. However, the point is that project assessment usually focuses on the supply-side view, ignoring the deeper issues of the demand-side impacts. Project assessment evaluation revolves around the stated objectives of the project and on implied project parameters such as completion time, completion within budgets, economic sustainability etc. The demand-side assessment too is limited to those specified by the objectives.

Bhoomi's objectives were specified on the basis of governance reform, with its supply-side perspective, rather than on the basis of development, which includes a larger perspective of the demand-side also. Limited governance and project objectives are achievable within the short time span available to government bureaucrats to plan, design and implement e-government projects. It was thus possible for a project like Bhoomi to be implemented efficiently and be declared a success. Had Bhoomi's objectives been defined by development goals, rather than governance goals, then, it is possible, Bhoomi's design may have been entirely different and it may have assumed an entirely different form.

## References

1. Yin, R.K.: Case Study Research: Design and Methods. Volume 5 of Applied Social Science Research Methods Series. Sage Publications, Thousand Oaks (2003).
2. Benbasat, I., Goldstein, D., Mead, M.: The case research strategy in studies of information systems. MIS Quarterly **11** (1987) 369–385.
3. Kothari, U., Minogue, M.: Critical perspectives on development: An introduction. In Kothari, U., Minogue, M., eds.: Development Theory and Practice: Critical Perspectives. Palgrave (2002) 1–15.
4. Escobar, A.: Encountering Development: The Making and Unmaking of the Third World. Princeton University Press (1995).

5. Minogue, M.: Power to the people? good governance and the reshaping of the state. In Kothari, U., Minogue, M., eds.: Development Theory and Practice: Critical Perspectives. Palgrave (2002) 117–135.
6. Bhatnagar, S.: E-Government: From Vision to Implementation. Sage Publications, New Delhi (2004).
7. Heeks, R.: Understanding e-governance for development. i-Government Working Paper Series 11, Institute for Development Policy and Management, University of Manchester (2001).
8. Heeks, R.: The approach of senior public officials to information technology-related reform: Lessons from India. Public Administration and Development **20** (2000) 197–205.
9. Basu, S.: E-Government and developing countries: An Overview. International Review of Law Computers & Technology **18** (2004) 109–132.
10. Krishna, S., Walsham, G.: Implementing public information systems in developing countries: Learning from a success story. Information Technology for Development **11** (2005) 1–18.
11. Madon, S.: Evaluating the developmental impact of e-governance initiatives: An exploratory framework. The Electronic Journal of Information Systems in Developing Countries **20** (2004) 1–13.
12. Gronlund, A.: State of the art in e-Gov research a survey. In Traunmuller, M., ed.: Proceedings of the Third International Conference, EGOV 2004. Lecture Notes in Computer Science, Springer-Verlag (2004) 178–185.
13. De', R.: The complex nature of e-Government projects: A case study of Bhoomi, an initiative in Karnataka, India. In Traunmuller, R., ed.: Proceedings of Electronic Government, Third International Conference, Zaragoza, Spain, Aug-Sep 2004. LNCS 3183, Springer-Verlag (2004) 556–557.
14. Chawla, R.: Roll out of successful e-governance projects: Bhoomi - a case study. Technical report (2003).
15. Lobo, A., Balakrishnan: Report card on service of bhoomi kiosks: An assessment of benefits by users of the computerized land records system in karnataka. Technical report, Public Affairs Centre, Bangalore (2002).
16. Sen, A.: Development as Freedom. Oxford University Press (2000).
17. De', R.: E-Government systems in developing countries: Stakeholders and conflict. In Wimmer, M., Traunmuller, R., Gronlund, A., Andersen, K., eds.: Proceedings of Electronic Government, 4th International Conference, Copenhagen, Aug 2005. LNCS 3591, Springer-Verlag (2005) 26–37.
18. Parthasarathy, B.: Information and communication technologies for development: A comparative analysis of impacts and costs from India. Technical report, International Institute of Information Technology - Bangalore (2005).

# ROI Analysis in e-Government Assessment Trials: The Case of Sistema Piemonte

Tommaso Carratta[1], Lucy Dadayan[2], and Enrico Ferro[1]

[1] Istituto Superiore Mario Boella
Via Boggio 61, 10138 Turin, Italy
{Carratta, Ferro}@ismb.it
[2] College of Computing and Information, SUNY,
135 Western Avenue, Albany, NY 12222
ld8318@albany.edu

**Abstract.** Assessing the returns of public investments in information and communication technologies (ICT) poses important practical and research challenges. Scholars and practitioners that have embarked in ICT assessment activities have encountered many difficulties which, to a large extent, have remained pending issues. This paper reviews the exiting literature on public return on investment (ROI) and presents an assessment conducted on an Italian circuit of eGovernment services. The paper intends to share the experience gained from our study with the rest of research community. Also, it proposes a perspective on public ROI that differs from a strictly bottom line approach to stimulate a debate on the role of such evaluation activities in the process of eGovernment implementation.

## 1 Introduction

The implementation of eGovernment services as well as streamlining of the public functions represents a strategic goal for most Western countries. Thus significant amount of financial resources are being devoted to ICT related investments. This modernization process still requires a considerable amount of effort and, in order to be sustainable overtime, must be supported by an adequate evaluation of the public returns generated.

Assessing the returns of public investments in ICT poses important practical and research challenges. Scholars and practitioners that have embarked in ICT assessment activities have encountered numerous difficulties which, to a large extent, remain as pending issues. Some examples include the intangibility of the benefits generated, the time at which benefits have to be measured, and the cross-sectional nature of information technologies. In such a situation there is room for some reflections on what role public ROI should play in the process of eGovernment implementation. In particular, the extent to which ROI should be considered as a process with a value in and of itself, rather than simply an objective oriented activity. This paper attempts to stimulate such a debate. The paper is divided into three sections. In the first section we define terms such as

M.A. Wimmer et al. (Eds.): EGOV 2006, LNCS 4084, pp. 329–340, 2006.

ROI, IT, ROI in IT, and provide a review of the existing literature on different methods and models utilized for measuring ROI in government IT investments. In the second section we present an ROI assessment experience on an Italian circuit of eGovernment services named Sistema Piemonte. In the third and final section we discuss lessons learned and propose a new perspective on ROI analyses that departs from a pure bottom line approach.

## 2 Assessing Return on IT Investment: Literature Review

### 2.1 What Is ROI in IT?

Research on ROI in IT and attempts to build models and methods for measuring both tangible and intangible benefits of IT is becoming increasingly widespread in the social science community. Measuring return in IT investment is complex and requires a thorough understanding and knowledge of both the business process and the context in which it is embedded. Therefore, it is necessary to understand the relationships between the costs, benefits and risks of IT investments as well as different contextual factors including organizational, institutional, and environmental. Currently more and more governments are investing in IT. While the average annual growth rate of IT investment is growing year over year[1], the benefits and value of IT investments are still being questioned by many researchers and practitioners. The inconsistency in the research results is viewed as a metaphor on the subject of IT investment decision-making, meaning that "there are no single, simple methodologies that will give a consistent, reliable and optimal solution to managers facing an IT investment decision" (Schniederjans et al. 2004).

Before analyzing the ROI in IT, it is important to define ROI in IT as well as to understand the meanings of IT, ROI, and IT investment separately. It is not the purpose of this paper to show similarities and differences between different definitions of IT, ICT, ROI, and ROI in IT. However, a quick overview of existing definitions is useful for understanding the concepts underlying the discussion.

*Defining IT:* The term information technology also used for information and communication technology and their abbreviations IT and ICT are used very frequently in different fields, across different disciplines, and across all geographical continents. However, there is still no universal consensus with respect to what IT/ICT is and what their main characteristics are. First, it is important to understand the difference between technology and IT/ICT, and that IT/ICT is not equal to technology. Interestingly, there is a difference between the definitions developed in Europe and the USA. According to the European Commission, the importance of ICTs lies in the ability to create greater access to information and communication, and not in the technology itself. On the other hand, many definitions of IT/ICT developed by US scholars, practitioners, and/or organizations

[1] Analysis of data extracted from Detailed Fixed Asset Database, U.S. Bureau of Economic Analysis (BEA) shows that the investment in ICT, and particularly in software, is growing year over year.

still tend to emphasize and separate the hardware, software, telecommunications and other means of technology used for creating the output – useful information systems. For purposes of this paper, information technology can be defined as modern technologies used for the creation, management, use, handling and retrieval of information.

*Defining IT investment:* There are different approaches to defining IT investment. On the one hand IT investment is viewed as investments in equipment, applications, services, and basic technologies (Keen 1995). On the other hand, IT investment is viewed as expenses associated with acquiring hardware, software, communications, networks and personnel to manage and operate management information systems (Weill et al. 1989). For this paper, an IT investment encompasses all of the following components: personnel, application software, system software, and hardware (Schniederjans et al. 2004).

*Defining ROI:* The definition of ROI is much more confusing compared to the definitions of IT and IT investment. There is a wide range of methodologies for defining both tangible and intangible returns on IT investments. The traditional definitions of ROI consistently focus on the financial returns to determine how the investment will repay the investor.

*In search of defining and measuring ROI in IT:* Currently there is no comprehensive and accepted definition of ROI in IT. ROI in IT is associated with both tangible and intangible benefits, costs, and risks. The intangible benefits, costs, and risks are sometimes the most important factors for IT decision-makers, but they are typically the most difficult to quantify and measure. Thus, there is a concurrent need for conducting a comprehensive literature review and categorizing research in ROI in IT.

### 2.2 Is There a Value from IT Investment? The Productivity Paradox

The productivity paradox refers to the absence of a positive relationship between spending on IT and its resulting contribution to productivity/profitability (Lucas 1999). "In the early 1990s, researchers found a productivity paradox concerning IT investments. This paradox showed IT investments with negative or zero returns" (Dehning et al. 2002). Since then many researchers and practitioners attempted to give different explanations, reasons, justifications, and solutions for the paradox of IT productivity. According to Dos Santos and Sussman, "even though organizations invest in the latest technology to increase efficiencies and profits, failure to redesign and reorganize delays the return on that investment" (Dos Santos et al. 2000). Brynjolfsson and Yang attempted to uncover the productivity paradox of IT investment by examining four different approaches: (1) mismeasurement of outputs and inputs; (2) lags due to learning and adjustment; (3) redistribution and dissipation of profits; and (4) mismanagement of information and technology. The authors noted that the first two approaches are based on shortcomings in research and methodology to measure ROI in IT, and not practice (Brynjolfsson et al. 1996). However, the last two approaches can be explained by shortcomings in management practice.

Today many organizations are employing a variety of methods to support their decision-making processes when investing in IT. Regardless of the method or combinations of methods employed for supporting decisions, investment in IT is associated with conditions of uncertainty and risk, indicating that some acts have more than one possible outcome, and "the decision maker cannot fully control which outcome will occur" (Edwards et al. 2001). Cost and expected financial return are important factors in IT investment decision-making processes, but so are expected non-financial returns provided by the IT investment, which are hard to measure and have multiple attributes. Intangible benefits such as increased quality, variety, customer service, speed and responsiveness are poorly accounted for in productivity statistics as well as in most firms' accounting numbers (Brynjolfsson 1994) leading to systematic underestimates of IT productivity (Brynjolfsson et al. 1996).

The probability of obtaining a positive return in IT investment depends on the type of IT investment (Lucas 1999). ROI in IT as a *strategic application* will be different from ROI in *transformational* IT. It is easier to estimate a range of possible costs, benefits and risks, and probability of each in the case of strategic IT investment. It is much harder to estimate the costs, benefits and risks associated with transformational or innovative in nature IT investments as often they change the nature of company, the industry, and even the way people live and work.

### 2.3 Return in IT Investments in Public Sector

There is a range of methods, strategies, and tools used to measure the value of IT and ROI in IT. Traditional ROI analyses are typically based on financial models (Arlotto et al. 2003). Recently traditional financial models and methods including net present value, return on sales, and return on assets have been criticized on different grounds. First, the traditional ROI models are criticized for not being able to accurately predict ROI due to uncertainty and difficult decisions involved in IT investments (Benaroch et al. 2000). Second, traditional ROI models are based on the assumptions that costs and benefits are always known and expressed in a common metric – dollar value (Laudon et al. 1999). Third, traditional ROI models do not take into consideration the political position in the organization. "While political position has very little to do with IT, it usually affects the period of time allowed for ROI" (Forrer et al. 2001). The traditional financial ROI models have more limitations including the exclusion of social and political returns.

Success through IT in the public sector is different from that in the private sector. In measuring ROI in IT, private sector organizations usually focus on the "bottom-line," while the public sector organizations usually focus on policy initiatives (Forrer et al. 2001). Public sector organizations, unlike private ones, are not primarily concerned with investing in IT with the expectation of gaining economic return; they are more concerned with fulfilling political goals such as collaboration among government entities, improved government services and citizens access to public services (Dufner et al. 2002). In addition, public sector organizations face more competing goals and are more bound to legal and staffing restrictions than private sector organizations (Guy 2003). Thus, what is actually considered a positive return and benefit in the private sector may well be considered a threat and potential risk in public sector. For example, private organizations may have an incentive to invest in IT targeted to automating tasks and reducing headcounts. However, reduced headcounts would be a potential risk for public agencies as they have limited discretion to fire and/or reassign employees in order to achieve similar efficiencies from IT (Chircu et al. 2003). "Job security, computer phobia, management freedom, and that ever-prevalent line "we've always done it that way" are among the reasons why it is difficult and sometimes undesirable to measure ROI" (Forrer et al. 2001).

## 2.4 Brief Overview of Public Sector Return in IT Investment Models

During the last decade a range of models were developed to measure the return on IT investments in the public sector with the purpose of creating a solid decision base for public managers (see Table 1).

**Table 1.** List of Public ROI in IT models

| Name | Acronym | Year | Source |
|---|---|---|---|
| Social Return on Investment Model | SROI | 1996 | Roberts Enterprise Development Fund |
| Value Measuring Methodology | VMM | 2001-2003 | US Social Security Administration and the General Service Administration |
| Balanced E-Government Index | BEGIX | 2002 | Bertelsmann Foundation and Booz, Allen and Hamilton |
| Federal Enterprise Architecture Performance Reference Model | PRM | 2003 | U.S. Office of Management and Budget |
| Public Sector Value Model | PSV | 2003 | Accenture in cooperation with Kennedy School of Government, Harvard University |
| Performance Reference Model | PRM | 2003 | US Federal Enterprise Architecture Program Management Office (FEAPMO) |
| Interchange of Data between Administration | IDA VOI | 2003 | European Commission, DG Enterprise |
| Demand and Value Assessment Methodology | DAM & VAM | 2004 | Australian Government Information Management Office |

The common similarity among the different models is that all of them evaluate IT investments in the public sector as a *portfolio problem* as opposed to traditional private sector way of evaluating IT investments as a single problem of measuring financial returns. Thus, all the models take into consideration a package of both tangible and intangible factors when assessing IT investments in the public sector – *cost* (analysis of both financial and non-financial investment cost), *benefit/value* (assessment of both financial and non-financial benefits and value), and *risk* (assessment of potential risks). Most of the models emphasize different levels of benefits and value created from IT investment, including political, social and economic. All the models attempt to develop a shared scale for quantifying and analyzing the package of factors, i.e. cost, benefit/value and risk associated with IT investments. The end result of each model usually is a calculated score and some kind of diagram that presents the IT investment results.

The wide range of the models suggests that no single model is universally applicable to all government IT projects and across different geographical areas. Thus, we developed a hybrid approach for the assessment of the case presented below. Our hybrid approach draws from best practices found in the literature and also includes additional components to make the analysis adherent to context peculiarities. In the next section of this paper we provide some background information and a description of the methodology adopted.

## 3 The Case of Sistema Piemonte

### 3.1 Background Information

The region of Piemonte has historically adopted a systemic approach towards the management of public IT implementation. In the 1970s the regional government established a public consortium (CSI-Piemonte) to support IT implementation projects throughout different administration levels. This decision was the result of two main considerations. To begin with, they acknowledged a high level of administrative fragmentation present on the territory. Second, they believed that a centralized and collaborative approach among the different administration levels would generate a number of benefits in terms of efficiency and effectiveness for the regional system. Following the same logic, CSI was given the responsibility to set up a project named Sistema Piemonte (Piedmont System) with the aim to promote the provision of public services via web-enabled interfaces. The project began in 2001 as a web-portal. Nevertheless, over the years it has evolved towards an integrated platform for the provision of eGovernment services. The structure of Sistema Piemonte was adjusted to increase its flexibility in order to respond to different needs present among local administrations.

Cantamessa et al. in their recent study highlighted how the evolution of eGovernment services at local level in the region has been stagnant over the last three years. Two types of issues in particular have been identified. The first issue is the inability for most small municipalities (below 5000 inhabitants) to set up any type of eGovernment activity. The second is the difficulty for medium-large municipalities to implement the back office solutions necessary to start providing fully transactional services through their websites (Cantamessa et al. 2005). Sistema Piemonte thus aims at responding to these two needs by offering a full-package service to the former and ad hoc back office support to the latter.

In 2005 CSI decided to undertake an ROI analysis to check the extent to which the logic behind Sistema Piemonte was economically beneficial. In addition, CSI identified a need for exploring applicable business models that could be sustainable over time. The case study presented below is the result of the ROI assessment conducted in collaboration with CSI.

### 3.2 Hybrid Model for ROI in Government IT Assessment

A literature review conducted on existing models for public ROI in IT represented a solid base for the creation of an ad hoc model that fitted the specific necessities of the Sistema Piemonte project. Although synthesizing existing models allowed us to create a new methodology, the intent of this article is not to propose our hybrid model as a better way for ROI in government IT assessments, but simply to share the lessons learned from its application. As a matter of fact, the main merit of the exercise was not so much in terms of methodology creation for IT assessments, but rather in terms of stretching the application of the existing methodologies to a further and more detailed level of quantification of costs and, most importantly, benefits.

The next two sections provide a brief description of the methodology implemented in the case of Sistema Piemonte. The description of the adopted methodology is divided into two blocks: the cost analysis and the benefits assessment.

*Cost analysis:* The primary goal of cost analysis was to discover and map the relationships between existing resources and the services offered. In this first phase it was important to distinguish between costs that could be directly associated with each single e-service and those that were common to all e-services. Thus, we conducted a background analysis in order to create a catalogue of e-services costs, which were divided into two main categories (see Figure 1):

- Costs associated with the development and management of each e-service,
- General costs associated with CSI's resources that are common to all e-services.

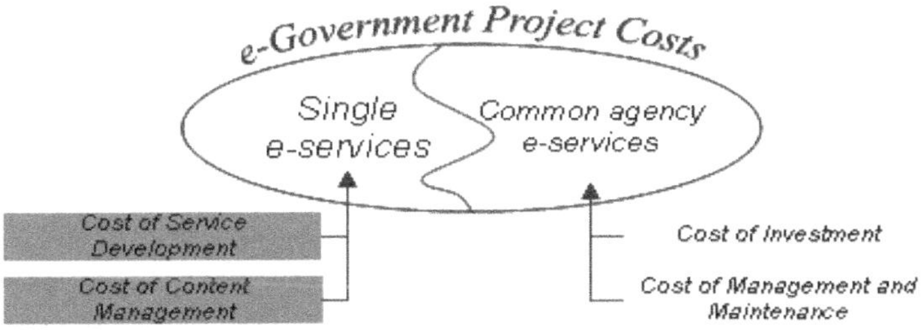


**Fig. 1.** Two categories of e-services costs

In order to create short-term and long-term scenario forecasts, both service specific costs and general costs were further divided into two subcategories: investment costs and operation costs. The calculation of service specific costs and general costs required the use of two different allocation procedures. While the former could be directly attributed to each individual service, a two step process was necessary for the latter:

1. A quota of the infrastructure's cost destined to Sistema Piemonte was calculated.
2. A cost driver (or a combination of cost drivers) adherent to the cost nature, was adopted to spread the cost across the services linked with the infrastructure.

In the end, the cost analysis helped us to reallocate the project costs among all the e-services. This was an important result for a number of reasons. First, it represented the basis for the evaluation of the added value generated by each service. Second, it allowed us to identify the main cost factors in the creation of different growth scenarios. Third, it permitted us to keep costs under control. Finally, it suggested what factors were most needed for the adoption of a sharing model. *Value/benefits assessment:* The goal of the benefits assessment was to develop a tool that could estimate the value created by each e-service for different stakeholders. The value is calculated based on an analytic comparison of the benefits introduced with government e-services implementations and the traditional way of providing services (before implementation). Our value/benefit assessment took into consideration the different aspects of value created from IT investments, i.e. economic, social and political, and was based on a two-stage process. The first stage began with an assessment of the models identified in the literature review presented earlier. The comparative analysis allowed us to identify a set of both tangible and intangible benefits associated with IT investments. At the end of this stage we developed a database containing forty generic benefits associated to the e-government services considered. In the second stage we developed a value assessment model. The model was based on MS Excel spreadsheet and tested for two different bundles of e-services and two hypothetical local administrations with five thousand and ten thousand inhabitants respectively. A detailed description of the second stage is provided below.

### 3.3 Assessment of E-Services Benefits

The fist step in the assessment consisted of linking each of the forty generic benefits with the e-services provided by Sistema Piemonte. Subsequently, benefits were categorized along three main dimensions: business line (or typology of value created), direction of value creation, and benefit unit of measurement. The categories presented in each dimension are listed below[2]

| *Business Line* | *Direction of value creation* | *Unit of measurement* |
|---|---|---|
| • Direct customer (user) value | • Government to Constituency | • Money |
| • Social (non-user/public) value | • Government to Business | • Time |
| • Government financial benefits | • Government to Government | • Quality Countable |
| • Government operational / foundation value | • Internal Effectiveness and Efficiency | • Quality Uncountable |
| • Strategic/political value | | |

The next step was to associate each benefit with an analytic indicator in order to quantify the amount of value created. The following are sample examples for translating the e-services into benefits:

[2] We adopted Booz Allen Hamilton's methodology as described in "Building a Methodology for Measuring the Value of E-Service." USA Social Security Administration (2002).

- *Reduction of displacement cost* ⇒ direct customer/user value – G2C – money
- *Faster implementation of procurement stages* ⇒ direct customer/user value – G2B – time
- *Improvement of service availability (24 hours x 7 days per week)* ⇒ direct customer/user value – G2C – quality countable
- *Increased citizen participation in public/political decision-making* ⇒ social (non-user/public) value – G2C – quality uncountable

The quantitative measurement of each indicator was based on an estimation of the value created per e-service request. At the beginning of the assessment process, the two local administrations considered had to choose among the list of e-services offered by Sistema Piemonte. Next, an estimation was produced about the improvements that the provision of the services via Internet could entail in terms of processing time and cost. The computation of the value generated by each service was based on the estimated average number of annual requests by a potential hypothetical e-government user.

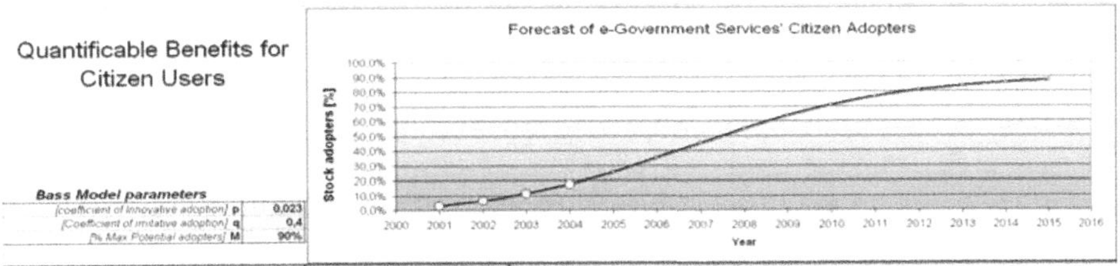


| | Statistical survey of e-governmnet adopters in the region | | | | Forecast of e-government citizen users (%) | | | | | | | | | | |
|---|---|---|---|---|---|---|---|---|---|---|---|---|---|---|---|
| | 2001 | 2002 | 2003 | 2004 | 2005 | 2006 | 2007 | 2008 | 2009 | 2010 | 2011 | 2012 | 2013 | 2014 | 2015 |
| E-Government services diffusion (statistical survey) | 2,6% | 6,0% | 11,0% | 17,5% | | | | | | | | | | | |
| Forecast e-Government services' citizen adopters (%) | 2,5% | 6,1% | 11,0% | 17,5% | 25,5% | 34,9% | 44,9% | 54,7% | 63,5% | 70,8% | 76,5% | 80,7% | 83,7% | 85,8% | 87,2% |

**Fig. 2.** Estimated number of citizens using of e-Government services

In order to forecast the number of potential adopters of the e-government services, we analyzed data from regional and national surveys on e-Government services diffusion. We applied the Bass model (1960) for the interpolation of the diffusion curve as shown in Figure 2. This process allowed to estimate percentage of e-Government citizen users and quantify the benefits for each given year. A similar procedure was adopted for the estimation of both business and government users.

The final step was to group benefits into two categories: value created for the public administrations in Sistema Piemonte network, and value generated for other stakeholders including citizens, business users, and public administrations outside the Sistema Piemonte circuit (see Figure 3 below). The aim of this final distinction was to explicit the direct and indirect benefits that a local administration could enjoy by joining the Sistema Piemonte initiative.

Concluding, the main merits of the ROI analysis conducted may be summarized as follows. First, it permitted to identify the main stakeholders and beneficiaries of each e-service: citizens, businesses, or governments. Second, it

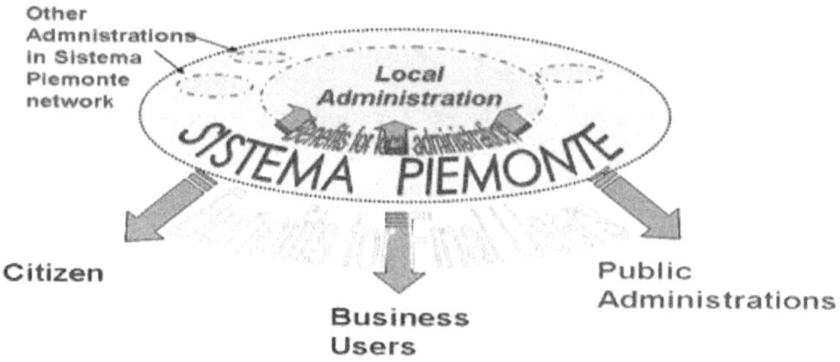


**Fig. 3.** The two fronts of benefits

made possible to quantify values and benefits created by the participation of a local administration in an e-government service network (Sistema Piemonte) and compare it with the related investment costs. Third, it allowed performing adoption simulations and identifying different probabilistic scenarios for the future diffusion of e-government services in the region. Fourth, it proved a useful decision-making support tool in the choice of the right business model for a sustainable e-service implementation. Finally, the hybrid model adopted for this case study may be used in assisting local administrations to understand the benefits brought to final users by the new e-services implementation.

## 4 Lessons Learned and Policy Implications

A number of lessons can be learned from the cost analysis and value/benefit assessment experience described above. During the study we faced different problems that led us to revisit the process. The first barrier we encountered when conducting the cost analysis had to do with the cross-sectional nature of ICT. Despite the fact that Sistema Piemonte was an initiative managed by a single entity (i.e. CSI), the information concerning the project was very fragmented and scattered among different departments. As a result, a considerable amount of effort had to be put in order to reach a comprehensive understanding of how the various components of the project were interacting among each other. Thus, the first important result generated from the cost analysis process was twofold. On one hand, we identified processes inside CSI that were involved in the development and management of Sistema Piemonte. On the other hand, the mapping of the services offered, allowed us to understand what areas needed to be further developed.

As per the benefit assessment, the main hurdle encountered was related to the scarcity of information about the impact of current and future ICT adoption. Although the procedure we adopted to estimate benefits was as rigorous and objective as possible, the uncertainty introduced by each estimation contributed to reducing the reliability of the bottom line result. Nevertheless, it must be emphasized that the model permits to easily identify best/worst and most likely scenarios, and thus provides an indication of the sensitivity of the final result.

Another important issue in the assessment of benefits was the time dimension. Some benefits manifest only years after a project has reached maturity. Thus, attempts to quantify them in the early stages of the investment may result as a difficult task highly based on "guesstimation".

All the issues described above, led us to think that a bottom line approach to public ROI analysis may be too risky and not extremely reliable. A legitimate question could then arise as to the value and purpose of carrying out such kind of analysis. The lessons learned with Sistema Piemonte experience has revealed that the merits of a ROI analysis in complex eGovernment projects should be searched for in the support it may provide to project management activities. As a matter of fact, the benefits generated from creating a complete, simple and understandable representation of the project for managers far exceeded the benefits stemming from reaching a final result stating that the project was generating a total value of "x" or "y". This thesis is reinforced by the fact that often managers base their decisions about whether to continue projects on a high amount of tacit knowledge as well as political reasons rather then hard figures. In conclusion if we consider that in 2003 Heeks estimated the world-wide rate of failure in eGovernment projects to be as high as 85% (Heeks 2003), it appears evident the need for some control and project management tools. In this respect, we believe public ROI analysis may provide a valuable contribution.

## References

1. Arlotto, P., and Oakes, J.: Return on Investment: Maximizing the Value of Healthcare Information Technology. Healthcare Information and Management Systems Society, Chicago, IL (2003).
2. Benaroch, M., and Kauffman, R.: Justifying Electronic Banking Network Expansion Using Real Options Analysis. MIS Quarterly, Vol. 24 (2000) 197-225.
3. Brynjolfsson, E.: Technology's True Payoff. In: Information Week (1994) 34-36.
4. Brynjolfsson, E., and Yang, S.: Information Technology and Productivity: A Review of the Literature. Advances in Computers, Vol. 43 (1996) 179-214.
5. Cantamessa, M., et al.: eGovernment Online Services in Piedmont. Istituto Superiore Mario Boella, Turin, Italy (2005).
6. Chircu, A., and Lee, D.: Understanding IT Investments in the Public Sector: The Case of E-Government. In: Proceedings of the 2003 Americas Conference on Information Systems (AMCIS). Tampa, FL (2003) 792-800.
7. Dehning, B., and Richardson, V.: Returns on Investments in Information Technology: A Research Synthesis. Journal of Information Systems, Vol. 16 (2002) 7-30.
8. Dos Santos, B., and Sussman, L.: Improving the Return on IT investment: The Productivity Paradox. International Journal of Information Management, Vol. 20 (2000) 429-440.
9. Dufner, D., et al.: Can Private Sector Strategic Information Systems Planning Techniques Work for the Public Sector. Communications of the Association for Information Systems, Vol. 8 (2002) 413-431.
10. Edwards, W., and Fasolo, B.: Decision Technology. Annual Review of Psychology, Vol. 52 (2001) 581-606.

11. Forrer, D., and Anderson, T.: The Dichotomy of Measurement: Information Technology Return on Investment in the Public Sector. In: Proceedings of the 12th Annual Conference of the Production and Operations Management Society. Orlando, FL (2001).
12. Guy, M.: Public Management. In: Defining Public Administration, Shafritz (ed.), Western Press. Boulder, CO (2003) 161-168.
13. Heeks, R.: Success and Failure Rates of eGovernment in Developing/Transitional Countries: Overview. Institute for Development Policy and Management, University of Manchester, Manchaster, UK (2003).
14. Keen, P.: Every Manager's Guide to Information Technology: A Glossary of Key Terms and Concepts of Today's Leader, 2nd ed. Harvard Business School Press. Boston, MA (1995).
15. Laudon, K., and Laudon, J.: Management Information Systems: Organization and Technology in the Networked Enterprise, 6th ed. Prentice Hall. Upper Saddle River, NJ (1999).
16. Lucas, H.: Information Technology and the Productivity Paradox: Assessing the Value of Investing in IT. Oxford University Press. New York, NY (1999).
17. Schniederjans, M., et al.: Information Technology Investment: Decision-Making Methodology. World Scientific Publishing Company. River Edge, NJ (2004).
18. Weill, P., and Olson, M.: Managing Investment in Information Technology: Mini Case Examples and Implications. MIS Quarterly, Vol. 13 (1989) 1.

# IT Auditing in E-Government

Reinhard Riedl and Manuel Juen

Department of Informatics
University of Zurich
Binzmühlestrasse 14, CH-8050 Zurich
riedl@ifi.unizh.ch, manuel.juen@gmail.com

**Abstract.** We first motivate the need for innovative IT auditing approaches for E-Government. Then we define the requirements and propose an own IT auditing concept for E-Government projects. It is based on established risk management procedures, project management concepts for multidisciplinary projects, and on past experience. Finally, we validate our proposed approach against the requirements.

## 1 Introduction

There are many different kinds of audits in use today [1], such as environment audits, health and safety audits, and various types of audits in the IT. In this paper, the focus lies on external IT project management audits. According to [2], the objective of an IT project audit is "to provide an early identification of those issues that may hinder an on-time, within-budget implementation of an application that is controlled, [and] documented [...]". Or in short, to increase a project's chances of success.

Audits are one of the tools to achieve this, others being for example the use of quality achievement methods and internal project controlling. The particular strength of (external) audits is that they provide an external view at the project. It is easier for external auditors to abstract from the seemingly particular nature of the project and and to compare the project status or planning with empirical experience gathered from similar projects. They have less emotional affiliation with the project and little or no unspoken implicit knowledge about the project. Thus they can easier separate the project-internal facts and the relevant project context from the purely motivational project context. And they can easier detect inconsistencies in the project design as well as communication deficits of the project management. This leades to a documentation-based, more objectively balanced look at the problems and the possibilities. It thus reduces the risk of underestimating challenges, costs, risks, and side-effects. Clearly, standard financial audit procedures are not sufficient to achieve such goals as an in-depth analysis of project contents is needed, together with a sound understanding of typical problems in the domain, where the project is situated.

Fortunately, apart from a missing, targeted e-government project auditing process, no fundamental obstructions exist. In many countries audit departments already exist on various levels of government. Most of these entities would need to

M.A. Wimmer et al. (Eds.): EGOV 2006, LNCS 4084, pp. 341–352, 2006.

employ only a few additional resources in order to regularly conduct audits in E-Government projects. No change of laws, organizational structure, and processes would be necessary. Even in case of future projects spanning several federalistic levels or administrational departments on the same federalistic level, the involved audit entities could conjointly conduct audits relatively easy.

The main goal of this study was to develop a holistic IT auditing approach, which is specifically tailored for E-Government. Similar activities in this field, conducted among others by the INTOSAI's and the EUROSAI's IT subcommittees ([3], [4]) indicate that there is a recognized need for such an approach, also on an international level. We shall first take a quick look at common problems in E-Government projects before we analyze the specific situation in Switzerland in chapter 3. Chapter 4 derives the requirements to such an audit approach and in chapter 5 and 6, we will present our approach and validate it, respectively.

## 2 Characteristic Problems in E-Government Projects

At the heart of an IT audit is technology and its application. E-government audits have to look at the handling of technology and the management of its implementation and installation process, whether this produces high value, low risk, controllable side-effects, and sustainably low costs. While programme and project portfolio audits will be more concerned with value, e-government project audits will more focus on the other listed aspects. For this purpose it is a must to understand, why e-government projects fail. Several reviews of E-Government projects ([6], [7], [8], [9]) and our own experience with big R&D projects and as project auditors have shown the following six typical problems. A similar discussion of such problems can be found in [5].

- Lack of top-down views: System goals and cardinal aims of the project are often only vaguely defined.
- Lack of comprehensive stakeholder management: Important stakeholders are left out or stakeholder management is done without a well-defined communication concept.
- Lack of transdisciplinary thinking: Some of the relevant disciplines for an E-Government project (e.g. law, management, politics, sociology, economics, etc.) are left out or they are considered only in an isolated manner.
- Old fashioned or unsuitable management methods: Public administrations have a strong tradition of law-oriented input controlling, wereas IT projects require a focus on pragmatic output controlling
- Unsatisfactory or inadequate project organization and controlling: IT project controlling is often missing in public administration and project management structures are often unsuitable for the project at hand.
- Lack of an appropriate risk management culture: Many leading players are highly skilled in managing their personal political risk, while lower ranking civil servants assume that 100.

All of these common problems have to be considered for the design of the audit approach. It should be noted that in many cases it is easier to introduce quality management in public administrations than in industry, and that the involvement of academic partners usually is not suited to decrease problems.

The listed observations imply that a straightforward translation of IT auditing processes from the private sector to the public sector is not possible. For example, multi-disciplinarity is more critical in e-government than in e-business, and there are no well-established approaches for auditing the transdisciplinary quality of multidiciplinary IT projects in industry.

## 3 Focused Study: State-of-the-Art in Switzerland

We have started our research with an investigation of the state-of-the-art in Switzerland. By 2005, 7.4 million inhabitants lived in Switzerland and the GDP amounted to around 445 billion Swiss Francs [10]. Three different levels of government exist, namely the centralized federal government, the state government in the 26 Cantons, and the municipal government. We have concentrated on the Swiss Federal Government and the Government of the Canton of Zurich and we have compared their current practices with those of larger Swiss banks. For this purpose, we have carried out a total of 16 semi-structured interviews, thereof six with members of the federal administration, four with employees of the administration of the State of Zurich, four in the financial sector, one with an IT Auditor in the Austrian Federal Government, and one with a Partner of a Big 4 public accounting firm.

### 3.1 Swiss Federal Administration

As in most countries, there is a supreme audit institution (SAI) on the federal level in Switzerland. It is called the "Swiss Federal Audit Office" (SFAO) and it employs around 100 people. Nine of them are currently working in the section "IT Audit". Since it is not subordinate to any of the seven administration departments, the SFAO can be regarded as an external audit entity. As its scope covers more than 30'000 employees, the available resources for IT audit are very scarce. However, they are not significantly smaller than in other countries' SAIs.

In e-government, the SFAO has only reviewed "Guichet virtuel" and "Vote éléctronique", which are the two most famous Swiss e-government projects by far. In 2003 ([6]) several quite shortcomings were found and reported, and mostly corrected in the aftermath. However, it turned out that many of them should have been fixed at a much earlier time in order to limit the damage. Recently, a follow-up audit [7] was conducted which found most issues to be resolved, along with some remaining ones.

In addition to the SFAO, there is an audit unit in the Federal Department of Defence, Civil Protection and Sports (DDPS) which also deals with IT. In analogy to the private sector, it can be regarded as an internal audit unit. Even though it has already conducted several audits in the field of IT, it has not yet had to deal with any E-Government project directly. Apart from that, there are no other internal audit units that deal with IT on the federal level.

### 3.2 Administration of the State of Zurich

The State of Zurich by the end of 2005 had more than 1.2 Million inhabitants and about 750'000 people working within it's boundaries [11]. According to [12], the GDP at the same time amounted to about 90 billion Swiss Francs, whereof about one third was acquired in the financial sector. As every state in Switzerland, Zurich maintains a so called financial control unit (FK) of the State. It consists of 26 people, 2 of which deal with IT issues. Considering the number of employees in the scope of the FK, which is even higher than on the federal level,[1] this is too scarce to allow for audits of e-government projects. Next to the FK, the section Privacy Protection of the State of Zurich also conducts audits in the IT domain [13]. However, it's resources are too scarce as well.

### 3.3 Swiss Banks

The fact that financial institutions rely heavily on the use of information technology for their core business has an impact on the way they handle their IT audits. Usually, more emphasis and accordingly more resources are employed therein than in most other industries. In addition, compliance necessities also contribute to the emerging maturity of the IT auditing in this sector. Thus, the IT audit function in banks can be seen as a sort of best practice. The most important lesson to be learned by public administrations from Swiss Banks is that considerable more resources should be spent on IT audits, as they really provide value for money, namely lower development and maintenance costs and shorter times-to-market. The first directly relates to one of the prime concerns of Swiss citizens, namely low taxes. The second is becoming increasingly important in the global of competition of regions for industrial investments. Since it is unlikely that the situation is going to improve dramatically, we may further identify efficiency of an e-government auditing process as one of its key requirements.

## 4 Existing E-Government Audit Propositions

In the course of this study, two other propositions on how to audit E-Government projects could be identified: “E-Government in an audit perspective” ([15]) by the EUROSAI and an audit framework by the Indian Court of Audit [14]. Both of them were developed in the last two years. Their main deficits are that they do not consider failure history of previous E-Government projects and that they do not take into account lessons learned from IT project management.

Unfortunately, apart from the traditionally low emphasis on output controlling and the high entanglement of legal, organizational, and process perspectives

[1] Mostly due to public health care, which in Switzerland lies in the states' jurisdiction.

with technological perspectives, it is an increasing public criticism of high payments for outside views, which hinders public administration to catch up with industry. In addition, the common belief has to be overcome that auditing is primarily concerned with financial correctness. Our approach intends to demonstrate that external e-government auditing can provide high value for very low costs if it proceeds due to the strategy "look at most critical risks first".

# 5 Requirements

One of the main lessons learned from the private industry is that there are no non-trivial zero-risk e-business projects and that risk management is the critical art of project management. This equally applies to E-Government. Therefore, an IT audit for E-Government projects should first look at how well risks are handled and for this purpose it can and should rely on past experiences with IT projects in general and on past experiences with E-Government projects in particular. The following five key requirements are derived from the main goals of IT project auditing, sketched in chapter 1, from characteristic problems in E-Government projects, described in chapter 2, and from the current situation in Switzerland as described in chapter 3.

1. Completeness: The approach should be holistic: it should take into account every internal and external perspective at the whole project cycle as well as every knowledge domain relevant for the project in order to detect every substantial problem that could potentially threaten the project's success.
2. Efficient arrangement: The approach should be as efficient as possible to limit the resources needed for auditing. Critical findings should be obtained first.
3. Generality: The approach should be designed in a way that it can be adapted easily to any e-government project, no matter its size or the executing entity.
4. Simplicity: The approach should be kept simple enough to support an easy communication of its intentions and results to all stakeholders.
5. Feasibility: The approach should be practically applicable in all modern public administrations and it should be easy to use even by non-experienced auditors.

# 6 Audit Approach for E-Government Projects

## 6.1 Scope, Ownership, and Preconditions

Information Technology is adopted by a government on three levels:

- Strategic level, with long-term strategies for the use of information technology in the public sector
- Program level, with programs and project portfolios as a means of accomplishing an IT strategy
- Project level, with projects as short-time, task-focused endeavors in order to achieve a clearly defined sub-goal of a strategy or as a preparation therefore

The scope of the audit approach presented in this paper is a single E-Government project's planning and realization phase. Since in a democratic country, the citizens are the legitimate owners of any audit report, we propose the use of the standard procedure in the publication of public administration audits, namely that the raw report is submitted to the audited entity first, which then comments on the findings made. Afterwards the report should be made available to the interested public.

One of the key preconditions is that enough resources are available at the executing entity. Further, it is crucical that the audit's results lead to a change of the project plan. This requires that the auditors and the auditees establish a good teamwork. In case of a disagreement, a standardized procedure should exist, involving the project's sponsor and domain specialists if necessary.

### 6.2 Audit Approach

The design of the audit approach reflects generic best practice in IT project management and makes use of some process structures presented in [16]. It is divided into two sections. The first section is executed if the audit is conducted during the concept phase of a project. Therewith, potential problems can be corrected at a very early point of a project. The second section should be used to check up on a project's progression and it's proper execution. However, even if it was not possible to conduct an audit in the concept phase, we propose to carry out section I and to decide whether identified shortcomings are severe with a look at the progress made. In case of severe shortcomings the expected costs of a change have to be compared with its benefits.

The general audit procedure for every item mentioned in the approach (e.g. System Goals, Side Effects etc.) is the following: First of all, it has to be checked whether it was considered and if necessary documented accordingly.[2] Only after this criteria has been met, the quality and the meaningfulness of these documents is audited in a second step.

**Section I.** Section I of the audit approach is designed to be conducted in the concept phase of a project. It consists of four parts, which should be executed sequentially, since they were conceived to disclose the most substantial problems in a top-down fashion.

1. *Cardinal Aims:* In this step, the auditor checks, whether the project's cardinal aims are clearly defined and documented, and if they are realistic and meaningful. Thereby, the system goal constitutes the main reason for starting the project in the first place. Side effects are other important conditions such as time constraints that have to be maintained. Whole life costs have to include all costs that accumulate not only during the project, but also during

[2] In smaller projects, such a document might not be necessary for every item, but it should nevertheless have been considered by the project members.

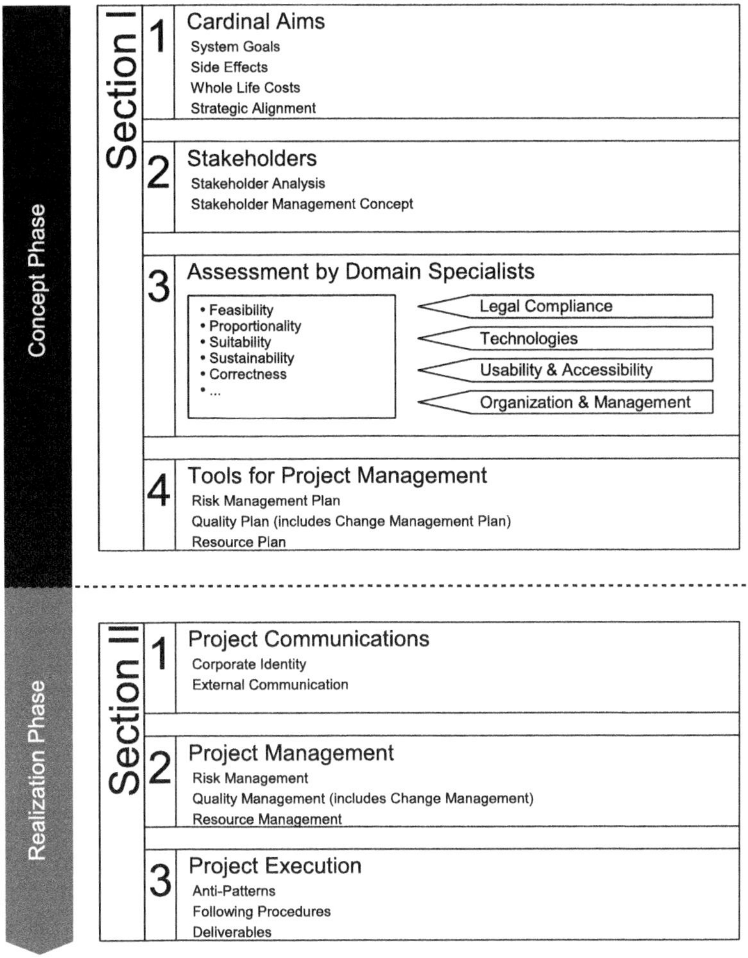


**Fig. 1.** Audit Approach for E-Government Projects

the rest of the life cycle of the product. The fourth important item to audit is the strategic alignment of the project in ccomparison with E-Government strategies, other or planned projects, and programs.

2. *Stakeholders:* Here, it is checked if all relevant stakeholders to the project have been identified and an according stakeholder management concept exists. This concept should be clear, set the right priorities and furthermore, it should be manageable by the project team.
3. *Assessment by Domain Specialists:* The project should regularly be assessed by specialists in the following domains:

   (a) Legal Compliance: Every E-Government project needs a legal basis from public law. Furthermore, privacy, information security and other relevant contraining laws have to be adhered.

(b) Technologies: The intended technologies to be used in the project should be suitable for the intended purpose. Furthermore, they should be sustainable, with respect to anticipated technological innovations.
(c) Usability & Accessibility: Depending on the presumed users of the project's product, usability and accessibility have to be assured.
(d) Organization & Management: The project's management structure, organization and controlling have to be feasible and match the size, complexity and the expected duration of the project.

In all of these four domains, the auditor ensures that a competent person has assessed all relevant details and documented them accordingly. It must be clear which person is responsible for each domain in the remainder of the project.

4. *Tools for Project Management:* Finally, the auditor checks whether a consistent and reasonable risk[3] management plan, quality plan and resource plan exists. The risk management plan should be realistic and neither too detailed nor too generic. The actual project plan (V, VP, XP, DSDM, etc.) should comply with the identified residual risk (and the task) (see [16]). The quality plan should describe the necessary means to ensure that each product in the development cycle has the quality attributes required. In the resource plan a detailed project planning that includes personnel assigned to tasks, deliverables and expenses should be provided. Its overall numbers for duration and costs should either fit with empirical evidence for similar types of project or the deviations should be justified.

## Section II

1. *Project Communication:* The audit examines if the project's communication works effectively both internally and externally. Every project member should be informed about the project's goals, its current status, risks and other important features. Furthermore, all relevant external stakeholders should be informed regularly about the project's goals and progress. Therefore, it may be necessary that the success of the external communication concept is empirically validated.
2. *Project Management:* Here, the auditor can rely on the plans that have been prepared in part 4 of section I. Thus, he can check if the risk register is up to date, if the change management is working properly and if the project is within time and budget.
3. *Project Execution:* First of all, known anti-patterns for E-Government projects have to be avoided. Secondly, the domain specialists have to sign off the documents in their responsibility as planned. Third, the produced deliverables can be analyzed more thoroughly. If the auditor finds that his knowledge is not sufficient to be able to make a proper statement, especially in this last part, he should consider calling in an external expert.

---
[3] A risk is anything that could potentially threaten any of the cardinal aims of a project.

# 7 Validation

The validation of the audit approach cannot be achieved easily, as it is hard to transform them into mearurable benchmarks. We have applied the proposed approach in a first step virtually to two different E-Government projects by making use of existing audit reports of those projects. Then we have informally checked, if all typical worst case outcomes are considered, as they were depicted in chapter 2. Finally, we have validated the requirements from chapter 4 directly.

## 7.1 Case studies

We have used the audit reports of the E-Government projects "Guichet virtuel" and "Vote éléctronique" by the SFAO [6] and the audit report by the Austrian Court of Audit (ACA) of the IT project "Papierlose Aussenwirtschaftsadministration" of 2004 [8] for assessment.

**"Guichet virtuel" and "Vote éléctronique".** For validation, we used the 10 most substantial findings made in this audit report. They range from missing change management, missing communication concept, violations of laws and federal procedures and inadequate controlling structures. Using the proposed audit approach, we could reobtain all of these 10 findings (see Appendix A).

**"Papierlose Aussenwirtschaftsadministration".** In this audit report, which was written in 2004 and published in 2005, some very severe findings were made which resulted in the opening of several legal procedures. Furthermore, other significant shortcomings were identified. Among those, missing segregation of duties, over 100% overrun of costs, missing or unsuitable contracts and missing control mechanisms. Again, we were able to recreate all of the substantial findings made in this report (see Appendix B).

## 7.2 Experiences

Past experiences are incorporated into our approach. All of the characteristic problems mentioned in chapter 2 could be detected: Cardinal aims are considered in the very first step of section I. The stakeholder management is reviewed in part 2 of section I of the approach. Transdisciplinary considerations are subject of part 3 in section I. Generic best practice project management, project controlling, and above all, risk management, are covered in part 3 of section I.

## 7.3 Requirements

From the two hypothetic applications in chapter 6.1, the following conclusions can be drawn:

1. Completeness: All substantial findings could be identified in the applications.
2. Efficient arrangement: The most severe findings could be made more or less right in the beginning. Severeness however can be very subjective.
3. Generality: The concept could easily be applied to the two projects, even though they differed considerably in size and complexity.
4. Simplicity: With a certain minimal experience in the domain, most findings could have been made by any auditor and they could have been clearly communicated to the project members. However, most probably they would not have agreed in some cases.
5. Feasibility: Auditors at the audit entities considered would most likely be able to follow our approach with their existing knowledge.

This validation does not provide full evidence that our audit approach will work in practice. However, such evidence can only be achieved with a broad empirical application, including monitored and evaluated auditings to verify the actual feasibility.

## 8 Conclusion

The comparison of IT auditing in the Swiss Government and in the Swiss financial sector has shown that there are significantly less resources spent for IT auditing in the Government than there are spent in the financial sector. In particular, there do not exist tailored approaches for the auditing of E-Government projects. Existing solutions in other countries ignore worst case experiences from past E-Government projects. Therefore, we have designed and partially validated an IT auditing approach which focuses on results, risks and professional IT project management rather than on correct procedures. For example, the financial auditing part focuses on the empirical validation of time and cost planning by way of comparison with similar projects and it is complemented with a multidisciplinary auditing of the content and compliance of activities and an auditing of internal and external communication.

Other than auditing single projects, it would make sense to take a closer look at E-Government programs as a whole, thus extending the proposed auditing framework. One possibility for this would be to combine our approach with the 4+2 concept, outlined in [17].

## References

1. Power, M.; The Audit Society : Rituals of Verification; 2nd edition; Oxford University Press; Oxford; 1999
2. Gallegos, F., et al.; Information Technology Control and Audit; 2nd Edition; Auerbach Publications; Boca Ranton Fl.; 2004
3. http://www.intosaiitaudit.org/aboutus2.htm
4. http://www.eurosaiit.org/9282201/v/indexdom.htm

5. Riedl, R.; Engineering E-Government Platforms and G2G Solutions; Presented at the INTEROP-ESA 2005 in Geneva, Switzerland; http://interop-esa05.unige.ch/INTEROP/Proceedings/eGovScientific/papers/2a2.pdf
6. Swiss Federal Audit Office; E-Government in the Federal Chancellery: Audit of the Projects "Guichet virtuel" and "Vote éléctronique"; September 2003; http://www.efk.admin.ch/pdf/3108BE_Bericht_BK_E_Government.pdf;
7. Swiss Federal Audit Office; E-Government and NOVE-IT in the Federal Chancellery; Follow-up Audit; October 2005; http://www.efk.admin.ch/pdf/E-Government%20und%20NOVE-IT%20in%20der%20Bundeskanzlei.pdf
8. Austrian Court of Audit; Audit Report of the Project "Papierlose Aussenwirtschaftsadministration"; April 2005; Pages 41ff; http://www.rechnungshof.gv.at/Berichte/Bund/Bund_2005_04/BUND_2005_04.pdf
9. Austrian Court of Audit; Audit Report of the Project "Projekt e-card"; April 2004; Pages 43ff; http://www.rechnungshof.gv.at/Berichte/Bund/Bund_2004_04/Bund_2004_04.pdf
10. http://www.statistik.zh.ch/publikationen/ktzhiz/ktzhiz05_00001.pdf
11. Zuercher Kantonalbank; Kanton Zuerich in Zahlen 2005; http://www.statistik.zh.ch/publikationen/ktzhiz/ktzhiz05_00001.pdf
12. Zuercher Kantonalbank; Wertschoepfung im Kanton Zuerich; 2005 retrieved from: http://www.standort.zh.ch/internet/vd/awa/standort/de/wirtschaft.html
13. Datenschutzbeauftragter des Kantons Zuerich; Taetigkeitsbericht 2004; Zuerich; 2005
14. Sharma, A.; Challenges when auditing e-government; UN/INTOSAI Seminar on the Application of Information and Communication Technologies (ICT) in the Audit of e-Government; Vienna, April 2005; http://www.intosai.org/Level6/6_18_VN_INT_Seminar/India_E.pdf
15. EUROSAI IT Working Group; E-government in an audit perspective; November 2004; http://www.eurosai-it.org/9282000/d/english_e_gov.pdf
16. Ould, M.; Managing Software Quality and Business Risk; John Wiley & Sons, Ltd; Chichester; 1999
17. Joyce, W., Nohria, N., Roberson, B.; What Really Works; HarperCollins Publishers, New York; 2003

# A Case Study 1

| # | Finding | Checks in Audit |
|---|---|---|
| 1 | Missing change management | Section I, Part 4, Item 2 |
| 2 | Knowledge concentrated in one person | Section I, Part 4, Item 3 |
| 3 | Missing communication concept | Section I, Part 2, Item 2 |
| 4 | Inadequate controlling and reporting | Section I, Part 3 (d) |
| 5 | Insufficient contract controlling | Section I, Part 3 (d) |
| 6 | Missing disclaimer on webpage | Section I, Part 3 (a) |
| 7 | No calculation of whole life costs | Section I, Part 1, Item 3 |
| 8 | Violation of WTO rules regarding bidding process | Section I, Part 3 (a) |
| 9 | No framework agreements | Section I, Part 3 (a) |
| 10 | General Terms and Conditions missing in contracts | Section I, Part 3 (a) |

## B Case Study 2

| # | Finding | Checks in Audit |
|---|---|---|
| 1 | Inadequate bidding procedure | Section I, Part 3 (a) and (d) |
| 2 | Inadequate project management | Section I, Part 3 (d) |
| 3 | Oral agreements without written contracts | Section I, Part 3 (a) and (d) |
| 4 | Illegal procedures for follow-up orders | Section I, Part 3 (a) |
| 5 | Missing system specifications for hardware purchases | Section I, Part 3 (b) |
| 6 | Unnecessarily high system availability defined | Section I, Part 3 (b) |
| 7 | Violation of WTO rules regarding bidding process | Section I, Part 3 (a) |
| 8 | Inadequate contracts with external personnel | Section I, Part 3 (a) and (d) |
| 9 | 100% cost overrun caused by non declared services | Section II, Part 2, Item 3 |
| 10 | Missing checks and balances | Section I, Part 3 (d) |

# Author Index

# Lecture Notes in Computer Science

For information about Vols. 1–4049

please contact your bookseller or Springer

Vol. 4180: M. Kohlhase, OMDoc – An Open Markup Format for Mathematical Documents [version 1.2]. XIX, 428 pages. 2006. (Sublibrary LNAI).

Vol. 4163: H. Bersini, J. Carneiro (Eds.), Artificial Immune Systems. XII, 460 pages. 2006.

Vol. 4162: R. Královič, P. Urzyczyn (Eds.), Mathematical Foundations of Computer Science 2006. XV, 814 pages. 2006.

Vol. 4159: J. Ma, H. Jin, L.T. Yang, J.J.-P. Tsai (Eds.), Ubiquitous Intelligence and Computing. XXII, 1190 pages. 2006.

Vol. 4155: O. Stock, M. Schaerf (Eds.), Reasoning, Action and Interaction in AI Theories and Systems. XVIII, 343 pages. 2006. (Sublibrary LNAI).

Vol. 4153: N. Zheng, X. Jiang, X. Lan (Eds.), Advances in Machine Vision, Image Processing, and Pattern Analysis. XIII, 506 pages. 2006.

Vol. 4152: Y. Manolopoulos, J. Pokorný, T. Sellis (Eds.), Advances in Databases and Information Systems. XV, 448 pages. 2006.

Vol. 4151: A. Iglesias, N. Takayama (Eds.), Mathematical Software - ICMS 2006. XVII, 452 pages. 2006.

Vol. 4146: J.C. Rajapakse, L. Wong, R. Acharya (Eds.), Pattern Recognition in Bioinformatics. XIV, 186 pages. 2006. (Sublibrary LNBI).

Vol. 4144: T. Ball, R.B. Jones (Eds.), Computer Aided Verification. XV, 564 pages. 2006.

Vol. 4139: T. Salakoski, F. Ginter, S. Pyysalo, T. Pahikkala, Advances in Natural Language Processing. XVI, 771 pages. 2006. (Sublibrary LNAI).

Vol. 4138: X. Cheng, W. Li, T. Znati (Eds.), Wireless Algorithms, Systems, and Applications. XVI, 709 pages. 2006.

Vol. 4137: C. Baier, H. Hermanns (Eds.), CONCUR 2006 – Concurrency Theory. XIII, 525 pages. 2006.

Vol. 4134: K. Yi (Ed.), Static Analysis. XIII, 443 pages. 2006.

Vol. 4133: J. Gratch, M. Young, R. Aylett, D. Ballin, P. Olivier (Eds.), Intelligent Virtual Agents. XIV, 472 pages. 2006. (Sublibrary LNAI).

Vol. 4130: U. Furbach, N. Shankar (Eds.), Automated Reasoning. XV, 680 pages. 2006. (Sublibrary LNAI).

Vol. 4129: D. McGookin, S. Brewster (Eds.), Haptic and Audio Interaction Design. XII, 167 pages. 2006.

Vol. 4128: W.E. Nagel, W.V. Walter, W. Lehner (Eds.), Euro-Par 2006 Parallel Processing. XXXIII, 1221 pages. 2006.

Vol. 4127: E. Damiani, P. Liu (Eds.), Data and Applications Security XX. X, 319 pages. 2006.

Vol. 4124: H. de Meer, J.P. G. Sterbenz (Eds.), Self-Organising Systems. XIV, 261 pages. 2006.

Vol. 4121: A. Biere, C.P. Gomes (Eds.), Theory and Applications of Satisfiability Testing - SAT 2006. XII, 438 pages. 2006.

Vol. 4119: C. Dony, J.L. Knudsen, A. Romanovsky, A. Tripathi (Eds.), Advanced Topics in Exception Handling Components. X, 302 pages. 2006.

Vol. 4117: C. Dwork (Ed.), Advances in Cryptology - Crypto 2006. XIII, 621 pages. 2006.

Vol. 4116: R. De Prisco, M. Yung (Eds.), Security and Cryptography for Networks. XI, 366 pages. 2006.

Vol. 4115: D.-S. Huang, K. Li, G.W. Irwin (Eds.), Computational Intelligence and Bioinformatics, Part III. XXI, 803 pages. 2006. (Sublibrary LNBI).

Vol. 4114: D.-S. Huang, K. Li, G.W. Irwin (Eds.), Computational Intelligence, Part II. XXVII, 1337 pages. 2006. (Sublibrary LNAI).

Vol. 4113: D.-S. Huang, K. Li, G.W. Irwin (Eds.), Intelligent Computing, Part I. XXVII, 1331 pages. 2006.

Vol. 4112: D.Z. Chen, D. T. Lee (Eds.), Computing and Combinatorics. XIV, 528 pages. 2006.

Vol. 4111: F.S. de Boer, M.M. Bonsangue, S. Graf, W.-P. de Roever (Eds.), Formal Methods for Components and Objects. VIII, 447 pages. 2006.

Vol. 4110: J. Díaz, K. Jansen, J.D.P. Rolim, U. Zwick (Eds.), Approximation, Randomization, and Combinatorial Optimization. XII, 522 pages. 2006.

Vol. 4109: D.-Y. Yeung, J.T. Kwok, A. Fred, F. Roli, D. de Ridder (Eds.), Structural, Syntactic, and Statistical Pattern Recognition. XXI, 939 pages. 2006.

Vol. 4108: J.M. Borwein, W.M. Farmer (Eds.), Mathematical Knowledge Management. VIII, 295 pages. 2006. (Sublibrary LNAI).

Vol. 4106: T.R. Roth-Berghofer, M.H. Göker, H. A. Güvenir (Eds.), Advances in Case-Based Reasoning. XIV, 566 pages. 2006. (Sublibrary LNAI).

Vol. 4104: T. Kunz, S.S. Ravi (Eds.), Ad-Hoc, Mobile, and Wireless Networks. XII, 474 pages. 2006.

Vol. 4099: Q. Yang, G. Webb (Eds.), PRICAI 2006: Trends in Artificial Intelligence. XXVIII, 1263 pages. 2006. (Sublibrary LNAI).

Vol. 4098: F. Pfenning (Ed.), Term Rewriting and Applications. XIII, 415 pages. 2006.

Vol. 4097: X. Zhou, O. Sokolsky, L. Yan, E.-S. Jung, Z. Shao, Y. Mu, D.C. Lee, D. Kim, Y.-S. Jeong, C.-Z. Xu (Eds.), Emerging Directions in Embedded and Ubiquitous Computing. XXVII, 1034 pages. 2006.

Vol. 4096: E. Sha, S.-K. Han, C.-Z. Xu, M.H. Kim, L.T. Yang, B. Xiao (Eds.), Embedded and Ubiquitous Computing. XXIV, 1170 pages. 2006.

Vol. 4094: O. H. Ibarra, H.-C. Yen (Eds.), Implementation and Application of Automata. XIII, 291 pages. 2006.

Vol. 4093: X. Li, O.R. Zaïane, Z. Li (Eds.), Advanced Data Mining and Applications. XXI, 1110 pages. 2006. (Sublibrary LNAI).

Vol. 4092: J. Lang, F. Lin, J. Wang (Eds.), Knowledge Science, Engineering and Management. XV, 664 pages. 2006. (Sublibrary LNAI).

Vol. 4091: G.-Z. Yang, T. Jiang, D. Shen, L. Gu, J. Yang (Eds.), Medical Imaging and Augmented Reality. XIII, 399 pages. 2006.

Vol. 4090: S. Spaccapietra, K. Aberer, P. Cudré-Mauroux (Eds.), Journal on Data Semantics VI. XI, 211 pages. 2006.

Vol. 4089: W. Löwe, M. Südholt (Eds.), Software Composition. X, 339 pages. 2006.

Vol. 4088: Z.-Z. Shi, R. Sadananda (Eds.), Agent Computing and Multi-Agent Systems. XVII, 827 pages. 2006. (Sublibrary LNAI).

Vol. 4087: F. Schwenker, S. Marinai (Eds.), Artificial Neural Networks in Pattern Recognition. IX, 299 pages. 2006. (Sublibrary LNAI).

Vol. 4085: J. Misra, T. Nipkow, E. Sekerinski (Eds.), FM 2006: Formal Methods. XV, 620 pages. 2006.

Vol. 4084: M.A. Wimmer, H.J. Scholl, Å. Grönlund, K.V. Andersen (Eds.), Electronic Government. XVI, 353 pages. 2006.

Vol. 4083: S. Fischer-Hübner, S. Furnell, C. Lambrinoudakis (Eds.), Trust and Privacy in Digital Business. XIII, 243 pages. 2006.

Vol. 4082: K. Bauknecht, B. Pröll, H. Werthner (Eds.), E-Commerce and Web Technologies. XIII, 243 pages. 2006.

Vol. 4081: A. M. Tjoa, J. Trujillo (Eds.), Data Warehousing and Knowledge Discovery. XVII, 578 pages. 2006.

Vol. 4080: S. Bressan, J. Küng, R. Wagner (Eds.), Database and Expert Systems Applications. XXI, 959 pages. 2006.

Vol. 4079: S. Etalle, M. Truszczyński (Eds.), Logic Programming. XIV, 474 pages. 2006.

Vol. 4077: M.-S. Kim, K. Shimada (Eds.), Geometric Modeling and Processing - GMP 2006. XVI, 696 pages. 2006.

Vol. 4076: F. Hess, S. Pauli, M. Pohst (Eds.), Algorithmic Number Theory. X, 599 pages. 2006.

Vol. 4075: U. Leser, F. Naumann, B. Eckman (Eds.), Data Integration in the Life Sciences. XI, 298 pages. 2006. (Sublibrary LNBI).

Vol. 4074: M. Burmester, A. Yasinsac (Eds.), Secure Mobile Ad-hoc Networks and Sensors. X, 193 pages. 2006.

Vol. 4073: A. Butz, B. Fisher, A. Krüger, P. Olivier (Eds.), Smart Graphics. XI, 263 pages. 2006.

Vol. 4072: M. Harders, G. Székely (Eds.), Biomedical Simulation. XI, 216 pages. 2006.

Vol. 4071: H. Sundaram, M. Naphade, J.R. Smith, Y. Rui (Eds.), Image and Video Retrieval. XII, 547 pages. 2006.

Vol. 4070: C. Priami, X. Hu, Y. Pan, T.Y. Lin (Eds.), Transactions on Computational Systems Biology V. IX, 129 pages. 2006. (Sublibrary LNBI).

Vol. 4069: F.J. Perales, R.B. Fisher (Eds.), Articulated Motion and Deformable Objects. XV, 526 pages. 2006.

Vol. 4068: H. Schärfe, P. Hitzler, P. Øhrstrøm (Eds.), Conceptual Structures: Inspiration and Application. XI, 455 pages. 2006. (Sublibrary LNAI).

Vol. 4067: D. Thomas (Ed.), ECOOP 2006 – Object-Oriented Programming. XIV, 527 pages. 2006.

Vol. 4066: A. Rensink, J. Warmer (Eds.), Model Driven Architecture – Foundations and Applications. XII, 392 pages. 2006.

Vol. 4065: P. Perner (Ed.), Advances in Data Mining. XI, 592 pages. 2006. (Sublibrary LNAI).

Vol. 4064: R. Büschkes, P. Laskov (Eds.), Detection of Intrusions and Malware & Vulnerability Assessment. X, 195 pages. 2006.

Vol. 4063: I. Gorton, G.T. Heineman, I. Crnkovic, H.W. Schmidt, J.A. Stafford, C.A. Szyperski, K. Wallnau (Eds.), Component-Based Software Engineering. XI, 394 pages. 2006.

Vol. 4062: G. Wang, J.F. Peters, A. Skowron, Y. Yao (Eds.), Rough Sets and Knowledge Technology. XX, 810 pages. 2006. (Sublibrary LNAI).

Vol. 4061: K. Miesenberger, J. Klaus, W. Zagler, A.I. Karshmer (Eds.), Computers Helping People with Special Needs. XXIX, 1356 pages. 2006.

Vol. 4060: K. Futatsugi, J.-P. Jouannaud, J. Meseguer (Eds.), Algebra, Meaning, and Computation. XXXVIII, 643 pages. 2006.

Vol. 4059: L. Arge, R. Freivalds (Eds.), Algorithm Theory – SWAT 2006. XII, 436 pages. 2006.

Vol. 4058: L.M. Batten, R. Safavi-Naini (Eds.), Information Security and Privacy. XII, 446 pages. 2006.

Vol. 4057: J.P.W. Pluim, B. Likar, F.A. Gerritsen (Eds.), Biomedical Image Registration. XII, 324 pages. 2006.

Vol. 4056: P. Flocchini, L. Gąsieniec (Eds.), Structural Information and Communication Complexity. X, 357 pages. 2006.

Vol. 4055: J. Lee, J. Shim, S.-g. Lee, C. Bussler, S. Shim (Eds.), Data Engineering Issues in E-Commerce and Services. IX, 290 pages. 2006.

Vol. 4054: A. Horváth, M. Telek (Eds.), Formal Methods and Stochastic Models for Performance Evaluation. VIII, 239 pages. 2006.

Vol. 4053: M. Ikeda, K.D. Ashley, T.-W. Chan (Eds.), Intelligent Tutoring Systems. XXVI, 821 pages. 2006.

Vol. 4052: M. Bugliesi, B. Preneel, V. Sassone, I. Wegener (Eds.), Automata, Languages and Programming, Part II. XXIV, 603 pages. 2006.

Vol. 4051: M. Bugliesi, B. Preneel, V. Sassone, I. Wegener (Eds.), Automata, Languages and Programming, Part I. XXIII, 729 pages. 2006.